It is never pleasant for a biographer to contemplate the *other* times that your subject may have died, but, in the case of David Bowie, 25 June 2004 saw him come closer than most to his end. It was on that date, as he performed what would be his final full live show in Scheeßel in Germany, that he suffered the latest in a series of near-fatal heart attacks. His illness saw the Reality tour draw to a premature close as he cancelled the sixteen remaining gigs that he was to have played everywhere from Vienna to Monte Carlo. At the time, his publicists played down the seriousness of his illness, ascribing his indisposition to a trapped nerve that needed emergency surgery. Only later did the full, shocking truth became clear.

Bowie was lucky to survive. He had suffered his first cardiac arrest two days earlier, during a concert in Prague, but out of a genuine desire to give his audiences a good time and a bloody-minded refusal to accept his own mortality, he carried on endangering his health, ignoring the entreaties of those around him to stop and rest. It would have been ironic if a man, whose hard-living lifestyle during his '70s heyday had often pushed him to the precipice, had died after abandoning all his various vices, from alcohol and drugs to myriad casual sexual encounters and cigarettes. But the human body can only take so much punishment. Bowie's slight frame had suffered more abuse in his fifty-seven years than a dozen others could have taken in their combined lifetimes.

Bowie survived and lived another eleven and a half years, albeit with a vastly reduced public presence. Yet it is tempting to play the game of 'what if' and speculate what the reaction would have been had he died, whether during a live performance or a few hours or days afterwards in hospital. He was then in the middle of a remarkable comeback that had begun with his iconic performance at Glastonbury Festival four years earlier, when he had performed a rapturously received greatest hits set that saw him make peace with a past that he had spent the previous decade trying to escape from. He had released two studio albums since then, the acclaimed *Heathen* in 2002 and the less well-received *Reality* the following year. The latter felt more as if Bowie was putting out something to justify a long and lucrative tour than offering the world a record that he could not live without making.

Had *Reality* been Bowie's final release, it would be viewed as a disappointing last hurrah from a great artist. It contains some superb songs – the opening four are as good as anything that he recorded in this period – but there is also the dragging sense of 'Will this do?' hanging over the record. Bowie was at his best when he was not influenced by trends or necessities, commercial or otherwise. When he released records that nobody else could have made, he justified the faith that his millions of admirers placed in him. But when his albums had the taint of obligation to them, it was hard to feel the same reverence.

Certainly, if Bowie had died, suddenly and tragically, the reaction would have been a grief-stricken one. It would have been a salutary reminder that even musical icons are mortal and that the demands of a long, gruelling tour sat uneasily with his hitherto unsuspected health issues. He would have been venerated as an icon, a legend, and his '70s and early '80s heyday celebrated. Perhaps the previous decade and a half – which had seen him bounce back from the ignominy of the late '80s to renewed critical and commercial respect – would have been treated generously, but nobody would have seriously suggested that *Reality* was his best work, nor a fitting epitaph to a remarkable talent. And this would, inevitably, have tempered the reaction. By the time that the initial outpouring of sorrow wore off, there would have been the faint but pervasive taint of missed opportunity clinging to the Bowie legend. Pick the final point at which he was great, whether it was *"Heroes"*, *Scary Monsters* or *Let's Dance*, and regard everything that came afterwards not as the flawed but often brilliant expression of a once-in-a-lifetime talent, but as a drawn-out epilogue to a career that had peaked long before its creator reached the age of forty.

# LAZARUS

# LAZARUS

## THE SECOND COMING OF

# DAVID BOWIE

### ALEXANDER LARMAN

new modern

new modern

First published in the UK in 2026 by New Modern
An imprint of Putman Publishing
Mermaid House, Puddle Dock, Blackfriars, London, EC4V 3DB

@newmodernbooks
@newmodernbooks

Hardback ISBN: 978-1-917923-44-6
eBook ISBN: 978-1-917923-46-0
Audio ISBN: 978-1-917923-45-3

A CIP catalogue record for this book is available in the British Library.

Publishing and editorial: Pete Selby and James Lilford
Typesetting: Marie Doherty

1 3 5 7 9 10 8 6 4 2

Every reasonable effort has been made to trace copyright-holders
of material reproduced in this book. If any have been inadvertently
overlooked, the publisher would be glad to hear from them.

New Modern is an imprint of Putman Publishing
www.newmodernbooks.co.uk
www.putmanpublishing.co.uk

FSC
www.fsc.org

MIX
Paper | Supporting
responsible forestry
FSC® C018072

Printed and bound in Great Britain by Clays Ltd, Elcograf S.p.A.

*For my beloved daughter*
*Rose Evelyn Bowie Larman, REBL herself,*
*and in memory of David Bowie,*
il miglior fabbro.

# CONTENTS

'Dying
Is an art, like everything else.
I do it exceptionally well.'

Sylvia Plath, 'Lady Lazarus', *Ariel*

'Jesus lifted up his eyes, and said, Father, I thank thee that thou hast heard me.

And I knew that thou hearest me always: but because of the people which stand by I said it, that they may believe that thou hast sent me.

And when he thus had spoken, he cried with a loud voice, Lazarus, come forth.

And he that was dead came forth, bound hand and foot with graveclothes: and his face was bound about with a napkin.'

**John 11: 41–44**

When I first came up with the idea for *Lazarus*, it was a reaction against the way that Bowie's latter-day career was marginalised and tacitly belittled, even by his admirers. We all know, and love, his canonical work from his so-called 'imperial phase', which began with the release of 'Space Oddity' on 11 July 1969 and came to an end just fewer than fifteen years later, when he put out 'Blue Jean' on 10 September 1984. Yet everything that came after that was tainted by association with unsuccessful albums, grandiose but somehow risible tours and, most crucially, Bowie's own growing discomfort with the pop stardom that management and record labels alike wished to shoehorn him into.

He refuted this. As he would later sing on the title track to his final album *Blackstar*, 'I'm not a pop star'. It took him every single conceivable permutation of toying with his public image – first ignoring it, then subverting it and, finally and most happily, celebrating it – to achieve the artistic and personal fulfilment that he craved. No longer the bright young thing who had staggered, unwashed and somewhat slightly dazed, through the '70s, the mature Bowie was a man whose apparent self-belief was undermined by a deep insecurity that crueller commentators both observed and took grim pleasure in mocking. He had been a Midas-like figure for comfortably more than a decade, moving through a fickle industry that he dominated with flair, poise and the ability to create musical alchemy with near-genius consistency. And then he lost that ability – and, for a long time, it showed no signs of returning.

*Lazarus* is, if you will, the pensive B-side to the triumphant A-side of his heyday. We are fascinated by our heroes not because they are flawless and perfect, but because we see in their imperfections the reflection of our own failings and foibles. Christ died on the cross calling out 'My God, my God, why have you forsaken me?' Alexander the Great wept when he realised that there were no worlds left to conquer. Nelson was half the man he had been when he met his end at the Battle of Trafalgar. And countless other musicians, or celebrities, have disappointed or underdelivered, because they were only mortal, rather than the gods their admirers wanted them to be.

My intention was never to venerate Bowie as a peerless, flawless genius. That I believe him to be the greatest British musician of the post-war era is simply personal opinion; other views are available. It was instead because I hold him in such high esteem that, in my exploration of the second quarter-century of his career, I constantly asked whether he achieved the things that he was truly capable of or if he made the mistake of believing his own hype. He faltered and stumbled more times, and in more ways, than most artists of comparable talent might be expected to. There were poor albums – praised to the skies by well-meaning but overly partisan critics – and misjudged attempts to diversify his appeal that only served to embarrass him. As an early reader of this book commented, 'for someone who is as great an admirer of Bowie as you are, you aren't half hard on him'.

And that, surely, is the point. Were he a less robust talent, I would not hold him up to the scrutiny that he merits. That – spoiler alert – the book ends with Bowie not simply respected but venerated beyond measure is testament to a simple statement of fact that is the more thrilling for its apparent obviousness: he was *David Bowie*. He left this world not with the mundane mortality of a heart attack, but with a triumphant ascendancy that saw him produce one of his greatest, and most enduring, albums as a final testament. It is impossible to think of how he could have planned his departure in a more inimitable, or satisfying, fashion.

Yet there is an awful lot else that happened between his stuttering attempts to regain his musical integrity with the Tin Machine project and the magisterial greatness of *Blackstar*. A continued source of frustration over the past decades has been an unwillingness of biographers to treat Bowie's latter-day career with the gravitas that it merits. The music critic Tom Hibbert's cruel, if witty, denigration of him as 'Dame David Bowie' stuck for years, taking his innate integrity away and instead turning him into yet another successful but bland middle-aged rock star whose music would probably do to soundtrack a car commercial or two before being forgotten about.

Bowie had his flaws, and I have been, I hope, unsparing in analysing his missteps and attempting to ask why these errors of judgement (and, sometimes, taste) took place. But I have also tried to celebrate a great musician and, I believe, a great man. Avoiding hagiography has not been hard, but conveying the very personal sense of why Bowie has been my idol – my lodestar – for so much of my life has gone hand in hand with an honest and unsentimental appreciation of where he let me, and others, down. Still, any suggestion of a compact of that nature between artist and fan is erroneous. Bowie never owed anybody anything. His greatest work was achieved when he wrote purely for himself and ignored fashion and fleeting trends alike. I would hope, as his close collaborator Mike Garson told me, that people will be listening to Bowie's music, and appreciating it, as long as we as a species still derive some visceral, deep-rooted satisfaction and happiness from the work of a man who could sing about space oddities, life on Mars, black stars and, yes, Lazarus and touch the hearts and souls of millions.

This has been an immensely personal book to write – and a joyful one. The pleasure that I have taken in researching it, and interviewing many of those who worked with and knew Bowie, has been a crucial feature of my own figurative journey upriver, without, thankfully, the looming presence of Mr Kurtz at its conclusion. At times, I had feared that I would discover some similarly compromised and, indeed, 'unsound' figure: another icon with feet of clay. It was therefore a relief and a pleasure to discover that Bowie – the 'real' Bowie, as far as anyone could know him – was not a cold-hearted and dictatorial monster, but a charming, goofily humorous, fiercely intelligent and thoroughly likeable figure who was also capable of resonant genius.

I have no idea what Bowie would have made of *Lazarus* had he lived to read it. He was often scathing about biographies of him, criticising them for factual inaccuracies and literary infelicity alike, and I owe it to his memory not to produce a dishonest or misshapen account of this vital portion of his life and career. I can only hope that he would at least have appreciated my intentions in writing it and approved of the idea of this less heralded but still vital part of his life and work being given the full and fair measure that it merits. I will leave the final words, appropriately enough, to his producer and friend Tony Visconti, who said, in the hours after his death, 'We are fortunate to have lived in the same time as him.' I can only concur and I hope that you do, too.

*Alexander Larman,*
*London, September 2025*

# PROLOGUE

## Brixton, 10 November 1991
## 'I wouldn't want to be this guy'

*'Sit down, man. You're a fucking disgrace.'*

There is little more dispiriting than a band going on a long and tedious trek around the world to promote an unloved album. Yet, as their tour bus rolled into Brixton on 10 November 1991, the quintet of musicians on board were doing what they could to keep their spirits up on a wet, cold Sunday evening. The rhythm section of the brothers Hunt and Tony Fox Sales were bounding about as energetically as ever, discussing what practical jokes they might play on Coco Schwab, the singer's PA – a woman who they believed, not inaccurately, did not approve of them or their antics. The lead guitarist Reeves Gabrels spent half his time intervening before these antics could get out of hand, earning him the scornful nickname 'Henry Kissinger' on account of his peacekeeping. The rhythm guitarist Eric Schermerhorn was a hired hand who had only joined the band on his old friend Gabrels's invitation and was still doing his best to understand the Fellini-esque carnival that he had become embroiled in.

The musicians constituted the band Tin Machine, which had formed three years before at the instigation of one of the best-known men in the world. Schermerhorn describes his induction into the madness pithily. 'It's May '91 and I'm in New York. My girlfriend broke up with me. My band broke up. *I'm* broke. Then I get a message from Reeves saying "We need a second guitar player for Tin Machine. [Rhythm guitarist] Kevin Armstrong's out, will you come audition?" So I said, "Of course, man" and flew out to LA. I remember at the end of the rehearsal, packing up my stuff, and then

1

*he* comes up and says "I'm really looking forward to working with you". And, just after that, I shook my head and just said "Oh, my God".'[1]

The initial atmosphere on the It's My Life tour – so named after the words tattooed on Hunt's broad shoulders – which began in Dublin on 16 August, was upbeat and cheerful. The Sales brothers were the sons of the well-known children's comedian Milton 'Soupy' Sales and were always on hand with some fool-born jest or gag to lighten up the mood. Gabrels, a professorial but friendly figure who had studied at the Berklee College of Music, kept the band together both musically and organisationally. Schermerhorn, meanwhile, slept in the bunk below that of his employer's on the tour bus, which gave him an opportunity of observing him at closer quarters than he could ever have expected. He was especially privileged to be listening to what he called 'his insane, self-deprecating, cutting humour' and was amused to hear that the singer's favourite comedians were the 1950s troupe the Goons, whose cultural inroads into the United States had been significant enough for Schermerhorn not to be totally perplexed by his bandmate's habit of talking, apparently nonsensically, about Bluebottle and Hercules Grytpype-Thynne.

Yet just as Bluebottle's best-known catchphrase was to say 'You dirty, rotten swine, you! You have deaded me!', so the star's good humour was to be dented by the appearance of the 2 September 1991 edition of *Melody Maker*, which contained its critic Jon Wilde's damning verdict on the second Tin Machine album. Once, *Melody Maker* had been an ally, allowing the singer to admit his apparent homosexuality in a 1972 interview with the magazine. His statement – 'I'm gay and I always have been'[2] – may not have been wholly accurate, but it was vital to the success of his career, something that he later acknowledged when he said 'Yeah, it was *Melody Maker* that made me. It was that piece by Mick Watts.'[3]

Now, with the star an apparently diminished figure, journalists sharpened their edges on his latest album, calling it a bored man's vanity project. The judgement of *Entertainment Weekly*'s Bill Wyman – no relation to the Rolling Stone – was typical, as he sighed about 'meaningless lyric after meaningless lyric',[4] although he was laudatory compared to *Spin*'s Jonathan Bernstein, who sneered that it was 'a follow-up as eagerly awaited as *Mannequin 2: On the Move*' and its frontman 'a man made ridiculous by adhering to rules he wrote for his most rickety and least publicly subscribed persona'.[5] Still, Wyman and Bernstein were both kinder than Wilde, a prolific journalist who had written sympathetic interviews with, among others, Laurie Anderson and Boy George. Yet this empathy was lacking when it came to his demolition of the second Tin Machine album, in which he concluded, both sorrowfully and angrily, 'Hot tramp! We loved you so. Now sit down, man. You're a fucking disgrace.'[6]

Whether or not it is true – as Wilde later claimed to have been told by the musician's PR manager Alan Edwards – that his target wept when he read the damning review, this, and other poor notices, had a grim effect on the atmosphere for the remainder of the European leg of the tour. Schermerhorn, the new boy, had already observed the tension that lay between the demands of Tin Machine as a band and its superstar singer. Few other acts touring their second album had to play host to Tom Cruise at a rehearsal in Dublin, and for all the act's much-vaunted 'democracy', the band's leader was the only person who the press really wanted to interview. And he was not in the best of spirits.

The singer had a much-documented drink and drugs addiction in the 1970s, reaching its nadir during the recording of the *Station to Station* album when he was said to subsist on a diet of milk and red peppers, and became so paranoid as a result of the snowdrifts of cocaine that he was consuming that he kept his urine in jars. When he was in his unlikely but lucrative world-conquering period as a pop star the following decade, he liked to distance himself from this troubled young man, but the urge to walk on the wild side was still strongly within him.*

---

\* This was despite his sanctimonious declaration in an August 1991 interview that 'I don't take drugs . . . life by example is the only thing to do . . . when I see an artist propagating the use of drugs as a good lifestyle, one wonders and hopes that when the drugs kill him the example will be even better, frankly.'

Schermerhorn observes that 'back then, he was just cleaning up from coke and booze, and you could tell that he was still at the in-between stage. Some mornings, he looked rough. I could tell "Oh, he got hammered last night".'[7] Some went further; the psychologist Oliver James commented to the author Dylan Jones that 'a friend of mine who is a coke dealer met [the musician] in the early '90s and he hoovered up huge amounts of coke, so much so, that my friend, who is kind of an expert in this stuff, said that he must have been doing some other drugs to protect him from the effect. Because if you took that amount of coke in one go, it could potentially kill you.'[8]

Perhaps in an attempt to overcome these urges, the star was in a phase, brief and unlikely though it seemed, of trying to be a regular guy. Even if his interactions with the press seemed defensive rather than warm – 'I'm a big boy,' he defiantly told *Rolling Stone*, 'and I find myself less and less interested with how I'm perceived anyway'[9] – he seemed torn between two worlds: the one where he was being feted by the great and the good, and the other, in which he was the frontman of a hard-rock band, going out on the road and playing venues the kind of size that he hadn't even considered in decades.

In the former category, Schermerhorn now observed how his employer was leading an existence that seemed like the regal tour of some theoretically beloved but faded imperial figure. 'Every night backstage, there'd be different people, actors, filmmakers, no matter what the city. And he'd always say, "Do you mind if Liz comes back?" And we're like "Liz who?"' The answer was, of course, Liz Taylor. Not that her host was ever cowed by mixing with the super-famous. 'Man, he could turn on the charisma; he could turn it on, when he needed to turn it on.' Yet there were many other times when he could be, in Schermerhorn's recollection, 'a shitty, pissy little asshole'. On one occasion, a journalist inveigled himself onto the tour bus, only to be thrown off by his quarry indignantly asking 'What the fuck do you think you're doing?' The guitarist noted that it seemed like a stagey demonstration of the musician's status. 'It was like "Damn, I'm the prima donna. I'm the fucking rock star."'[10]

This sense of self – or sense of doubt – extended into his ill-fated attempts to be conventional. Schermerhorn got on well with his boss, who, in his recollection, thought of him as 'the new kid who's gonna get his mind blown on tour'. The guitarist was savvy enough not to bug the singer, nor to ask him stupid questions, but instead observed his cigarette ash falling from the top bunk as he smoked one of the three packets that he got through a day, all the while reading voraciously. Yet when they ventured outside, as incognito as they could be, the results were almost tragicomic. As Schermerhorn says, 'We were walking by a pawn shop in Minneapolis, selling radios, old shit. And we go in, and he sees a portable CD player, used for 90 bucks. And he says "I'm gonna offer the guy 70 bucks." And I'm like, "Why didn't he just buy a new one somewhere or send his assistant to get it?" And then I realised. "Oh, he's trying to be a normal guy." But he was trying to rebuild himself from the inside.' Schermerhorn concluded, wistfully, 'I think he was lost. And I think Tin Machine was him trying to say "I'll be in a band again, and that'll sort it all out."'[11]

It did not. His employer had said of his better-known repertoire, 'for a long time, I've wanted to stop fucking doing those songs. I mean, it's really hard for me to get it up for Major Tom at this point. I absolutely loathe singing "Young Americans".' And he boasted with pride that, on their previous gigs, 'no one screamed out for "Heroes"'.[12] Unfortunately, nobody was screaming out for 'Shopping for Girls' or 'Prisoner of Love', either. For all his bravado – 'I'm an adult, and with this band we're not trying to fake anything. What we're trying to do is take rock and roll along with us. I love it way too much to just leave it behind'[13] – the musician was unable to escape the world's suspicion that he was, indeed, faking it. Once, he had sneered at the same old thing in brand-new drag. And now he was trying to convince people that it really could shine, after all.

At the outset of the tour, the singer made a joke out of his new act's reduced circumstances. Giving a joint interview in a press conference – he stuck to the agreement that all publicity appearances would be equally divided between all four official members of the band, a Stalinist edict that most publications ignored by only printing what its most famous member said – he quipped, of the uninspiring surroundings of the Los Angeles Marriott airport hotel in which he was speaking, 'you know, fellows, when I look out on all this splendour spread before us and consider all that we've accomplished in our short time together to bring us here – well, I'm sorry, but I can't help but feel a little bit choked up'. Nor was he under any illusion as to his new band's popularity. When one eager journalist asked him whether he considered their debut album was misunderstood, he laughed and replied, 'Oh, I don't know about misunderstood. How about unheard?'[14]

By the time the tour of unheard songs arrived in the UK, the running jokes were wearing thin. It may have seemed like an amusing shift to embrace the life of jobbing musicians – travelling by bus, eating unadventurous meals in cheap chain restaurants where nobody bothered them – but it was also repetitive and grimy. Britain, in the aftershock of Thatcherite government, was a place devoid of colour or energy, and the determinedly low-key tour reflected this. Yet the star, who took delight in (inaccurately) telling interviewers that 'I haven't really been in England since 1973',[15] took a certain grim delight in recapturing his past, even if nobody else did.

The singer and Gabrels referred to themselves as 'tarnished cranky people', singing the words to the tune of R.E.M.'s 'Shiny Happy People'. When the singer pointed out that they had 74 years' worth of touring between them, making them, in his estimation, 'the very poor man's Muddy Waters', Hunt Sales merely replied 'Shit.' Despite the 'mire of sexual innuendo' that the band claimed they had slipped into, in large part because Gabrels chose to play his guitar on stage using a vibrator and the singer saying that he was 'trisexual – I'll try anything once',*[16] the sheer banality of the venues that they were playing to indifferent audiences would have defeated even the most vibrant of musicians.

---

* He recycled this not wildly original joke on numerous occasions, most notably in his fiftieth birthday interview with the BBC, in reply to the Pet Shop Boys' Neil Tennant asking him if he genuinely was bisexual in the 1970s: a classic evasion covered with a gag.

The last time the star had played the Wolverhampton Civic Hall had been in 1973 on the Aladdin Sane tour, to fans dumbstruck with adoration. Now, if any of the same admirers were there, two decades later, the only enthusiasm that they were displaying was that of nostalgia, even as the star and Hunt Sales, trying their hardest, would take to the stage wearing T-shirts emblazoned with the legend 'Fuck You, I'm In Tin Machine'. The unkind might have suggested, given the amount of drugs that the two men had taken, that it was as much a reminder of what they were supposed to be doing as a statement of intent.

The singer tried to be as cheerful as he could. When the journalist Charles Shaar Murray asked him whether, after his 'decidedly mixed' experiences in the 1980s, he now wanted to be in a band rather than remain a solo artist, his subject attempted to deflect, saying 'I didn't think it would really come to this. I never thought I'd sink so low! This is the first band that I've been in – as opposed to led or directed – since The Kon-Rads (in 1963!).' Then there was an attempt at PR ('the fact that it evolved very quickly into a band format was just great, and that it's become what it's become is just wonderful'), but the description of what the faithful could expect from the shows was hardly inspiring. 'I think we'll probably look right for our ages. We'll spend a bit of money, dress up nicely, play our music and hopefully not look like mutton dressed up as lamb.'[17]

As if tiring of the tour before it was even halfway done, or brooding on Jon Wilde's dismissal of him, the star opened up about his past life to Schermerhorn during the interminable hours on the tour bus.

Of how he'd gone through a period of being drunk every day since he was 16.

Of trying, and failing, to clean up his act in the 1980s on the Let's Dance tour, and beyond.

Of his current literary interests (Philip K. Dick was a great favourite, but he couldn't stand *The Sheltering Sky* author Paul Bowles).

Of his friendship with Marc Bolan when the two were teenagers, and how they would sit in Bolan's front room while his mother brought them tea, and how they would systematically analyse sheet music of Broadway musicals, working out how they fitted together and what made a classic song a classic.

Of the joys of his recent engagement to Iman, to whom he had proposed in Paris while travelling on a boat beneath the Pont Neuf bridge a couple of weeks before.

He even offered a candid opinion on one of Schermerhorn's bandmates. 'When Hunt gets high, it annoys me, and I've said that if he doesn't quit, he'll be out. We've got replacement drummers waiting. And then we'll be in some insane restaurant in Italy, eating absurd food at two in the morning, and he'll have toilet paper stuck to his shoe. And then I'll start laughing hysterically, and an "Oy Vey!" becomes an "Oy Vey, Baby!"'[18]

The latter observation would find its own regrettable sequel, but as the circus came into town, it was all the star could do to find humour where he could. It was clear, given both Tin Machine's artistic ambitions and commercial fortunes, that the London venue they would play for two nights was not going to be Wembley Stadium. Or even Wembley Arena. The band had played some smaller venues in 1989, including the Town & Country Club in Kentish Town and the National Ballroom in Kilburn, but those had been secret, invitation-only shows. Now they were faced with the knowledge that they would fail to sell out anything larger than a mid-sized theatre. Whether they considered the then Hammersmith Odeon, scene of Ziggy Stardust's last stand in July 1973, is unknown, but it would be the Brixton Academy, a relatively new venue in south London, that would see their sole performances in the capital, on 10 and 11 November 1991.

It may have amused the singer that the recently installed prime minister, John Major, had also lived in Brixton between 1955 and 1965, and that his supposedly humble origins would become part of the Conservatives' successful campaigning slogan the following year: 'What does the Conservative Party offer a working-class kid from Brixton? They made him prime minister.' Such was the 'authenticity' that Brixton was supposed to connote that Major was compelled to return there for an election broadcast in 1992, being filmed awkwardly buying kippers at the market and reacting with joy and surprise to the sight of his father's old shop. Yet the musician's intentions were rather different, and considerably less public.

As the bus arrived in Brixton, he said, 'That's where I grew up', to which Schermerhorn nodded and said 'Oh, cool.' Then the singer suddenly made a request. He asked if the bus might divert past 40 Stansfield Road, the house where he was born and lived until he was six. Nobody was going to argue with him, even if the impromptu detour ran the risk of exposing him to obsessive fans or delaying the beginning of the show. So the bus drove past a row of nondescript three-storey Victorian houses, many of which were in advanced states of decrepitude, given the area's insalubrious reputation, until it arrived outside one, no more noteworthy than the rest, and then stopped.

The star disembarked from the bus in the rain and walked over to the house. Schermerhorn, who had been sitting behind him, glanced outside the window. To his surprise and faint embarrassment, he saw that the musician – a man who he had come to admire; someone who he said working with was 'like being strapped into the best ride at the amusement park'[19] – was weeping. And his bandmate's only thought was *Man, I wouldn't want to be this guy.*[*,20]

There could have been any number of reasons for his emotional state, ranging from a cathartic rush of nostalgia at this anonymous homecoming of sorts to simply the overwhelming exhaustion that he must have felt on what proved to be a punishingly lengthy tour for a roundly ridiculed album. Or it was something closer to home. When the star reboarded the bus, he spoke quietly to Schermerhorn. 'My mother never accepted me. She adored my brother and thought that he was the genius. She's always asking me when I'm going to get a real job. But it's all a miracle. I should have been an accountant.'[21] They drove on and the incident was not

---

* Gabrels was also present, but in his recollection, 'I was perhaps less impressed with the situation than Eric was at that point . . . I was more "OK, yeah, house" when I saw it.'

mentioned again. They played the gig, as they would the next night, when the singer would be struck in the eye by an over-enthusiastically chucked packet of Marlboro cigarettes. True to form, he seized the advantage by briefly donning an eye patch that made him look like a rakish pirate. Tin Machine never returned to London to perform again.

Schermerhorn remains mystified as to why he was the recipient of such a confidence – if, of course, it was sincere. As he says, 'For me, I was like, "Whoa, why is he talking to me like this? Why is he confiding this in front of me?" Then you realise that maybe he treats everyone like this. Maybe anyone else who could have been there would have heard exactly the same.'[22]

The star would often offer similar amounts of never-before-heard candour to delighted journalists, who would be thrilled with their apparent scoop, only to find that their interviewee had offered the same information, often word for word, to their colleagues and rivals. Those who expected the unvarnished truth from him were often to be disappointed. Yet those who cynically anticipated nothing more than falsehoods from the former Thin White Duke would also be undone by their own lack of belief in him.

In John 11, Jesus says – when he is confronted with the apparent death of Lazarus, the brother of Mary, she who anointed him with ointment – that 'I am the resurrection, and the life: he that believeth in me, though he were dead, yet shall he live. And whosoever liveth and believeth in me shall never die. Believest thou this?' Mary indeed does and is soon vindicated when her brother returns to life, wrapped in the same clothes in which he was buried. Jesus had told the truth. Yet what he has neglected to mention is that Lazarus, raised from the dead to prove a complex theological point – or alternatively because his benefactor enjoys his and his sister's company and doesn't want such a boring thing as mortality to get in the way of having him at his table – is unique in that he now knows what death is, and will one day, inevitably, have to return to such a state again.

Nine years after his near-fatal heart attack, David Bowie would return to Stansfield Road one final time in 2013, this time accompanied by his wife Iman and their 13-year old daughter Lexi, as part of what became his valedictory visit to Britain. On this occasion, he was anonymous, cloth-capped and furtive, now just another late middle-aged man showing his family sights of personal significance to him. But as he stood outside the house, weeping, that November evening two decades earlier, he could never have anticipated what would be an extraordinary resurrection of his own, accomplished in ways that he could barely have imagined.

# TIN MACHINE AND SOUND + VISION

## 'How long will you tolerate this?'

*'Our Father, who art in heaven. . .'*

'I don't know what the *fuck* they wanted.'
Gabrels, Bowie, producer Tim Palmer and Sales, Mountain Studios, 1989.

Tim Palmer

On 20 April 1992, the Freddie Mercury Tribute Concert for AIDS Awareness was held at Wembley Stadium, just outside London. The event was designed both to commemorate the Queen lead singer Freddie Mercury, who had died of AIDS at the age of 45 the previous November, and to raise funds for the Mercury Phoenix Trust. What none of the organisers had considered – or wished to consider – was, a few years after Live Aid and its less celebrated offshoot Farm Aid, the participating artists being fully attuned to the reach that such a high-profile event would inevitably have, thanks to its being televised worldwide. Should one of the participants wish to become the centre of attention, they would have to do something so off-kilter and unexpected that it would become the *de facto* talking point of the concert.

Most acts performing at the concert would have regarded such a display of one-upmanship as undignified and attention-seeking. After all, virtually everyone playing at the Freddie Mercury tribute was world famous and not in need of the extra exposure – and consequent publicity – that such a moment would bring. There were only two exceptions to this. One was George Michael, long emancipated from Wham! and developing a solo career as the biggest pop star in Britain, thereby filling the gap left by Mercury. His barnstorming rendition of Queen's 'Somebody to Love' therefore stole the show, musically, which led to inevitable rumours that Queen would have recruited him as a replacement for their lead singer. If, of course, anyone *could* have replaced Freddie Mercury.

The other exception was a more specific case. Playing to a stadium audience for the first time since the end of his Sound + Vision tour at the end of September 1990, David Bowie, recently returned from what would be his final gig with Tin Machine in Tokyo on 17 February 1992, had something to prove to the in-person crowd of 72,000 and a global multitude of as many as a billion people. Unbeknownst to everyone – including the musicians he had been playing with a couple of months before – he had decided to call time on the Tin Machine project and to return to his solo career, albeit now with, he hoped, a wisdom and maturity that his post-

*Let's Dance* work had so sorely lacked. He had to show the world that he was back and at the top of his game, both musically and performatively.

It was a musical triumph. There was a duet with Annie Lennox on 'Under Pressure', the song that Bowie had recorded with Queen in Switzerland in July 1981; a froideur had set in between Bowie and the band's guitarist Brian May, who icily referred to 'Mr Bowie' and later candidly admitted that 'it was hard, because you had four very precocious boys and David, who was precocious enough for all of us'.[1] For the second song, the precocious one reunited with his fellow Spider from Mars guitarist Mick Ronson,* with whom he had not played since Ronson performed a guest appearance on 'The Jean Genie' in Toronto on the Let's Dance tour in September 1983. The two tore through an appropriately ferocious version of Bowie's 'All The Young Dudes' as part of a makeshift supergroup that included the remaining members of Queen, Mott the Hoople's Ian Hunter and Def Leppard guitarist Phil Collen. And, finally, Ronson (looking haggard, thanks to the liver cancer that would kill him within a year), Queen and Bowie united for a mighty '"Heroes"', which would, under normal circumstances, have made for a fitting finale to the three-song set that he had come on for. But the star had other ideas.

Dressed in a bilious mint ice-cream-coloured suit, Bowie dutifully paid tribute to 'our great friend, Freddie Mercury', before going on to hijack the show by discussing all those who had been 'toppled by this relentless disease', including a friend of his, 'Craig'. Bowie then dramatically fell to his knees and proceeded to recite the Lord's Prayer, word-perfect. The presumably dumbstruck audience observed this remarkable moment of theatricality in virtual silence, after a few initial (ironic?) whoops could be heard from a few observers. Then, a moment later, Bowie, looking relieved,

---

* The two had reconnected again at the Brixton Tin Machine gig that took place after Bowie's emotional return to his childhood home. Gabrels recalled how 'everybody left as per usual and went back to the hotel, and I stayed with Mick for four hours and hung out'. If they discussed how to be Bowie's chief lieutenant – and the pitfalls involved in such a thing – it could only have been useful advice.

15

concluded and departed to cheers and applause, and the concert could once again resume, with its talking-point moment firmly established in the minds of a billion people.

Reaction to the stunt varied. May commented caustically that 'he didn't do *that* in rehearsals'. In *Melody Maker* – clearly by now established as the anti-Bowie music title – Paul Mathur sighed that 'he is now officially completely redundant as anything other than a caricatured object of ridicule'. Bowie's publicist Alan Edwards says – tactfully perhaps – 'To be honest, for some reason that one's a bit of a blur. We had an inkling David was going to do something special, but we were slightly astonished when he got down and did the Lord's Prayer.' Ever the PR supremo, Edwards still describes it as 'a brilliant moment, though'.[2]

As for its performer, he discussed it occasionally in subsequent interviews, including with *Rolling Stone*'s David Sinclair the next year, and in *Q*'s 'Cash for Questions' in 2000. Admitting to Sinclair that many had been surprised by his actions, Bowie suggested 'it wasn't for them', before equivocating as to his own motivations. 'I've never bought in to any organised religion. But now I have an unshakeable belief in God. I put my life into his hands every single day. I pray every morning.' He concluded that, 'For me, it's a universal prayer. I was as surprised as anyone that I'd said it at that concert. But I was pleased that I'd done it.'[3]

He went further in the *Q* interview, presumably feeling that he could now be candid. 'I had no idea whether I was going to carry it out or not until that break at the end of ['"Heroes"'], then, whoosh . . . I was down. I felt as if I were being transported by the situation and that I no longer had any control. In hindsight, as it was so alien a gesture within the context of rock, it remains a favourite personal rock "moment" for me. It was astounding to find that I could complete the prayer in front of so many thousands of people without hearing a pin drop (*sic*). It was a magical thing. I was so scared as I was doing it, as I felt the jaw-dropping quotient fill the stadium.'

Bowie then claimed – inaccurately, but it's a good story, so let it stand – that 'the most extraordinary aspect was that the producer of the American televised link of the show found it so hard to handle it, that he refused to allow it to be transmitted in the States'. He then owned up to having acted less out of awareness-raising and more from a desire to be dramatic. 'I have to admit there's an aspect of my personality which continually asks my audience '"How long will you tolerate this?"''[4]

The nature of the *Q* interview was that such questions could not be followed up on, and so Bowie escaped further interrogation. Yet if a journalist had wanted to pry further – and if his or her quarry would cooperate – then they might have delved into Bowie's convenient but transitory belief in a deity, briefly exhibited on 'Word on a Wing' and the title track from *Station to Station*, and suggested that, like so much else in Bowie's life and career, it was little more than a pose, adopted on a whim and discarded at will. He might have smiled and concurred, or vigorously disagreed. Or he might have gone on to make a joke about it, before changing the subject to something he was more comfortable with.

Success has many fathers, but failure is an orphan. When Bowie discussed the Tin Machine project later in his career, it was usually difficult to discern what his true feelings were. He described it as 'a dreadful commercial failure, but an artistic success' to Sinclair, and there was the bullish suggestion that there would be a further album, despite the fact that 'it doesn't seem to be England's cup of tea at all . . . Judging by some of the antagonistic letters we had, it's almost as if I'd let the side down. Very strange.'[5] He was laconic to Simon Witter in 1995, describing the project simply as 'success', but the following year he was more balanced with Mick Brown in the *Daily Telegraph*, calling it 'a disaster touched with glory. A glorious disaster.'

Still, he refused to disown the project, saying that 'for better or worse, it helped me to pin down what I did and didn't enjoy about being an artist. It helped me, I feel, to recover as an artist.'[6] It would be easy for the committed Bowie fan, beguiled by their idol's literate sales patter, to reimagine the years that he spent in the world's least likely hard-rock band not as a grim wallow in existential misery but as a healthy, exciting process, in

17

which he worked alongside brilliant musicians and succeeded in rescuing his artistic mojo from whatever swamp it had descended into after the embarrassments of the late 1980s. To which I can only suggest that he wasn't known as a master of reinvention for nothing.

The previous decade had seen Bowie encounter triumph and disaster, both of which he had reacted to, publicly at least, with the nonchalance that characterised his career. *Let's Dance*, released in 1983, had been comfortably his most successful album commercially, but then its successors, 1985's *Tonight* and his artistic nadir, 1987's *Never Let Me Down*, were ashen imitations of the art-pop blend that Bowie and his producer Nile Rodgers had honed to near perfection on the world-conquering behemoth that had brought the musician, wild-eyed and slightly dazed, into the mainstream for the first time in his career. It was not a comfortable place for him to tarry in. The only logical – only imaginable – solution was for him to reach deep inside himself and summon up whatever remained of his artistic soul that had not been steadily eroded away by the drudgery of first-class travel and class A drugs, to say nothing of a stream of sycophantic admirers who would genuflect, or more, at the coming of the former Ziggy Stardust.

When Bowie met Reeves Gabrels, the man who would become his most consistent, and important, collaborator throughout the 1990s, he soon realised that he was in the presence of neither sycophant nor court jester. In 1987, Gabrels was accompanying his then-wife Sarah Terry on tour for her work as Bowie's press officer. Trying to while away the time while she arranged interviews on the Glass Spider tour, Gabrels was perusing a book about Persian perspectives on art. He then heard a familiar voice say 'Hi, I'm David. What are you reading?' Gabrels showed him, the two hit it off and then spent the afternoon sitting in Bowie's trailer watching *Fantasy Island* and improvising their own storyline with the sound turned off.

Gabrels may have thought it was a surreal, if enjoyable, encounter, but there was soon an unexpected development. Bowie had assumed, given Gabrels's choice of reading matter, that he was a painter, but Terry gave him a tape of her husband's demos, also informing him that she and he would be moving to London from Boston for her work. A few weeks later, the guitarist picked up an answerphone message, delivered in what Gabrels describes as 'not exactly what my cartoon Monty Python version of a British accent is supposed to be . . . not this horrible Nigel Tufnell accent . . . more transatlantic.' The voice was friendly, but business-like. 'I'm calling from Morocco, where I'm filming *The Last Temptation of Christ*. Well, I hear you're moving over to London. So I'll see you when you get there. Look forward to it.'

It was less an enquiry and more a command, and it was not long until their collaboration began. As Gabrels recounts, Bowie called and said '"What are you doing this weekend?" And I was like "Well, Mr Bowie, nothing that I can't cancel." And so I went over to his place and what was supposed to be a weekend turned into a month.'[7] After passing the audition – Bowie asked Gabrels to play 'Ziggy Stardust', at which the guitarist excelled – the pair headed over to Montreux in August 1988, and Bowie set about recruiting personnel for his new, as yet-mysterious project.

The brothers Sales had worked with him on the 1977 Iggy Pop album *Lust for Life*, which Bowie produced. They were brilliantly talented musicians, but also a liability because of their hard-living ways and their refusal to take direction. Bowie later acknowledged this by saying, not without admiration, 'The Sales brothers would never accept having another boss. They are far too stubborn and aware of their own needs. They're not in the market to be anybody's backing band, either of them. You do not fuck with the Sales brothers.'[8]

Less experienced, but also less abrasive, was the 26-year-old producer Tim Palmer, who Bowie immediately christened 'young Tim'. He had endeared himself to the musician by telling him that his favourite album by him was the overlooked *Lodger*. 'Ironically,' Bowie replied, 'that's very appropriate for the direction that the new music would be going in.' When Palmer headed over to Montreux to begin work on the project, he had grandiose ideas as to what the studio would be like. 'I had these images in my head of a huge control room with big glass windows, and out of the glass windows, you'd be seeing people skiing down mountain slopes.' He was swiftly disabused. 'The studio was basically a little room on the side of the casino, with a very, very small control room with no frills at all and very, very cramped. There wasn't really anywhere to sort of hang out or do anything entertaining, save make tea on a kettle in the hallway.' Palmer concluded, with English understatement, 'it certainly wasn't the sort of studio that I was expecting'.[9]

It was clear from the outset that Bowie wanted to shake things up and challenge both himself and those around him with the new project, which he suggested would become a full-band record, rather than a David Bowie one. This did not necessarily sit well with Gabrels, who became his main co-writer on the first Tin Machine album. 'David was approaching it differently. He felt like he had already been writing songs for two thousand years at that point. He didn't need to keep writing songs, he wanted to just go all out.' The classically trained Gabrels disagreed. 'I wanted to build the house first. I wanted the structure standing.' On the song 'I Can't Read', Bowie insisted on a blues refrain that began to drive Gabrels mad with its constant repetition, before he eventually snapped and shouted, 'I have to keep listening to this track over and over again! It's going to drive me nuts!' Bowie smirked, and replied, 'There's *always* room for blues.'[10] The saying would become a mantra within the band.

Initially, the relationship between the musicians was a tense and awkward one, something that Bowie may have enjoyed stirring up in the spirit of creative tension. The Sales brothers looked down on Gabrels as milquetoast – 'Henry Kissinger from Boston'. 'I was the new guy that had to find my way in and it took them purposefully pushing me to the point where I lost my temper' before he could be accepted into 'their' band.[11] They had not inherited the sense of humour of their father, the comedian Soupy Sales; their jokes were typically laden with a mixture of sexual innuendo and menace. It made for a wearying environment.

Bowie, meanwhile, stuck to his usual technique of improvising lyrics at the microphone, his words treading a fine line between profundity and gibberish. The first song that they recorded was 'Heaven's in Here', followed by a shouty cover of Roxy Music's 'If There Is Something', which Bowie claimed had been done for reasons of expedience. 'We were so exhausted that we didn't have it in us to write another song, so we used an old song to show how we as a band would approach someone else's material.'[12]

The guitarist Kevin Armstrong, who had played at Live Aid with Bowie, came into the sessions midway through, and his presence brought about balance, as he was instinctively on the calmer, more collegiate side of Gabrels and Palmer. 'I joined in the mayhem,' he later recalled, 'while wondering what it was all about . . . I was caught up in the Bowie-verse in a new way.'[13] At the beginning of 1989, the band decamped to Nassau to continue recording, which made for a more harmonious experience; Bowie had fancied some sun and spent the sessions residing in singer Robert Palmer's palatial beach house. The darker side of the Bahamas inspired one of the band's least distinguished songs, the clunky 'Crack City' – Bowie attempting to lecture his listeners on any social issue was eternally a mistake – but nonetheless, after recording 35 songs in a mere six weeks, the group had enough material for their debut album.

The band took the name Tin Machine almost at random. 'We really weren't interested in what kind of band name we had,' Bowie later remarked, 'so it was almost arbitrary – *Ah, let's just pick a song title*', while Gabrels's irreverent suggestion of The Emperor's New Clothes was vetoed. Then it was time to play their first gig in a local club in Nassau. Patrons reacted with surprise and disbelief to the presence of Bowie in their midst. 'It was all unannounced,' says Tim Palmer, 'so they literally turned up, set up a few amps and played to an unsuspecting crowd. I tried my best to mix the sound, but the place was basically a disco and the sound mixing board was actually tiny and on the stage itself.' Nonetheless, it was a lively, if chaotic, night that suggested that Bowie's latest project might have legs, although some of his colleagues had their own reservations. 'Leaving Nassau, I cannot deny that I was disappointed,' says Palmer. 'I had arrived in Nassau co-producing the new David Bowie album, and left producing Tin Machine.'[14]

This sense – that the audience was being short-changed somehow – was the prevalent critical reaction when the first Tin Machine album was released on 22 May 1989, less than a year since the inception of the project. The front cover was depressingly banal, a quasi-Patrick Bateman fantasy of four well-dressed, affluent-looking banker types set against a white background: a yuppie reverie at odds with the heavy rock quotient of the songs on it. Bowie's label EMI were less than enamoured by what they received, too. An internal memo referred despairingly to 'repetitive tunes . . . lyrics that preach . . . minimalist or no production' and a paucity of radio-friendly singles.[15] Unsurprisingly, the relationship between artist and label soon soured. EMI may not have expected another *Let's Dance*, but this wasn't even *Tonight*.

The 42-year-old Bowie had embarked on the project with intent and now, publicly at least, seemed to believe that he had fulfilled that desire, cheerily boasting to *Q* that 'I'm so up on this I want to go and start recording the next album tomorrow'. He told the journalist his plans before discussing them with the rest of the band, announcing that there would be 'another two albums at least. Oh, yes, this will go for a while. While we're all enjoying playing with each other so much, why not?'[16] It sounded like a threat as much as a promise. Certainly, publicity comments did not necessarily indicate a simpatico group; when Tony Sales suggested, ironically, that they were 'one big happy family', his brother was quick to come back with the riposte 'with child abuse!'*,[17]

All the same, the initial critical reaction to *Tin Machine* was not as dismal as might be imagined. *Rolling Stone* called it 'Sonic Youth meets *Station to Station*', and there was praise for its punchy, direct qualities, with the Sales's rhythm section and Gabrels's innovative guitar coming in for particular approval. *Spin* described the album as 'noise rock without the noise.

---

* God bless Adrian Deevoy, of *Q* magazine, for noting that Hunt Sales said this 'triumphantly'. Any fan of the thunderous, unforgettable opening of (the Bowie co-wrote) 'Lust for Life', with *that* drum intro, must be in Sales's debt, but working with him – as his former colleagues recount – must have been a challenging experience.

Aggressive, direct, brutal and stylishly plain, it combines the energy of the rock avant-garde with traditional R&B rhythmic punch.'

Decades later, this seems like empty hyperbole, written by over-excited journalists who confused a significant change of pace and style from Bowie with an improvement in his songwriting. It is undeniably true that *Tin Machine* might be described as 'proto-grunge', as Palmer called it, and that it could be compared to Pixies, Dinosaur Jr and similar alternative American hard-rock bands who were making a cult splash at the time.

The difficulty was that the songwriting was far removed from what Bowie was capable of. Listened to today, the album is an ugly, hectoring, noise devoid of melody and subtlety. If it is superior to *Never Let Me Down*, that is because the closing track, 'Baby Can Dance', has a stylish swagger that briefly elevates the whole enterprise, while 'Amazing' possesses a rare tunefulness largely lacking from the rest of the album. The remainder of *Tin Machine*, meanwhile, lies somewhere between lumpen and distasteful. Viewed objectively as an album in its own right, it is a failure; viewed as the first step in Bowie returning to artistic fulfilment, it is regrettably vital.

Today, few would seek to praise it, but its creators are anxious that it be seen on its own terms. A few years after its release, Bowie suggested, possibly ironically, that he thought it was 'the best album of that year . . . a cracking classic'.[18] 'I was surprised at the level of hostility and vitriol the first record received,' says Gabrels, 'because it's just music, you know?'[19] Palmer remains proud of his 'very important' work with the band, but still maintains that it would have received more respect had it been a Bowie solo album. 'I just feel that the whole project was slightly tarnished, because people were a little bit cynical about the idea of it being a band and didn't really take it that seriously.'[20] Yet perhaps the most succinct criticism came from, of all people, Tina Turner's mother, who sighed that she 'liked it better when David was singing songs'.[21]

Nonetheless, the album was commercially successful (Bowie said it had done '*phenomenally* well' and Gabrels suggests, perhaps optimistically, it sold 2 million copies worldwide\*) and so there was a brief tour in the summer of 1989, before they decamped to Sydney for a few weeks in September to lay down some demos for a future album. The stripped-back, uncompromising shows were the opposite of Bowie's Glass Spider grandiosity two years before, consisting of a dozen appearances in small club venues. Bowie had, by now, decided to sport a slightly unfortunate beard. Allied to the expensive but oddly unflattering Prada suits that he began each evening wearing, he looked like a bit-part actor from one of the lesser action films of the era, the kind of character who insults the hero and ends up shot, garrotted or otherwise punished for his insolence.

Not that anyone was answering back to Bowie, who now decided, in between Tin Machine albums, that he would like to make a great deal of money. The Glass Spider tour had been expensive and he needed to recoup its vast costs as swiftly and easily as possible. Firstly, there was the lucrative release of some of the obscurities from his back catalogue by the record label Rykodisc. It was issued as a three-disc set, entitled *Sound and Vision*, and sold as many as 200,000 copies. Additionally, Bowie – nobody's fool – agreed to the Rykodisc reissue of all his albums from his 'imperial phase' between 1969 and 1980, featuring never-before-heard songs on each CD, cassette or LP.

Bowie then took matters the logical step further. It may have seemed surprising that, just a matter of months after telling any interviewer who would listen that he was committing himself to his new band, and that they were vital for him to regain his artistic integrity, he was taking to the stage at a press conference, clean-shaven and corporate, to promote a 106-date, 24-country tour, again named Sound + Vision, that would last for much of 1990 and would see him perform a greatest hits selection, wisely eschewing

---

\* Bowie's biographer Christopher Sandford suggested in 1996 that it had sold a million copies by then, and he is usually reliable when it comes to sales figures. It is possible that, somehow, it shifted another million in the intervening three decades. Certainly, unloved copies used to be prevalent in second-hand record stores and charity shops.

any of his recent output. There was, however, a kicker. Bowie announced that he would retire all his most beloved songs after the tour concluded, reasoning that 'I'm sure by the end I'll never want to do it again, so what about if I do these songs for the last time – just do them on this tour and never do them again?'[22]

Bowie decided, in an apparently egalitarian moment, that he would allow his admirers to choose their favourite songs to be performed on the tour, via a telephone poll. This idea was quietly scuppered after the *NME* launched a campaign for his much-derided (although secretly quite fun) 1967 novelty single 'The Laughing Gnome' to be performed on the tour, indicating the irreverence that the popular music press felt towards Bowie at this stage of his career. He assembled a five-piece band that included his previous collaborator Adrian Belew as musical director and guitarist (Gabrels turned down the job on the dual grounds that it would be a distraction from his work with Tin Machine, as well as running the risk of aggravating the Sales brothers), the Turkish multi-instrumentalist Erdal Kizilçay on bass, Michael Hodges on drums and Rick Fox on keyboards. It was a less extravagant undertaking than the Glass Spider tour of 1987 – no backing dancers or horn sections here – and was designed by the Canadian choreographer Édouard Lock to have something of the feel of Bowie's grand '70s touring spectacles, the Stage and Station to Station extravagances.

Aesthetically and visually, it was a triumph; Bowie worked in sync with Lock to create something marvellous. The show began with a 50-foot-high video projection of the singer looking down at the audience, as a spotlight illuminated Bowie himself, singing the consistent show opener 'Space Oddity' while accompanying himself on acoustic guitar. Yet if the concerts were a feast for the eyes, they were a rather less satisfying auditory experience. The stripped-back band was thin and struggled to fill the vast spaces in which they were performing, and as the tour wore on, Bowie lost interest in the vast endeavour. He was superior towards the band members – who were reminded, coldly, that they were hired hands who could be dispensed with if they displeased their patron – and they, in turn, found themselves disappointed that their input was not valued. Bowie began the tour engaged to his former dancer Melissa Hurley, but the engagement ended during the six-month campaign. It was not a happy time.

Still, its intended purpose – to make a great deal of money and to exorcise the past – was accomplished without unnecessary incident, and Belew, who escaped the more dictatorial treatment that his colleagues faced, found Bowie friendlier and calmer than when they had worked together in the '70s. Yet even though his employer was more philosophical about life, openly admitting his embarrassment at the excesses of the Glass Spider tour, Tin Machine had not yet fulfilled its purpose. 'More than anything else,' Belew recalled, 'he was once again unsure of where to move his career to.'[23]

The answer seemed inevitable and so Bowie reformed Tin Machine in the winter of 1990. The band's previous personnel all reunited, although Tim Palmer had recently had a baby and asked to be allowed to resume production duties after the basic tracks were completed. However, numerous things had changed. For a start, Bowie had parted ways with EMI, who had lost interest in pandering to their quixotic star when other, more pliable rock gods were available to make them more money. He had made EMI a huge amount of money in the '80s, and so their actions seem almost laughably ungrateful, but expensive vanity projects do not go down well with bean-counting record company executives. *Tin Machine II*, as it was unimaginatively called, would eventually be released on the Polygram offshoot label Victory Music. However, Bowie had other matters on his mind. He had fallen in love.

The presence of the model, occasional actress and philanthropist Iman Abdulmajid in Bowie's life was vitally important in making him the more rounded and accessible figure that he became. They met when she was 35 and he was 42 – a considerably smaller age difference than existed between Bowie and his previous partner Melissa Hurley, who was in her early twenties when they separated – and both described their first meeting on 4 October 1990 as love at first sight; Bowie later said that he was thinking of their children's names on their initial encounter. They began dating almost immediately and were engaged within the year.

Happiness writes white and so the cynical may have expected the second Tin Machine album, conceived as it was when its creator was in a happier and more stable mindset than before, to be a gentler and less abrasive experience. *Tin Machine II* may not have been a Ronettes album, but it was a far more pleasurable listening experience than its cacophonous predecessor and remains one of Bowie's most overlooked releases – not least because, at the time of writing, it is unavailable on any streaming service, in part through confusion as to who the rights belong to, as well as being long since out of print as a physical record. It's hardly *Scary Monsters* or *Station to Station* – or, for that matter, *Blackstar* or *Outside* – but it deserves greater credit than it has received.

Gabrels, who co-wrote virtually every song, suggests that his intention was 'to make the compositions more harmonious, and make it musically richer'[24], and Palmer agrees that it's underrated. 'It was a little bit more textured and a little bit more produced. But I don't think anything is lost by that. I think that some of the songs that are on the *Tin Machine II* album are as good as anything in the Bowie catalogue and it's such a shame to me that people don't get the chance to finally hear that album and stream it and learn to love it. I believe that if people heard it a little more, they would see the beauty that I see that's within that album.'[25]

Technically, Bowie was at his finest. Palmer recalls, admiringly, that 'when we recorded a song called "Amlapura", David went out and sang a vocal at one point, and I was in the control room, and I just thought it was absolutely fabulous. But David himself was a little disappointed with that, so I asked "What was it about the performance that you didn't like?" because, to me, it seemed perfect. And he said that he didn't feel that the sadness was coming through enough from the lyric for his song and he wanted to perform it again. And I said, "Well, how will you approach it to make it sadder?", and he said, "I'm just going to sing it just a little tiny bit flat, and it will give it a more of a melancholic feel." And he went out and did exactly that.'[26]

It was a bravura display of technique, which Palmer remains impressed by. 'To this day, I've never seen a vocalist do anything like that in the studio. It was quite incredible. And it's worth noting that this was a time before the manipulation of vocal pitching that we have today. There was no autotune when we made those records.'[27] And this achievement stretched to about half the album, from its weary, beautiful closer 'Goodbye, Mr Ed' – prefiguring 'Slip Away' / 'Uncle Floyd' in its wry cynicism about American pop culture, written by an outsider looking in – to the initial single, the tightly controlled and pulsating 'You Belong in Rock 'n' Roll', which reached the dizzying heights of number 33 in the UK singles charts and so became Tin Machine's biggest hit. There are plenty of other highlights, too, such as 'Shopping for Girls' – a song about child prostitution in Thailand that was, perhaps, a rebuke to the then wildly successful glamorisation of sex work in *Pretty Woman* – and the lively opener 'Baby Universal'. But, alas, something terrible happened: Hunt Sales was permitted, even encouraged, to sing.

We will tactfully pass over the merits, or otherwise, of the songs that showcase Sales's vocals ('Sorry' and 'Stateside', if you're a masochist*), but their presence on the album suggested a flaw that became dominant during the '80s and would remain constant up until almost the end of Bowie's life and career: he was incapable of judging what was brilliance and what was filler, or worse, and presented them back to back. *Station to Station* and *Low* were conspicuous by the absence of dull filler, but over the course of *Tin Machine II*'s dozen songs, torpor soon sets in. Had half a dozen been omitted, and a tight, 20-minute EP been released instead, it would be regarded far more highly today than it is.

Some critics were blindsided into overrating *Tin Machine*. They would not make the same mistake again and so proceeded to go far in the opposite direction. Edward Bell's cover illustration of four naked statues was the first

---

* I'm with Nicholas Pegg, who calls them 'the most frighteningly bad songs ever to find their way into the Bowie canon'.

thing to attract ridicule – not least because the puritanical American market insisted on the censorship of the genitalia of the statues – and then it was open season on the rest of it. Adrian Deevoy, in a *Q* review snappily entitled 'Are Tin Machine crap?', swiftly provided assent, and few were kinder, although the ever-contrary *Creem* dutifully proclaimed that it offered 'the best music Bowie's released since 1980's *Scary Monsters*'.

Whether or not it was, the record-buying public had lost interest by the time the album appeared on 2 September 1991. Bowie may have declared in 1989 that 'I've never been worried about losing fans'; this was confirmed in brutal fashion, as the millions who saw him on the Sound + Vision tour expressed precisely no interest in his latest release. The album peaked at 23 in the British charts, and stumbled to a pathetic 126 in the US. The future of Tin Machine, such as it was, now lay in live performance, rather than record sales, which were minuscule compared to those of its predecessor.

A comprehensive tour was arranged, beginning in August 1991 in Dublin and ending the following February in Tokyo. It was with poised boastfulness that Bowie declared 'Sometimes, we can be absolutely dreadful on stage. Other nights, I don't think there is a band to touch us.' There was a desire to provoke – the then-disgraced comedian Paul 'Pee Wee Herman' Reubens* was mooted as an opening act, but, as Gabrels says, it was 'too soon' – but it swiftly faded. After all, as Bowie wryly acknowledged, 'we're all of a certain age, we're all divorced. At one point, that was going to be our name. Four Divorced Men or Alimony Inc.'

The opportunity to see the band live was one that Bowie's most committed fans could not pass up but, once again, there was a dedication to ignoring his back catalogue that disappointed all but the Tin Machine faithful. Well-received covers of Neil Young's 'I've Been Waiting for You' – sung by Gabrels, and later to be recorded on *Heathen* – and Pixies' 'Debaser' showed up the weakness of much of the material that the act had recorded, although rehearsal and recording, as well as the presence of the able

---

\*    He had been arrested for indecent exposure at an adult cinema in July that year.

Schermerhorn,* saw the band play as a tight, cohesive whole on stage, albeit with one exception.

Hunt Sales had unblushingly told one journalist that he did not take drugs, but this was a lie. Bowie, attempting to commit to sobriety himself to make his new relationship with Iman work, found himself both frustrated and angered by his drummer's behaviour. He later complained that the tour had been a 'nightmare' because 'one of our members had a serious drugs problem, and that really destroyed the band more than anything else. It got to a situation where it was intolerable. You didn't know if the guy was going to be dead in the morning. We just couldn't cope.'

Bowie had consistently said, both publicly and privately, that he wanted to make three Tin Machine records, but the dismissive critical and commercial response to *Tin Machine II* meant that even the most committed of his admirers was unlikely to finance its recording and promotion. A compromise was hit upon. Eight of the band's songs – ranging from the decent ('You Belong in Rock 'n' Roll', 'Goodbye Mr Ed') to the unspeakable (a full *eight minutes* of 'Stateside') would be recorded on the North American and Japanese legs of the tour, and then released through London Records in July 1992. The collection would take its title from Hunt Sales's joke, *Oy Vey, Baby*,† although the name was understandably believed to be a sour allusion to U2's considerably more successful and beloved *Achtung Baby*, which had seen the band reunite with Bowie's erstwhile producer Brian Eno and sell millions of copies worldwide.

Gabrels, at least, likes *Oy Vey, Baby*. 'We achieved what we wanted to achieve with the live album, and we were playing the more complicated

---

* Of the many interviews that I conducted for this book, Schermerhorn – who has no financial stake in any of Bowie's releases – was the most enjoyably candid, suggesting at one point that he thought, vis-à-vis Bowie and Tin Machine, 'it wasn't his best songwriting . . . it wasn't even his middling songwriting . . . most of my friends pitied me for being in that band.'

† Another, thankfully dismissed, Sales suggestion was 'Two Live Jews', a pun on the name of the then-notorious hip hop act 2 Live Crew.

and less complex stuff alike.'[28] Yet nobody else shared his views and *Melody Maker*'s dismissal that its singer 'had ceased to exist as an artist of any worth whatsoever' was met by a complete lack of commercial success. *Tin Machine II* may have underperformed, but *Oy Vey, Baby* flopped altogether, achieving the doubtful distinction of becoming Bowie's first album since 1967 not to chart at all. The suggestion – or threat – that there would be another live release, this time called *Use Your Wallet* – a nod to Guns N' Roses' considerably more successful *Use Your Illusion* albums – was not followed up on.

In any case, Bowie seemed to have made his peace with the end of the Tin Machine experiment. His all-powerful PA Coco Schwab was overheard by Gabrels remarking that 'Tin Machine was driving down the value of David's currency' and that work had to be done. Within a month of the release of *Oy Vey, Baby*, Bowie released 'Real Cool World' as a single. The theme song to the forgotten Brad Pitt picture *Cool World* – a film most notable for being directed by Ralph Bashki, responsible for *Felix the Cat* in a former life – it was unexceptional, but marked the reunion of Bowie with Nile Rodgers, which would go on to pay far greater dividends commercially in due course.

Over the previous couple of years, the singer had shown himself at his best and at his worst. Schermerhorn saw his personal generosity when the guitarist was summoned to Bowie's suite after the band had played Tokyo's Budokan venue. Schermerhorn was surprised to see that Bowie was clad only in a dressing gown, and, for an irreverent moment, wondered what his employer's intentions were, before Bowie profusely thanked him for his work on a long and often difficult tour and asked him, almost conversationally, which acts he'd most like to work with in the future. Schermerhorn, placed on the spot, stammered 'Chrissie Hynde and Iggy Pop', to which Bowie nodded and said that he'd see what he could do. A matter of a couple of weeks later, Schermerhorn was offered work playing with both Hynde and Pop, something for which he remains grateful: 'it gives me chills to this day, because no one's done anything like that for me since'.[29]

Yet Bowie was also capable of being petulant and difficult, the very model of a modern music egomaniac. He was often short with fans when they had the temerity to approach him in public, and appeared to resent their ingratitude, hissing that 'I don't know what the *fuck* they wanted' when it came to Tin Machine.[30] The band conducted interviews as a four-piece, which Alan Edwards called 'a bit more challenging media-wise as we were trying to make sure the press didn't just focus on David'.[31] This combative element could spill over into publicity commitments once the charm waned or boredom dominated.

A particularly grim occasion arose when Bowie appeared on Terry Wogan's BBC show with the rest of Tin Machine on 14 August 1991. He came across as bored, sarcastic (when asked whether that was 'a real guitar' Gabrels was playing, Bowie answered 'No, it's my lunch, Terry'*) and prone to bizarre surrealism. At one point, he interrupted a question by shouting 'Hello, Ron' into the audience, off-handedly explaining 'He's a mate of ours from Dublin', only for the usually affable Wogan to say, sharply, 'I've got a few mates in Dublin as well'. The broadcaster subsequently said of Bowie that he was the most difficult interviewee he'd encountered in half a century of broadcasting and that he 'thought a solid slap would have helped the situation', although he qualified this by saying 'I didn't hit him, of course. But it came close.'[32]

The Tin Machine era is one of the least-loved aspects of David Bowie's career. There are those who will defend its individual songs, albeit without especial passion, and it was important both for introducing him to Gabrels and for, in Bowie's own estimation, whetting his almost blunted purpose and teaching him how to be a rock star again, rather than an increasingly bland pop performer; it gave him his demon back. But commercially and critically, it was a nadir for Bowie, who would soon have to find new ways of developing his talents without relying on the fallback

---

* Gabrels had also chosen to use a vibrator to play his guitar with, as was his custom: this may have been a step too far for the smiling face of the BBC.

option of his considerable back catalogue or on unquestioning respect from those who had once slavishly adored him. That he had already broken his own resolution by performing '"Heroes"' and 'All The Young Dudes' at the Freddie Mercury concert was not remarked upon by anyone sensitive in his presence.

Alan Edwards, unsurprisingly, takes a more favourable view of the period. 'Tin Machine imbued David with a fantastic energy and sense of purpose, so it was really exciting to be around him during this time. There were some really good songs, such as "Goodbye Mr Ed", which were a bit overlooked. All the guys in the band – Hunt, Tony and Reeves – were fun to be with so I enjoyed going on the road with Tin Machine. I've got a lot of happy memories from those shows.'[33]

And even while embarking on an unlikely career as the frontman of a hard-rock band with American leanings, the man who once jokingly referred to himself as 'the Swiss Larry Grayson' was nothing if not a contradictory figure. It was now time to put away childish things, marry the woman he loved and get on with the next phase of his life and career: conquering the world, all over again.

# 2

# *BLACK TIE WHITE NOISE*

## 'He was running from success'

*'I have never been so happy'*

Bowie went into *Black Tie White Noise* bloodied but unbowed,
as this shot from the video of its lead single 'Jump They Say' suggests.

F. Scott Fitzgerald once wrote 'Let me tell you about the very rich. They are different from you and me.' One of the most obvious ways in which Fitzgerald's dictum has been proved correct is in how the wealthy choose to wed. David Bowie's first marriage, to Angela 'Angie' Barnett, took place on 20 March 1970 at the Beckenham Register Office. It was a determinedly no-frills affair conducted in order for Angie to receive a work permit, which in turn expanded her husband's horizons by enabling him to more easily travel to and perform in the United States – of which her Cypriot-American birth made her a citizen. The laissez-faire nature of the union was demonstrated by the night before the wedding being spent in bed with a mutual friend, who would then serve as best man, and the wedding evening itself was an uproariously drunken affair in the Three Tuns in Beckenham.

Nearly a quarter of a century later, Bowie's second wedding was a decidedly different undertaking, lighter on loucheness and drunkenness, and considerably more elevated in setting, guestlist and the reputation of the couple marrying. Bowie's initial marriage, taking place not long after 'Space Oddity' had given him his first hit, was covered in the *Beckenham and Penge Advertiser* and the *Beckenham Journal*. His second saw the exclusive rights sold to *Hello!* magazine. This might have been viewed as infra dig, but there was no doubt that, in exchange for a series of posed photographs showing Bowie and his new bride Iman looking suitably tense and unrelaxed, the substantial cheque that the celebrity publication offered would have been welcome.

The first half of 1992 was one of the more productive periods in Bowie's life. It saw him conclude the Tin Machine tour (and Tin Machine itself) in Japan, dramatically return to stadium performance at the Freddie Mercury tribute concert, and begin sessions for a new solo album at Mountain Studios in Montreux – where *Tin Machine* was recorded – and at The Hit Factory in New York. Bowie also turned his attention to domestic matters. He bought a £2 million Irish estate and announced his intention to move to Los Angeles with his new wife, too. Whatever else Tin Machine had done, it had shaken Bowie out of his torpor and inertia, giving him a new vitality that would soon translate into both personal and creative momentum.

Bowie and Iman's actual marriage was itself little more eventful than the Beckenham event, being a small civil ceremony conducted in Lausanne on 24 April 1992 by the local magistrate. Both dressed in stylish monochrome; Bowie donned a black suit and tie accessorised with a white rose, while Iman wore a white trouser suit with a black jacket. They then headed to Los Angeles to begin their house hunt, an intention that was soon dropped after their 29 April arrival on coincided with the unleashing of social and racial tensions sparked by the acquittal of the policemen accused of savagely beating Rodney King. The Los Angeles riots began the same day and lasted for five more, resulting in 62 deaths, thousands of injuries, 12,000 arrests and a billion dollars' worth of damage. The newly-weds watched the violence unfold from their hotel, with their celebratory plans cancelled, but rather than castigating the proponents of the riots, Bowie sympathised. 'The whole thing felt like nothing less than a prison break by people who had been caged up for too long with no reason.'[1]

With the idea of a California residence forgotten, Bowie now began writing music inspired by two very different events: the riots and a larger wedding celebration, which would be held in Florence on 6 June, in the Saint James Episcopal Church. Rumours that it would take place in Mustique were disseminated by the Bowie camp to throw opportunists off the scent, but more than a thousand fans still turned up outside the church on the day.

It was a grander affair than the Beckenham or Lausanne ceremonies, but still relatively low-key by A-list musician standards. A mere 68 guests were invited, who included Iman's family, Bowie's mother Peggy, the omnipresent Coco, Edwards and a smattering of celebrities, among them Monty Python's Eric Idle and the homonymic trio of Yoko Ono, Bono and Brian Eno.*

---

\* It may have inspired the later song 'Eno Collaboration' by Half Man Half Biscuit, with its lyric 'I know Bono and he knows Ono and she knows Eno's phone goes thus.'

The reunion with the first three was enjoyable, as might be expected, but his re-encounter with Eno would prove to be vital.

Edwards, who served as chief usher, has detailed memories of the day. 'It was the most beautiful setting and such a happy occasion. David was totally in love with Iman. I was obviously responsible for looking after the guests, including Iman's very friendly but large family, so there was quite a lot of running around and working out who was who and where to seat them. Also, I was liaising closely with Brian Aris, the photographer who was taking the pictures for *Hello!*. I had to try to get little items for the story and make sure I was writing down all the names of the guests etc.'

In his memoir, Edwards expressed vague surprise about the sale of the wedding photos to *Hello!*. 'I suspect the deal was pushed along by Iman,' he observed, 'as this wasn't in keeping with Bowie's typical media positioning.'[2] But he also says, 'I was just aware that it might have been greeted with scepticism in some quarters of the music press, being that David was such a credible artist and this was a celebrity magazine. As it happens, there wasn't any real pushback. I wasn't aware of any creative or artistic decisions being made by Iman. I think David always knew exactly what he wanted to do.'[3]

Carefully briefed by Edwards, *Hello!*'s eager readers were duly given privileged information about every aspect of the ceremony and celebration, from the designer of Bowie's suit (Thierry Mugler, who was present) to the choice of music, composed by the groom himself, in which the anonymous journalist may have inadvertently betrayed a lack of familiarity with Bowie's *oeuvre*. *Hello!* wrote vaguely about 'an atmospheric composition, soothingly beautiful' and gushed that 'the strains of a saxophone alternated with exquisite solos and keyboards creating a mesmerising effect on all'.[4]

Eno, meanwhile, paid greater attention to the instrumental than many of the other guests did, noting its similarity to several of the tracks on the albums they had co-written together in Berlin, *Low* and *"Heroes"*. Hot off the enormous success of U2's *Achtung Baby*, an album intended in part as a gracious homage to the work of Bowie and Eno, the producer took the opportunity to reconnect with the newly married man at the reception that evening, congratulating him on both the ceremony and the music that he had made for it. Bowie mentioned that he had begun recording once again and the two began to make enthusiastic but vague plans to work together again. The unspoken suggestion, on both sides, was that even Eno would have struggled to work his alchemy on the last few albums that Bowie was responsible for.

Still, this reunion would have to wait, as the morning after the ceremony saw Bowie and Iman submit to *Hello*'s softball questions (Sample: 'What was your first impression of Iman, David?'). Yet even this revealed a few facets of personal and professional interest, from Bowie admitting that he 'was a bit cautious because I have a silly sense of humour and I was scared it might put her off me' to his going into greater detail about his personal faith after the Lord's Prayer recitation a few weeks before. 'I'm not a religious person – I'm a spiritual person. God plays a very import-ant part in my life – I look to him a lot and He is the cornerstone of my existence – even more as I get older. But it is a one-to-one relationship with God. I believe man develops a relationship with his own God. I tend to judge a man or a woman by their actions – the way they are with me and the way they are with their friends.' Anyone who had listened to the dramatic anguish of 'Word on a Wing', from 1976's *Station to Station* album, in which Bowie addresses the Almighty himself with Hamlet-like intensity, would be aware that this was familiar – if comfortingly theatri-cal– territory for him.

Yet a more revealing insight was elicited when Bowie compared his second wedding to his first. 'For my part, I got married when I was very young. It was an unfortunate marriage and it didn't work out even remotely. The most glorious thing that came out of my last marriage was my wonderful son Joe, whom I love dearly. And, fortunately, all through my indiscretions, obsessions, addictions and whatever else went wrong in my life, we have been able to form a mutual tie.' Joe – now the film director Duncan Jones – served as his father's best man at the second wedding, something that Bowie professed himself 'absolutely privileged and honoured' by – although, true to form, he couldn't resist a frivolous joke about his responsibilities ('He was absolutely terrific and he didn't lose any of the rings!'). Still, looking at his life, friends and new bride, Bowie could at least allow himself a moment of reflection that referred to the ceremony, but may also have had greater resonance beyond that. 'This for me is so exciting and so invigorating. I have such great expectations of our future together. I have never been so happy.'[5]

Once Bowie's honeymoon in Bali – which he suggested would be 'extensive', dedicated to the exploration of 'many wonderful lands' and to the purchase of 'lots of fabulous clothes'[6] – was concluded, he returned to work in earnest. It was clear, after the commercial disappointment of *Tin Machine II* and the outright failure of *Oy Vey, Baby*, that there had to be considerable change if Bowie was to remain a mainstream commercial prospect in the eyes of record buyers and companies alike.

Gabrels describes the situation pithily. 'There was a lot of pressure from his business office to do *Let's Dance* part two. Once they put that team together, they could go into a meeting with the record company and say, "Look, now I want to produce David again."' Declining commercial fortunes led to declining record company advances, too. Gabrels observes that 'David pretty consistently got around $4 million per record, until we did Tin Machine, when he got $3.27 million. It was like they were saying, "You're almost worth $4 million, but not quite."'[7] In any case, Bowie's relationship with EMI had fallen apart after the first Tin Machine album and he was now looking around for two separate people: someone who would fund the new record, and a producer.

In the case of the former, Bowie swiftly found a berth. The Mimrans, a father-and-son team, had made a great deal of money in the European automotive industry and they believed that they could transfer this success into the music business by forming a new company called Savage Records. The 24-year-old David Mimran declared that Bowie would be 'absolutely . . . the artist to break the label wide open [and be] everything I would hope for'. Therefore, according to Gabrels, 'they got a deal out of

Savage for I don't know how many millions but it was a ridiculous amount because David was going to be their kick-off artist'. Such were the hopes from all parties that Bowie's substantial financial deal was centred around the belief that this would, again, be the album that would sell well in the States. Looking for a guaranteed hit, Bowie decided to turn to Nile Rodgers and suggest a reunion. After all, if *Let's Dance II* was going to be the means of reviving his commercial fortunes, who was better suited to producing it than the original maestro? Money was of no concern; Bowie blithely said to Rodgers, 'Let me know when it comes to somewhere around three million bucks.'[8]

Like Eno, Rodgers had been in touch with Bowie since their all-conquering earlier collaboration, but they hadn't worked together in that time. He remarked, in a rather disconsolate way, that he thought he 'probably would have been his first choice for *Tonight*, but that didn't happen'. (In the event, Bowie hired Derek Bramble, with whom he fell out, and Hugh Padgham; imagining what songs like 'Loving the Alien' and 'Blue Jean' would have sounded like produced by Rodgers is one of the more frustrating 'what ifs' in contemporary music.) Their first, tentative reunion in the studio together produced the 'Real Cool World' single and, with Bowie already revitalised by the Tin Machine project and keen to have a successful record, it should have been as harmonious a collaboration as *Let's Dance*, if not more so.

It was not. As he ostentatiously disowned everything from the substance abuse of former incarnations to his much-proclaimed bisexuality ('I was never gay,' he said in 1992. 'I was physical about it, but frankly it wasn't enjoyable . . . it was almost like I was testing myself. It wasn't something I was comfortable with at all. But it had to be done'[9]), Bowie was regaining control over his persona and career alike. The Tin Machine albums had enabled him to make the music he had wanted to, but he had also had to battle the Sales brothers and critical and commercial ridicule. Now he had the resources and the impetus to do what he liked once again, and everyone working on the album – from Rodgers downwards – was in no doubt as to who was in charge. Bowie's name, figuratively speaking, was once again over the door.

If Tin Machine had been meat-and-potatoes rock, with a side order of modish grunge, then the album that would become *Black Tie White Noise* would be an eclectic smorgasbord of influences and collaborators that Rodgers would be tasked with marshalling into coherence. The jazz trumpeter Lester Bowie (no relation) was prominent on around half the album, and there was an eclectic roll call of special guests who included Bowie musicians both recent (Gabrels) and legendary, with the Spiders from Mars' Mick Ronson and keyboardist Mike Garson returning to the fray – in the ailing Ronson's case, for the final time.

The final track list hinted at a confused and difficult recording process, although both Bowie and Rodgers were swift to praise their collaboration in contemporary interviews. Four of its 12 songs would be covers, with another two being the instrumentals originally composed for Bowie's wedding. And the song that should have been, and probably would have been, its big hit single, 'Lucy Can't Dance', was ditched, relegated to bonus track status on the original CD release. If one wanted to be cynical, it is likely that Bowie had walked into the studio with less material than his comeback album truly merited and was relying on two things to salvage it: Rodgers' technical wizardry and his own spontaneous genius.

It was not the first time that a lack of preparation led to greater trouble later down the line. In an interview with *Rolling Stone* to mark the album's release in April 1993, Rodgers contrasted his experience with what had happened a decade before. '*Let's Dance* was the easiest record I've ever made – three weeks total; *Black Tie White Noise* was the hardest – one year, more or less.' Yet in the same discussion, Rodgers praised the now drug-free Bowie, noting that he was 'a hell of a lot more philosophical and just in a state of mind where his music was really, really making him happy'.[10]

One reason for Bowie's newfound happiness was that he was calling the shots entirely. 'With all due respect to Nile,' he told *Rolling Stone*, 'I didn't listen to *Let's Dance* that much. It wasn't all me. It was a lot of Nile. On the first side particularly, I was really letting Nile run with it. This time when I went back in with Nile, I thought, 'Not again.' So it was very much my album that we made this time, and Nile contributed to it, as opposed to Nile doing everything and me just suggesting we get Stevie Ray Vaughan in or whatever. That's probably why it's so identifiably me.'[11]

Some would argue that it was a waste of time and money to recruit a super-producer like Nile Rodgers and then tell him precisely what to do, but Bowie's micromanagement hit new heights. As Rodgers later said, 'he was really different on that record because it was David steering the ship. It was more his vision, whereas on *Let's Dance* he showed me his vision and allowed me to interpret it. With *Black Tie White Noise* it was more "This is what I want to do."' This reached its zenith when Rodgers performed the solo on 'Miracle Goodnight' and Bowie gave him precise instructions as to how to play it: 'Nile, I want you to play this solo as if the '50s never existed.'[12]

Other collaborations proved happier affairs. Garson, who played piano on 'Looking for Lester', had not worked with Bowie since *Young Americans*, but when the telephone rang and the words 'Hi, it's David' could be heard on the other end, Garson describes the feeling as being 'like ten minutes had passed since we last spoke'. He was very much a supporting player this time around; 'my playing on [*Black Tie White Noise*] didn't kill me,' he drily remarks. 'A lot of the focus was on Lester's trumpet, and there weren't the kind of spaces that he left for me on, say 'Diamond Dogs' and 'Sweet Thing' and 'Candidate', which means that there wasn't a whole lot for me to do, other than be a small presence in footprint.'[13] But it would lead to more substantial work together later, not least on the song 'Bring Me the Disco King', which Bowie and Garson began developing in the sessions. The pair would sporadically work on it until it finally reached fruition a decade later, on the album *Reality*.

The drummer Sterling Campbell, meanwhile, played on *Black Tie White Noise* – his first appearance on a Bowie album – but he had been a fan of the musician since he first saw him perform on the "Heroes" tour in 1978, at the age of 14. Bowie's drummer Dennis Davis lived in the same building as Campbell and, knowing that the boy wanted to be a drummer himself, gave him a ticket to see Bowie and his band at Madison Square Garden that evening, which proved to be a formative experience. When Rodgers introduced him to Bowie 15 years later, Campbell married the enthusiasm of an ardent fan with the committed technique of an enthusiastic drummer, which meant that his contributions to the album, along with those of the jazz drummer Poogie Bell, are some of its most distinctive.

Working with Bowie, Campbell says, was a blessedly straightforward experience. 'He was very nice, and very enthusiastic. I had a lot of ideas about making music, because I'd really studied David's music and felt I really understood it, thinking *How can I make that '70s stuff sound '90s?'* Bowie appreciated Campbell's commitment and expertise, and their work together took on a straightforward pattern. 'We'd talk first, shoot the shit about what's happening in the world or something funny that's happened, and then he'll say "Okay, okay, let's go. Let's go record now." There was no conflict or argument that I could see. Instead, he'd just say, after a conversation and a cup of tea, "Here's this song. What're you going to do?"'[14]

Yet all of these collaborators, old and new alike, were insignificant compared to the brief return of Ronson to the studio for a cover of Cream's 'I Feel Free'. He hadn't played on a Bowie album since *Pin Ups* in 1973, as their once-close relationship had foundered after Ronson had attempted his own solo career with the 1974 album *Slaughter on 10th Avenue*, which featured several songs co-written by Bowie but conspicuously failed to achieve the same success as his own, more epochal albums. However, after their reunion in Toronto the decade before, their friendship resumed. Bowie was especially amused by the back-handed homage that their work together on 'Rock 'n' Roll Suicide' received on the 1992 Morrissey album *Your Arsenal*, which Ronson produced. Not only did the album's title have a touch of performative camp that Bowie relished,* but the song 'I Know It's Gonna Happen Someday' climaxed with a guitar part that deliberately mirrored the rising crescendo of the earlier song.

The feeling that *Black Tie White Noise* was an attempt on Bowie's part to make sense of his past – hence the guest collaborators, the return of Rodgers and the covers – reached its most brain-twisting when Bowie decided to cover 'I Know It's Gonna Happen Someday' on the album. He described his thought process with amused briskness. 'It occurred to me that [Morrissey] was possibly spoofing one of my earlier songs, and I thought "I'm not going to let him get away with that". I do think he's one of the best lyricists in England, and an excellent songwriter, and I thought his song was an affectionate spoof.'[15] Bowie therefore gave the Morrissey–Mark Nevin co-write a knowingly baroque treatment, reaching heights of grandiosity unheard on a Bowie album since his syrupy cover of 'God Only Knows' on *Tonight*. There was a gospel choir, the blues-rock guitarist Wild T. Springer and a veritable Wrecking Crew of supporting musicians. It is *big* and (somewhat) clever. Appropriately enough, when Bowie played the song to Morrissey, he wept, saying 'Oooh, it's so grand!'

He was not wrong and it remains one of the most cohesive highlights of the album. Of the other covers, the Ronson collaboration on 'I Feel Free' has appropriate pizzazz and energy, belying its guitarist's ill health – Bowie, channelling Freddie Mercury, referred to his ailing sideman as 'the dear old thing' and was seen affectionately embracing him in the studio – but is less interesting as an artistic statement than 'Nite Flights', Bowie's cover of the Walker Brothers song from the eponymous album. Written by Noel Scott Engel, better known by his stage name Scott Walker, and openly inspired by '"Heroes"', the original is a portentous, scary walk on the very wild side, whereas the Bowie–Rodgers version gives it a disco-funk

---

* When they were on good terms, Bowie described Morrissey as 'a sort of sexual Alan Bennett, because of his attention to detail. He'll take a small subject matter and make a very grandiose statement of it.'

makeover that increases the accessibility while toning down the terror. It was 'The Electrician', the fourth song on *Nite Flights*, that was most important for Bowie, but this highly listenable and idiosyncratic cover showed his strengths as an interpreter of others' music, something he had demonstrated as far back as 1969 when he began covering Jacques Brel's 'Amsterdam' – a song made famous, in its English-language version, by none other than Walker.

If *Black Tie White Noise* contains rich seams of allusive pleasure both in its musical and cultural references, it is not always so sure-footed. The fourth cover, 'Don't Let Me Down & Down', was obscurity itself, being a version of a song by a Mauritanian princess called Tahra who, far from coincidentally, was a friend of Iman's. The title alludes both to the Beatles and to Bowie's own 'Never Let Me Down', but the finished song is nothing more than a pleasant but forgettable interlude between more interesting music. Much the same can be said of the opening and closing tracks, 'The Wedding' and 'The Wedding Present', which might, charitably, be said to be examples of the newly married Bowie's uxoriousness – or allusions to 'It's No Game' and its two contrasting versions on *Scary Monsters* – or alternatively be seen as self-indulgence.

Yet where the album really came to grief was in its potential singles. After all, if you were making a spiritual sequel to *Let's Dance*, you might realistically expect something as joyful, exhilarating and distinctive as that title track as the first release. Instead, the lead track released, 'Jump They Say' – an incongruously upbeat meditation on the suicide of Bowie's schizophrenic half-brother Terry Burns, who killed himself in January 1985 by throwing himself under a train – was certainly distinctive but hardly the stuff of the *Billboard* hit parade. It did, though, reach number 9 in the UK singles chart, Bowie's first song to do so since the rather catchier 'Absolute Beginners' in 1986. It might be best remembered for its brilliant, disturbing Mark Romanek-directed video, depicting Bowie as a corporate drone in an eerily bright dystopia, on the verge of either committing suicide or being executed. Abounding with allusions to directors including Hitchcock,

Kubrick and Chris Marker,* it is one of Bowie's best promotional films, and superior to the song it accompanied.†

It was considerably better than the album's second single 'Black Tie White Noise', a collaboration with R&B star Al B. Sure! that tries to be a meditation on the Los Angeles riots. It is one of those Bowie songs that simply doesn't work, either musically – the duet is teeth-grindingly embarrassing to listen to – or intellectually. Bowie is attempting a commentary on racism, via the prism of his own interracial marriage, and also trying to offer a sardonic dismissal of the way in which such songs as the McCartney–Wonder duet 'Ebony and Ivory' can attempt to promote racial harmony in the most superficial of ways.

The problem with the song is that Bowie simply can't pull off the inherently contradictory conceit he is reaching for and the result becomes dismally unsuccessful, as well as patronising: a millionaire white man trying to lecture his listeners on racism. Gabrels summed it up briskly and accurately when he said 'You're putting out a solo album with Nile, and the big single has Al B. Sure! rapping on it. What the fuck? I said to him "You're not the tail, you're the dog. Don't let them wave you around."'[16]

When the album was eventually released, there was a sense of relief and happiness that Bowie was back as a solo artist, and that he had taken rather greater care over the album than anything he had done since his last collaboration with Rodgers. The cover image, a photograph by Nick Knight of Bowie in 'mature' mode, encapsulated what the musician was trying to do: reassure his long-standing admirers that he was producing a classic Bowie album that could stand comparison with his '70s and early

---

* An experimental French filmmaker, whose most famous picture, 1962's *La Jetée* – a short science-fiction feature almost entirely constructed from still photographs – would go on to inspire Terry Gilliam's 1995 picture *12 Monkeys*.

† One person who was deeply offended by 'Jump They Say', both as a song and a video, was Bowie's aunt Pat, who called it 'macabre and pathetic' and accused Bowie of using the memory of his late brother 'to put his record in the charts'.

'80s work, while drawing in a younger audience who might be impressed by the suavity and poise of the 46-year-old star.

Heralded by remixes of the singles by the hip likes of Leftfield and Brothers in Rhythm, Bowie now basked in the best reviews he had had in a decade. True to form, *Q* praised it as 'an album which picked up where *Scary Monsters* left off in 1980' and trumpeted that 'if any collection of songs could reinstate [Bowie's] godhead status, this is it'.[17] *Billboard* called it 'trail-blazing and brilliant', while *Rolling Stone* cooed that it was 'one of the smartest records of a very smart career'. It went to the top of the UK charts, selling more than 100,000 copies and restoring a reputation that had teetered and tottered dangerously over the past decade.

The album's success was helped by Bowie – who had decided not to tour the album, instead releasing a six-song concert film directed by David Mallet, who was responsible for the videos of 'Ashes to Ashes' and 'Let's Dance', among others – giving a series of interviews that appeared to be more candid and straightforward than the gamesmanship and persona-adopting of the Tin Machine era, and before. In a lengthy interview with the BBC's Simon Bates on Radio 1, he spoke about everything from race relations in the US to his feelings of confusion and guilt around his brother's death. He called the album's third single 'Miracle Goodnight' 'a very simple song' with a good riff, praised his collaborators and suggested that the release of *Black Tie White Noise* saw him in a good place. 'This one I really feel is a fairly accurate reflection of my state of mind. It doesn't have the same pain as some of the other albums. There's almost a joy in there, which is nice to see peeking through at long last.'

David Bowie, the happily married man, producing an album that is a paean to everything from the joys of reconciling with your old bandmates and covering the songs of artists you admire to your love for your new wife. Happiness writes white (noise). It is now clear, three decades after its release, that *Black Tie White Noise* represents one of the most audacious bait-and-switches that Bowie ever participated in during his career, elevating a series of mediocre-to-good songs into the pantheon simply through charm and by telling people that it was an important, enduring album: his best since *Scary Monsters*. *Q* wrote that 'the album deals primarily with the moods and experiences of the "real" David Bowie, unmediated by any fictional third party or arch dramatic irony'. This was wishful thinking, the magazine choosing to swallow the publicity gruel. *Black Tie White Noise* is no more autobiographical than *Ziggy Stardust* or *Low*, and perhaps even less revealing than many of his earlier albums, for all its apparent candour. Just because someone swears blind they're telling you the truth doesn't mean that you can trust them.

Dave Thompson, writing in the *Rocket*, was one of the few critics not to be taken in by the blandishments. 'In a strange way, when Bowie was weird, he defined our normalcy. It was inevitable that, when he straightened out, he'd lose our attention. *Black Tie* is a very straight album. The skills which were once Bowie's by default have been irretrievably passed on to the kind of talents he used to eat for breakfast, and he is left flapping alone, a mudskipper when the mud's dried up . . . The hunter has finally been caught by the game.'[18]

The album's reputation has suffered considerably in recent years, not least because Rodgers has subsequently been candid about his frustrations working on it. 'I felt my hands were tied to a large extent,' he told the biographer David Buckley. 'It was like "Hey David, let's try this." "No, I don't wanna do this." "Hey, David, let's try this, then" "No, I don't want to do that either. This record is really about my wedding."' When a justifiably frustrated Rodgers cried 'But David, no one cares about your wedding. Let's make a hit!', Bowie coldly replied, "No, I don't want to compete with *Let's Dance*." Rodgers attempted to recruit Iman, an old friend, to his corner, but she, loyal to her husband, simply said, 'I agree with David'. Rodgers miserably concluded that 'when we finished that record, I knew it wasn't cool . . . I think there's some really clever, interesting stuff on it. But the point is, it ain't as good as *Let's Dance*.'[19]

One of the major, and understandable, sources of Rodgers' frustration was that 'Lucy Can't Dance' – an upbeat, danceable song that takes lyrical aim at Madonna, who was decried as a bratty opportunist, and that would have been a considerable hit if released as a single – was not even included on the album proper. 'Everyone around him was totally perplexed when it only appeared as a bonus track on the CD,' said Rodgers. 'He was running from success and running from the word "dance". Imagine David Bowie and Nile Rodgers together, and we come out with a song 'Lucy Can't Dance'. Smokin'! I was already accepting my Grammy. But he was not budging. It was an exercise in futility. No matter who I tried to call, it fell on deaf ears.'[20]

Rodgers' opinion is mirrored by Reeves Gabrels, who played guitar on the Tin Machine do-over 'You've Been Around', but was otherwise absent from the album; his guitar solo on 'I Feel Free' was overdubbed by Ronson, something that the guitarist was happy to stand down from ('It's Mick fucking Ronson!'). Yet he remains unconvinced by *Black Tie White Noise* now. 'I think it's a period piece. Some things are timeless. And some things aren't. That one isn't. To me, the question is: does it hold up? And the answer is: no, not for me.'[21] The album has many of the same failings of the second *Tin Machine* LP, as well as those of some of Bowie's subsequent '90s releases. Individual tracks are strong, at times extremely so, but it feels like a grab-bag of ideas loosely structured around a tenuous concept rather than a satisfying and coherent collection of songs.

When compared to the records of his heyday, it was inevitably a disappointment. But that was not the album's sole purpose. Like a politician taking over a debased party who must haul it out of incompetence and decadence and transform it into something fit for purpose and electability once more, *Black Tie White Noise* had to make its creator respectable again. Bowie knew that what he joked was his 'Phil Collins' period in the late '80s had made him a figure of ridicule. Tin Machine had not broken through into public consciousness enough for him to rehabilitate himself, so this album was the first time that many people had heard Bowie's new material since *Never Let Me Down* in 1987, if not before. It did enough, with the European sales and the generally positive reviews, to put him back in the field and to ensure that the open antipathy he had faced for years would die down. Still, this was not the same thing as the adulation that he had once received. For a man who cared about being taken seriously, it was not enough.

There was also to be another unpleasant professional development for Bowie. He was especially keen that *Black Tie White Noise* be a commercial success in his newly adopted home country of the US, not least because its music, performers and lyrical concerns were all geared towards it. Unfortunately, Savage had paid far too much money for the album and so it collapsed shortly after it was released in the States, reaching an unimpressive 39 in the *Billboard* charts, before plummeting down further.

As one Bowie insider commented in an unflattering news story headlined 'When David Bowie signed to Savage, he took a long shot – and missed', 'the record is a proven high-profile failure in America. It's been out eight weeks, it peaked at number 39, and is now heading down towards 200. It's almost certainly going to get more difficult to buy in the shops and I can't really imagine another label would be brave enough to take the record on. America is a very difficult market; it's a lot less forgiving than Britain, where records can fail first time around but then get re-released.'[22]

David Mirman, embarrassed by his hubris, now filed for bankruptcy. Out of spite, he decided to sue Bowie for $65 million – covering the $1 million loss he claimed that his label made on *Black Tie White Noise*, as well as breach of contract, claiming that Bowie was expected to record another three albums for Savage. (This would only apply to the US; in the UK, where Bowie entered into a four-album deal with Arista, there was no such difficulty.) The case was dismissed by the New York State Court of Appeals, although not until July 1998, and Bowie's lawyer Paul LiCalsi declared that 'this drives a stake through the heart of this ridiculous case'.

All the same, Bowie was now left without an American record label and, with no tour planned for the album, he found himself at leisure for the first time in several years. He would not perform live again until September 1995, although he was prolific during the next couple of years, in many different fields. But the most significant professional encounter he was to have that year was with an unlikely figure: a 25-year-old from Haywards Heath who was the frontman of the hottest new band in Britain.

Brett Anderson was a man out of time. While his contemporaries looked enviously over to the mega-success of Nirvana and Pearl Jam, wishing desperately that they could front bands that could bid for serious commercial success in the US, Anderson's lyrical concerns were kitchen-sink drama with a coating of poetic desperation: Mike Leigh meets Byron. His band Suede swiftly established themselves as the hottest act in Britain through dint of their guitarist / composer Bernard Butler's technical and musical prowess and Anderson's knack both for conveying on-stage charisma and dispensing witty (if slightly stagey) one-liners that the music press fell over themselves to reproduce.* Comparisons were made with the Smiths, Roxy Music and even the Pet Shop Boys, but there was no greater or more important influence on Suede than David Bowie.

It was pure coincidence that Suede's eponymous debut album was released the week before *Black Tie White Noise*, but anyone listening to the two of them back to back would be struck by the cathartic, vibrant energy of the one – an album on which even the ballads and slower songs could send fans wild at gigs, such was the drama with which Anderson would perform them – and the moneyed complacency of the other. Steve Sutherland, an *NME* journalist, had the bright idea of attempting to bring the two together after Bowie responded enthusiastically to a mixtape of Suede's early singles and bootleg live tracks. Bowie agreed, organising a conversation between the two as a self-conscious echo of his own interview with William Burroughs in 1973.

He had been largely dismissive of most of his other admirers – he especially loathed Gary Numan, who he saw as a derivative upstart, and asked

---

* My own favourite being 'America is a thing to be broken, like an insolent child'.

for him to be removed from a 1980 Kenny Everett Christmas TV show before he would participate in it – but either because he had mellowed with age, or because he was genuinely excited by Anderson and Suede, Bowie now willingly took on the role of elder statesman and mentor, albeit wholly on his terms. The dynamic of the interview was gratifying. Anderson, who had made his name by declaring that he was 'a bisexual man who had never had a homosexual experience', was clearly in awe of an assured Bowie, who took the opportunity to reminisce about his '70s career and, once again, to murmur that 'I found out I wasn't truly a bisexual but I loved the flirtation with it'.

Bowie praised the first Suede album, albeit with just a hint of condescension ('the poignancy of the everyday is very apparent in your work') and skilfully drew a distinction between his own theatricality ('I may not have had any real understanding of why or how, but what I was doing was a fabrication') and the more authentic, heartfelt expression of self that Anderson and Suede exemplified. When Anderson earnestly remarked, of the band's frenetic live shows, that 'I'd never wanna appear like a media fabrication, which I'm sure lots of people think we are . . . premeditated is one thing we're completely not', Bowie could only reply, sardonically, 'therein lies the difference'.

The two men parted with expressions of mutual regard (the starstruck Anderson told the interviewer Sutherland that '[Bowie] was actually one of the nicest people I've ever met . . . so, so charming . . . he came in and he smelt beautiful, that was the most important thing . . . he smelt of Chanel – but not poor person's Chanel') and Bowie would continue to be a fond admirer of Suede throughout his life, although he never went so far as to collaborate or perform with the band. Yet the most revealing section of the interview came at its conclusion, when Anderson suggested that he was able to rely on friends for companionship and understanding. Bowie scoffed at this. 'You do have to remain empty of relationships and all those things . . . it sounds very pretentious, but that is the sacrifice one makes. You do sacrifice a lot of real, honest, internal psychological safety by doing what we're doing. You end up as some sort of emotional casualty because you learn how to keep relationships away from you. And breaking that habit suddenly becomes very hard.' Anyone who had been dispensed with by Bowie would know this to be painfully true.

Bowie concluded with a couple of Wildean aphorisms, which also appeared to express an antipathy to the work that he was undertaking. 'Art is a burden, isn't it?' When Anderson enthusiastically agreed, Bowie dispensed a parting *bon mot* that appeared to epitomise his present-day attitude to his musical career, theatricality and artistic invention firmly in place: 'Genius is pain. Oh, dear me.'[23]

Life also brought its share of pain. The week after the *NME* published the interview, Bowie rang his old friend, the drummer John Cambridge, and reminisced about Ronson, saying, affectionately but with irritation, 'the silly sod won't stop smoking'.[24] This might have been hypocritical, coming from a man with a committed nicotine habit that saw him consume packets of cigarettes a day, but the next time Cambridge heard from Bowie, on 29 April, it was with sombre news: Ronson had died at the age of 46.

Of all Bowie's vital musical collaborators – from Tony Visconti to Brian Eno, Reeves Gabrels to Nile Rodgers – Mick Ronson occupied a unique place in his life and work. Not only was he vital in transforming Bowie from the effete figure of the late '60s into the dynamic, dramatic world-conquering Ziggy Stardust that he became, but he did it all wholly without ego or a desire to upstage the singer. His final cameo on *Black Tie White Noise* was just as distinctive as every other appearance that he had on Bowie's albums, and the great affection that he felt for his one-time bandmate was demonstrated by his rising from his figurative sickbed to perform with him one last time.

It might therefore have been expected that Bowie would have reacted to his friend and collaborator's death with deep, sincere grief. However, whether through recalcitrance or an excess of feeling, the tributes he paid to Ronson were almost rote in their expression, such as when he commented that 'he was really up there in the so-called hierarchy with the great guitar players . . . [he was] superb, absolutely superb'.[25] A more honest expression of how he felt came when he rang Ronson's widow Suzi,* in tears, the day after he heard of her husband's death. 'I loved him,' he said, only for Suzi to respond, cuttingly, that 'you haven't done anything to help'.[26]

It was this stasis – or self-regard – that saw Bowie absent from the funeral, but this attracted less criticism than his not performing at a benefit concert held in Ronson's memory the following year. Many, including Mott the Hoople's Ian Hunter, speculated that Bowie's non-appearance was related to the necessarily lower-key guests than had performed at the Freddie Mercury tribute, and supposedly said that 'if that fucker shows his face here tonight, I'll smash his fucking face in'.[27] Those who wish to defend Bowie suggested that he was uncomfortable with his name and fame overshadowing that of Ronson, but this hardly precluded him from sending a message of support or a video. The only comment that he made about his absence was in 1998: 'The truth is I was not convinced by the motivations of this event, but, frankly, I prefer to stay silent.'[28]

If Bowie's interpersonal relationships, both personal and professional, left something to be desired, then this was the prerogative of the man who, depending on your point of reference, either sold the world or fell to earth. As he weighed up the various American record deals he was offered, basked in the happiness of life with Iman and considered his next option, Bowie was now presented with one of the most unorthodox, and rewarding, opportunities that he had ever had in his career. It would compel him to re-examine a past that, even as he tried to escape it, showed no signs of letting him go.

---

\* With whom Bowie had also been sexually involved, at points.

*3*

# THE BUDDHA OF SUBURBIA AND LEON

## 'This swaggering, violent and ignorant millennium'

*'I've suffered badly when I've pandered to the marketplace'*

The Bowie–Eno reunion – pictured here in September 1994 – was productive,
occasionally fraught, and produced a masterpiece in the form of *Outside*.

Dave Bennett/Getty

S ome writers regard their schooldays as the most formative of their lives, but the author Hanif Kureishi did not. He attended Bromley Tech School in Keston, south London, and hated it. It was an undistinguished establishment. 'It is important to note what a shithole it was,' Kureishi later reminisced, 'bullying, violent, with incompetent teachers. Education, in those days, for working- and lower-middle-class children, was hardly considered essential or even necessary.'[1] Most of those who attended the school loathed the atmosphere and got out as early as they could, with university, or even A-levels, seen as an impossibility. The lucky, literate ones got drudge jobs in the civil service or in insurance, whereas the less fortunate were condemned to manual labour, or a lifetime on the dole, grimly queueing up at the labour exchange once a week for a pittance.

Kureishi compared the average Bromley Tech School leaver's fate to that of H. G. Wells's Kipps, a draper's assistant, whose simple nature seems to mark him out for a similarly undistinguished existence. Yet there was a similarity between Kureishi, whose Oscar-nominated 1985 screenplay for the film *My Beautiful Launderette* catapulted him to fame and success, and Kipps, in that both were offered a way out of the suburban hell in which they were placed. In the case of Kipps, the *deus ex machina* was an unexpected inheritance of a fortune and a property from his grandfather, but when it came to Kureishi, it was the example of another former student of Bromley Tech: David Bowie.

As the author described it, when he was studying between 1966 and 1970, the influence and presence of the former David Jones hung heavy over the school. Although the popular art teacher Owen Frampton had his own dealings with the music world, thanks to his son Peter achieving success as the guitarist for the band Humble Pie,* most of the staff regarded their former pupil as a satanic influence. As Kureishi recalled, 'There was a picture of [Bowie] in the school and the teachers would say "If you don't behave yourself, Kureishi, you'll end up like him"'[2] – to which

---

* Whose 1976 live album *Frampton Comes Alive!* was a notable commercial success.

58

the young man's response was 'How do I achieve such a thing?' After all, 'Bowie was this ruling god . . . he was a figurehead for us . . . he liberated all suburban teenagers.'[3]

Once Kureishi had achieved success in theatre and on screen, he wrote his first novel, *The Buddha of Suburbia*, which was published in 1990 by Faber. The publisher regarded it as a very big deal indeed – the cover designer was Peter Blake, who did not come cheap – and their faith in it was justified by both the stellar reviews and the Whitbread Award for best first novel. It would be turned into a television series, directed by Roger Michell, and adapted by Michell and Kureishi himself, with the author very clear as to whose songs he wanted to soundtrack it. But the use of Bowie's '70s music would not come cheaply, and BBC dramas did not have the budget for large amounts of cash for the rights. What Kureishi had to do was to meet his idol and charm him. He succeeded, and the result would lead to one of Bowie's most intriguing and important, if still overlooked, albums.

Kureishi managed to meet Bowie for the first time in early 1993 for a brief conversation for the American magazine *Interview*.* Bowie was not especially forthcoming, discussing fashion, androgyny and bisexuality with the air of a man who had given similar answers ten times or more, but when Kureishi asked, bluntly, 'Did you think that sadness was necessary to you as a musician?', he was jolted into a more interesting reply. 'I never thought I would be very happy, ever. I presumed that's what I had given up to have this ability to produce magic with music. And then you look at other artists in history and say, "Well, they were like that. They were always very stoned and had miserable lives, but look what great art they did." You're not willing to look at the artist who was balanced and harmonious in his life and still was a great artist. And so you kind of resign yourself to it.'[4]

It was a more revealing answer than he may have intended. His personal life was the most content that he had ever known it, but *Black Tie White*

---

* A title founded by Andy Warhol, who Bowie would soon go on to play in Julian Schnabel's 1996 film *Basquiat*.

*Noise* was not the all-conquering comeback it had been intended to be. The idea that Bowie could somehow make himself miserable was undesirable, but his own balanced and harmonious existence was not producing great art. Something else had to occur.

Kureishi was able, via the ubiquitous Alan Yentob* – who had famously made a 1975 BBC film, *Cracked Actor*, about Bowie – to arrange a further encounter with the musician for dinner at the River Café in Hammersmith, where he broached the subject of using his music in the adaptation of *The Buddha of Suburbia*. He found Bowie at his most charming and personable, determinedly sticking to mineral water but keen to impress the writer, who observed 'he obviously really liked to be liked and worked hard at being liked'. When the moment came to beg permission for the use of Bowie's songs, he wryly replied 'I thought you'd never ask',[5] before countering with a further, unbelievable suggestion. He would write the original music for the television series, thereby giving it the kudos of being the first (and last) full soundtrack that he would ever compose – although he had arranged and performed some songs for Alan Clarke's 1982 TV adaptation of Brecht's *Baal*, in which he had starred.[†]

It is not hard to see what the appeal of the book was, over and above Kureishi's obvious literary ability and the Bromley connection. *The Buddha of Suburbia* revolves around Karim Amir, a mixed-race teenager drowning in suburbia in the '70s, whose horizons are expanded by his spending time in New York and London, and absorbing, as if by osmosis, the sexual, cultural and musical mores of the bohemian big cities. Chief among these is his relationship with his stepbrother Charlie Kay, who reinvents himself as an all-conquering, otherworldly figure known as Charlie Hero, before eventually settling for lucrative but artistically stagnant life as an '80s rocker.

---

\*　The then controller of BBC1

†　He had been supposed to compose music for Nicolas Roeg's 1976 film *The Man Who Fell to Earth*, but a combination of his heroic drug use and Roeg's demanding specifications meant that his half-formed compositions were abandoned, although they may have been revived, in part, for the *Low* album.

Kureishi did not deny suggestions that Charlie was a dig at the punk star Billy Idol – another one-time Bromley resident – but the other inspiration for the character was not publicly discussed, although the casting in the series of Steven Mackintosh, an actor who did not look wholly dissimilar to Bowie, may have given the game away.

While *Black Tie White Noise* had been an expensive, expansive undertaking that used high-profile musicians and the services of Nile Rodgers, Bowie's *Buddha of Suburbia* project came in two distinct acts. The first was composing brief instrumental pieces, to order, at his regular haunt of Mountain Studios in Montreux. It proved an awkward and potentially embarrassing experience for Michell and Kureishi to have to give their idol direction, and indeed they had to be candid about how his inexperience in composing soundtracks meant that some of his music was either inappropriate or didn't fit the images on screen. However, Bowie took criticism in good spirit* and the score, which was later BAFTA-nominated, was soon finished. He had worked for love, rather than money, and then announced to Kureishi that 'because the BBC pays you shit, I'm going to make an album.'[6]

His main collaborator on what would become his next studio album was the multi-instrumentalist Erdal Kizilçay, a Turkish musician who had played on *Never Let Me Down* and who had toured with him as a guitarist on the Sound + Vision tour. That had not been a pleasant experience for Kizilçay, who had found Bowie tetchy and belligerent. He and his bandmates had been hidden on the side of the stage, and one night in Canada, Kizilçay had mistaken Bowie waving at him for an invitation to emerge from the shadows and come to the front. This transgressed some unwritten law, and a furious Bowie threw his guitar on the ground and stormed off, later shrieking at Kizilçay that 'Erdal, I've spent 11 million fucking dollars

---

* He wrote in the liner notes that accompanied the album that '[The] project was manoeuvred and focused primarily by Roger Mitchell [*sic*] the director, who guided me around the usual pitfalls of over arranging against small ensemble theatre'.

on this show, and if I need a dancer I can find a better one than you. And if you're not happy you can just fuck off.'[7]

Initially, Kizilçay was only too prepared to fuck off, but once Bowie calmed down, the two reconciled and the singer began talking airily about a jazz album that he was planning on making next. Although *Black Tie White Noise* had elements of jazz, not least in Lester Bowie's trumpet, Kizilçay was not asked to participate, but he was Bowie's first choice for its follow-up, which could scarcely have been more different. The earlier album had taken more than a year to record, whereas *The Buddha of Suburbia* had the bulk of its music recorded in a mere six days, albeit with later overdubs requiring the starry services of Mike Garson and Lenny Kravitz, who played guitar on the title track. Kizilçay was, fortuitously, another Swiss resident, and the two men convened at Mountain Studios to take many of the sketches or motifs from the television series and flesh them out into fully fledged songs, with the aid of co-producer David Richards, who had worked on *Never Let Me Down* and would later also collaborate with Bowie on *Outside*.

Although the relationship between Bowie and Kizilçay had improved since the singer's hissy fit on tour, the enforced creative intimacy between the two led to Kizilçay being leant upon in new and often taxing ways. As Bowie described it a decade later to the comedian Ricky Gervais, '[Kizilçay] had to become proficient on every instrument in the orchestra. This led to a lot of testing on my part. I would produce an oboe from my jacket pocket. "Hey, Erdel, don't you think oboe would be nice here?" He would trot off to the mic and put down a fluent and beautiful solo then say, "That's quite good, but how about if I doubled it with the North Albanian Frog Trembler?" And he would. I would seethe, as I would have placed bets on his not being able to play such and such an instrument with our engineer. I never once was able to catch him out.'[8]

Kizilçay's task was a demanding one. Bowie presented him with the low budget and limited resources as a *fait accompli*, but said 'Let's go, let's do it', and it became an exciting and satisfying opportunity. The sense of risks being taken and trusted collaborators doing their best work in consequence grew when Garson was asked to do piano overdubs on two tracks, 'South Horizon' and 'Bleed Like a Craze, Dad'. As he describes it, 'David called me up the day before, and said "Can you be in such-and-such a studio in Burbank tomorrow?" So I showed up, and he said "I've finished the entire album with Erdel and now I need you." Then he put the tapes on, and he said "Just play".'[9]

Garson found the improvisational nature of his work thrilling and reflected on what it meant as regards his wider collaboration with Bowie. 'He got the best of me. And if someone treats me that way, I'll give them 150 per cent, because they trust me. If they don't trust me, I can go to 90 per cent, 80 per cent, 70 per cent, down to -20 per cent, depending on how much of an asshole they are. I'm not even an average musician at that point, I'm *horrible*, because unlike a studio musician who turns up and can be steady and white toast, I'm an artist.'[10]

Bowie acknowledged this when he wrote of Garson's playing on 'South Horizon', which he described as his favourite song on the album. 'I personally think Mike gives one of his best-ever performances on this piece and it thrills on every listening, confirming to me at least that he is still one of the most extraordinary pianists playing today.' Garson only discovered this praise after Bowie's death and was deeply moved. 'I had never seen that he had written that before . . . it was very touching.'

Once Garson's parts had been recorded, along with Kravitz's cameo,* it was time to mix the album, which proved to be an unusually complicated process, owing to various technical difficulties. It would take 15 days, rather than the six the music had taken to record. It was then time to put best foot forward and see how the public would react to the second Bowie release of the year, coming a mere seven months after *Black Tie White Noise*.

---

* Which I cannot describe better than the Bowie chronicler Chris O'Leary, who called it 'proficient, perfectly-played and soulless, top-rate simulacrum-music from one of the '90s most pointless artists'.

There was obvious concern that the record would be regarded merely as a soundtrack album to the series, rather than an LP in its own right. As Bowie wrote in the atypically serious sleeve notes, 'this collection of music bears little resemblance to the small instrumentation of the BBC play of *Buddha* . . . these same pieces just took on a life of their own in the studio, the narrative and '70s memories providing a textural backdrop in my imagination that manifested as a truly exciting work situation. In short, I took the TV play motifs and restructured them completely except, that is, for the theme song.'

He then went into considerably greater detail as to his intentions, providing Bowie musicologists with a degree of unvarnished insight into his working methods. 'I took each theme or motif from the play and initially stretched or lengthened it to a five- or six-minute duration. By means of time-code I experimented with various rhythmic elements, drums, percussion, temple blocks, et al until I found a sense of companionship to the primary motif. Then, having noted which musical key I was in and having counted the number of bars, I would often pull down the faders leaving just the percussive element with no harmonic information to refer to. Working in layers, I would then build up reinforcements in the key of the composition totally blind so to speak. When all faders were pushed up again, a number of clashes would make themselves evident. The more dangerous or attractive ones would then be isolated and repeated at varying intervals so giving the impression of forethought.'

Bowie's cut-up style of lyric writing has attracted praise and criticism in equal measure and he was remarkably candid about his intentions. 'Fifty per cent of the lyrical content is used merely semiotically, the rest either with implied abstruse connotation or just because I like the sound of the word. There has always been a hazy rootlessness to my writing. I put it down to an overwhelming sense of transience, or is it a case of imagination being memory rearranged? This leads me often to re-complicate much of my composition writing, something I'm working earnestly away from.'

If the results had been unsatisfactory, then all this would be nothing more than the emperor's new clothes, flashy verbiage being used as a fig leaf to cover the paucity of ideas or achievement underneath. Yet over the album's 55-minute duration, there was a remarkable amount of intellectual and musical playfulness and experimentation that showed up *Black Tie White Noise* – to say nothing of Tin Machine – for the less accomplished work that it was. This innovation begins with the title track, a perfect pastiche of Bowie's early '70s work accomplished with brio; the only piece from the album actually used on the series' soundtrack, it prefigured the acoustic sounds of the album *hours*. . . later in the decade, and was more immediately accessible than anything he'd done since 'Absolute Beginners' seven years before. It could have been a hit in another universe, but it was given a perfunctory release in late November 1993 and crawled to 35 in the UK charts. It is reprised at the end with Kravitz's guitar overdubs and should be treated with due suspicion. The original is far superior.

Thereafter, Bowie and Kizilçay appear to be having a near-indecent amount of fun subverting expectations. The ambient shimmer of 'The Mysteries' undoubtedly owes a great deal to Brian Eno (whom Bowie praised in the liner notes for '[occupying] the position in late 20th century popular music that Clement Greenberg had to art in the '40s or Richard Hamilton in the '60s'). Even if it sounds not dissimilar to the kind of music that one might hear in a very upmarket spa while having a massage, it's part of a wonderfully rich musical palette that includes everything from Roxy Music-esque art rock ('Strangers When We Meet') to ebullient, Blondie-inspired new-wave pop ('Dead Against It').

If you're after *Low*-esque boundary-pushing, then 'Ian Fish UK Heir' (an anagram of Hanif Kureishi) will delight, while Garson's work on the jazz-tinged instrumental 'South Horizon' is, as Bowie suggested, some of his finest and most distinctive playing to occur over the two men's long and distinguished time together. Forget *Black Tie White Noise*; this is undoubtedly the more energetic and accomplished of the two records that Bowie put out in 1993 and should, under normal circumstances, have been a substantial hit. 'I felt really happy making that album,'[11] Bowie later reflected. It shows.

However, as was now increasingly the case, its merited success was stymied by his British record label, Arista, failing to comprehend what was on their hands and choosing not to publicise it. It was typical of their inexperience that, rather than featuring images of Bowie, they choose to use pictures taken from the show on the album cover instead. It would only be much later that someone at the label wised up to the idea that they had A David Bowie Album on their hands – following up a UK number one hit earlier that year – rather than a television soundtrack, and attempted to market it accordingly. But by then it was far too late.

Bowie described it pithily. 'The album itself got only one review, a good one as it happens, and is virtually non-existent as far as my catalogue goes. As it accompanied the TV play of the same name, it was designated as a soundtrack by the record company and got zilch in the way of marketing money.'[12] It may therefore have been with a touch of the defensive that he described it as his favourite afterwards, but like many an underappreciated child, it was down to its parent to extol its virtues if nobody else would notice them. It has been reassessed since its re-release in 2007, but remains the least-heard and most unduly neglected of all Bowie's studio albums.

Still, the process of working with Kureishi and Kizilçay had led Bowie to delve into his past and the results were hugely worthwhile. In the sleeve notes, he includes a series of bands, places and things – 'the stockpile of residue' – that had influenced him on the album. It makes for a fascinatingly eclectic selection:

> Free association lyrics
> Pink Floyd
> Harry Partch
> Costume
> Blues clubs
> Unter den Linden

Brücke Museum

*Pet Sounds*

Friends of the Krays

Roxy Music

T. Rex

The Casserole

Neu

Kraftwerk

Bromley

Croydon

Eno

Prostitutes & Soho

Ronnie Scott's club

Travels thru Russia

Loneliness

O'Jays

Philip Glass in

New York clubs

Die Mauer

Drugs

He then moved away from discussing his creative process for *The Buddha of Suburbia* to offering a statement of artistic intent that was miles away from the largely unrevealing interviews that he had given to promote his previous half-dozen albums. His major concern was in tearing up the status quo and replacing it with something more vibrant and daring. 'A major chief obstacle to the evolution of music has been the almost redundant narrative form. To rely upon this old war-horse can only continue the spiral into the British constraint of insularity. Maybe we could finally relegate the straightforward narrative to the past. On the other hand, modern circumstances having had a dysfunctioning [*sic*] capacity upon pure chronological perspective, my writing has often relied too arbitrarily on violence and chaos as a soft option to acknowledging spiritual and emotional starvation. I know I'm not alone with his dilemma.'

Bowie praised the new wave of American artists, such as Pixies and Sonic Youth, for expressing chaos artistically, but, as the new millennium approached, felt that the growing necessity to harness this energy and make something worthwhile and striking out of it was all-important. 'It could be reordered within a formal harmony to recreate focus and, to some degree, rebalance the often loutish nadir into which we have blundered. Our pro-digious British talent is more than able to reveal the real gems submerged under this swaggering, violent and ignorant millennium.'

If Bowie could have done with the services of a good editor to express his sentiments more concisely, many of the points he made were fascinat-ing. Not long after his joint interview with Brett Anderson, he decried what he saw as the industry's lack of interest in home-grown music ('We have so much un-nurtured talent in this country that it borders on criminal') and compared the likes of 'Pollock, Springsteen, Warhol and Nirvana' and 'the Great American Cultural Blanket' to the rapidly diminishing British arts scene. 'No other country, least of all the States, has been able to smoothly incorporate unpatronisingly so many diverse cultural elements into a cohe-sive and socially stable music form as we have on this isle.'

Bowie knew that his own magpie-like tendency to steal ideas, allusions and motifs could lead to him being called a self-plagiariser, even a thief ('I am completely guilty of loading in great dollops of pastiche and quasi-narrative into this present work at every opportunity'), but his argument, which seems stronger and more seductive with every year that passes, was that it was not enough to accept the bland corporatisation of music as an art form,* but to fight vigorously to maintain its individuality. He concluded, dramatically, that his 'own personal ambition is to create a music form that

---

* The top-selling albums in the UK in 1993 were Meat Loaf's *Bat Out Of Hell II: Back Into Hell* and Whitney Houston's soundtrack to *The Bodyguard*. The only album of Bowie's to make the top 100 was his best of compilation, *The Singles Collection 1969–1993*, which still charted below releases from Phil Collins, Sting and, naturally, Suede.

captures a mixture of sadness and grandeur on the one hand, expectancy and the organisation of chaos on the other. A music that relinquishes its hold upon the 20th century yet searches out that which was stimulating and productive as a basis from which to work in the 21st century.'[13]

Veteran Bowie watchers could probably guess what was coming next. The pivot away from the jazz-funk of the previous album, to say nothing of the hard-rock dynamic of Tin Machine; the renewed appreciation for Eno, with whom he was beginning to bounce around new ideas; the intellectualisation of music as an art form, offering one of its most distinguished and intelligent creators the opportunity to create a *magnum opus*; and the chance to work with some of the most able and talented musicians he had encountered during his career, who would rise to the considerable occasion that he presented. Kureishi and *The Buddha of Suburbia* had reignited his fire. The results would be incendiary.

Towards the end of 1992, Bowie gave an interview to *Architectural Digest* from his home in Mustique. Most of it was rote – a rich man in paradise telling a journalist the secrets of his success – but it concluded with one interesting nugget: 'My ambition is to make music so incredibly uncompromised that I will have absolutely no audience left whatsoever and then I'll be able to spend the entire year on the island.'[14] Neither *Black Tie White Noise* nor *The Buddha of Suburbia* could be described as uncompromisingly difficult, but ever since Bowie had reconnected with Eno at his wedding, he was brooding on what his next step should be. His back catalogue was retired, he had no American record label (although suitors vainly hoping for the next *Let's Dance* soon came forward) and he was enjoying the first extended period of rest that he had had in years, going for long walks in Mustique and thinking about what to do next.

It helped that, for all of his high-minded dismissal of 'the Great American Comfort Blanket', one of the practitioners that he named helped put him back on the cultural map with younger people. When Kurt Cobain and Nirvana headed to Sony Studios in New York on 18 November 1993 to record an *MTV Unplugged* special, they chose to include a cover of 'The Man Who Sold the World', as Cobain was a committed Bowie fan. Although many Nirvana fans were unfamiliar with the song, Cobain graciously chose to acknowledge 'the debt that we all owe David'.[15] At a stroke, Bowie was rehabilitated in a country that had treated many of his previous albums with either suspicion or disinterest. Bowie's biographer Christopher Sandford wrote that 'it would be hard to exaggerate the shove to his career';[16] after the MTV show was broadcast on 18 December, it did more to revive interest and attention in Bowie than either of the two albums that he had released that year. Cobain committed suicide fewer than six months later, choosing to burn out rather than fade away, but his patronage of his idol meant that Bowie began 1994 in high-minded and playful mood. It was time to bring the band back together, with the professorial figure of Eno as its guiding spirit.

Bar a brief appearance co-hosting an AIDS benefit at Wembley Arena on 1 December, Bowie completely disappeared from view between his promotional responsibilities for *Black Tie White Noise* and the eventual release of *Outside* in September 1995. He gave few interviews during this time, bar some jolly remarks to *Mojo* magazine in late 1994, when he declared 'Eno and I are working on five different projects at once, stockpiling them for release next year. On some of them we're not quite sure how far the spin-offs will go, whether in the theatre or television . . . We should be going so much further. We're working on how far you can prod and push it, to make it do things it shouldn't do, which is what we're both good at.' He concluded that 'we've got hours of stuff to sort out – we've had no notion of marketplace in mind. It's an honest, healthy approach for an artist, to work only for yourself. I've suffered badly when I've pandered to the marketplace.'[17]

He was correct. This time round, there would be no needy attempts to produce a hit single, but simply the untrammelled pursuit of artistic fulfilment, helped by a committed group of musicians who were able to interpret and execute Bowie's wishes to the best of their ability. It is no exaggeration to suggest that, until *Reality*, there was no latter-period Bowie album that featured such an accomplished ensemble, and it says a lot about the creative, collegiate spirit in which *Outside* was recorded that several tracks on it credit not only Bowie, Eno and Reeves Gabrels, but also Mike Garson, Erdal Kizilçay and Sterling Campbell, all of whom gave their absolute best in unorthodox but inspiring conditions.

It was the fifth album that Bowie would record at Mountain Studios (it would have been the sixth consecutive one, from *Never Let Me Down* onwards, but the second Tin Machine album was instead recorded in Sydney and Los Angeles) and it was the first one where the location seeped into the DNA of the record. Switzerland is a strange and contradictory place, where the sense of wealth, calm and prosperity only barely conceals the oddness of a country where the money concealed in its bank vaults is often of dubious provenance, where the spas are both vastly expensive and faintly sinister in their promise of maintaining eternal youth at all costs, and where, if all else fails, you can have yourself discreetly killed, courtesy of the Dignitas organisation.

It was this sense of mortality and dread that the author Thomas Mann tapped into in his 1924 novel *The Magic Mountain*, a clear but unacknowledged influence on *Outside*,* in which Mann attempted to further the arguments he had made in his 1922 essay 'On the German Republic', in particular his contention that 'no spiritual metamorphosis is more familiar to us than that where sympathy with death stands at the beginning and resolve to live and serve, at the end'. Issues of mortality permeate *The Magic Mountain,* as they would *Outside.* Its protagonist Hans Castorp is confined to an Alpine sanatorium with what initially seems like a mild bronchial infection but soon worsens to tuberculosis, and then when he is eventually

---

* As well as on the underrated 2016 Gore Verbinski film *A Cure for Wellness*, to say nothing of its inadvertent anticipation of the secretive Davos summit every January.

71

allowed to leave the sanatorium, his eventual death in the killing fields of the First World War is sardonically foretold by Mann:

> There were moments when, as you 'played king,' you saw the intimation of a dream of love rising up out of death and this carnal body. And out of this worldwide festival of death, this ugly rutting fever that inflames the rainy evening sky all round – will love someday rise up out of this, too?[18]

This fascination with 'adventures in the flesh and spirit' would prove one of the great intellectual influences on *Outside*, in which the heart teaches filthy lessons, minds are deranged and the body is something to be mocked, disparaged and torn apart. There are numerous other parallels between *The Magic Mountain* and *Outside*, too. Castorp, like *Outside*'s nominal protagonist Nathan Adler, is confronted by a heightened cast of characters who inhabit the sanatorium, itself every bit as surreal an environment as Bowie's imagined Oxford Town in New Jersey. These include Mynheer Peeperkorn, an elderly Dutchman who is described as both 'a blurred man' and a Dionysian figure, and Castorp's love interest Madame Clavdia Chauchat, an enigmatic but erotically enticing figure who comes laden with promise, or vice. They would easily have fitted into the world of *Outside* characters Algeria Touchshriek and Ramona A. Stone.

*The Magic Mountain*'s chapter titles surely inspired Bowie's 'segues' and song titles on *Outside*, too; there is little to choose between 'The Voyeur of Utter Destruction (as Beauty)' and 'Segue – Ramona A. Stone'/'I Am with Name' and Mann's 'Teasing/Viaticum/Interrupted Merriment' or 'An Outburst of Temper/Something Very Embarrassing', just as 'I'm Deranged' is not so very far from 'Danse Macabre' or 'The Great Stupor'. (Amusingly – coincidentally? – one chapter of *The Magic Mountain* is simply entitled 'Changes'.)

It was a strange oversight that, when Bowie produced a list of his 100 favourite books in 2013, Mann's work was not included. He certainly knew it – and indeed teasingly alluded to its title, albeit backwards, in his song 'The Supermen' from *The Man Who Sold the World* – but perhaps the themes that Mann referred to throughout his books cut a little too close to home. After all, he was the author who produced one of the great tragic works about society's obsession with youth and beauty in *Death in Venice* and also teasingly revisited the Doctor Faustus story in his eponymous 1947 novel in which the composer Adrian Leverkühn sells his soul in order to obtain 24 years of genius. By the time that Bowie came to record *Outside*, he had been a significant figure in the music industry for a shade under quarter of a century, after the release of 'Space Oddity' on 11 July 1969. Had he been familiar with Mann's *Doctor Faustus*, he may have been wondering if his own time was up.

Such metaphysical considerations may have permeated the album, but they did not weigh heavily for those making it, who arrived at (magic) Mountain Studios in March to find that Bowie had adopted an unorthodox approach to creativity. 'When I turned up, there weren't any songs,' says Sterling Campbell. 'David didn't do anything except paint.'[19] Montreux was in the out-of-tourism season, and it was quiet and isolated. When 'the magician' Eno appeared, he was able to cite another Mann maxim: 'art is to the community what dreams are to the individual'. Bowie had fought Rodgers for artistic control with *Black Tie White Noise* and had won, but the album's lacklustre results meant that he may well have been better off ceding influence to the experienced producer. However, when it came to Eno, there was no question of who was in charge. He remained the only artistic collaborator of Bowie's who could, and did, give him direction.

In the early days, a pattern formed. Campbell and Eno would breakfast each morning and discuss what would happen in the studio, and then they would walk in and begin work. 'Brian really controlled everything at that point,' noted Campbell, 'with him directing all of us.' His favourite game, the 'Oblique Strategies' cards, in which the musicians were instructed to do something wholly out of their comfort zone in order to achieve unexpected results, was in full swing; Campbell remembers how 'he would have us playing "Baby Love", but deliberately not in the style of the Supremes, and so on. Some of these things went on for a long time. And then it was just Brian choosing ideas, because we were basically experimenting and just trying out ideas and with Brian pushing us in the direction that "nothing was normal".'[20]

When Gabrels arrived in the studio, a week before Eno turned up, he found Bowie in an intentionally aimless state, without any songs or ideas prepared, painting and experimenting. As he describes it, with heroic understatement, '*Outside* was a little odd because it was just David and I in the studio for a week, and then Brian turned up, and Brian was Brian.'[21] There was also a third producer, David Richards, who died in 2013 and who has been almost entirely airbrushed out of the picture. Most would recognise Bowie and Eno, but few would acknowledge the contribution of the other man, who nonetheless should be posthumously saluted for what was surely the difficult and challenging task of keeping everything together.*

With the cast of characters now assembled, Bowie, still without any US record label, self-funded the project (Gabrels estimates to the tune of $2 million) and then the recording process began. As Campbell says, 'David did not give really us any direction. He just got a whole bunch of 30-minute tapes of us just trying out ideas. There's no shape, no verse. There's no chorus, no melody, the whole time. He was painting about five feet away from me, doing little charcoal sketches of the musicians. He didn't say anything. He just let Brian do his thing. And then they found that they had a bunch of material and said "Now let's shape it into songs".' Campbell calls it 'a really, really cool way of making music', but is also cautionary. 'You've got to be able to do that type of stuff. You've got to be one of those guys. And that's what separates David from other people. He could sit down and write from a piano, he could take pieces of papers and throw it up in the air and come up with lyrics.'[22]

---

\* In his diary, Eno describes him simply as 'engineer on the Bowie record'.

The album's proper piano player, Mike Garson, had not worked on an Eno–Bowie production before and found the entire experience thrillingly bizarre. 'We'd go in for a few weeks for several hours and they had two Sony tape machines locked together. And we'd play, as they'd play recordings in our ears of God knows what, rock and soul music and all sorts of thing. Brian would be putting these little notes on us, telling us to play like we're spacemen in the year 3007 or something.' He may have been bewildered by Eno's very oblique strategies – 'None of it meant anything to me. I wanted to get to that piano and just play but I got what they he was trying to do to loosen up' – but he valued the inspirational chaos and uncertainty. 'The environment allowed me to play this crazy way, even crazier in some ways than on *Aladdin Sane* because it didn't have the same kind of guitar and bass and heavy drums.'[23]

Ironically, given the intensity of the music, its creation proved to be the most enjoyable studio experience that Garson had with Bowie. 'Brian would do all sorts of stunts in the morning and surprises and crazy things. We were at Mountain Studios, overlooking a lake in a gorgeous hotel we were staying in, living a beautiful life. The notes just found you. You didn't have to search for them or anything. They were in the walls and the piano and *Outside* was the easiest album I think I ever did.'[24]

The only musician uncomfortable with this new regime was Kizilçay, who had thrived on the intimate musical relationship that he had developed with Bowie during the *Buddha of Suburbia* sessions and now found it frustrating not only that Eno was clearly in charge, but that the Oblique Strategies were dominating proceedings. As he later complained, 'Eno wrote me something like that I was an Arab sheikh and I wanted to marry this guy's daughter – so I needed to show him I could play psychedelic, arabesque funk. But I don't need a letter to play Oriental stuff!'[25]

As recording proceeded, and hours' worth of formless but thrilling jams and improvisations were captured on tape, the question arose as to what it was all going to be turned into. 'The whole idea originally was to put out a white label album,' says Gabrels, 'or any other colour you want.

Because there was already a *Black Album*, and there was already a *White Album*. And, of course, not tell anybody who it was by.'[26] The existing music, known as 'the Leon tapes' after the central character of *Outside*, were summed up by Gabrels as 'a three-hour improvised opus', and are undeniably intense, difficult listening. However, had they been released in any form, they could have revitalised Bowie's reputation as an experimental artist. 'If you listen to [the tapes],' says Garson, 'then you can hear that, psychologically, mentally, emotionally and spiritually, everyone is giving phenomenal contributions.'[27]

Had *Leon*, or whatever it would eventually end up being called, been released in even lightly edited form in early 1995, it would undoubtedly have been the most intense and uncompromising album of Bowie's career. Yet there was precedent for megastars to release challenging music, whether under their own names (Lou Reed's notorious and unlistenable 1975 album *Metal Machine Music*) or a pseudonym, such as the Paul McCartney–Youth side project The Fireman, which released its debut album, *Strawberries Oceans Ships Forest*, in 1993. After the advent of the internet, the *Leon* tapes leaked, and today it is possible, with time and patience, to reconstruct a version of what *Leon* would have been; Bowie historian Chris O'Leary suggests that it would have been three lengthy suites, named 'Leon Takes Us Outside', 'I Am With Name' and 'The Enemy Is Fragile', and I see no reason to dissent.

It is unlikely that *Leon* will ever receive an official release, not least because when record companies heard the early version of what Bowie, Eno et al. had recorded, they balked at it as being commercially poisonous. *The Buddha of Suburbia* had flopped, and *Black Tie White Noise*'s unsuccessful US release meant that, Nirvana-derived cachet aside, Bowie had not had a successful album in the US since *Tonight* had sold more than a million copies there in 1985. If he wished to achieve any significant commercial success again, Bowie would have to compromise, to combine his commendable desire to expand his artistic repertoire with something that he was exceptionally good at: writing songs. After a few months of occasionally frustrating, mainly joyous improvisation in Switzerland, it became clear that Bowie would have to impose some sort of narrative structure on the music that he had created or risk releasing an album that would alienate his remaining fans. After all, he was now a very long way from *Let's Dance*.

It would be back to the studio in early 1995 – this time in New York – with a completely new and streamlined approach, a world away from the artistic improvisations of Switzerland. A chance commission from *Q* would help immensely in creating an artistic world for Bowie and his music to inhabit, but even as he prepared to knuckle down, word reached him that his idol Scott Walker was returning with a new album, *Tilt*, for the first time in a decade. In 1978, Eno and Bowie had listened to *Nite Flights* in the studio, awestruck with admiration. Now, it seemed as if he would challenge them on their own terms when it came to innovation and gutsiness. Nineteen ninety-five would be the tale of two comebacks. Only one of them would end up being successful.

# 4

# *OUTSIDE*

## 'Like something no one else would have done'

*'Prepare ye the way of the Lord, make his paths straight'*

Bowie and Reeves Gabrels.
The great undersung creative bromance of this era.
Reeves Gabrels

After Bowie and Eno had digested *Nite Flights* in 1978, they immediately offered to produce any album that Scott Walker wished to make. *Lodger* was a record made in the shadow of Walker's towering achievement, just as *Nite Flights* was reportedly influenced by *"Heroes"*, and Bowie himself was a lifelong aficionado of the enigmatic, reclusive musician. Walker had come to fame as a member of the '60s group the Walker Brothers,* which had begun as a mainstream pop act specialising in covers of songs by popular composers of the day. Yet even from early on, there was something odd and askew about the Walker Brothers, with Scott's sumptuous baritone voice delivering mournful songs of heartbreak and loss over swelling orchestration. He may have looked like a teen idol – at their peak, the Walkers' fan club supposedly had more members than that of the Beatles – but he was intent on sabotaging any commercial benefit that this might have brought him.

By the time he pursued a solo career, combining his own material with morose covers of the songs of Jacques Brel, initial success gave way to incomprehension and dismay from his former admirers. His 1970 album *Scott 4* was released under the name Scott Engel, rather than Scott Walker, and flopped, but then again it isn't difficult to see why; those who had merrily bought singles like 'Make It Easy on Yourself' and 'The Sun Ain't Gonna Shine Anymore' were not, perhaps, the target market for songs like 'The Old Man's Back Again (Dedicated to the Neo-Stalinist Regime)'. Ironically, compared to what would come later, *Scott 4* now sounds like a finely crafted and intelligent collection of accessible yet challenging music that should, by rights, have established Walker as the towering talent of his generation. Instead, it sent him into a downward spiral of alcoholism and resentment, in which he became a beautiful voice for hire and little else.

Bowie, whose album *David Bowie* was released a fortnight before *Scott 4*, was always an admirer of Walker's, who was four years older than him,

---

* Although none of them were called Walker or indeed related to one another.

practically to the day.* When *Vanity Fair* asked Bowie in 2003 to discuss his favourite albums, he recalled that 'in the mid-'60s, I was having an on-again, off-again thing with a wonderful singer-songwriter who had previously been the girlfriend of Scott Walker. Much to my chagrin, Walker's music played in her apartment night and day. I sadly lost contact with her, but unexpectedly kept a fond and hugely admiring love for Walker's work.'[1]

Bowie once suggested that his singing voice was a straightforward cross between that of Walker's and the once-popular, now-forgotten Cockney singer Anthony Newley, and many of Bowie's soaring orchestral early songs, from 'Wild Eyed Boy from Freecloud' to 'Five Years' – and, naturally, 'Life on Mars' – bore a heavy debt to Walker's work, both musically and vocally. Yet while Bowie's career rocketed throughout the '70s, Walker's was largely becalmed. A reunion with the Walker Brothers produced the top-ten hit 'No Regrets' in 1975, but neither that eponymous album nor 1976's *Lines* contained any songs written by Walker. Then *Nite Flights* came along and the whole trajectory of Walker's career changed forever, even as its commercial failure ended any mainstream success that he might have aimed for.

Stephen Kijak, who made the 2006 documentary *Scott Walker: 30 Century Man*, worked with both men on the film. Walker agreed to be interviewed for it, offering candid insights into his eccentric creative process, while Bowie paid homage to his idol by serving as executive producer for the picture, as well as appearing on camera. Although it was suggested in the press that Bowie had financed the documentary, Kijak says that this is untrue. 'I said "All I need from you is your name and an interview. And if you want to pay for the movie, even better." But he picked the interview and name of course. Smart man.' Although Kijak is clear that 'he didn't give me a penny', Bowie was immensely helpful. 'His presence was really all we needed. It just opened the floodgates and made people realise that this was a serious thing, and that Scott Walker is someone that they should

---

\* Walker was born on 9 January 1943, Bowie on 8 January 1947.

be paying attention to. It helped enormously. He was just so supportive. It was really such an honour and privilege to have him bless the project and just be there supporting it.'[2]

During the documentary, in which Eno also appears as an interviewee, the story of the two men attempting to produce a Walker album is brought up once again. While this would undeniably have been a commercial coup, Walker refused to consider it. Kijak's impression was that 'at the time, it was like "Whoa, no, too much" . . . Bowie may just have been too bright a flame for him.'[3] Walker's then-label boss Dick Leahy put it more simply. 'Scott just wasn't interested. He told me to tell Bowie he didn't want to do it. He insisted he didn't want to work with other people.'

Walker did work briefly with Eno in some abortive sessions for what became his 1984 album *Climate of Hunter*, but the two men, aided by Daniel Lanois, did not gel. Contemporary accounts suggested that Lanois and Eno wanted to create complex, layered backing tracks through Eno's time-honoured process of improvisation, whereas Walker had a far clearer idea of what he wanted his music to sound like and resented any interference. Rumour has it that six instrumental tracks were eventually created but that Walker was so unhappy with them that he threw the masters into the Thames and ended the collaboration that way. The only public comment that he ever made on the matter was to the *NME*, when he dolefully quipped that 'I thought rather than destroying Eno's career too I had to do [that] on my own'.[4] His orchestrator Brian Gascoigne claimed that 'Eno hadn't the faintest idea of what Scott was up to . . . [Scott] is happy to listen to suggestions . . . as long as nobody tries to insist on one that's been sidestepped. And they, as hired producers, never understood that.'[5]

He may have been advised to listen more closely to Eno, who later remarked to *Q* that he didn't think 'that Scott threw the tapes in the river – that sounds like too much of a dramatic flourish for him. He wasn't in a great state of mind at the time, mind you.'[6] *Climate of Hunter* flopped, reaching a pitiful 60 in the UK charts, and legend suggests that it was Virgin Records' lowest-ever selling album. Its failure soon saw Walker withdraw from the public eye altogether for the next decade. Apparently, he spent the years he wasn't releasing music sitting in pubs drinking, playing darts and watching people, all of whom were blissfully unaware that the middle-aged American sitting in a cloth cap had written some of the greatest music of the twentieth century. Meanwhile, Bowie released a further four solo albums and his two Tin Machine records.

On paper, there was little obvious comparison between the two men. One was an international A-list celebrity who could still sell out stadiums if he deigned to play his most popular songs, whereas the other was a cult artist who attracted a small but fiercely loyal band of admirers.* And yet Walker sat there, godlike in Bowie's estimation; a kind of Colonel Kurtz figure, who had travelled through the jungle of the music industry and now allowed those who still worshipped him to join his cult if they wished to discover inner peace. Should he now return with a new album that could change the music industry, the results would be impossible to predict.

'I want to leave here with some kind of result – not just more promising bits and pieces, all half-finished.'[7] So Eno wrote in his diary on 11 January 1995. When his work with Bowie had concluded in Switzerland the previous November, *Leon* was initially thought to channel something of the spirit of Walker's more esoteric work, if he had been given the backing to turn *Nite Flights* and *Climate of Hunter* into a triple-album version and damn any commercial necessities into the bargain. What, unfortunately, became clear was that if Bowie and Eno produced their version of a Scott Walker album, it would not sell any better than Walker's last releases had done.

---

* Including the musician Julian Cope, whose 1981 compilation of Walker's music, *Fire Escape in the Sky: The Godlike Genius of Scott Walker*, did a great deal to bring his work to a younger, post-punk audience.

Although Gabrels bullishly suggested in 2003 that 'we hoped [*Leon*] would have come out intact and uncompromised by financial/commercial pressures' and that 'it would have been a very serious musical statement and maybe pissed off more people than Tin Machine',[8] it was entirely clear that no major record label would put out something as uncompromisingly difficult as *Leon*, even with the names Bowie, Eno, Gabrels and Garson – to say nothing of the others – attached. It was up to the creator of the work not only to refine it into something more viable, but to do so in an artistically interesting and intellectually respectable way.

Salvation came from *Q*, which was then Britain's most respected music magazine and unafraid of allowing musicians (and journalists) to take more esoteric approaches to their art than the usual cycle of record-promotion-tour-repeat. In its January 1995 issue, the publication went Bowie-heavy – a remarkable leap of faith given that the subject hadn't released an album in more than a year and had no new record imminently planned, to say nothing of the previous one being a flop. It included both an 'internet conversation' between Bowie and Eno, recorded on 26 October 1994, and probably the strangest 'artist's diary' ever put on paper.

The former was arch and self-conscious in the extreme, full of in-jokes and strained puns (Eno: 'You leave my Kant out of this'; Bowie: 'In fact, [Abba] were initially known as Abattoir'), but did throw up one line of interest to their excited admirers, when Bowie suggested, apparently sincerely, 'I must tell you I'm overjoyed with the new mixes you sent. I really feel we are in an extremely exciting and uninvestigated area. Same goose bumps as 1977 and a Tuesday in late 1984.'

And the latter came about because *Q* asked Bowie to write a diary of his experiences recording what would subsequently become *Outside*. Conscious, as ever, of not wanting to expose his inner workings to the world, he declined. 'I kind of felt that the daily recording and itemization of my habits was really boring frankly – "went to studio, recorded, went home, had dinner, went to bed" – I mean, it was not a real riveting slice of life.'[9] Instead, he wrote a fictionalised three-page diary revolving around a detective, Nathan Adler.

It would be entitled *Diary of Nathan Adler, Or the Art Ritual Murder of Baby Grace Belew*, subtitled 'A Non-Linear Gothic Drama Hyper-Cycle' and would be largely incomprehensible, even as it cribbed sections from David Lynch's hit show *Twin Peaks*. *Q* prepared its readership by saying 'he's written a short, strange, story, bits of which may or may not be autobiographical. The computer illustrations/portraits are by him as well.' Bowie's first work of published fiction was a tongue-in-cheek exercise in befuddling the gullible and those lyrical trainspotters who, even in the pre-Reddit age, would eagerly mine every line of their idols for some hidden nuance that their rivals and competitors had missed. Adler, the last man of integrity in hell, has found himself in a world where murder is committed as a work of art, where serial killers roam the streets with impunity and where 'we're mystified by blood. It's our enemy now. We don't understand it. Can't live it. Can't, well. . . y'know.'[10] Readers were largely mystified, but at least one young filmmaker, soon to make his masterpiece, took note. As did Eno.

Therefore, when producer, musician and the rest of the ensemble reconvened at the Hit Factory studio in New York at the beginning of January 1995, circumstances had changed considerably. Although Bowie had been spending a considerable amount of time in Switzerland over the previous years, where he had lived in Lausanne, he had also acquired a New York apartment in 1992, on the ninth floor of the Essex House Hotel to the west of Central Park. The city would subsequently become an invaluable creative base for him. *Let's Dance*, which had been recorded at the city's Power Station studios, had been his first record imbued with the energy and excitement of Manhattan, and now *Outside* would continue that trend.

On 11 January, Eno assessed the work that they had recorded in Switzerland. He was less impressed and excited by it than Bowie was, describing it as 'very underdisciplined . . . rambling, murky, over-and-underdubbed – things just left where they happened to fall'.[11] He called himself 'the sculptor to David's tendency to paint', and described it as 'a good duet',[12] the inference being that he was bringing structural rigour to Bowie's more impressionist flourishes. He later summed up the 'deal' thus: 'I start on a musical landscape to develop a sense of emotional place; DB does all the singing and thus discovers the voice in the wilderness.' As Eno knew, the allusion here was biblical, to the book of Isaiah 40:3, namely 'The voice of one crying in the wilderness: Prepare ye the way of the Lord, make his paths straight.' He expressed his admiration of their working methods, writing that 'the result sounds like something no one else would have done'.[13]

The first song that was recorded in these new sessions was 'Dummy', which would later be resurrected as 'I'm Afraid of Americans' on the *Earthling* album, and the structural emphasis now lay with turning the fascinating but formless material improvised the previous year into disciplined, listenable songs. Sometimes, inspiration struck from simple good fortune. Kevin Armstrong, returning on guitar duties, was able to resurrect an old song of his and see it turned into *Outside*'s title track. As he says, 'David heard me playing the riff from an old song of mine called "Babylon Bridge" that was written in about 1980. I was playing it at a Tin Machine rehearsal or soundcheck. He jumped on it and asked me if he could have it as the basis for a song. We worked it up with Tin Machine and played it live at a few gigs as a piece called "Now", but later it became changed to "Outside". I was very pleased to have contributed to the title song of such a great album.'[14]

As matters progressed, Eno oscillated between despair and excitement. He called 'I'm Deranged', which would become one of *Outside*'s highlights, 'a poorly organised song with no meaningful structure', but was far more impressed by the improvisations that occurred when Bowie's veteran guitar-playing collaborator Carlos Alomar and the singer took a Gabrels composition entitled 'Moondust' and turned it into something electrifying and pummelling, helped by Bowie's vocal improvisations about a space-boy. 'When he's on, he's really on,' the producer wrote admiringly of his collaborator. 'Perhaps I should accept that he's the hunter to my pastoralist – he hangs round for a long time and then springs for the kill, whereas I get results by slower, semi-agricultural processes.'[15]

The new, more accessible album slowly came together. A song originally known as 'Toll The Bell', which Eno called 'the most infectious song
we've ever written together',[16] began as something obscure and incomplete
before slowly gathering pace and confidence. It eventually became the
poppiest and, indeed, most infectious song on *Outside*, in the form of 'I
Have Not Been to Oxford Town'; an obvious single, although it was never
released as one. 'Moondust' would metamorphose into one of the album's
most thrilling moments, the hard-rock 'Hallo Spaceboy', which brilliantly
combined Bowie's extra-terrestrial lyrical fascinations with an electrifying
fusion of guitar and Joey Barron's frenzied drumming. 'Don't change anything,' said a pleased Bowie when recording was completed on 18 January.

Bowie now seemed to be thriving on the greater discipline that this
new environment was offering him. Ironically enough,* one of the best
songs on the album, 'No Control', was recorded within an hour, and Eno
had particular praise for his theatrical manner of singing on it. 'There's a
stunning section in it when he alludes to that style of singing you get in
Broadway musicals, when the hero looks up into the sun, one arm extended
to the future, and sings in this gloriously open-throated, honest, touchingly
trusting way.' It's impossible not to notice this, which is, as Eno writes,
'[tuned] to just the right pitch of sincerity and parody', and it remains 'one
of the most fascinating things I've ever seen in a studio'.[17] Just as Bowie, the
cracked actor himself, was able to take Tim Palmer's suggestion to alter his
pitch just a millimetre on a Tin Machine song and thereby transform it, so
Eno's tutelage here paid off handsomely. The producer may have written
in his diary, 'I wonder if he realises how good an artist he is at that kind of
thing . . . people often take their own talents for granted', but it is safe to
assume that Bowie knew exactly what he was doing at that time.

Much of *Outside*, then, came into focus thanks to Eno's careful and
painstaking production, but it would never have been the work it became
without Bowie's quicksilver talent, darting off in unexpected and sometimes

---

* Eno called his performance 'a paradigm of control'.

perverse directions, but always coming back to the starting point: superb, sometimes disturbing songs that built on *The Buddha of Suburbia* and his previous work with Eno alike, and resulted in something memorable and inimitably David Bowie. Yet there was another presence, too. The influence of latter-day Scott Walker, which could be faintly discerned on most of the album, became explicit on its centrepiece, 'The Motel', the longest song on the album at nearly seven minutes and probably its best.

In the context of *Outside*, it is supposedly sung by the character of Paddy, one of Nathan Adler's informants, but to regard this as anything other than a truly virtuoso performance by Bowie would be to do it down. It is a slow-paced, gradually escalating piano ballad that eventually explodes into a crescendo that can only recall an angrier, more feral version of 'Life on Mars', as well as 'Sweet Thing' from 1974's *Diamond Dogs*. Vocally, lyrically and musically, the song – which owes much to 'The Electrician', itself inspired by Bowie and Eno's 'Warszawa', but is also, proudly, its own creation – is far ahead of anything that Bowie had done since *Scary Monsters* and hinted at a thrilling new direction for his career. He continued to perform it live right up until the end of his touring career, and I can attest that seeing him play it on the Reality tour at Wembley in 2003 was an astonishing, goose bumps-inducing moment,* the more so because its creator had, a few moments before, been cheerily bantering with the audience.

Garson, whose piano playing on 'The Motel' is extraordinary, remains justly proud of his contributions to the song. 'It's actually in my top five Bowie songs. It's amazing. He'd already written it, so I just helped him fix it up with a few chords, but I added in a few harmonies to make it stronger, too.'[18] Bowie was appreciative of Garson's contributions to the album and

---

*   Looking at the setlist, I can see that it comes in the middle of an astonishing run of songs. 'Under Pressure', 'Life on Mars', 'Ashes to Ashes', 'The Motel' and then 'Loving the Alien'. Some might then claim that quality dips with 'Never Get Old', but then the main set ends with 'Changes', 'I'm Afraid of Americans' and '"Heroes"'. The next night offered 'Be My Wife', 'Fantastic Voyage' and 'She'll Drive The Big Car' instead; I think I went on the right evening.

knew that the straight-talking Brooklyn native would not be trifled with. In an interview after *Outside*'s release, he recalled that, when Eno was handing out his Oblique Strategies cards with instructions to the musicians as to which identities they should adopt, 'I think he gave to Mike Garson: "You are Mike Garson". You don't really have to put Mike anywhere other than where he actually is. He's totally out there.'[19]

Yet the presence of a revived Walker caused some trepidation. When his new album, 1995's *Tilt*, was announced, Eno feared that it might lead to *Outside* being scrapped altogether. As he wrote in his diary on 11 April, a month ahead of *Tilt*'s release: 'Realise that possibly Scott Walker's album could occupy much of the territory of David's. If it does, David won't release those things and as time passes more will get chipped away, or submerged under later additions.'[20] This uncertainty lasted until 27 April, when Eno wrote that 'Bowie called and played an amazing Scott Walker song* from *Tilt* down the phone – in awe of his singing but relieved that the record's in different territory from ours'.[21]

Bowie was able to be magnanimous about *Tilt* when it became clear that it was not going to be a serious challenger to *Outside*, either commercially or in terms of reviving Walker's public reputation. He would later say in a webchat that 'the best album that came out this year in terms of being an adventurous album was Scott Walker's *Tilt* which of course died after about a week. It was bought by three people, me being one of them.'[22] He also declared that he found it 'a sensational record, very brave too. I've got a lot of respect for his integrity. He's true to himself, whereas other artists are traitors to themselves. He really works without compromising and there are very few artists like that.'[23] The irony was that, if *Leon* had not been massaged into a more commercial shape, Bowie would have been

---

* Which one? Obviously, Bowie would have had an advance copy of the record, so it might have been any of the eight tracks on it, but I would hazard a guess at its being the first, most accessible song, 'Farmer in the City', an ode to the murdered film director Pier Paolo Pasolini.

looking at his very own *Tilt*, which may have been received ecstatically by the faithful, but could just as easily have vanished without trace.

Walker and Bowie had, at this point, never met. This would later change on 15 November 1995 when Bowie was touring the *Outside* album and Walker briefly came backstage at London's Wembley Arena at the star's instigation. According to the journalist Steve Pafford, who was present, Bowie excitedly said to Iman 'Quick, go and get the camera!' when he realised that Walker had come to say hello, and then the two chatted briefly before Walker made his excuses and left.* A buoyant Bowie then excitedly said to Pafford, 'I left him the tickets but I didn't think he was gonna turn up! That was Scott Walker! Oh, wow, that's made my tour!'[24] They would never meet again, but their paths would cross, and their final interaction would be a memorable, and affecting, one.

*Outside* is Bowie's longest studio album by a considerable margin. At an exhausting 74 minutes, it is nearly 20 minutes longer than the first Tin Machine album or *Black Tie White Noise* – both themselves records that could have done with some judicious editing and removal of songs. Even committed aficionados of *Outside*, such as me, would admit that it could do with losing those 20 minutes, if not more.† Both Bowie and Eno would come to concur with this; Bowie suggested that 'I should never have made it as long as it is',[25] while Eno sighed his hope that 'it was shorter. I wish nearly all records were shorter.'[26]

Eno described it with the clear-sighted attitude of one who has seen it all before and can offer the detached aspect of a prophet, or a Stone Age man. 'Strong, muddy, prolix, gritty. Garsonic, modern (self-consciously,

---

\* When Pafford, coincidentally bumping into Walker a couple of years later in London, asked him his opinion of his biggest fan, Walker replied: 'He's a great artist. He's been very kind with the things he's said about me, so I was more than happy to return the favour. He deserves it.'

† Since you asked. . . I'd remove 'Leon Takes Us Outside', all the segues, 'Wishful Beginnings', 'We Prick You' and consider taking off 'Strangers When We Meet', for reasons outlined above, which would turn the album into a rather more manageable 47 minutes.

ironically so.) . . . some acceptable complexity merging into not-so-acceptable muddle; several really beautiful songs ("Motel", "Oxford Town", "Strangers", others). The only thing missing: space – the nerve to be very simple. But an indisputably "outside" record.'[27] It was bold, challenging, gleefully uncommercial and the epitome of what a pre-millennium David Bowie album ought to be, taking the experimental leanings of his previous work and compressing them into a fascinating whole.

By rights, it should have been the album that restored Bowie to a triumphant place in the mainstream. When compared to some of the other key releases of 1995, including Radiohead's *The Bends*, Pulp's *Different Class* and Bruce Springsteen's *The Ghost of Tom Joad* – to say nothing of Alanis Morrisette's ubiquitous *Jagged Little Pill* – it is a majestic, timeless work that still stands up brilliantly three decades later. The only nod to commercial demands is the inclusion of a re-recorded version of 'Strangers When We Meet' as the album's final song. It sounds fantastic, ballsier and more dynamic than the original, but it has nothing to do with the remainder of the album structurally or thematically and therefore its presence must be viewed as a desire on someone's part – Bowie's? Eno's? Arista's? – to ensure that the album would have a hit single.* Its B-side, 'Get Real', is a fascinating anomaly; a Bowie–Eno co-write, it's a three-minute pop song that could easily have fitted onto *Let's Dance*.

In preparation for *Outside*'s release in September 1995, Bowie signed a new contract in June with Virgin America, which would not only see his new album given the all-bells, all-whistles treatment, but enable the entirety of his post-*Scary Monsters* albums to be reissued. After a few years in which money and status had both been a source of concern for him, the deal that he agreed with Virgin – spearheaded by Ken and Nancy Berry, both committed Bowie aficionados who were desperate to get him onto their label, whatever the cost – gave him both security and the assurance that he was

---

* Naturally, when it was released – as a double A-side with a new live version of 'The Man Who Sold the World', memories of Nirvana's version still fresh – it reached an unimpressive 39 in the British charts.

not washed up. Instead, as he approached 50, he retained both dignity and poise in an industry often geared towards the next big thing.

The only downside was an unseemly squabble that ensued over songwriting credits on the album, and therefore the royalties that its various participants were due. When Bowie and Eno had worked together previously in the '70s, it was relatively straightforward. Eno received co-composing credits on several songs on *Low*, *"Heroes"* and *Lodger*, occasionally with Carlos Alomar, and Tony Visconti was credited on all three albums as producer. However, nearly two decades later, the more unorthodox composition of *Outside*, with its origins in the improvisation of the *Leon* project, led to bad feeling, especially between Gabrels and Eno.

Although the two men had been on good terms during recording in Switzerland ('I had roughly 60 dinners with Brian,' says Gabrels, 'because David had gone home after recording every night'), the guitarist was surprised, after the initial sessions had been completed, to be handed a form which, in his recollection, 'amounted to an NDA'. In it, the wording stated that 'the artist and the producer could claim any performance on the record as their own'. Gabrels, who by now had worked on four albums with Bowie and had co-written several songs, was appalled, calling it 'heinous' and blaming Bowie's business managers for sharp, even dishonest practice. Today he says, 'David came out of a different generation, where lyric writing was 50 per cent of the song, but his use of the Verbasizer\* called that into question. Are you going to send 50 per cent of the royalties to Apple? So I said to him, "David, this is just wrong, because you can't claim that my performance on guitar is yours, or Brian's."'[28]

According to Gabrels, Eno and Bowie were working from the assumption that 'any music that is made in the studio, by musicians that have been picked by the producer or the artist, as a byproduct of their improvisations in the studio, is owned by the producer and/or artists'. Eno had even

---

\*  An innovative form of software that was developed by Ty Roberts and used by Bowie on his signature 'cut-up' technique of lyric writing on the album.

attempted to implement a mathematical system of sorts to quantify this, writing in *Modern Recording and Music* in 1982 that 'I'd make a judgement on the writing of [a] piece as if I had nothing to do with it . . . what we got was everyone's opinion of what you've done, except his or her own.'[29]

Gabrels vehemently disagreed with this, from both an artistic and a commercial standpoint. There was extra wrangling because, in his recollection, 'Brian wouldn't sign the contract for the songwriting arrangements, even though the album had already been out a couple of months . . . it seemed like he was holding out.' He concluded, of his experiences working on the album, '*Outside* was a blast, right up until the last two months, which threw me quite a bit. But everything was fine between me and David, and a few months later, we were working together again. Brian and I . . . I never saw him again in the studio. I've run into him socially, but I don't think he's ever quite forgiven me for going to bat for the little guy.'*,[30]

In any case, Gabrels was sidelined during the publicity campaign for the album, which began in late summer 1995, after Bowie had shot a video for the first single, the industrial, Nine Inch Nails-accented 'The Heart's Filthy Lesson'. It would later be used by David Fincher over the end credits of his brilliantly grim serial killer thriller *Se7en*, ensuring that the dazed and gut-punched audience would be given an extra fillip of intense misery on their way out of the cinema. (It's a shame, incidentally, that Bowie never acted for Fincher; the two men share a blackly comic sensibility that could have been harnessed in intriguing and memorable ways on screen.) A revitalised Bowie planned a variety of activities to celebrate *Outside*'s release. There would be his first solo tour since 1990, in which he would visit the US and Europe, followed by festival shows in the summer of 1996. And, of course, he would talk to the press once again: the first significant interviews that he had given in years.

---

*    Eno's own recollection was very different. He wrote in his diary on 27 September: 'Talked to Bowie re *Outside* splits on phone . . . his straightforwardness in matters like this always agreeably surprises me.'

For a man who claimed that he had 'run out of charisma',[31] Bowie certainly gave some of the most entertaining and apparently candid comments to favoured journalists of any of his peers. To Paul Gorman of *Music Week*, he was evangelical about the prospects of continuing the story of Nathan Adler et al. beyond the confines of *Outside* – which was officially named 1. *Outside* as if in the expectation of further updates – and declared 'this is an ongoing series of albums. This is a once-in-a-lifetime chance, by a narrative device, to chronicle the final five years of the millennium. The over-ambitious intention is to carry this through to the year 2000.'[32] The second album was tentatively entitled *Inside Outside*, consisting of what Bowie called 'pretty far-out stuff' and intended for release in 1996. There was grandiose discussion of staging an eight-hour version of the work, possibly in association with the American experimental stage director Robert Wilson, somewhere at the 1999 Salzburg Festival to celebrate the coming of the year 2000. It never amounted to anything, although, according to Gabrels, Bowie spoke with complete sincerity, rather than attempting to give journalists interesting copy. 'He *always* believed what he said.'[33]

In any case, Bowie was talking about *Outside* with greater confidence than he had displayed in his work for years. His particular skill in these interviews, which he would deploy throughout the rest of his career, was to flatter his interlocutor into believing that they were just as talented and brilliant and multifaceted as he was, and that, were it not for the tiresome demands of the publicity circuit, they could easily be friends and mutual confidantes.

Some moments of candour slipped through the net. When asked how he'd describe the record to his long-term fans, Bowie quipped that he'd 'probably say that it's neo-paganism in search for sense in a fragmented society', before further elaboration. 'I have to feel that what I'm doing right now is artistically the most successful thing that I've ever done. For a long time . . . I'd be really scared of feeling that I'd got somewhere, because, for me, art is about searching . . . I think the search is the thing.' He openly disowned some of his earlier work, saying 'the [albums] I hate the most are the ones that sold the most, like *Tonight, Never Let Me Down*. I don't seem to like the things that are commercially successful as much as I like my commercial failures. I like all my commercial failures, generally.' And his best jokes were blackly funny, shot through with a career's realisation of both triumph and disaster. When asked 'What makes a real rock star and to what extent do you fit the bill?', Bowie responded, mordantly. 'A tombstone, mate! That's when you really become a rock god. Dead icon!'[34]

If he cared about the critical reaction, he was studiously nonchalant, saying, 'when Brian and I work together, we tend to work very much for our own enjoyment and for whatever fulfilment we get out of it. We just hope and presume that somebody else will also like the things we find interesting.'[35] Although 'The Heart's Filthy Lesson' failed to excite much interest – bar its grotesque video, which featured depictions of ritual violence and was consequently banned on MTV in its original form – when the critics were finally played *Outside*, the reaction was enthusiastic in the extreme.

It was *Q*'s reviewer Tom Doyle who boldly charged in with the oblig-atory 'best album since *Scary Monsters*' quote,* but he was far from an outlier, with the consensus being that Bowie had built on the promise of *Black Tie White Noise* and produced his finest album in 15 years. This was, admittedly, a harsh judgement on *The Buddha of Suburbia*, but 'his best album since the previous one' would have sounded like faint praise indeed. The veteran writer Charles Shaar Murray, writing in *Mojo*, spoke for his peers when he declared: '*Outside* is David Bowie's comeback album, and about fucking time, too.' He perceptively observed that 'Bowie has spent most of the last decade making "comeback albums", most of them fairly embarrassing; praised on release, and subsequently disowned, by invet-erate wishful thinkers, and bought by comparatively few'.[36] There was the residual concern that *Outside*, which lacked an obvious hit single, was

---

*    'A bold and fascinating trip to offer his devoted listenership, *Outside* is undoubtedly Bowie's most dense and uncompromising work since *Scary Monsters & Super Creeps*' is the precise quotation.

destined to flop commercially and be nothing more than a *succès d'estime*. This may have suited Bowie and Eno, but certainly wasn't what Virgin America had opened their chequebooks for.

In the event, the album was a reasonable commercial success without being a smash hit. After it was released on 25 September, it reached number eight in the UK charts, considerably below *Black Tie White Noise*, but an improvement on *The Buddha of Suburbia*'s 87th placing. In the USA, it peaked at 21 on the *Billboard* Top 200, his highest placing for a decade and a welcome indication that Bowie had, indeed, returned from the grave. Eventually, *Outside* would sell more than a million copies worldwide. It was a considerable return for such a wilfully difficult and opaque album, and proof that Bowie's re-evaluation by the mainstream had come at precisely the right time.

It helped that he had chosen to support the album with a large-scale tour, on which he would be supported by Nine Inch Nails, then performing their own Self Destruct tour. Rather than the Nails being a straightforward support band, Bowie had an innovative idea; the two acts would perform separately, but there would be a crossover section in the middle in which Bowie and his musicians and Nine Inch Nails would perform some of their songs together, including 'Hurt', 'Scary Monsters' and 'Hallo Spaceboy'. The presence of Trent Reznor and co ensured that the US leg of the tour, at least, would be commercially viable, but with a bleak twist. It soon transpired that the audience was primarily there for the Nails, and once they had finished performing, Bowie and his band often saw a substantial exodus.

Not that he had ever intended to offer the audience the comforting certainty of a greatest hits set. 'Like I said in 1990, I'm done with all that,' he declared in a *Music Connection* interview. 'I'm not doing any of those songs again. Basically, the stuff that would have taken up 75 per cent of my previous shows doesn't exist for me anymore. But the rest of the material that makes up what we're doing onstage now are things from the new album and basically older stuff that I've only done once or twice onstage, or stuff that I've never done onstage in the past.'[37] It is possible that some of his more committed fans would thrill to the inclusion of 'Teenage Wildlife' and 'Moonage Daydream' – I certainly would have done – but the only universally recognisable songs that Bowie chose to perform were 'Breaking Glass', 'The Man Who Sold the World' and 'Under Pressure', the latter of which Bowie sang as a duet with his new bassist, the singer-songwriter Gail Ann Dorsey, who would go on to be a consistent presence in his work for the following decade.

Dorsey, who had been working with Tears for Fears, has nothing but fond memories of her time on the *Outside* tour and of working with Bowie. 'David was fantastic. He was very kind, very patient, very funny. He never stressed me out. And I think he was very intuitive, so I'm sure he could tell I was very stressed-out. I had a couple of allies in the form of Mike Garson and Carlos [Alomar], who held my hand and kept me from freaking out, because touring was scary. I just hunkered down and learned the material as best I could, which is what I do, and, and tried to serve the song.' The excitement and nerves of being on a large-scale tour with Bowie led her to ask him one day: 'You could have had any bassist in the world playing with you. Why did you choose me?' His answer was simple. 'I was in a hotel, watching a music programme, and you were on TV playing a guitar and I thought *I'd like to work with her.*'[38]

Dorsey was particularly impressed because this would have happened when she was touring her excellent 1988 album *The Corporate World*. It was typical of Bowie's magpie-like tendencies – as well as his knack for spotting and nurturing talent – to have remembered her and, when the time was right, to have called upon her services. 'He can remember all sorts of facts,' she says, 'whether it's things from his own life, something from an encyclopaedia, something from 13th-century history or some verse from the Bible. He will remember it as soon as he's read it. He had that kind of a brain and was super-intelligent.'[39]

Both Garson and Gabrels, veterans of the Bowie show, regarded the Outside tour, especially in its American leg, as less successful than the album that spawned it.* It did not help that, for whatever reason, Bowie decided to launch the tour on 14 September, a week and a half before *Outside* was released. He may have gaily announced to *USA Today* 'How do you commit commercial suicide? Well, you do this: play songs from an album that hasn't been released yet, and complement it with obscure songs from the past that you've never done on stage',[40] but what sounded like a joke soon proved to be accurate. Earlier in 1995, Bowie had suggested that the album would never translate into live performance, calling it 'far too ambitious a project'. He was, unfortunately, vindicated in this.

Garson suggests that 'he asked us to match the sound of Nine Inch Nails, which was much louder and more bass-heavy than anything we normally did. I felt a little awkward about that because it took a little away from who he was, but he wanted to be able to reach our audience. So we pumped it a little bit.'[41] As for Gabrels, he saw the potential difficulty of touring with a younger, more zeitgeisty band. 'We knew the job was going to be a tough one when we took it to go out on the Outside tour. The crowd that came to the gigs, they were there for Trent, as at the time there was no bigger deal.'[42]

The reviews were not kind. Eric Weisbard contrasted the two acts in *Spin*, writing '"Hallo Spaceboy" (performed here by both bands as they changed over; 11 musicians, two superstars, and prerecorded gibberish), from Bowie's overcooked new album *Outside*, made me suspect Major Tom of a new incarnation: *Absolutely Fabulous*'s Patsy, desperately flouncing at the contemporary . . . Bowie's act made intellectual demands: recognizing cuts like "Joe the Lion" and thinking about their legacy in 1995. Reznor, bouncing off of a crack quartet capable of playing in multiple drum, keyboard, and guitar combinations, and skilled at trumping backing tapes with spontaneous outbursts, only tasked his listeners physically, but the results

---

* Bowie did, however, have the amusingly incongruous experience of visiting the Oval Office on 6 October 1995 and being enthusiastically greeted by President Clinton. The two would later meet again in 2007.

were light years more inspirational. Wonderful noise versus outsider ambiguities: For rock fans, the fight isn't even close anymore.'

It did not help that the technical complexity of performing the album's songs was a logistical nightmare. Gabrels, frustrated by the challenges the band faced on tour, nearly got into a physical fight with Peter Schwartz, who was serving as musical director. 'I'm just about to get up and grab him by the throat and hit him,' he recalled, 'and so simultaneously my ex-wife and Gail Ann Dorsey each kick a leg out from under me. I fall back in my seat, before I can do any damage, or before anyone even senses my intent, they both look at me and go, "No!".'[43]

Matters improved when a stripped-down version of the tour, by now only featuring Gabrels, Garson, Dorsey and Zachary Alford on drums, headed to Europe. Even here, though, there were personnel difficulties. As his cover of 'I Know It's Gonna Happen Someday' demonstrated, Bowie had long admired Morrissey, whose own commercial fortunes had remained buoyant since the glory days of the Smiths. The Mancunian miserabilist had even stronger feelings towards his erstwhile idol; he wrote in his autobiography of his memories of handing him a fan note in the early '70s, while Bowie was on his Ziggy Stardust tour, and how 'thus I touch the hand of this inexplicably liberating reformer; he, a Wildean visionary about to re-mould England, and I, a spectacle of suffering in a blue school uniform'.[44]

The two had duetted on Marc Bolan's 'Cosmic Dancer' as an encore at one of Morrissey's concerts in Los Angeles in 1991 and had remained in touch,* so Bowie asked him to be his support act on his European dates. As with Nine Inch Nails, the plan was for the two acts to cross over, and then for Bowie to take over. However, Morrissey was not intended by nature to be one of life's supporting players and disliked playing to Bowie's audience,

---

* Their brief friendship produced one glorious exchange. Over breakfast one morning, Bowie confided in Morrissey, 'You know, I've had so much sex and drugs that I can't believe I'm still alive,' to which the eternally suffering one replied: 'You know, I've had SO LITTLE sex and drugs that I can't believe I'm still alive.'

rather than his. After petulantly hissing at one of the Wembley concerts, 'Don't worry, David will be on soon' – and this news being greeted with glee rather than sorrow – he quit, declaring 'I left the tour because he put me under a lot of pressure and I found it too exhausting'.*,45 Bowie was not impressed and remembered the slight all his life.

The Outside tour eventually ground to a halt in Paris on 20 February and Bowie could assess the previous two years with clear-sighted ruthlessness. He was working with the best musicians of all generations, from the veteran Garson to the brilliant Dorsey; he had recaptured much of the critical acclaim and respect that he believed that he had lost for good; he was once again a mainstream commercial prospect, albeit off the back of an album that was an inevitable compromise between his most esoteric artistic instincts and the demands of an industry that had increasingly little space for dreamers; and his domestic life, helped by his move to New York, was the happiest and most settled that it had ever been. Yet even as a whole new generation of musicians, alternately in thrall to him and attempting to make a name by rejecting his influence, came forward, it was time for him to look beyond music and find other ways in which he could cement what would become the most multifaceted and chameleonic of legacies.

---

* The tour promoter John Giddings told Dylan Jones: 'I tried to sue Morrissey for the £20,000 I'd paid him, but then someone pointed out that nobody had complained.'

# BOWIE ON SCREEN

## 'I don't really think it's a career'

*'I know what it's like to be appreciated
as well as degraded'*

Bowie dabbled in film throughout this time, not always with
success, but *The Linguini Incident* is an underrated charmer.
Richard Shepard

Imagine, for the sake of argument, that you were an aficionado of Westerns who was in the mood for an English-language treat around Christmas 1998, and that you were walking past one of Rome or Milan's many cinemas. There, the new picture *Gunslinger's Revenge* – or as it is more evocatively named in Italian, *Il mio West*, 'My West' – had recently been released. You may not have heard of its star, the actor-writer-comedian Leonardo Pieraccioni, but the presence of the stalwart Harvey Keitel is always a reassuring one. You pay your couple of thousand lira and take your seat in the cinema, hoping to be entertained.

The film, unfortunately, is a saddening bore. You realise swiftly that it has the usual Euro-pudding failings of a wildly eclectic cast who do not appear to be acting on the same continent, let alone in the same picture, and although Keitel, in the lead role of the stoic cowboy Johnny Lowen, is as gruffly reliable as ever, you are bored and start to wonder what's going to happen next. Your answer comes around the 45-minute mark, when a familiar face appears as the bizarrely named 'Jack Sikora', whose first line – delivered in an extraordinary mixture of cockney, Deep South American and what could be Australian (or equally a poor take on Jamaican patois – it is hard to tell) – is 'Well now this place stinks worse than a mule's ass . . . and somebody's already shittin' their pants!' You sit up, newly engaged. David Bowie – for it is he – has come to town, and he is a gunslinger, out for revenge. The film will be dreadful – it *is* dreadful – but at least it won't be boring any more.

Bowie filmed *Gunslinger's Revenge*, apparently for a lark, over a fortnight in Tuscany in June 1998, in an otherwise quiet year after the efforts and excursions of 1997. Thirty years before, on 26 February 1966, he had given one of his first interviews about acting to *Melody Maker*. The then 19-year-old singer-songwriter was promoting his single 'Can't Help Thinking About Me', which he had recorded with his band the Lower Third. It would not be his commercial breakthrough, although it would later find another lease of life decades later, but the conversation between Bowie and the anonymous journalist had several nuggets of interest, from the perceptive opening observation – 'Without doubt David Bowie has talent. And also without doubt it will be exploited' – to Bowie's precocious statement, said 'modestly', that 'I want to act. I'd like to do character parts. I think it takes a lot to become somebody else. It takes some doing.'[1]

It is often mystifying as to why rock stars – those most demonstrative, egotistical, larger-than-life characters – choose to develop a sideline in acting. Most significant figures in music have, at some time or another, appeared in at least one film or television series. Sometimes, this has been with distinction: Lady Gaga is an Oscar-nominated actress, the Who's Roger Daltrey moved with alacrity into character roles – and back again – from the mid-'70s onwards, and the likes of Cher, Barbra Streisand and Frank Sinatra have all been iconic presences on screen. Yet there are many other examples of toe-curling embarrassment. Prince and Rihanna – hugely powerful, vital presences on stage – failed to translate this charisma into acting ability, and for every half-decent Madonna performance, there are another half-dozen dismal misses that demonstrate that the Material Girl should stick to music.*

Bowie, on the other hand, had a fascinatingly hit-and-miss thespian career. He may have declared to *Newsweek* in 1972, dismissing any connection to his recent statement that he was bisexual, 'I'm an actor, I play roles, fragments of myself,'[2] but it became clear that he was at his best when he was allowed to inhabit parts that came close to who 'David Bowie' was, or at least appeared to be. He was therefore perfectly cast as the otherworldly alien Thomas Jerome Newton in Nicolas Roeg's sci-fi drama *The Man Who Fell to Earth*, but he was miserably out of place as a Prussian gigolo in David Hemmings's dismal *Just a Gigolo*, which he ruefully described as 'my 32 Elvis Presley movies contained in one'.[3]

It continued in the same vein throughout the '80s. He was extraordinary on the Broadway stage in *The Elephant Man*, stylish but uncomfortable

---

* Her writing and directing career has been even worse. I had to watch her Wallis Simpson–Edward VIII drama *W.E.* as research for my 2020 book *The Crown in Crisis*, and mere words cannot describe my horror at being subjected to that dismal film.

in Tony Scott's *The Hunger*, understated and brilliant in *Merry Christmas, Mr Lawrence*, a redeeming feature in *Absolute Beginners* – not least because his title track may be his single finest song from the decade – and so deep in self-parody as Jareth, the Goblin King in *Labyrinth*, that it's a wonder that his increasingly elaborate wigs and costumes don't fall apart, so obvious it is that he's having to restrain himself from laughing at the absurdity of the whole enterprise. What he very seldom did was to play recognisable human beings. Even his Major Celliers in *Merry Christmas, Mr Lawrence* is as much a symbol as a man, a blond-haired vision of a stiff upper lip barely concealing enormous emotional pain.

It was therefore a significant step for Bowie that he worked with the most important filmmaker he had yet collaborated with in late December 1987, in the form of Martin Scorsese. He had recently turned down the role of the megalomaniac villain Max Zorin in the Bond film *A View to a Kill* – it would subsequently be assumed by Bowie's future co-star Christopher Walken – and was looking for a greater challenge.\* He had long been an admirer of Nikos Kazantzakis's novel *The Last Temptation of Christ* and had followed its halting progress towards film adaptation with interest, commenting to *NME* in 1984 that 'strangely enough, they can't raise a cent of finance for it in America'.[4]

At the time, Bowie believed that none other than Keitel was cast as Pontius Pilate, with Aidan Quinn as Jesus and the Kinks' Ray Davies as Judas Iscariot, but in fact Scorsese had cast Sting, following in the age-old Hollywood tradition of having Romans played by Englishmen. When scheduling difficulties meant that Sting had to drop out, Scorsese briefly toyed with offering the role to Lou Reed – which would have been a fascinatingly strange piece of stunt casting, given that Reed was not known for his thespian abilities – but in the end he decided that Bowie was a better fit.

---

\*    He later said, 'It simply was a terrible script and I saw little reason for spending so long on something that bad, that workmanlike. And I told them so. I don't think anyone had turned down a "major" role in a Bond before. It really didn't go down too well at all.'

The two men had met in New York earlier in 1987, when the Glass Spider behemoth had arrived in town. 'I wanted to play against the traditional biblical epic,' Scorsese would later say. '[Bowie] was the first person I thought of. It was his charisma, his look, and ultimately the way he moved.'[5]

The part of Pontius Pilate in the finished film was nothing more than a cameo – a three-minute performance that only needed Bowie to spend two days in Morocco on set, during which, as Pilate, he offers a suitably world-weary portrayal of a high-ranking administrator bored with both the politicking and bloodshed involved in his job, as he sentences Willem Dafoe's Jesus to death on Golgotha. Scorsese's main direction to him was to be a still, poised presence, without a hint of Hollywood villainy. In his brief scene, Bowie manages to deliver some memorable, Paul Schrader-scripted lines, as he says, matter-of-factly, 'it's one thing to want to change the way that people live, but you want to change how they think, and how they feel'. His Pilate is not unsympathetic, but a protector of the status quo at all costs, asking his captive to perform some magic tricks for him with no belief that he will actually be able to do so. His response to Jesus's refusal – 'that's disappointing' – is a particularly elegant piece of understatement.

Scorsese was thrilled with Bowie's performance. 'There I was face-to-face with the ancient world,' he later said of the first time he saw him on set, 'a being from the ancient world. I suddenly looked into the face of history. His face was right up close to mine and he was smiling and his hair was done as Pontius Pilate. He was in his toga and his eyes, of course, one was one colour and the other another colour. It was the most shocking, beautiful thing I had seen. This was the ancient world and it has come alive! He was an alien in the best sense of the word!'[6]

The two had warm exchanges about cinema during their time on set – Scorsese was especially interested to hear about Bowie's experiences working with Nagisa Oshima, who had directed him in *Merry Christmas, Mr Lawrence* – and although the two never worked together again, Scorsese had toyed with the idea of casting him as Fred Astaire in a Schrader and John Guare-scripted biopic of George Gershwin, to be made around 1993;

Astaire suggested before his death in 1987 that Bowie was the sole actor who he would allow to play him on screen.

Had the film come off, it's likely that Bowie would have happily reunited with his director. In 1995, he said of his casting in *Last Temptation* that 'I wonder what Scorsese's like – well, you'll find out, he's offered you a role. Right! With somebody like that you don't even question the role. You say – Scorsese? Yeah, I'm doing it.'[7] Many years later, in one of his final interviews, Bowie was still reminiscing fondly about the experience, saying in 2004, that 'it's wonderful when Scorsese asks if I want to wander on and do Pontius Pilate – that's terrific', before noting, self-deprecatingly, 'but Russell [Crowe] can sleep safely'.[8]

Due to Tin Machine obligations, Bowie would not work on another film until late 1990, when he accepted a role in Richard Shepard's second picture, *The Linguini Incident*. Shepard, who went on to be a success-ful filmmaker responsible for such pictures as the Pierce Brosnan–Greg Kinnear film *The Matador* and the Jude Law vehicle *Dom Hemingway*, was 24 years old when he made it, and, by his own admission, 'I was not Orson Welles making *Citizen Kane* at that age.' An offbeat and quirky romantic comedy based around the dynamic between Bowie's barman Monte – an Englishman adrift in New York and mired in debt – and Rosanna Arquette's waitress-cum-aspirant escapologist Lucy, it was a critical and commercial flop on release and set Shepard's previously promising career back several years. However, a 2024 director's cut – running, unusually, five minutes shorter than the brief theatrical release – reveals that, while no classic, *The Linguini Incident* is a smart, funny piece of cinema that is especially notable for Bowie's remarkably low-key and effective performance. For the first time in his acting career, he wasn't playing a heightened or tragic character, but instead was the closest he had yet come to being himself on screen.

The film features two choice comic cameos by Buck Henry and Andre Gregory – both of whom had previously acted in Bowie pictures, namely *The Man Who Fell to Earth* and *The Last Temptation of Christ* – as the owners of the restaurant in which Bowie and Arquette work. As Shepard explains, 'we sent the script to Bowie and Mick Jagger to play Buck Henry and Andre Gregory's parts. But we did it without any knowledge of how the movie business worked. We just thought "Yeah, let's just offer it to them", not even thinking why Mick Jagger and David Bowie would do this movie for no money with this director they didn't know, while they're touring the world.' Shepard now admits 'it was truly a case of "ignorance is bliss"'. Yet to his surprise, he swiftly heard back from Bowie's management, who conveyed an unexpected message. 'He said "I don't want to play that part. But I would like to play the lead part."'⁹

Shepard, a committed fan of *Withnail and I*, had envisioned Richard E. Grant in the role of Monte,* but swiftly adapted. Even as his financiers suggested that Bowie was not a tested commercial prospect in cinema, the director replied, 'He's one of the most famous people in the world. What are you talking about?' The appeal for Bowie and Shepard was that Monte was a down-to-earth role, and while Grant – estimable actor though he is – would have gone big, Bowie underplayed it. 'I thought how fun would it be to see him play not *The Hunger* and not the man who fell to earth,' says Shepard, 'but to play a real human being or whatever. And so we had to fight for David to be in the movie, and now, thirty years later, *he's* the value of the movie.'¹⁰

Although Shepard now allows that 'it was not a particularly enjoyable shoot for me', because low-budget cinema does not make for a relaxing or pleasant environment, Bowie had a glorious time making *The Linguini Incident*. Able to decompress from the stadium demands of the Sound + Vision tour, and taking a break between Tin Machine albums, he was at his most laid-back and comfortable. 'I think this movie offered him a chance to be funny,' says Shepard now, 'and he was charming and relaxed, and there was no tension from him at all. In fact, he couldn't have been more encouraging as he also improvised a lot of dialogue. He never left to sit in his trailer, but just got on set from the beginning of the day until we

---

\* Actor and director would later work together on *Dom Hemingway*.

were done. And he would just talk to everyone; if you were to track down every single member of the crew of that movie, they would have a photo of their kids, or themselves, with David Bowie. He was enjoying himself the entire time.'[11]

One plausible reason for Bowie's new-found contentedness was that he had recently met Iman, who has a brief, amusing cameo in the picture as a well-heeled socialite who tries to bid on a date with Monte but is restrained from doing so by her irritated paramour. ('It was funny before you even knew their history,' notes Shepard. 'But then, of course, knowing their history, you couldn't ask for a funnier cameo.') When Bowie and Shepard were not filming, they spent time together in Los Angeles, seeing bands and going for dinner, something that the director would later describe as 'an incredible experience during a surreal part of my life'. Bowie was, he remembers, 'low key and doing his job and having a good time'. Iman was the major reason for this happiness. 'He was open to falling in love in a serious way, which he did, obviously. It wasn't just some dalliance. She was the love of his life and the person he'd spent the rest of his life with.'[12]

As always, star and director parted ways when filming completed, although Bowie's company Isolar took on some limited financial responsibility for the picture when it became obvious that it could not be finished otherwise. Yet it was recut, against Shepard's wishes, to reduce the levels of quirk and then dumped in cinemas on the weekend of the LA riots. The reviews were largely disparaging, although the *New York Times* praised Bowie's 'amusingly level-headed presence' and how he was 'looking elegantly sunken and sounding wonderfully debonair'.

The film flopped at the box office and Bowie's short-lived career as a romantic comedy leading man was over, although his real-life relationship had begun gloriously. Shepard encountered Bowie again once more, by chance, in New York a decade later. He felt it incumbent on him to apologise to him for the film's failure, saying 'that was really one of the toughest experiences of my life, because the movie was taken away from me, recut and bombed'. Bowie smiled happily and said, 'I met my wife on that movie so, yeah, I will always look fondly back on that film.' For Shepard, 'that's the greatest, greatest thing in the world'.[13]

*❀*

Bowie remained riddled with self-doubt about whether he had any serious acting ability, despite the success of both *The Man Who Fell to Earth* and *Merry Christmas, Mr Lawrence*. In 1987, he suggested that he didn't know 'if I do have a career as an actor. I do some acting jobs occasionally, but I don't really think it's a career. It's something that I get offered every now and again and if it seems witty or silly or something that I might enjoy doing, then I do it. But it's not like a second career or anything.'[14] Yet after his revitalising experience on *The Linguini Incident*, he was considerably more engaged, saying to the *Irish Times* in 1991 that 'as regards movies, I did two this year. I did a comedy with Rosanna Arquette called "Linguini" [*sic*] which comes out in the fall and I've done a film with John Landis and Sylvester Stallone for television which comes out later this year. And I'm directing my own first movie next year. So with movies I'm still in there.'

The Landis TV picture that Bowie refers to, *Dream On*, was in fact an adult-themed sitcom, in which he makes a brief appearance as Sir Roland Moorecock, a tyrannical British film director who is prone to making remarks like 'I don't generally fraternise with the help, but as I don't have any friends of my own, I'm going to invite you all to my little shack in the country this weekend.' It allowed Bowie to be bitchy, and funny, and although the show has long since been forgotten, nobody has ever delivered the words 'Hello, Francesca' with more world-weary contempt.

In an interview that he gave to *Movieline* magazine in April 1992, Bowie talked freely about many of the projects that he had been offered, or had wanted to be in, that never came to fruition. After he and Mick Jagger had duetted, indifferently but to chart-topping effect, on the 1985 cover of 'Dancing in the Street', there was much interest in reuniting the two of them for a film. Mooted ideas included *Mountains of the Moon*, which would have starred them as the Victorian explorers Burton and Speke and followed their ill-fated journey to central Africa to discover the source of the Nile,* or a picture in which they would have played Byron and Shelley. Bowie, especially, hankered after the Byronic in both his life and career† – in the Julien Temple-directed video for his song 'Blue Jean', *Jazzin' for Blue Jean*, he had played a flamboyant rock star character called 'Screamin' Lord Byron' – so this would have been an intriguing, but sadly never-realised project.

Other films that Bowie wished to make included *At Play in the Fields of the Lord*, adapted from Peter Matthiessen's 1965 novel and in which he would have played the missionary Martin Quarrier, opposite Richard Gere, optimistically cast in those pre-outrage days as an Indian pilot. 'I would have given my right arm to play the role of [Quarrier],' said Bowie. 'It would have been a glorious film to participate in.' He and Jagger were also interested in appearing in a remake of the Marlon Brando/David Niven romantic comedy *Bedtime Story*, which eventually became *Dirty Rotten Scoundrels*; the script ended up being made with Michael Caine and Steve Martin. 'Mick and I were a bit tweezed that we lost out on a script that could have been reasonably good.'[15]

Yet it is the never-realised idea of Bowie's directorial debut that is more intriguing. Ever since he worked with Roeg in the mid-'70s, he had become interested in the idea of making his own feature film, in the style of a less magisterial Sir Roland Moorecock. Concept albums of his – such as *Diamond Dogs, Outside* or (less successfully) *Never Let Me Down* – often feel like the soundtracks to grandiose motion pictures that only time, or money, prevented from being filmed in all their glory. He had gone a relatively long way towards developing a frenzied, drug-fuelled bacchanal back then that would have combined elements of the kabbalistic philosophy that he explored on the title track of *Station to Station* with good old-fashioned

---

* It was eventually made by Bob Rafelson with Patrick Bergin and Iain Glen in the lead roles.

† Jagger famously recited Shelley's 'Adonais' at the Stones' free Hyde Park concert in memory of Brian Jones on 5 July 1969.

provocation, involving Jesus as a freedom fighter who ends the film being captured by a cloven-hoofed Satan. By Bowie's own admission, it was 'the most alarming piece'. He once recalled that 'John Lennon looked over it and said "Why do you want to make this?? This is so fucking evil!" And I said "But it's going to look great!"'[16]

A decade and a half later, Bowie's ambitions had fallen to earth, but, as he said, 'now I feel I can at least accomplish the task, and hopefully with some degree of elegance.' He gave away few details in interviews, but let slip that his directorial debut was not a big-budget, special effects-laden film, but would be a character-driven picture, set in contemporary Los Angeles (a place so crucial to the narrative that Bowie called it 'the fifth performance') with four main characters. He described it as 'about person-alities, and the destructive effects of one person's challenge and control over another person's life'. Bowie suggested that he was excited about the visual aspects of directing, but was unconvinced that he had done a sterling job with the screenplay, saying '[Writing the script] is not like writing a song at all. It's stunningly hard. The first thirty-five pages were fun. Then I hit a wall.' Veteran Bowie observers may have listened to his concerns – 'I'm a ball of sweat when I think about what I have to do. It really is terrifying.' – and laid considerable bets on the film never being made. When he said 'I'm being secretive about this because I want the film to come out without any expectations whatsoever,'[17] he might have added that his own expectations of making it were not high. And so it proved. The intriguing prospect of a Bowie-directed picture never came to fruition.

He did not lack for filmmakers who wished to work with him, how-ever. David Lynch, the quixotic visionary whose previous forays into cinema had alternated between brilliance (*The Elephant Man*, *Blue Velvet*) and self-indulgent posturing (*Dune*, *Wild at Heart*), had decided to bring his much-acclaimed '80s television show *Twin Peaks* to cinema, and he wished to recruit a stellar cast for its big-screen incarnation. Bowie was a long-standing fan of Lynch's work, in particular his terrifying debut, 1977's *Eraserhead*. In the pre-video and streaming days of 1980, Bowie announced to *Melody Maker* that his ambition for the decade ahead was 'to own a personal copy of *Eraserhead*'.

Although Bowie's performance on Broadway as Joseph Merrick, aka the Elephant Man, was accomplished with mime and movement, rather than the heavy make-up that John Hurt wore in Lynch's 1980 film, the fact that both projects took place in the same year nevertheless displayed an impressive degree of synchronicity between the two men. Therefore, when the chance came for Lynch to cast Bowie in a small but pivotal cameo in his 1992 film *Twin Peaks: Fire Walk with Me*, he leapt at the opportunity. According to the film's co-writer Robert Engels, his casting came about as part of a running joke. 'When we were writing *Fire Walk with Me* at David [Lynch]'s house, his assistant at the time would be in the other room, and she would come in to give David a phone message or something. She would hear what we were talking about and she would always jokingly say, "as played by David Bowie". We'd always laugh. When we got done with the script, David said, "I think we should get David Bowie". That's what that comes from. Of course, David being David, he can just call him up. It was pretty funny.'[18]

The part that Bowie was given, that of FBI Special Agent Phillip Jeffries, was created especially for the film, and he appears to bewildering and terrifying effect. He filmed his cameo in the summer of 1991 and it is probably the darkest role that he ever played on screen. As with his appearance in *The Last Temptation of Christ*, it is a brief and striking jolt, in which the character of Jeffries, long since presumed missing by his FBI colleagues, briefly reappears, as if from hell. Amid barely glimpsed but horrific images, Jeffries says, in a Louisiana accent, 'It was a dream . . . we live inside a dream', and then, after a cry of 'I found something!', disappears once again, his purpose for reappearing unknown.

Lynch was, naturally, a great admirer of Bowie. In a 2017 interview with *Pitchfork*, he described him as being 'unique, like Elvis was unique. There's something about him that's so different from everybody else. I only met him during the time I worked with him and just a couple of other times, but he was such a good guy, so easy to talk to and regular. I just wish he was still around and that I could work with him again.'[19] A few weeks later, reflecting on a collaboration that he described as 'a thrill', Lynch elaborated about Bowie's accent. 'Someone made him feel bad for the accent he put on at the time of *Fire Walk with Me*. I thought it was fine, but in our last phone call, he asked me to cast a real Louisiana actor with a real Louisiana accent for the voice acting of his character, and so I did. Funny enough, that actor sounded just like David Bowie.'[20]

There were spin-offs from the collaboration, however. Bowie would later record a sepulchral, haunting cover of Gershwin's 'A Foggy Day in London Town' with Lynch's regular composer Angelo Badalamenti in 1998 for a charity album, and – appropriately given the shared DNA that *Outside* and *Twin Peaks* both possessed – Bowie would later donate 'I'm Deranged' from that album to Lynch's masterly 1997 horror picture *Lost Highway*; it was used both in the opening and closing credits of that film. Certainly, for this writer, it is impossible to separate the song from the picture, meaning that 'I'm Deranged' feels as if it was composed especially for *Lost Highway*. Its presence on the *Outside* album two years previously therefore feels nothing less than a Lynchian touch of time-hopping surrealism that forges an appropriate connection between Bowie/Jeffries and Lynch himself. The character would reappear in Lynch's 2017 miniseries *Twin Peaks: The Return*, but as Bowie was no longer able to participate, the part was now played by what looked a large kettle with a glowing white orb on its end: an ingenious piece of inventiveness that the character's creator would surely have appreciated.

From the terrifying to the trivial. The next acting role that Bowie accepted, in late 1992, was a self-parodying cameo as himself in the 1993 Dick Clement and Ian La Frenais sitcom *Full Stretch*, a comedy in which Reece Dinsdale's hapless limousine driver attempts to transport his celebrity passenger around London, with the usual mildly amusing consequences. The only moment that lingers in the memory – save the image of the former Thin White Duke asleep in the back of a limo that has been impounded – is a reasonably droll exchange in which, as Bowie attempts to read Ian McEwan's *Black Dogs*,\* Dinsdale, wishing to flatter his charge, says 'I really like Tin Machine'. The awkward pause – lengthened in the edit by its director Antonia Bird?[†] – lands all the better 30 years on. Yet it says much for Bowie, an international rock star and household-name celebrity of decades' standing, that he would take on inconsequential parts like this. The next time that he would appear in a British sitcom as himself would be more than a decade later, and would be rather more significant. But before then, he had to answer the call of an old friend.

On his 1971 album *Hunky Dory*, Bowie included an acoustic song about the American pop artist Andy Warhol, which was affectionate but not without a certain element of bite. Over Mick Ronson's acoustic guitar riff, Bowie sings 'Andy Warhol looks a scream / Hang him on my wall' and with a touch of English humour that would have been anathema to Warhol, declares 'He'll think about paint and he'll think about glue / What a jolly boring thing to do.' The song is fondly regarded – as Bowie biographer Nicholas Pegg observes, the song has long been a cult favourite among aficionados – but when it was written, Bowie had yet to meet the man who was its inspiration.

This was remedied in September 1971, when he headed over to New York to sign a record contract with RCA. During his visit, he was granted an audience with the great man at his Factory studio. It was never likely to have been a meeting of minds, and so it proved. After Bowie awkwardly passed on good wishes from an unidentified mutual acquaintance, who

---

\*   He would place McEwan's 1978 collection of short stories, *In Between the Sheets*, in his top 100 books of all time.

†   Who went on to make the excellent *Priest* and the still-underrated cannibal black comedy *Ravenous*, which was shot by Anthony B. Richmond, who also filmed *The Man Who Fell to Earth*.

Warhol chided as a 'sick boy', Bowie played the impresario the song that bore his name. It did not go well. As Bowie later recounted, 'he absolutely hated it . . . he was cringing with embarrassment. I think he thought that I really put him down in the song and it really wasn't meant to be that – it was kind of an ironic *homage* to him.'[21] Warhol left the room to gather himself and, returning, made the characteristically dry comment that 'I like your shoes'. Bowie, always the peacock, was wearing a pair that were a gift from Marc Bolan – 'brilliant canary yellow, semi-wedge heel, semi-point rounded toe'. Warhol took some Polaroid photos of the shoes, then filmed an acquiescent Bowie performing mime for a few moments, before bidding him farewell by saying 'Goodbye, David. You have such nice shoes.'[22]

If Bowie had hoped that he would develop a similar relationship with Warhol to the one that his friend Lou Reed enjoyed, he would be disappointed. He later commented to the artist Tracey Emin that he always felt stupid in Warhol's company; this lingering feeling of insecurity never truly disappeared.* Although his attempts at developing a cultural centre in London, in the form of the Beckenham Arts Lab, owed a great deal to Warhol's influence on the Factory, he could not successfully emulate what the other man had done. Many of the public remarks that he made about Warhol over the next few years – such as saying to William Burroughs in 1974 that 'this man is the wrong colour to be a human being' and remarking, of their ill-fated meeting, that 'he had nothing to say at all, absolutely nothing'[23] – can be seen as attention-seeking, the bright but frustrated pupil trying to catch the teacher's eye. It did not work.

Warhol attended several of his concerts, most notably the Ziggy Stardust performances, and was a guest in the audience for *The Elephant Man* in 1980. Yet when the artist died in 1987, at the age of 58, the relationship between him and Bowie was formal at best, non-existent at worst.

---

* A visitor to the 2018 Warhol retrospective at New York's Whitney Gallery observed that 'the footage of the excruciating mime played on a small screen. It felt more like it had been included to heap ridicule on DB, which supports Bowie's lingering insecurity, even after both artists had died.'

Warhol may have remarked that 'David always tried out combinations that no one else would have dreamt of',[24] but he never invited him into his inner circle, unlike a talented, youthful and self-destructive artist named Jean-Michel Basquiat, who took the American art scene by storm in the '80s before dying of a heroin overdose in 1986 at the age of 27.

Shortly after the deaths of Warhol and Basquiat, Bowie began building up a serious art collection. One of the pieces that he bought was Basquiat's *Air Power*, for which he reportedly paid $3.5 million.* It was a piece of synchronicity that he also owned artworks by the painter Julian Schnabel, who had known Basquiat in the '80s and who now wished to make his directorial debut with a biopic of his near-contemporary. Some naysayers suggested that it was the height of self-indulgence for a painter to make a film about another painter, to which Schnabel pugnaciously responded: 'I know what it's like to be attacked as an artist. I know what it's like to be judged as an artist. I know what it's like to arrive as an artist and have fame and notoriety. I know what it's like to be accused of things that you never said or did. I know what it's like to be described as a piece of hype. I know what it's like to be appreciated as well as degraded.'[25]

Schnabel had begun thinking about the Basquiat film shortly after his subject's death and, by 1990, he had written a script, which he sent to Bowie, whom he thought would make an admirable Andy Warhol: one icon incarnating another. Unfortunately, as Bowie would later confess to Simon Witter, 'I turned it down, because I didn't think I had the time. I didn't really know Julian and I was as hypocritical as the rest of society, and I thought, *Well, he's a painter. How come he can make movies?*' However, New York cultural high society is a small enclave, and so Bowie and Schnabel came face to face at a soirée a few years later. They hit it off, with Bowie later recounting that he thought, 'This guy actually does have vision. I'm sure if he turns his hand to making movies, he'll do a half-decent job of

---

* This proved to be a typically canny investment. When much of Bowie's art collection was auctioned off after his death, the Basquiat sold for $8.8 million.

it. So, he re-represented the script to me and I said, "Yes, I'd really like to do this."'[26]

Schnabel self-funded the picture, on a tight $3 million budget, and – with then-little-known Jeffrey Wright cast as Basquiat – called in a mixture of favours from New York glitterati in order to assemble a suitably star-studded supporting cast that would give the film proper gravitas. As Bowie described it, 'I was not a little persuaded by the fact that several of my friends were in it: Dennis Hopper, particularly, who I've known for something like 20 years, and Gary Oldman, who I know very well, Chris Walken, who I've had many run-ins with. William [sic] Dafoe, who I've worked with. So, we all knew each other, and they in turn knew each other, so it had a workshop atmosphere to it. I loved the hell out of it, mainly because it was only ten days' work.'[27]

In interviews, Bowie liked to play down the seriousness with which he approached playing Warhol. 'I only had 7,000 words, and once I got them in the right order, it was a doddle. I mean, a most challenging role.'[28] This was disingenuous. In fact, he had prepared carefully for the role, bearing in mind Warhol's dictum that 'If you want to know all about me, just look at the surface of my paintings and films, and there I am. There's nothing behind it.' He borrowed Warhol's clothes, including one of his many silver-blond wigs, a pair of glasses and a jacket from the Warhol Museum in Philadelphia. 'They still smelt of him. I even had his little handbag – a very sad little bag with all kinds of devices to make you better.'[29]

Bowie is only in the film for about 15 minutes, but Schnabel's hunch – that you need an icon to play an icon – paid off handsomely. From his first scene, in which Basquiat hustles his way into a restaurant to sell an amused Warhol his 'ignorant art', Bowie, complete with mid-Atlantic accent and notes of feline camp, brings Warhol to the screen in a captivating and seductive way, never sentimentalising or humanising him too much but keeping him a chilly, detached figure – another alien who fell to earth. It is a testament to the subtlety of Bowie and Schnabel's work that the writer Bob Colacello, who edited Warhol's *Interview* magazine throughout the

'70s and '80s, compared his performance favourably to others who had impersonated Warhol. 'Bowie looked the most like Andy. When I first saw Bowie on the set, it was like Andy had been resurrected.'*,[30]

Bowie was unsurprised by its lack of commercial success, but later called it 'a very, very good movie', going into greater detail about his intentions for playing Warhol. 'I'm so fed up of people portraying him as this cold, calculating man. Because he wasn't. I just thought that he was this rather insecure queen who didn't quite believe how big he was and didn't quite know why. I found it very funny, he was just very funny. Unwittingly, half the time. He was a human. He wasn't this machine at all. He's always made out to be such a menacing figure and he wasn't. He was just this guy living a life like everyone else and struggling through it most of the time.'[31]

One of *Basquiat*'s most affecting moments is a scene in which Basquiat, informed of Warhol's death, tearfully watches old home movies of him. A moment that could easily have been sentimental in a lesser film has a genuine emotional heft to it. Bowie was pleased with this representation of Warhol. 'Those people who knew him really were moved when he died. It was so unexpected and it shouldn't have happened.'[32] Although he would later suggest that he and Warhol 'never particularly got on', his sympathetic and subtle work here would be his most significant appearance in cinema until Christopher Nolan's *The Prestige* a decade later.

Just as Bowie's directorial debut never came to be, so there were many other pictures during the '90s that could have been fascinating but, thanks to the vagaries of the film industry, failed to attract enough funding or fell victim to Bowie's music schedule. He was a great admirer of Ridley Scott's work and once admitted that 'the only Hollywood movie I regret having passed on was a piece that [he] wanted me very much to do. He even determined that if I didn't do it, he wouldn't make it. Unfortunately,

---

* A dissenting voice was the photographer David Bailey, who called Bowie 'awful . . . He played him as camp, and Warhol was never really like that.'

I was touring at that time so it became an impossibility. He never did make it, so at least I know that I don't have to kick myself too hard.'[33]

For many, the greatest loss of Bowie's cinematic career was that he was never able to collaborate with the artist and filmmaker Derek Jarman, who was, in many regards, a kindred spirit. His first feature film *Sebastiane*, a homoerotic quasi-biopic of the martyr St Sebastian, not only cast Bowie's old mentor Lindsay Kemp* in the role – appropriately enough – of a dancer, but it was soundtracked by Brian Eno, who worked on *Sebastiane* shortly before collaborating with Bowie on *Low*. Jarman would cast Tilda Swinton – who would later become a friend and co-star of Bowie's – in many of his films, and directed music videos for several bands who were themselves in thrall to Bowie, from Suede and the Pet Shop Boys to the Smiths. Had Bowie not worked so closely with David Mallet in the '70s and '80s, it is likely that he, too, would have commissioned Jarman to work on his short films. The thought of 'Ashes to Ashes' and 'Boys Keep Swinging' accompanied by Jarman-directed films is deeply enticing.

Many of Jarman's feature films share a similar sensibility with Bowie's music. In their themes of fluid sexuality colliding with high-blown literary allusion, the likes of *The Tempest* and *Edward II* could almost be seen as parallel works to Ziggy Stardust and the riotous, confrontational queerness of the *Lodger* and *Scary Monsters* albums – although the defiant straightness of *Let's Dance* has no such answering chord in Jarman's work. It is an enormous shame that the two never worked together, but this was due to a mixture of ill fortune and bad timing. Bowie agreed to play the role of the Devil in a short promotional film for some Marianne Faithfull songs, including the single 'Broken English', but failed to turn up for shooting, leading Jarman to say to the young Julian Sands, who was acting as his assistant, 'Well, listen, Julian, you're devilish. You can play it!'

---

* Lindsay Kemp was an actor and mime artist who mentored the young Bowie in the ways of movement and expression. In Kemp's own description 'I taught David to free his body.'

Yet there was an unrealised project, *Neutron*, that would have brought Bowie and Jarman together. Jarman originally conceived of it in the early '80s and would work on it off and on until terminal ill health brought on by AIDS ended his filmmaking career in 1993. Although details of its storyline are sketchy, it is believed to be a post-apocalyptic science fiction drama – thereby returning Jarman to the setting of his second film *Jubilee* – that would have starred Bowie along with the actor-cum-playwright Steven Berkoff and been filmed in the then-disused Battersea Power Station. Jarman described it thus:

> There are six published manuscripts of *Neutron*, which zig-zag their anti-heroes Aeon and Topaz across the horizon of a bleak and twilit post-nuclear landscape. 'Artist' and 'activist' in their respect-ive former lives, they are caught up in the apocalypse, where the PA systems of Oblivion crackle with the revelations of John the Divine. Their duel is fought among the rusting technology and darkened catacombs of the Fallen civilization, until they reach the pink marble bunker of Him. The reel of time is looped – angels descend with flame-throwers and crazed religious sects prowl through the undergrowth. The Book of Revelations is worked as science fiction.[34]

If it sounds like a stranger, more esoteric version of *Good Omens*, the Terry Pratchett comic fantasy that would later be filmed with Michael Sheen and David Tennant in the lead roles, then it would undeniably have been intri-guing and a considerable stretch for Bowie the actor. When asked about it in 1999, he expressed regret that it had never come off. 'I still have the script and Derek's drawings. It's so sad that things get left behind. I tend to want to do too much. I want to approach his family at some time to see if we could do something with it. I even know down to the music how he wanted to do have things done. And it would be lovely posthumously to do his piece. It would be fabulous. A wonderful script – very scary piece of work.'[35]

Bowie also revealed, tantalisingly, that 'it had some quite spectacular scenes in it. It did require proper sets. There weren't existing properties around London. He went back to his set designing ideas for it and came up with these amazing Neo-Fascistic buildings for it.' Finally, he took the opportunity to debunk one of the more entertaining urban legends that has grown up around his association with Jarman. The story went that, when Bowie was considering making the picture, he visited the filmmaker at his Dungeness home, Prospect Cottage, only for the musician – a noted student of the occult – to see a skull on Jarman's writing table and, believing it to be a kabbalistic symbol, fled without discussing matters further. Amusing though the tale is, it has no basis in truth whatsoever. Bowie denied it, saying 'I would've given my arm to work with Jarman . . . [but] I don't think that anybody was willing to put up the bread for [*Neutron*]'. One of the great 'what ifs' of modern cinema continues to fascinate and frustrate in equal measure.

Bowie may have, in his words, 'enjoyed the hell' out of *Basquiat,* but such an experience was a rarity. When asked if making the picture had reignited an interest in acting, he replied: 'Not if I can help it. I don't enjoy the process. Unless you're the director, it's extremely boring and I'm not a born actor in terms of film.' This was unduly modest. While a misfiring Bowie on screen is undeniably embarrassing, at his best he was a subtle and powerful presence who gave beautifully modulated performances that put his thespian peers to shame – and, in the case of *The Linguini Incident*, he made a fine, if offbeat, everyman, too. He may never have been a star of the silver screen the way that he was of music, but he could be, and often was, a highly dynamic and endlessly watchable presence.

Still, as he promoted *Basquiat,* free from the improvisations and baroque indulgences of *Outside,* he knew that it was time to leave cinema and return to music once again. It was fortuitous for him that, at the very moment that he chose to embrace the unknown once again, his stock among his admirers had never been higher.

# BRITPOP AND *EARTHLING*

## 'Sometimes I feel so happy I depress people'

*'I don't know where I'm going from here,*
*but I promise I won't bore you'*

At the Brit Awards, 1996. Bowie half-relished, half-endured
his status as elder statesman of Britpop.

Getty

It may seem strange now, but in early 1996, the Labour politician and leader of the opposition, Tony Blair, was one of the most popular people in the UK. As John Major's Conservative government miserably imploded, mired in scandal and sleaze and general tomfoolery, Blair's New Labour promised a new contract with the British people, of hope and prosperity and colour, as opposed to the drabness and wastefulness of the Conservatives. Blair, a highly intelligent and opportunistic man, absorbed the economic lessons of Margaret Thatcher to offer a combination of social liberalism and financial frugality, epitomised by his dour shadow chancellor Gordon Brown.

This meant that, as he did on 16 February that year, he could make a speech calling for elected mayors throughout the country in the morning, and then skip off to the Brit Awards in the evening at the now-demolished Earls Court Exhibition Centre in west London to present the key prize of the night. The Brits, as they were known, had been established in 1977 and popularised in 1982. The event was intended to celebrate the industry's most successful artists, both British and internationally, but had suffered reputationally in the '80s, culminating in a disastrous 1989 event, co-hosted by Mick Fleetwood and Samantha Fox, that is rightly regarded as being to awards ceremonies what Hunt Sales was to singing.

By 1996, the event had regathered much of its lustre, helped by a well-refreshed audience of music industry worthies and rock stars that ensured that the record labels' 'fruit and flowers' bill would spiral into absurd figures, thanks to the scale of liquid and chemical indulgence. There had been some silliness along the way – Annie Lennox was named Best Female Solo Artist a total of five times in a decade, apparently because the organisers had trouble thinking of any other women recording music – but there was a different spirit in the air, encapsulated by a word that would come to be regarded with contempt, but at the time had a different, more celebratory feel: Britpop.

When Bowie had sat down for his *NME* conversation with Brett Anderson in 1993, he was pleased and gratified by the younger man's obvious adoration for both his music and his wider legacy to the pop culture of the day. Fewer than three years later, Suede – who released their most obviously commercial album, *Coming Up*, that September, after the dark, brooding Bowie-meets-Scott Walker masterpiece *Dog Man Star* failed to sell – were by no means the outlier among the nominees. Of the records nominated for Best British Album that year, Pulp's *Different Class* and Radiohead's *The Bends* both owed heavy debts to Bowie,* albeit from wildly different eras. Jarvis Cocker's act tried to emulate the sound of *Ziggy Stardust* and *Aladdin Sane*, whereas Thom Yorke's group split the difference and owed equal debts to the acoustic balladry of *Space Oddity* and *Hunky Dory* and the Eno-led experimentalism of *Low* and *"Heroes"*, a sound that would later be perfected on their early 2000s albums *Kid A* and *Amnesiac*.

Of the other acts nominated, Paul Weller's *Stanley Road* was a gruff shoulder-charge of an album, with its frontman almost at pains to disassociate himself from the prevailing trend for all things Bowie.† So were, in different ways, the two main acts nominated that evening, the feuding Blur and Oasis, whose albums *The Great Escape* and *(What's the Story) Morning Glory?* channelled, respectively, the Kinks and post-Beatles solo John Lennon. Although all three would, eventually, pay homage to Bowie in different but specific ways, it was a tale of two different kinds of influence: those who were only too happy to admit their debt to Bowie and those who seemed to not regard him as the godfather to the musical movement that they were now embracing. Nonetheless, when compared to the younger acts, Bowie had not had any significant commercial success for years and thus occupied a nostalgic place in Britain's musical and cultural sphere that he barely merited. *Scary Monsters* had, after all, been a decade and a half ago, *Let's Dance* also more than ten years. What had he done to merit such adulation since?

---

* Yorke even explicitly called *The Bends* 'our David Bowie pastiche'.

† Like most men of taste, Weller eventually came round. Not only did he write a song about him, simply entitled 'Bowie', in 2018, but he named one of his twin sons after him, too.

It was in this spirit, and no doubt reinforced by whatever stimulants he had happened upon that evening, that Oasis's charmless lead singer Liam Gallagher had squared up to Bowie a couple of months previously while the two were waiting backstage at the BBC to perform on *Later . . . with Jools Holland*. The show's producer Mark Cooper had decided that Oasis would open and close the show, a decision he now regrets – 'If I had my time again, I probably wouldn't do it that way'[1] – not least because a drunk, haggard Gallagher turned up in the aftermath of a bender, unable to sing a note. He decided to pick a fight with Bowie, announcing that he was 'a washed-up old fart' and trying to punch him. He was duly thrown out of the BBC and lead vocals for the show were assumed by his brother Noel instead, who made no attempt to speak to Bowie on the evening.

Bowie, unsurprisingly, was therefore subdued, even diffident when the ebullient Holland tried to interview him, but his performances of 'Strangers When We Meet' and 'Hallo Spaceboy' were magisterial, with Cooper raving that 'Bowie was at his operatic best . . . When he finished ['Strangers'], there was a wonderful, exhausted-but-triumphal sigh from him.'[2] It remains one of his greatest televised performances, making the former's debt to '"Heroes"' explicit, and fully utilising a beefed-up band that featured no fewer than three keyboardists, including Mike Garson.

Still, when he was waiting in the wings at the Brits a couple of months later, watching as Oasis took the Best Album prize for *(What's the Story) Morning Glory?*, he might have been forgiven for feeling a certain weariness, to say nothing of wariness.* *Not these chancers again.* It was Noel's turn to be ghastly that evening, alternately insulting his audience – 'Got nowt to say except I'm extremely rich and you lot aren't' – and belittling the man who presented him with his award, INXS singer Michael Hutchence, of whom he sneered: 'Has-beens shouldn't present fucking awards to gonna-be's.' Such was the state of mainstream British music in 1996.

---

* He may well have been more cheered by the British Producer of the Year award being given to Brian Eno.

The spirit of the evening, hosted by the radio DJ Chris Evans, was an uncertain, jittery one. Michael Jackson performed his dirge 'Earth Song', surrounded by fawning children, and Cocker, understandably provoked by the King of Pop's pomposity, jumped on stage and shook his slender derriere at him; a noble act for which he was arrested, although released without charge. By the time that the evening reached its last award, for Outstanding Contribution to Music, there had been enough event and absurdity to last a dozen ceremonies, but the night was not yet through.

When Blair appeared, wearing a suit that was too large for him, in the fashion of the day, and looking a little like the '80s satirical character Max Headroom, he was cheered as enthusiastically as any of the rock stars by the audience. His intro music was Bowie's 'Fashion' – 'We are the goon squad and we're coming to town' – and he adequately delivered a paean to British music in which he namechecked the usual suspects before calling Bowie 'an innovator – he's pushed the frontiers back, he's a man not afraid to go up the hill backwards.' After a brief montage of music videos, which included 'Jump They Say' and somehow omitted 'Life on Mars' and 'Let's Dance', an uncomfortable-looking Bowie took to the stage, in high heels and wearing a large earring saying 'SEX' on it.* He did not embrace Blair, as is the custom of these events, but instead said 'Thank you, Tony. Thank you, everyone else. I think I'll go and sing at you.' Then it was time to perform the Pet Shop Boys' remix of 'Hallo Spaceboy' with Messrs Tennant and Lowe, a brief medley of 'Under Pressure' and 'Moonage Daydream', and then he was off once again, preserving his reputation before some fresh horror could occur at one of the event's innumerable afterparties.

On its own terms, the 1996 Brit Awards ceremony was eventful, generally in a bad way, and Bowie was one of the few participants who managed to retain his dignity. Yet it was the apex of a series of events that took place between the release of *The Buddha of Suburbia* and the Glastonbury Festival

---

\* It was somehow typical of the evening that Bowie's backstage rider was not sushi, or caviar, or wagyu beef, but a ham baguette.

in June 2000, all of which, in their various ways, showed Bowie flirting with Britishness once again. He even said, when asked late in 1996 whether he still felt British, 'more so than ever before'. This may have been a sop to the tabloid press, something he occasionally offered when in an indulgent humour. The only times that he had spent any extended periods in Britain since the early '70s, when he first moved to the United States, had been for filming commitments, and he maintained his primary residence in New York throughout this time. This suggested that, for all his newly acquired Anglophilia, he was hardly about to move back to Brixton, Beckenham or, indeed, the Norfolk Broads.

Still, he was in pensive mood when he was interviewed by *Q* around the time of his Brits appearance. 'Do you find it a little ironic that as you continue to explore new avenues, there's an entire new generation of bands discovering your past?', asked the journalist Lucy O'Brien. Usually, Bowie would deflect or equivocate rather than give a straightforward answer to such a question, but, on this occasion, he openly discussed the way in which American music had acknowledged his influence, from Nine Inch Nails and Nirvana to Pixies and the Smashing Pumpkins. 'I must admit that my ego was massaged like you wouldn't believe, because I've always been aware that in Europe I've carried a certain amount of weight and I kind of know what my contribution to European music has been over the last 25 years. But in America, I've never really been sure. It's always been fairly ephemeral. I sort of come over and do a tour and go away again. You never hear people say, "Oh yeah, Springsteen, Pearl Jam and David Bowie" . . . You don't think of me and American music.'[3]

He would not return to the US until August 1996, when he began the sessions for the album *Earthling* in New York. Before then, he had to contend with an unexpected but welcome return to the British charts in the form of the Pet Shop Boys' collaboration on 'Hallo Spaceboy'. Neither 'The

Hearts Filthy Lesson' nor, surprisingly, 'Strangers When We Meet' had had any significant commercial impact when released as singles, and so Bowie, who had been impressed by the Trent Reznor remix of 'The Hearts Filthy Lesson', contacted the Pet Shop Boys, who had had significant commercial success with a series of spectacularly ambitious, intelligent and musically rich albums, the most recent of which was 1993's magnificent *Very*. The duo's singer Neil Tennant was a lifelong Bowie fan who had fought his way to the stage door of the Newcastle City Hall in the early '70s to get his idol's autograph – while, naturally, sporting a Ziggy-influenced hairstyle – but did not meet him properly until the two were introduced backstage at one of the Wembley shows on the Outside tour. Tennant said how much he admired 'Hallo Spaceboy' and that it would make a brilliant single. Bowie replied: 'You should remix it!'

Such pleasantries are commonplace in musical circles, but, as many other collaborators of Bowie discovered, he seldom suggested artistic projects without serious intent behind them. Tennant was both surprised and pleased that his idol telephoned him a few days later to reiterate his interest in the release; he later called the entire experience 'a career high point'. However, when Tennant and Lowe convened in the studio, they realised that the song's punchy, aggressive qualities all but disguised the relative paucity of lyrics on it. There is only one repeated verse, and a chorus that is not so much minimal as elliptical, like much of the lyric writing on *Outside*.

It seemed to offer relatively little to work with, but Lowe then had a mischievous idea. Bowie, after all, was the cut-up king when it came to mixing around his lyrics, even down to using the Verbasizer software to automate them. Why not play him at his own game and transpose the mucked-around-with lyrics of 'Space Oddity' into the song, thereby turning it into the third instalment of a trilogy that had begun with the exploits of Major Tom and continued into 'Ashes to Ashes'? The second, Tennant-sung verse now had the words 'Ground to Major bye-bye Tom / Dead the circuit countdown's wrong'. It was affectionate and irreverent at the same time – very Pet Shop Boys – but, as Tennant recalled, it did not necessarily meet with Bowie's initial approval. 'Bowie phoned up to ask how it was going and we said, "We've cut up the lyrics of 'Space Oddity'." Silence. "Sounds like I'd better come in."'[4]

Thankfully, the result proved to be one of the most purely enjoyable things that Bowie released in the '90s, reaching number 12 in the British charts. It would be his biggest hit until 'Where Are We Now?' in 2013, and that, admittedly, was a rather different case. The Pet Shop Boys themselves continued to perform a disco-heavy version of the song on stage, presumably in the belief that appropriation was the sincerest form of flattery. And the collaboration had its jolly moments, too. When Tennant said 'It's like Major Tom is in one of those Russian spaceships they can't afford to bring down', Bowie replied, in faux-innocence, 'Oh wow, is that where he is?'[5]

The one-time Major Tom may have enjoyed his work with the Pet Shop Boys, but it was to his touring band of Reeves Gabrels, Gail Ann Dorsey et al. that he felt his greatest loyalty, enthusing to Alan Yentob that they were 'probably the most enjoyable set of musicians I've worked with . . . [and] the greatest fun and satisfaction I've had with a band since the Spiders'.[6] As they trooped across Europe in the early months of the year, Bowie decided that he should record his next album in the same fashion as he had put *Aladdin Sane* together: swiftly, without endless studio time (and expense) and with his core group, as well as refining the sound that he had developed on his previous album. Heading back to Mountain Studios by himself – for the final time – he recorded a demo of a song, 'Telling Lies', that would sound like an offcut from *Outside* if the music on that album had been placed in a blender and then the residue been spiked with amphetamines.

In fact, its origins lay in the prolonged recording of *Outside*. 'I changed the arrangement all the time,' Bowie told *Mojo*. 'We must have tried 20 different approaches for that song.' He took his cue from the driving aggression of 'Hallo Spaceboy' and the intense drama of 'I'm Deranged', but also sought to combine its sonic assault with the then-modish sound of drum 'n' bass, as popularised by the British act the Prodigy, Bowie's later collaborator Goldie and LTJ Bukem, all of whom had come into fashion in the mid-'90s. The Prodigy, the best-known of them all, had released their signature song, 'Firestarter', in March 1996, a few weeks after the remix of 'Hallo Spaceboy' and it had galvanised the charts, selling more than a million copies in the UK and – significantly – more than half a million in the US as well. Its success led to commercial recognition of a musical movement that, a few years before, had been confined to dance clubs and the back pages of the trendier music magazines.

The reason for the success of 'Firestarter' was that it was immediate and somehow *threatening*, helped by the presence of the green-haired, tongue-studded Keith Flint, who delivered the song in a ranting, uncompromising yell, as well as looking like a nightmarish, Mephistophelean figure. It was probably no coincidence that the look that Bowie adopted for much of the latter half of 1996 – spiked red hair, an immaculately styled goatee and an earring – owed a significant debt to Flint, as well, of course, as nodding to his original flame-haired Ziggy incarnation. If ever Bowie wished to acknowledge those who paid homage to him,* it would always be with the recognition of his own history inherent in it.

When Bowie had finished 'Telling Lies', he recruited Mark Plati, a New York-based musician, to remix it. 'I met David in the spring of 1996,' Plati recalls, 'at the Looking Glass Studios in New York, which Philip Glass owned. Glass had just done his orchestral version of *Low*, so there was an existing connection between them.' The idea behind the hiring of Plati was that he was, in his words, 'more of a "rock" guy than the other engineers in the studio.' The collaboration was a fruitful one from the start. 'We really clicked from the get-go on a lot of levels, not just musically. We shared a similar sense of humour, too. At that point, I was just being an

---

* Not that the Prodigy's songwriter Liam Howlett was a particular aficionado of Bowie. He later admitted that 'I remember Bowie coming into the dressing room when we did gigs together in Germany. We had some great chats about drugs and stuff. He was someone I gained a lot of respect for very quickly.' But he also said he'd turned down an offer to remix his singles: '[he] didn't mean anything to me [musically].'

engineering-synthesiser programmer person, which was fine by me too, because I thought it was a week with David Bowie, which is great. So it just seemed like a nice little gig. I just didn't know that it wouldn't ever really stop.'[7]

When Plati had remixed 'Telling Lies', Bowie cheerfully said to him, 'Well, we're going to do a European festival tour. But when we come back, we're going to do a whole album of stuff like this with you, here at the Looking Glass.' Plati was sceptical, thinking 'Oh yeah, sure you are'. As he says, 'everybody would say things like that and you don't put too much stock in it, because you never know what's going to happen.' This was an altogether different case. A couple of months later, Plati had begun preliminary work in Berlin on the album that would become *Earthling*, which he describes as consisting of 'Reeves, David and I, the three of us in a room, putting these little ideas together from scratch'.[8]

Gabrels believes that the impetus for the hard-edged, drum 'n' bass and jungle-inflected sound of *Earthling* came about from the musical company that Bowie had been keeping earlier in 1996. 'At the end of the Outside tour, I had ten tracks that I had already worked out, as a starting point. We had been doing shows where we were on the same bill as Prodigy and Underworld, as well as Roni Size and Tricky. And just as I'd turned David on to Nine Inch Nails, he, in turn, turned me on to drum and bass and combined that what we already had done together and what he had already been doing for years. All that came together with *Earthling*.'[9]

It was an invigorating, experimental occasion, with Plati and Gabrels serving as co-producers along with Bowie. 'It was like a playground,' says Dorsey, 'but also a really creative situation. And you're working with someone who has unlimited resources, so you can go anywhere, and he is very excited when you explore. He always came in knowing exactly what outcome he wanted, but he's like a kid, he likes to play. One thing he said to me, of the creative process, is for him to throw everything into the pot and the art becomes the act of stripping away to reveal it, as opposed to building it one piece at a time, which served as his mantra.' For her, it was invigorating and supportive to have someone who was open to experimentation. 'As musicians, to think in that way – "What else can I try?" – was brilliant. Something that was really exciting for me, when I worked with David, was not feeling locked into any kind of structure.'[10]

Although Gabrels has co-writing credits on every song on the album bar 'Telling Lies' or 'I'm Afraid of Americans' (an Eno co-write left over from *Outside*), it is Plati who was the dominant musical influence this time around, not least because he rose to the technical demands of the recording, which would take Bowie's inimitable cut-up style of lyric writing and transpose that to music. 'We basically took pieces of songs we liked and put them into others. Previously, doing something like this would just take forever. The technology was not quite there and the people running it were not quite up to it. They weren't really musical enough to see how to do it. About a year before we started *Earthling*, I got pretty knee-deep into this stuff thinking, *Right, this is coming, and I really need to be on the case*. On the first day, we started working on something and they had all these ideas, and they wanted me to put this with this and that with that. Previously, it would take days, lots of splicing tapes together, but now I could just say "Give me a list and come back in a few hours". And when Reeves and David came back, they were, like, "Whoa". We were off to the races.'[11]

This spirit of adventure, accomplished swiftly, became the guiding principle for the entire record. Had Plati worked on *Outside*, he suggests, the album could have been finished far quicker, thanks to the advances in technology that he had mastered. In the event, *Earthling* took around six weeks to record, starting at the end of August. It was being mixed by late October and Gabrels remembers that it was completed on 11 November, Veterans Day. This was all the more impressive as an achievement because Bowie was playing gigs throughout September as part of the 'East Coast Ballroom' tour, meaning that the album was recorded during a four-day week.

It was one of the most purely enjoyable experiences of Bowie's career so far. Revitalised by both his new, committed and brilliant band and the influences that he had been absorbing from both British and American music, the recording of *Earthling* was fast, frenetic and fun. Plati describes life in the studio in similarly fond terms to Dorsey. 'David liked having fun and he liked being part of a band. There were no boundaries on what I could try or what I could do. If it worked, it worked. And if it didn't, it didn't. But he was always up for trying it, or if you tried an idea and he was uncertain, but then he twisted it a little, and then it becomes something else. As a vocalist, he was definitely old school. He would only stop if he blew a word on a line or if he wanted to change a lyric. It all made me think this is how music used to be done.'[12]

The lyric-writing process was similarly experimental. 'He didn't use the Verbasizer this time round,' says Plati. 'It was all done on Post-it notes. He was sitting on a couch at the back of the studio writing lyrics, and when he had enough, he gathered them up, stuck them on the music stand and that would be that.' Sometimes, the inspiration would be magnificently unorthodox, as with the lyrics for the album's first single proper, 'Little Wonder', with their intentionally nonsensical allusions to the Seven Dwarfs ('Dopey morning doc, grumpy gnomes' etc.). 'That was inspired by a Disney catalogue. My daughter was three and I was getting mail at the studio and that was one of the things I received. Reeves, David and I were having a laugh over it, to the point where Reeves actually bought a Tigger costume. It was ridiculous. But, yeah, we were just like making fun of the Disney catalogue and the Seven Dwarfs and all that and then, boom. I thought, *If a song comes from a Disney catalogue, it can come from anything.*'[13]

Mike Garson, meanwhile, was a less prominent presence than he had been on *Outside*, but his typically baroque and avant-garde contributions were as distinctive as they had ever been on any of Bowie's albums. 'I was always the secret sauce,' he explains, 'or the special sauce. And I wasn't used on every song, like a drummer would be, or a bassist or guitar player. He used me when he heard a space for my sound and you've got to respect that.' His take on *Earthling* was very simple. 'I thought *Why don't you add some good melodies to drum and bass sounds? They have great groups, but they don't know there's such thing as melody. You do.*' On 'Dead Man Walking',

Bowie encouraged Garson to play the last couple of minutes as an old-school bebop solo, while a particularly lunatic piece of improvisation came on 'Seven Years in Tibet'. 'It was a stupid Farfisa organ sound coming from a Kurzweil synthesiser, and I'm playing this bizarre solo like something that you might have heard from the Doors in the '60s. He loved it. I almost did it as a joke. And he told me that was one of the favourite things I ever played for him.'[14]

The only one of Bowie's regular musicians who felt somewhat short-changed was Zachary Alford, who came in for a week to perform overdubs, but by then was working on a completed album, rather than being given the freedom to improvise that the other musicians had. 'It was very fleeting,' he confirms. 'I did the best I could, but I thought of the stories of Woody Woodmansey talking about recording all those seminal albums. And it's the same. You're just getting to know the song and he says you're done. And he moves on to the next song.' Yet, rather than being annoyed by the experience, Alford suggests it gave him a greater insight into Bowie's creative process. 'David liked things to be fresh and raw and a little bit unsure. Somehow, that was charming. Knowing that changed the way I listened to his records afterwards. When I would go back and listen to, say, *Diamond Dogs*, I'd know that these guys were just winging it and that they didn't rehearse these things to death. A lot of whatever you hear that sounds spontaneous really *is* spontaneous.'[15]

If the ethos of *Earthling* was a renegade, laissez-faire one, unburdened by commercial imperatives, this was largely thanks to the extraordinarily generous deal that Bowie had been given by Virgin in the US, which allowed him creative control to produce whatever he liked. As Plati recalls, 'a lot of my work up to that involved people that were trying to copy some of this and that and American record labels saying, "Well, we need another Nirvana or we need another Pearl Jam." Here, there was no boundary on what we could or couldn't do. There's no record label police, because it's David Bowie. There was just such a great feeling of freedom. It was not a typical album making experience to me at all.'[16]

The final mixing session took an afternoon and then *Earthling* was ready for release. Had Bowie conquered the world all over again? Or was the halo in danger of slipping?

*ø*

The cover of the album depicts Bowie photographed from behind, wearing a tattered Alexander McQueen frock coat with a Union Jack emblem on it. It was the same coat that he had been wearing at concerts in the summer of 1996, inspired by a Graham Turk exhibit named 'Indoor Flag'. He described it as 'the ultimate anti-icon. A retelling of the British flag joke, again torn and stained . . . the tatty remains of a metaphysical empire.' At a time when patriotism and nationalism were making a comeback of sorts in the British music industry – after having been heavily frowned upon a few years before, when Morrissey draped himself in the Union Jack at a concert at Finsbury Park on 8 August 1992, signalling the beginning of a long, slow decline in his once-godlike status, as the *NME* were driven to ask 'Has Morrissey gone too far this time?' – Bowie had, once again, captured the feeling of the age while offering an ironic meta-commentary on it.* As he stands, gazing over an idealised British scene of green fields and blue skies that he has been superimposed onto,† the uninitiated might be forgiven for thinking that this was going to be either Bowie's Britpop album, or even a collection of wistful folk songs.

Anyone who had heard 'Telling Lies', which was released as a download-only single – the first example of its kind – in November 1996, would have been disabused of this idea. It was abrasive and noisy, the sound of *Outside* turned up to 11. But those who had consistently admired Bowie

---

* This was seen when Geri Halliwell, the de facto frontwoman of the inescapable, inexplicably popular manufactured girl group the Spice Girls, took to wearing a Union Jack dress, most famously at the 1997 Brit Awards.

† Appropriately, the picture of Bowie himself was taken in New York.

as a songwriter as much as an icon could be forgiven for asking a simple question: where is the tune?

The first single proper, 'Little Wonder', released the week before the album came out on 3 February 1997, was a similarly confusing experience. It began with a wild, out-of-control percussion assault, clearly inspired by 'Firestarter', and segued into Bowie's nonsensical, self-parodic lyrics ('Dame Meditation, take me away' presumably refers to his status as 'Dame David Bowie' in the British music press), before the chorus takes the song in the direction of '"Heroes"'-esque anthemic rock. Then there is some noise, another blast of the chorus, and the whole shebang is over. Purchasers of *Earthling* could, at least, not say that they hadn't been warned.

With the films of one of Bowie's heroes and inspirations, the director Stanley Kubrick, there was a pattern that developed sometime around the release of *Barry Lyndon* in 1975. Kubrick's new film would come out, be received politely – sometimes not even that – by the critics and then, over the coming decades, be reappraised and eventually come to be seen as a masterpiece. In the case of Bowie's albums from *Black Tie White Noise* onwards, the opposite would often occur. Music writers, excited by the idea that this was Bowie's finest album since 1980, would rush to offer laud-atory comment, declaring that this was a staggering work of heartbreaking genius, etc. And in the case of *Earthling*, Bowie was fortunate in that many of those who had originally dismissed *Outside* had now re-evaluated it over the previous 18 months, meaning that he was now about to enjoy the best reviews he'd had in years.

'His best since 1980's *Scary Monsters*,' *Rolling Stone* decided. 'Shot through with a gnarly atmospheric chill not encountered since *Scary Monsters*,' *Q* raved. *Billboard* demurred only very slightly – 'Bowie's most inspired, most cutting-edge, and most promising effort since *Let's Dance*' – and called it 'a work of infinite possibilities'. Some of the weekly music magazines lambasted it – in a particularly amusing review, Ian Harrison wrote in *Select* that '*Earthling* is splendidly coiffured and presented . . . but the selling point – Bowie goes original junglist nutty – is so negligible as to be non-existent. And what remains is not good' – but their readership and Bowie's fanbase had grown apart from one another over the previous years. It would be a commercial hit, reaching number six in the British charts and ultimately selling more than a million albums worldwide. There was also a Grammy nomination for Best Alternative Music Performance, which it lost to Radiohead's *OK Computer*.

Many of those involved in its creation speak extremely highly of it today. Garson says, simply, 'I love *Earthling*',[17] while Plati declares that 'it's aged really well' – although he does allow that 'in the early aughts, I thought maybe it was of its moment, and it was, of course. But now I hear things that sound like that, so I guess we weren't so far off the mark.'[18] Gabrels, meanwhile, calls it his favourite of the records that he did with Bowie. '*Earthling* just came together and came together so quickly.' When it comes to Bowie's biographers, there is a divergence of opinion. Nicholas Pegg calls it 'a very fine album indeed'[19] and David Buckley says '*Earthling* is the last David Bowie album to break new ground . . . the album has hardly ever been given the respect it is due.' Chris O'Leary, meanwhile, is typically nuanced and thoughtful when he suggests '*Earthling* is an aging man stealing toys from the young and throwing them into his own trinket pile, a man murmuring about religion, decay and exile on a flashy, noisy album that's riddled with pieces of sonic garbage and which sounded dated before its release. It's bloody with distorted life. *Earthling* may be his most misunderstood album; maybe even Bowie misunderstood it.' Yet Paul Trynka (admittedly, a biographer who has limited time for any album between *Let's Dance* and *Heathen* save for *The Buddha of Suburbia*) dismisses it as being on 'a drearily repetitive loop' and 'conservative and formulaic'.[*,20]

For this writer, it is comfortably the weakest studio album Bowie produced since *Tin Machine* and, in places, all but unlistenable. The songs

---

* Dylan Jones has an amusing story about irritating Bowie at an album playback session by damning *Earthling* with faint praise – 'I can see what you're doing there'. Although he reassured the irked artist by saying it was one of his finest works, he concludes that '*Stereogum* rated it his 17th best album, although I think they're being kind.'

divide into two categories: the melodically strong ones that have been ruined by the horribly dated and artificial-sounding production ('I'm Afraid of Americans', 'Seven Years in Tibet', at a push 'Telling Lies') and those that feel like studio improvisations left unfinished ('Little Wonder'; 'Law (Earthlings on Fire)'; the dismal 'The Last Thing You Should Do', a song I struggle to get to the end of). It is the anti-*Outside*. That album sounds magnificent three decades on, full of fear and fire and beauty, whereas *Earthling* is nothing more interesting than the sound of a fading star who has spent too long listening to Goldie and the Prodigy and has convinced himself that they are the future of music and that he should fall in with the new regime, pronto. In an ideal world, Bowie would have junked the album and recorded *Toy* instead, but such things can only be wished for.

Still, although Bowie was treated like royalty by virtually every journalist who encountered him, the best could still see through the facade. When Mick Brown interviewed him for the *Daily Telegraph* in December 1996, shortly before the album's release, he, too, was hoodwinked by *Earthling*, perhaps because he had to listen to it in Bowie's presence – 'rich with the sort of commercial hooks that have been absent from his more recent work'. Yet over the course of a long, perceptive conversation, Brown allowed Bowie his theatrical flourishes – 'Sometimes I'm so happy I depress people' – but was alert to two of his signature evasions, the faux-intimacy ('the warm handshake, the south London mateyness, the air of breezy candour – all conspire to effect that great social trick of leading you to believe after five minutes acquaintanceship that you've known Bowie all your life') and the nonsense that he spouted if unchecked.

'I do love communication,' Bowie told him. 'These days more than ever I feel like a very social animal, which I wasn't at one time. And I love the freedom of it. I love the joy it brings. And I love the conflicts and the debates which go with being much more a fully active member of society'. To this, Brown wrote, incisively: 'There is something disconcerting about this peroration. It is almost as if you are hearing someone talking about rejoining the human race.'[21] If *Outside* and Bowie's immersion in the art world had seen him purposefully detach himself from contemporary concerns and produce brilliant, iconoclastic work in the process, *Earthling* was the sound, once again, of the Starman falling to earth. The fact that he turned 50 on 8 January 1997, with all the concomitant thoughts of mortality, may have concentrated his mind wonderfully.

There are two particular vignettes of his birthday celebrations that linger. He appeared for a lengthy interview on the Mary Anne Hobbs show on BBC Radio 1, recorded from New York on 7 January, in which – in her words – 'scores of top international celebrities [are] clamouring to wish you a happy birthday'. Bowie was on relaxed and geezerish form. 'I didn't want to make it to 50. It seemed so unglamorous.' Given that this was the man who had written 'Don't want to stay alive when you're 25?', this seemed unusually consistent, but the new-look Bowie now suggested that '[when] I was about 43, 44, then I started to feel there might be some point in getting old'.

As usual, he declined to answer questions with any remote hint of seriousness. When Echo and the Bunnymen's Ian McCulloch tried to elicit details about his most decadent behaviour, Bowie replied, 'Some days I wore green *and* red, it got that bad.' There was a lot of laughter, a mock-apology for giving up alcohol ('I'm aware I'm talking to an English public here, but I'm afraid it happens no more') and some banter with Bono, naturally enough. Then the mood changed, and Hobbs and her listeners had a sudden, fleeting insight into the real, unvarnished David Bowie.

Of everyone who contributed, there was one anomalous figure, who was not interested in putting forward some rote enquiry or laddish in-joke,* but instead wished to offer his sincere good wishes and appreciation. In a remarkable coup for Hobbs and the BBC, none other than the perennially reclusive Scott Walker had been recruited to offer 'a personal message they wanted to deliver by carrier pigeon'. Bowie, initially unaware that it was his

---

* In a sign of the times, of the ten musicians who contribute questions to the programme, not one of them is female.

hero, laughed 'Oh no', only to be silenced when Walker, 'coming to you via a very crappy, old, handheld tape machine', said: 'There'll be [messages] about how you always embraced the new and how you freed so many artists and this is, of course, true. Like everyone else, I'd like to thank you for all the years, and especially for your generosity of spirit when it comes to other artists. I've been the beneficiary on more than one occasion, let me tell you. So have a wonderful birthday, and by the way, mine's the day after yours, so I'll have a drink to you on the other side of midnight. How's that?'

Bowie biographer Tom Hagler describes it as 'the most emotionally raw moment of David Bowie ever caught on tape', and he is correct. When Walker finished speaking, there is a lengthy pause – edited down in the broadcast version from around 30 seconds to about seven, but still tangible – and then a deeply affected Bowie, moved to tears, said 'Oh, I see God in the window'. He then haltingly admits: 'You really got to me there, I'm afraid . . . He's probably been my idol since I was a kid. That's very moving.' Asking for a copy of Walker's message, his usual articulacy has deserted him. All he can say is 'That's really thrown me. Thank you very much.'[22] It is a powerfully moving moment, as the carefully constructed image of Bowie disappears, just for a matter of a couple of minutes, before he recovers himself and normal service resumes.

It was the public face of Bowie that was on triumphant show the following evening at his fiftieth birthday concert at Madison Square Garden in New York. It was the single highest-profile public appearance he had made since the Freddie Mercury Tribute Concert. He gathered together his touring band, with Gabrels now serving as musical director, and emphasised that he was an Englishman in New York now, rather than a true Brit; there was to be no corresponding concert staged in London. And the choice of special guests, with the exception of the Cure's Robert Smith, was decidedly American in nature: the Foo Fighters, Sonic Youth, Pixies' Frank Black and Smashing Pumpkins' Billy Corgan.

By far the most enthusiastic response was reserved for Bowie's old colleague, friend and – on occasion – literal sparring partner, Lou Reed, who came on to perform on an electrifying medley of Bowie's 'Queen Bitch' and Reed's 'Dirty Blvd', 'White Light/White Heat' and 'Waiting for the Man'.* Some carped that there should have been more older collaborators – Iggy Pop, Carlos Alomar, Nile Rodgers, even Brian Eno – and fewer Grohls-come-lately. But the overall atmosphere of the concert was a joyous and celebratory one, even if the setlist was light on genuine hits – '"Heroes"', 'The Jean Genie' and 'Space Oddity' snuck in, but there were considerably more songs from *Outside* and the as-then unreleased *Earthling* album being played to an audience who, it is fair to judge by their reactions, were unfamiliar with Bowie's newer and less accessible material.

None of it mattered. Bowie, at 50, had revitalised himself, through a mixture of clever positioning, a couple of genuinely brilliant albums and an innate knowledge of how to sell himself at the cusp of the new millennium. Content and happy in his personal and professional lives alike, he looked out at the capacity crowd and made a declaration that seemed to encapsulate the glorious excitement of his life. 'I don't know where I'm going from here, but I promise you I won't bore you.' The audience applauded and cheered wildly, the covenant duly made.

Nineteen years later, almost to the day, that remark would be the single most cited in the early reports of his death.

---

\* Gabrels, awkwardly trying to make conversation with Reed during rehearsals, quipped when Reed's driver was late, 'Perhaps you should change "Waiting for the Man" to "Waiting for the Car".' To his surprise, 'he just thought that was the funniest thing he'd ever heard. And unknown to me, and the majority of the world I guess, he had a very high-pitched girly laugh.' Gabrels pronounced himself 'charmed' by this unexpected development.

# MODERN PAINTERS, NEW AFRO/PAGAN AND NAT TATE

## 'The artist's most profound dread'

*'I must have things now'*

When Bowie (pictured here with Jeff Koons) and author William Boyd
set out to hoodwink the international art world, neither could
have expected how successful their plan would be.

Steve Azzara/Getty

On 10 November 2016, the well-shod, terminally curious and rapacious alike all gathered at Sotheby's in London to witness the dispersal of the highlights of an art collection that was dismissed by the *Guardian*'s critic Jonathan Jones as 'disappointingly tasteful' and its former owner belittled as 'a repressed art snob'. As so often, David Bowie had the last laugh, when the first 47 works that he had once possessed sold for £24 million: more than double the initial estimate, a still-punchy £10 million.

Admittedly helped by their provenance from a famous owner's collection, many lots went for vastly more than the highest estimate, including Basquiat's *Air Power* – selling for more than double its anticipated £3.5 million price – and Frank Auerbach's *Head of Gerda Boehm*, which had been expected to sell for a relatively affordable £500,000, but instead realised a substantial £3.8 million or thereabouts: this was all the more impressive because Bowie's debt to the artist was considerable. 'Somebody I like very much indeed is Frank Auerbach,' he told the *New York Times* in 1998. 'I think there are some mornings that if we hit each other a certain way – myself and a portrait by Auerbach – the work can magnify the kind of depression I'm going through. It will give spiritual weight to my angst. Some mornings I'll look at it and go, "Oh, God, yeah! I know!" But that same painting, on a different day, can produce in me an incredible feeling of the triumph of trying to express myself as an artist. I can look at it and say, "My God, yeah! I want to sound like that looks."'[1]

The sale was not brought on by financial necessity, but by Bowie's family wishing to create space. A spokesperson for the estate explained that 'David's art collection was fuelled by personal interest and compiled out of passion. He always sought and encouraged loans from the collection and enjoyed sharing the works in his custody. Though his family are keeping certain pieces of particular personal significance, it is now time to give others the opportunity to appreciate – and acquire – the art and objects he so admired.'[2] Yet £24 million is still £24 million. The less headline-grabbing paintings were sold the following day, for a still-staggering £8.9 million;

Sotheby's observed that 'a total of 59 new records for artists were set over the course of two days'. And the greatest surprise for many – including Jones from the *Guardian* – was seeing what, exactly, Bowie had chosen to collect, and why.

Just as the list of Bowie's 100 favourite books that he sent out into the world in 2013 was much pored-over, and even inspired John O'Connell to write a 2019 title, *Bowie's Bookshelf*, that was equal parts literary criticism and speculation as to how the works informed Bowie's life and art, so the 255 artworks that were sold at Sotheby's led to considerable debate as to what Bowie's collection said about him as both a man and an artist.

Looking at the art for sale, Jones sneered that 'it is hard to stifle a yawn . . . Where are the vulgar pop art provocations? Where is the camp outrage, the punk iconoclasm? And where's Andy Warhol?' Instead, there were plenty of what Jones called 'very unglamorous artists' – 20th-century British painters like Winifred Nicholson, Graham Sutherland and Ivon Hitchens, of whom Jones wrote: 'If you took Bowie's collection on the whole and put it in a museum, you'd have the kind of gallery that gets three visitors on a rainy weekday afternoon to look sadly at the Henry Moore and the Bernard Leach pots.'[3]

It is doubtful that Bowie would have cared too much about Jones's scorn. After all, when the *David Bowie Is* exhibition sashayed its way into the V&A in 2013, the art critic was a lone dissenting voice in the general rapture, complaining that, after a recent bereavement, Bowie's music seemed to him 'as brittle as broken glass'. After comparing him unfavourably to Springsteen and Lou Reed, Jones concluded that he felt 'plenty of nostalgia when I listen to Bowie – but it cloys quickly, this old masquerade'.[4] But everyone has their own view of Bowie, and Jones is as entitled to his as the rest of us.

Yet there is something dispiriting about an art critic for a national newspaper simply dismissing Bowie's carefully curated collection as boringly tasteful, the acquisitions of a middle-aged expatriate nostalgic for the idealised England of his boyhood. Instead, his interest in art – both as collector and practitioner – was sincere and heartfelt, and if this opened him up to mockery, then his involvement in a spectacular reverse heist of sorts was a fitting riposte to a notoriously cliquey and snobbish industry that did not take kindly to a *rock star* – of all the debased professions – trying to become one of their number.

One thing that Bowie was frequently accused of throughout his career was fundamental insincerity, manifested through a dilettantish approach to life and music alike that saw him absorb whatever he wanted from people, places and situations, vampire-like, serve them up again with an inimitable twist on the original – 'same old thing in brand-new drag comes sweeping into view', as he once sang himself on 'Teenage Wildlife' – and expect the world to worship him for it.

Yet when it came to art, he was nothing if not respectful, even awe-struck, by the figures whose work he collected, whether they were contemporary artists he befriended and associated with or some of the most interesting figures of the twentieth century. Nor was he cowed by controversy. It was unsurprising that, when his collection was dispersed at Sotheby's, there were several works by Eric Gill, the sculptor and artist-craftsman who has been notorious for decades ever since it was revealed that he sexually abused his daughters, committed incest with his sister and had bestial relations with the family dog. Bowie acquired at least one of these works, a study for a sculpture at Ratcliffe College near Leicester, at auction in 1994. By then, Fiona MacCarthy's wholly damning biography of Gill had already run his reputation into the mire.

Bowie was not a dedicated follower of fashion. Instead, he worked closely with two curators, Kate Chertavian and Beth Greenacre, between the mid-'90s and his death, to build up a collection of neglected but interesting modern British art, which would later expand into an eclectic but coherent collection; as Greenacre said, 'He also collected African art, Memphis furniture, outsider art, and a number of Scottish artists. I don't see his collection as diverse at all because there is a line – a narrative thread – that runs throughout the collection.'[5] Bowie himself quipped that 'my left eye is for the avant-garde, my right for highly traditional work. The left is [*Time Out* art critic] Sarah Kent, the right [*Evening Standard* writer] Brian Sewell,* as far as I can see – or, rather, half-see, haha.'[6]

He took his art collecting seriously, paying several visits to the Cornish town of St Ives[†] – where several of the artists he collected, including Nicholson, lived – and frequently lending his work to exhibitions. According to Greenacre, 'David never "owned" the work in the sense that it was not about physically owning the objects. Instead, he valued the ownership of ideas and conversations with the artists. He was a custodian who was always sharing his passion for the artists – whether through private donations he made to institutions in his lifetime or gifts to friends.'[7]

When Bowie died, the auction could be interpreted as a continuation of this attitude towards the art: that one never owns a painting but merely takes charge of it for a certain amount of time, always in the knowledge that it will eventually be passed on to another collector, or custodian. Certainly, it is to be regretted that the collection could not pass into public ownership, to be kept in one place and, hopefully, to be seen by rather more people than the three visitors on wet weekday afternoons Jonathan Jones had anticipated. Yet we have plenty of other things to be grateful for when it comes to Bowie and art, both in the form of his own painting and his wider interest in the art form, which all began when he accepted an invitation from a respected but niche magazine to join its board.

*Modern Painters* was a small but highly thought-of London-based publication that had originated as the brainchild of the Cambridge-educated Peter Fuller, who, before his untimely death in a car crash in 1990 at the age of

---

* Sewell did not repay this admiration, calling Bowie's 1995 *Zenzi* painting 'ghastly' and 'messy' and grandly declaring: 'It simply doesn't work. The hand which drew it is clumsy.'

† He was, for instance, one of the guests at the opening of Tate St Ives in 1995.

42, had written several books and monographs about art. He was in thrall to the ideas of the critic John Ruskin, who famously declared not only that 'the most beautiful things in the world are the most useless; peacocks and lilies for instance', but also, in lines that could have anticipated Bowie's career a century after his own, wrote: 'The first test of a truly great man is his humility. By humility I don't mean doubt of his powers or hesitation in speaking his opinion, but merely an understanding of the relationship of what he can say and what he can do.'

This humility would be tested for Bowie four years after Fuller's death, when he was invited to join the board of *Modern Painters* by its editor Karen Wright, after being introduced to her by a mutual friend, the art dealer Bernard Jacobson. It was an exciting and fecund time in the world of British art, as the term 'Young British Artists' or 'YBAs' had recently been coined to describe a group who shared three attributes: they were mostly graduates of Goldsmiths, where they had studied fine art in the late '80s; many of them were represented by the White Cube gallerist Jay Jopling; and all of them were ambitious, provocative figures who sought to establish themselves on the scene – or canvas, if you will – of a country where post-Thatcherism was giving way to a different kind of meritocratic opportunity and where artists would be treated with equal respect and admiration to actors, musicians or – somewhere down the pecking order, admittedly – writers.

Bowie, who was all three at one time or another in his career, was introduced to the author William Boyd, who had also become a *Modern Painters* board member. By his own admission, Boyd was a casual admirer rather than committed fan of Bowie's. 'I remember listening to *Hunky Dory* again and again and again at university, and I was aware of him as a phenomenon, but I never saw him in concert and the whole *Ziggy Stardust* era wasn't really my cup of tea.' The two had first met at the Ivy restaurant in London when Bowie had strolled over to Boyd and said 'William Boyd? I absolutely love your books. I've read them all', to which the flustered author made the 'crap sort of response' that 'I really like your music'.[8]

Still, the meeting did at least have the positive consequence that, when Boyd and Bowie attended the first board meeting on 22 February 1994, which was invariably held in the private room of the Ivy, they were the 'new boys' and sat next to one another. As Boyd describes it, 'we were both out of our comfort zone, amid the professors of fine art and art critics, so we bonded over that, and began to see one another socially. The tone of the *Modern Review* meetings wasn't exactly chilled-out and relaxed.' A pattern developed. 'We'd meet in Bernard Jacobson's art gallery off Cork Street, drink coffee and talk very seriously about art. He'd ask searching questions about particular artists, and say "Why are there no great women artists?" I rather wanted to say "Dave, lighten up. It's a bit early in the day", but it was the passion of the autodidact, and that's what got him ticking over.'[9]

Boyd's recollection of Bowie was of an 'achingly thin' and 'gaunt and ravaged' figure who was both a chain smoker and a chain espresso drinker 'because he couldn't take any other drug in the world'.[10] He wrote in his diary that 'I had numerous conversations with Bowie. He was incredibly gaunt and didn't drink, eating cigarettes instead. It was the usual academic crowd of art critics. It's a small world, the art world, and these types are completely caught up in it. At the end of the evening Bowie took me aside to talk about a film project that his wife, Iman, was considering. I gave him my phone number so we may hear something about it further.'[11]

As a bestselling author himself, he wasn't overwhelmed by his colleague's fame, but then nor were the other board members; 'I think that at that first board meeting, quite a few people in the room hadn't a clue who he was, and I think he probably found that reassuring.' He was also struck by the compartmentalisation that Bowie was demonstrating in his life by this point in the '90s. 'I never talked much about books with him, or music for that matter. Art and painting were the common meeting ground, and there, there was no ego on display whatsoever. He was a very, very nice guy, but there were aspects of the rock star life that he could never get away from. For instance, he had a house in London, but I was never invited there, nor do I know where it was. And the first time

I wanted to communicate with him, he said "You have to write to this address in Geneva, to a 'Mr Schmitt'." I think he was in tax exile, or something like that.'[12]

Bowie's involvement with *Modern Painters* was not simply the self-indulgence of a wealthy middle-aged man, but born of a deep love and identification with art. To this end, his first interview for the title was not with some modish young artist, but with the 86-year-old painter Balthus, who was then living in Switzerland and averse to publicity. 'My original intention was just to be the liaison in all this,' Bowie explained. 'I gave him a call and proposed a meeting, suggesting I would bring a "qualified" journalist with me, to which he replied, "Good heavens, no. I can't stand art journalists. They are always so intellectual. I'd prefer you to do it, dear boy."'[13]

Bowie – who wryly observed 'I haven't been referred to as "dear boy" in decades' – made the journey to Balthus's chalet in Rossinière, and the two men formed a rapport. He had taken his preparation seriously; Boyd remembers that 'we had long discussions about Balthus, because nobody else would have been allowed to interview him, but I think that Bowie just liked being David Jones, journalist'.[14] The result was a 20-page article that was rich in both anecdote and detail, from Balthus recounting his friendship with Marlon Brando to his early tutelage at the hands of his mother's lover, the German poet Rainer Maria Rilke. Balthus was either unaware of the extent of Bowie's fame or chose to ignore it, asking him, when they were being shot for the magazine, 'Are you used to photographers?' One of the most photographed men of the century was able to assure him that, yes, he was accustomed to having his picture taken.

Bowie, like any good journalist, was largely able to put himself out of the picture, although there were occasional moments when he offered a figurative glance to camera, such as when Balthus, reminiscing about his friend, the artist André Derain, said '[he was an] extraordinary man . . . because he changed his opinions every day like a cloud'. The master of reinvention then asked 'And did he have a throughline? A sense of continuity about what he did as a painter, or did he change that as well?'[15] Had Balthus had a greater idea as to who Bowie was, he could have responded robustly in kind.

Bowie would write another six articles for *Modern Painters*, all of which would be both incisive and authoritative. (Boyd remarks 'he was a good writer and a smart guy . . . both things that were pleasant surprises.'[16]) His subjects included everyone from Tracey Emin and Julian Schnabel to Jeff Koons and Damien Hirst, and his writing is devoid of the self-conscious artfulness that could be found in his other published journalism for *Q* and *Time Out*.\* And he enjoyed the convivial (although, for him, strictly tee-total) get-togethers and meetings with artists that the quarterly *Modern Painters* lunches allowed him to partake of.

There was only one occasion where it went awry. 'We had a dinner at the Dorchester,' recalls Boyd, 'and Bowie wanted to meet Lucian Freud. It was arranged that the two should meet in a little anteroom off the private dining room. Bowie was very edgy about it. Anyway, Freud turned up and the two sat down opposite each other at a table and started talking. Then, after about 20 seconds, Freud just got up and ran away. Bowie came up to me, looking aghast, and all he could say was "What did I do?" He was horrified that somehow this great meeting had gone so hideously wrong.' Boyd never discovered the cause of the tension and can only speculate. 'I think Freud was very uncomfortable. He obviously knew who Bowie was by then, and might have been thinking "Who is this rock star?" So he decided to cut and run and just left . . . That was the one time I ever saw Bowie discombobulated. Otherwise, he was very cool, incredibly wealthy and famous.'[17]

His interest in art also saw him dabbling in politics, for one of the few times in his public life, although it could be argued that his interest was purely aesthetic. Peter Howson, who was the official war artist of the

---

\*   Christopher Sandford calls him 'very nearly a fully fledged journalist in his own right', which, I am afraid, reminds me somewhat of Alan Partridge saying 'Wings – the band the Beatles could have been'.

Bosnian War, produced a number of shocking and controversial works, the most discussed of which was his painting *Croatian and Muslim*, a 1994 picture that depicted a woman being brutally raped by two jeering men. Howson, who had witnessed the aftermath of similar atrocities first hand, was not attempting to play for shock value; 'I'm not aiming to be controversial. But I wanted to cut out all the reportage. It's not my job to do that. My job is to do the things you don't see, that the army doesn't even get to see, not to be an illustrator, not to tell stories, but to produce strong images of things . . . I suppose I think I have the right because I was there and because as an artist I can do anything.'[18]

The painting was originally commissioned by the Imperial War Museum, who balked at the work and refused to display it, despite including it in their catalogue of Howson's work. It ended up at the Flowers Gallery in London, until it was rescued by Bowie, who bought it for his own private collection in a move that, unsurprisingly, resulted in a good deal of publicity. Bowie himself remarked that 'it's a great picture [and] I think it's ridiculous that it wasn't shown . . . I don't *like* it. I think that is a completely inappropriate word, but I do think it's very powerful, and, obviously, very important.'[19] Howson later said, of the controversy, that 'I ended up having to go on to the radio and explain it. But then that thing happened with David Bowie buying the main painting. But things would be different now.'[*,20]

An artistic bond formed between Bowie and Howson, which resulted in the artist painting several studies of the musician. 'David Bowie came to the studio. I did a drawing of him. I asked him to pose for me so he said "Fine." He took off his coat and I put him on a plinth and he fell asleep. He fell asleep as he was posing, fell off the plinth and ripped his shirt. It was quite a weird feeling to have Bowie, this godlike creature, lying on the floor.' But his subject was not immune to vanity, browsing Howson's record collection. 'He was looking for his own CD, but he couldn't find it.'[21]

---

* The painting was eventually sold after Bowie's death, realising £130,000, ten times the amount of the highest estimate.

While Bowie was hobnobbing with artists and art critics alike, he was also developing his own interest in painting. He had begun experimenting with the format when he was in Los Angeles and Berlin in the '70s, having already established himself, in a small way, as a collector, spending any royalty cheques he acquired on art and interesting *objets d'art*. He would later recall that, when he wrote 'Life on Mars', his work space already contained 'a bargain-price art nouveau screen ("William Morris", so I told anyone who asked)'.[22] Yet he was ambivalent about his artistic abilities, saying in 1983 that 'it's a struggle and [paint and I] hate each other, but it doesn't have to mean you can't eventually get something onto a canvas that has a lot of spikiness to it'.[23]

'I met Bowie through Brian Eno in the late '70s,' says Bowie's biographer and friend, the designer Kevin Cann, 'and we really connected through art and design. Art was always a real passion of his, and in the mid '70s, when he really started to feel the pressure of fame, and was falling out with his management and all kinds of things going wrong, as well as being strung out a lot on cocaine – which certainly didn't help his mental health – he reverted back to art and started to do drawings and just became interested in Germany and Germanic art and Christopher Isherwood. When he got back to Europe, part of the battle was to sort of stay clean or as clean as possible. And one of those coping mechanisms was to throw himself into art.'[24]

Throughout 1994, Bowie had been cautiously experimenting with the art world, both in his *Modern Painters* writing and interviewing, and in collaborating with Eno on designing wallpaper for Laura Ashley, now a much-sought after collectors' item but greeted with a degree of ridicule at the time. One critic asked if Bowie had written 'an artistic suicide note'; another suggested he would buy a few rolls for his downstairs toilet 'as a constant and poignant reminder of what became of one of my all-time heroes'.[25]

Cann, who was closely involved in bringing Eno and Bowie together to design the wallpaper, admits 'he was always going to get a bit of a kicking, because that's what the British press do, and the art world was very, very snobby. But you still had a lot of people showing him a lot of respect at the time, which pleased him a lot.' Bowie himself remarked, defensively, 'Well, it's not very original. Robert Gober and a number of others, even Andy Warhol, did them. It's just part of a tradition.'[26] The design featured a minotaur set against a traditionally English, even chintzy background, something that both tied into Bowie's fascination with the minotaur as an artistic symbol and reflected his desire to provoke and startle, as well as being the art equivalent of Harold Pinter's 'the weasel under the cocktail cabinet'.

Although Bowie had been toying with the idea of exhibiting his work before he worked with Cann, he kept his intentions characteristically opaque. 'He was probably already gearing up to it when we first met, although whether he mentioned it to me exactly at that point, I don't know. But it was very soon after, when we started working on the wallpaper, because Laura Ashley understood that the work was going to be used for an exhibition and David had already arranged The Gallery in Cork Street.'[27]

Bowie had booked a space for his first solo show in April 1995 at the appropriately named The Gallery, but although he had a few works dating from the early '90s, and even a couple of pieces that he had completed in the '70s, it was clear that he could not stage an exhibition without enough artworks to justify it. Therefore, throughout 1994, Bowie would sporadically come to a rented house in Fulham and paint. As Cann describes it, 'he'd fly in on a Monday morning from Switzerland and spent five days painting in this little studio on the first floor. We would meet there, religiously, most Mondays and he'd bring a suitcase with various things that he needed. When he turned up, the house was immaculate, but I remember once that I walked into the lounge after an hour and it looked like a bomb had hit it. There were books and notebooks and bits of paper all over the place, and he was sitting cross-legged on the floor, working.'[28]

When Bowie was creating his art, he was a different figure to the benevolent dictator who dictated the environment in the studio. 'He was off duty,' says Cann, 'but only 50 per cent. If he was in the mood, then it was fantastic – you could chat about anything, ask him anything. If not, then the conversation was purely about work. From time to time, he got pretty touchy, and he was actively rude to me a couple of times, when I thought "Oh, give it a break". It was only later on that I realised that he couldn't help it, and it was his way of trying to cope with the worry. He was out of his comfort zone. Put him on stage or in a studio and he was perfectly fine, because that was his natural environment. But he'd also say "This is my show and I just want it to be great", which was understandable.'[29]

By the time that the exhibition was ready to open on 18 April 1995, Bowie had assembled an eclectic collection of works that included everything from the charcoal sketches he had made of his band from the *Outside* sessions, more minotaur images, oil portraits that he had painted of him and Iggy Pop from their time in Berlin and a return to the racial politics of *Black Tie White Noise* in the form of a couple of paintings inspired by a trip to South Africa, *Dry Heads* and *Ancestor*.* The exhibition, portentously entitled *New Afro/Pagan and Work 1975–1995*, opened to the usual blitz of publicity and interest, which Bowie dealt with with his usual calm aplomb. Cann remembers that 'on the night, he was fairly relaxed. There were a few dedicated fans outside, as there had been every day, but inside it was pretty frantic. David took the attitude that "I'm in charge, and this is my show", and that kept him going.'

Alan Edwards, who can be seen marshalling the press in contemporary ITN footage of the exhibition opening, knew that it would be a considerable change of scene for his client and that the art critics would be far

---

\* During his visit, he and Iman met with Nelson Mandela, as was virtually obligatory for any self-respecting celebrity in the '90s (Bono was practically a house guest of Mandela's). In the photos of the encounter, taken by Bruce Weber, Bowie looks smug, Iman looks enraptured and Mandela looks vaguely bemused as to who his guest is. It is hard to imagine, say, *Lodger* being on the stereo system at Robben Island.

harder to impress than music writers – who, as we have seen, were hardly sycophantic towards Bowie. 'There was always a change of scene just around the corner with David and that's what made working with him so stimulating and interesting. I'd always been interested in art, so I was fully involved. I even remember attending a meeting with the board of *Modern Painters* on David's behalf. I was by no means an expert, so I was having to do a lot of getting up to speed. You were always having to stretch yourself around Bowie. You couldn't just follow the formula.'[30]

As for the show, Edwards 'thought it was great and I remember the launch at Cork Street gallery, with some of his great paintings from the minotaur to Iggy and a great self-portrait'.[31] Bowie, immaculately attired in a long grey coat and silver top, seemed fully at ease with the many journalists asking him questions, suggesting that 'the style that I tend to adopt is whatever the job in hand is' and that 'I am anti-consistency in style in art, much as I am in music'. (His accent, incidentally, was wholly different to the Sarf London intonations that he would usually adopt on stage, or in chat-show interviews.)

Bowie kept dropping in countless quotable lines that he knew would be picked up and excerpted – 'I must have things *now* . . . I'm very much a product of the end of the 20th century, so it's immediate gratification I want' – and said, of his creative urge, 'it's like lifeblood. I can't conceive of a world in which I'm not painting and making music.' He even suggested that art was more important to him than music – 'it becomes an existence' – although he was quick to insist that he would never give up music for art: 'I'm fortunate to have the time, inclination and, possibly, the talent, to work in both mediums.' And when asked how he would feel if the critics were uncharitable, he had a ready reply. 'I've sold nearly all the art already! I've been in the rock business nearly thirty years and have developed an understanding of the difference between critique and criticism.' Summing up his status with music writers as 'reviled, applauded or sorely missed', he disagreed with any suggestion that the show was him laying himself bare. 'That's for me to know, and others to purchase.'

The show was, as anticipated, pilloried by the art writers. One critic described the artwork on display as 'post A-level, pre-art school', while another, who had been invited to the opening night, left tight-lipped, with his only comment to the press being a simple 'embarrassing'.[32] In truth, even a committed Bowie admirer would struggle to describe the work as being the equal of his music. Although there are flashes of interest, it is best to regard Bowie's sudden flare-up of artistic zeal as being one of the many projects that captured his attention for a short period. He all but admitted this in a 2003 interview with the *New York Post*. 'I've been so taken with the music side of my life over the last couple of years that I've done nothing I'm particularly excited about. But I've always found painting or sculpting has helped the progress of my music, especially in the early '90s.'[33]

As regards the bad reviews, Cann admits now that 'I think he was expecting them, but what he was really thinking about was "how much?". Of course, he was funding everything himself, so partly he was measuring success in whether he could even cover his costs. And that was the way his ambition worked. He could have put on a dozen shows and lost money. They could have just been vanity projects. But I think the fact that he was trying to gauge the success of it on what was sold was a measure of him in trying to prove that this isn't a vanity project. And I think to a degree that was successful.' After the exhibition, Bowie continued to be active in the London art world, collaborating with the artist Damien Hirst on a painting that riffed on *Outside – Beautiful, Hallo, Space-boy Painting* – and forming friendships with everyone from Tracey Emin to Gavin Turk. Yet the sense that he had of being an outsider rankled, and despite his cheery dismissal of the critics and the art world in general, he wished to settle scores, which he would do a few years later in the most considered and spectacular of ways.

It is the prerequisite of every wealthy middle-aged man to have his own boutique publishing business, and so when Bowie founded 21, a small fine art publisher that involved Karen Wright, Bernard Jacobson and the wealthy art collector Sir Timothy Sainsbury, one might have expected well-written monographs about obscure mid-twentieth-century artists. Which, in a manner of speaking, is what William Boyd produced, when he wrote a melancholy short book about a forgotten American painter named Nat Tate who died at the age of 32. It was soulful, respectful and did a fine job in bringing Tate back into the public view. There was only one problem with this: Tate had never existed.

By the beginning of 1998, *Modern Painters* no longer existed, either. 'The magazine was sold to Louise Blouin,' explains Boyd, 'who single-handedly sacked virtually every member of the editorial board, including me and David. You may have thought that, if you were going to keep on anyone, you'd keep on David Bowie, but instead we were all erased from the magazine, like some sort of Soviet era-purge.'[34] Before they were sent off to the figurative gulag, however, Bowie and Boyd had conceived a daringly subversive idea, as the latter explains.

'During a board meeting, Karen Wright said, "I'd really like to try and get fiction into this art magazine somehow, but I don't know how." So I just said, "Why don't I invent a painter?" She said "Great idea", so off I went and did it. I'd been collecting anonymous photographs for [his 2002 novel] *Any Human Heart* and so I had quite a cache of very good or interesting photographs of total strangers. I thought I could cook up this fake biography – pre-Google, of course – and trick it out with photographs and all the apparatus of a small monograph. So I did it. And then it was published in the magazine, and it was published in the *Daily Telegraph*. And then Bowie said, "Why don't we publish it as a little book?"'[35]

By this stage, 21 was establishing a reputation as a provocative, daring imprint, with Bowie's financial muscle meaning that it was able to publish books that a larger house would have avoided. As he himself explained, 'everything was either art at an academic level or so dense with art-talk that it excluded 90 percent of the reading market. We thought it might be a good thing to go at least halfway to changing that. I say halfway because some of us are maybe more populist than others.'[36] Its name alluded to what Bowie called 'a quick take on the awareness of the imminent next century' – much of Bowie's work in the '90s could easily have been described as 'Millennium Approaches', if the playwright Tony Kushner had not already taken that name for the first part of his *Angels in America* saga – and he happily declared that 'the great freedom within a small indie company like ourselves is that we get the last word on how something is presented and which books we publish. I would only be a tenacious contributor of ideas at a big house. As long as we break even at year's end, I think we'll be happy.'

Yet *Nat Tate: An American Artist, 1928–1960* would be rather different to, say, art critic Matthew Collings's *Blimey! From Bohemia to Britpop: The London Artworld from Francis Bacon to Damien Hirst*, 21's launch title. Boyd and Bowie, who had now evolved from friends to co-conspirators, were clear that nobody must be let in on the scam, which would be presented straight-faced, even down to the blurb that Bowie supplied for the book. He wrote: 'The small oil I picked up on Prince Street, New York, in the late '60s must indeed be one of the lost Third Panel Triptychs. The great sadness of this quiet and moving monograph is that the artist's most profound dread – that God will make you an artist but only a mediocre artist – did not in retrospect apply to Nat Tate.'

Boyd had anticipated that the story would be of mild interest to the art world. 'I had imagined it to be a slow burn, expecting that in six months, somebody would say, "There is no Janet Felser gallery on 57th Street" and I would have to say, "Well, there was, but you know . . ." Instead, the project quickly gathered momentum. Boyd prevailed upon the novelist Gore Vidal and the art critic and Picasso biographer John Richardson to offer their own quotes for the book, with Vidal suggesting that 'Tate was essentially dignified, though always drunk and with nothing to say', while Richardson offered an anecdote about Tate lunching with Picasso, as if it had been an offcut harvested from one of his biographies. And then Bowie persuaded the modish pop artist Jeff Koons to lend him his studio to give the book the launch that it deserved. An international media frenzy began.

Although book promotional duties in France prevented Boyd from being at the New York launch of *Nat Tate*, the stories of what happened on the night have become legendary. It took place, appropriately enough, on 1 April 1998, and Bowie read out excerpts of the book in Koons's studio with deadpan authority to an audience that consisted of many of the US's most respected art critics. When they were asked about their impressions of Tate, the majority, not wishing to be exposed as ignorant or behind the curve, spoke with passion and authority about their love of Tate's work, their regret at his having died so young and how pleased they were to have been able to attend a small retrospective of his work held in the late '60s. As Boyd recalls, 'there's a very funny photograph of Bowie holding *Nat Tate* and a slightly paranoid-looking Jeff Koons in the back. I think Bowie and Koons fell out as a result, because Koons felt he'd been used because he'd offered his studio as a venue, but he hadn't been told that *Nat Tate* was a fiction.'

In retrospect, even in the pre-Google era, the clues were there for the taking. Tate's name combines two of the most famous London art galleries, and Boyd, although an estimable novelist, was nobody's idea of an art biographer. Nonetheless, the gullibility of many of the most self-important members of the art world was what both men wanted to play on, and the resulting news story played out wonderfully. 'It was blown sky high a week later after the Koons party,' says Boyd, 'which rather got me off the hook. In a way, my conscience was eased because the hoax was exposed so quickly in the gossip column of the *New York Herald Tribune* and then everybody enjoyed that aspect of it. But if it had dragged on for a year or so, I'd be digging a deeper and more mendacious hole for myself. So although I was annoyed at first, thinking it was meant to be an exercise in my rather grandiose ambition to make fiction seem so real that you forget it's fiction, it proved its point brilliantly well.'[37]

Boyd is also very clear as to why the story has been such a captivating one. 'Without Bowie's involvement, there's no doubt people would have forgotten about it now. His fame made the story far more interesting.

I couldn't have supplied a blurb and hosted a launch party, and *Modern Painters* couldn't have done that. So there's no doubt that the fact that he was integral to the whole thing has made it extraordinarily enduring.'[38] Bowie himself never commented on the whole affair, leaving Boyd to shoulder the publicity duties, and given his extraordinarily eclectic range of work in the late '90s, it is tempting to imagine that he saw the whole *Nat Tate* affair as a lark, the schoolboy from Bromley Technical High School cocking a snook at authority.

And yet there is also something deeper and more resonant about his involvement. By this point in his career, Bowie was tearing through ideas and personae with the vigour of a Renaissance man in a hurry. If he suggested that the artist's most profound dread was, indeed, to be mediocre, he did everything in his considerable power to fight against such a fate through sheer eclecticism of interest and accomplishment. One moment, he would be declaring a lifelong interest in everything from the longevity of Tin Machine to a career as a painter, and then it would be discarded or archived without sentimentality or hesitation as soon as it behoved him to move on to another project. He has sometimes been described as ruthless for the way in which he dispensed with once-trusted, even beloved, collaborators, but in fact all he was doing was moving from one project to the next without any sense of regret, although he increasingly did look back to the past, sometimes with nostalgia and at other times with weary resentment.

Bowie embraced the artificial and the ephemeral with glee, challenging preconceptions of what a musician or an artist should be. If he could bankroll and promote the creation of an entirely fake painter, it was no less an artistic statement than what would follow subsequently in his career. But his new horizons would be his most ambitious venture yet.

8

# BOWIENET

## Fooling around with the internet

*'We are on the cusp of something exhilarating and terrifying'*

Bowie's early adoption of the internet's possibilities led him to allow fans to
compete to write a song with him – including the winner pictured here, Alex Grant.

Ke.Mazur / Getty

During most of the interviews that Bowie gave in the late '90s and early '00s, he was treated with the veneration that a much-beloved member of the rock royal family would merit: a thin white duke in all regards. Yet there was one notable exception to this and it occurred on 3 December 1999. Jeremy Paxman, then-presenter of the BBC's flagship current affairs programme *Newsnight*, had built a reputation as a tough interviewer, most notoriously in 1997 when he repeatedly asked the former home secretary Michael Howard whether he had over-ruled the head of the prison service. Paxman – who later claimed that he was stalling for time because his next item was not yet ready – demanded an answer from a squirming Howard no fewer than 14 times, which made for electrifying television and won him awards. It also earned him the nickname 'the Grand Inquisitor' and ensured that anyone who took part in an interview with him had to be on their guard for fear of looking foolish, or worse.

Bowie, whose jovial public exterior could only be maintained when he felt he was being treated with appropriate deference, did not wish to be questioned by Paxman. In the midst of promoting the *hours. . .* album, he was happier giving interviews to the more appreciative likes of Conan O'Brien and Rosie O'Donnell than he was sitting down with the combative Rottweiler, perhaps because he knew that Paxman – who was by no means a fan of his work – would make for a rigorous, forensic questioner and there was the inevitable risk that something might slip. It was therefore unsurprising that he berated Alan Edwards for agreeing to the conversation in the first place. 'I thought it was a master-stroke,' Edwards would later recall, '[but] he thought I'd gone crazy and was nervous that it would be a car crash . . . David told me that I would be fired if it wasn't a good interview.'[1] A great deal would be riding on the outcome.

The sixteen-minute interview remains fascinating more than two and a half decades on; it is worthy of comparison to the musician's more spontaneous conversation with Alan Yentob in the 1975 *Cracked Actor* documentary. Bowie begins the conversation obviously nervous and ill-at-ease,* fidgeting with his earlobe as Paxman announces, with a faintly disbelieving air, 'I've been thinking back over your career and it seems to me that there's been a constant reinvention', before – deliberately? – mispronouncing his surname to rhyme with 'How-ie' rather than the more appropriate 'Showy'. Yet Bowie swiftly regains his confidence, declaring that 'I have nothing to do with the [music] industry' and that 'I can't write or produce much in a place I find relaxing. I have to have a set of conflicts going on around me, not necessarily of my own doing.'

Throughout, Paxman alternates between being apparently interested and sceptical, offering his patented half-frowning expression of tempered incredulity with his famous subject. This proves an effective technique at times, as when Paxman quizzes Bowie about his drinking – 'not even a glass of wine?' – to be met with a surprisingly blunt reply. 'It would kill me. I'm an alcoholic, so it would be the kiss of death for me to start drinking again . . . It's very hard to have relationships when you're taking drugs and drinking.' And then, seven minutes in, in response to a question about what a young Bowie would choose to do with his life in 1999, rather than 1969, the musician announces 'it's now the internet that carries the flag for the subversive, possibly rebellious, chaotic and nihilistic'.

The tenor of the interview then changes, allowing Bowie to take the initiative and to make what would be one of his most prophetic and widely discussed statements. As Paxman sceptically asks him whether he is in favour of the free speech and, by extension, free action brought about by the internet, Bowie replies with 'I embrace the idea that there is a new demystification process between the artist and the audience.' Paxman describes the internet as incohesive and asks whether 'some of the claims made for it are hugely exaggerated', only for Bowie to cite the example of

---

* Edwards observed that Bowie was so keen to charm Paxman that he bought several books about fishing in order to prepare for their chat, knowing that the interviewer enjoyed angling when he wasn't reeling in politicians on camera.

Alexander Graham Bell, inventor of the telephone, who was once casti-
gated for his audacity in declaring that 'one day there will be a telephone
in every town in America'. He notes that 'I don't even think we've seen
the tip of the iceberg . . . The potential of what the internet is going to do
to society, both good and bad, is unimaginable . . . We are on the cusp of
something exhilarating and terrifying.'

When Paxman incredulously says 'It's just a tool, isn't it?', Bowie,
fully in control of the situation now, replies. 'No, it's not. It's an alien life
form . . . It's life on Mars, and it's just landed here. The actual context and
state of content is gonna be so different to anything that we can really
envisage at the moment, where the interplay between the user and provider
will be so simpatico that it will crush our ideas of what the medium is all
about.' He cites Duchamp and other disruptive figures in early twentieth-
century art, before prophesising that 'the idea that the piece of work is not
finished until the audience come to it, and add their own interpretation,
and what the piece of art is about is the grey space in the middle. That grey
space in the middle is what the twenty-first century is going to be about.'

The interview concluded amicably, if less incisively – the musician
suggested that he would like to start a new internet company of his
own – and when Bowie left, an anxious Edwards was reassured when
his client walked out, 'made an imaginary tick in the air with his hand
and said "One to you!" before walking out.'[2] Yet the impression that
Paxman and his questioning made on his subject lingered, and rankled.
Asked about his experience in an interview in Q magazine the following year, Bowie initially called his inquisitor 'very amiable and interested
– curious about things', but then went on to damn him by saying,
'Unfortunately, for some reason, he reminded me of an old friend, the
late Graham Chapman from Monty Python . . . I kept waiting for him to
say "That's enough. This interview's too silly." He didn't say it, but I bet
he thought it at times.'[3]

It was a classic Bowie technique: make a serious point and conceal it
beneath a joke, thereby diluting the sting. Yet Bowie believed that Paxman

had been less than appreciative about something that had become not just an interest of his, but a near-obsession. After all, wasn't it the clearest example of the future that he had prophesied throughout his career, one of simultaneous mass communication and compartmentalised isolation, one that the doom-laden songs of both *Ziggy Stardust* and *Diamond Dogs* appeared to allude to? The internet was more than a hobby for Bowie. Like his acting, or his art, it was a vital means of moving outside of music into the contemporary zeitgeist. Long before Kim Kardashian broke the internet, David Bowie fixed it, turning what was a niche fascination into a mainstream proposition. And, like so much else in his career, his relationship with it was complex, contradictory and eventually transitory, but, while it lasted, it was magnificent.

A few years before, it was another story. Bowie made little or no public comment about the internet, save remarking in one late 1995 interview, when asked about three things he hated: 'Ballet shoes. Absolutes. Whether that's one God, one political system, one art system, one anything, style of life. I think that's absolutely criminal. And the internet.'[4]

As seasoned observers knew, Bowie excelled at making statements in interviews that ran against, even flatly contradicted, what he privately believed. He had been using email as far back as 1983, and when he – appropriately enough – appeared at the NetAid concert at Wembley Stadium on 9 October 1999, he revealed that 'by '87, '88, I had the first artist newsgroup up, so I've been fooling around with the internet for a really long time.' Bowie's use of language was carefully chosen; 'fooling around' could either mean to mess about with or to engage in a non-marital sexual relationship. If he had been engaging in a fling with the internet, with all its vast, concomitant possibilities, events would unfold the year after his sardonic dismissal of it that would swiftly turn a series of one-night stands into a deeply committed relationship.

Bowie had always been a pioneer when it came to technology. His early music videos, from 'Life on Mars' to 'Ashes to Ashes', are regarded as masterpieces of the form, and when he chose to take matters further, the results were invariably interesting and original. His extended *Jazzin' for Blue Jean* short film not only won him a Grammy Award – the only one he received during his lifetime – for Best Music Video, but demonstrated that even if you detested the single, 'Blue Jean', that the film was promoting – and it was undeniably one of Bowie's best releases of the '80s – it was possible to enjoy Julien Temple's film, written by playwright Terry Johnson, on its own terms. It was a witty piece of self-deprecation, as Bowie played both an exaggerated version of himself ('Screaming Lord Byron') and the awkward, ill-at-ease Vic, caught out in a lie in an attempt to impress a woman.

He was nothing if not adventurous. Sometimes, these adventures would lead him down artistic cul-de-sacs, such as a brief flirtation with the CD-ROM format in 1994, when he released *Jump: The David Bowie Interactive CD-ROM*, which offered curious users the once-in-a-lifetime opportunity to 'enter Bowie's creative universe'. The product, which is now a minor collectors' item, was designed as a promotional gimmick to keep interest in *Black Tie White Noise* alive – and it is tempting to imagine that its release a year after the album suggested that there had been some significant technical hitches along the way, resulting in a delay. But there is some mild pleasure to be had from the quirkier touches, including the chance to listen to a muzak version of 'Jump They Say', along with the opportunity to edit a bespoke video of the song, using alternate angles and takes.

The artist behind it, however, was not satisfied. 'I hated it. I absolutely loathed it,' he later declared. 'There were aspects of it I thought had potential, but then again, there was so much information on the disc itself that made the idea of anybody using it interactively a joke. Interactive, as far as I'm concerned, is when the person who's operating the computer has as much to say as what's on the screen. That is interactive. And at the moment, it's just the ABC options. Even the most sophisticated CD-ROMs are just

"Here's the hard information. Now, you can take one of these three steps.'"
Bowie sought something more exciting, and innovative, with which to
make his mark, and also to find a new means of communication with his
acolytes and admirers, one in which he would always remain fully in control, no matter how forthcoming or candid he might appear to be.

One figure in the Bowie nexus was Robert Goodale, a New York lawyer who served both as his business manager, running his company Isolar,
and acted as his employer's point man for anything technology-related.
Goodale is credited as executive producer on *Jump* and on Bowie's original, perfunctory website, and by the summer of 1996, he wished to
diversify his interests, and involvement with Bowie, from Isolar to internet
and technological projects. He contacted a multimedia producer named
Robert Roy with a view to developing 'really cool innovative things', the
first of which was the chance to provide technical support and band-
width for the release of Bowie's download-only single 'Telling Lies' that
year. Although this did not ever occur, Goodale and Roy had now formed
a close association, with the former suggesting that this could go further: 'Let's figure out something to take David that will knock his socks
off, and he hasn't heard before.' The idea that they came up with would
become BowieNet.

Given the ubiquity of the internet today, it is salutary to remember that,
three decades ago, it was treated as something between a novelty – a one-
stop resource for pornography, gambling and shopping – and a cautionary
tale. Hollywood films, such as *The Net* and *Hackers*, presented the online
world as full of dangers and risks, as well as IT experts who looked like
Angelina Jolie and Sandra Bullock. These films might now seem fanciful as
well as laughably dated, but the prescient could see potential in setting up
businesses and websites that married the potential for instant worldwide
mass communication with the kudos of a well-loved brand or artist. Step
forward David Bowie.

As Roy recalled, 'we came up with this idea of "What if we could take
the backend technology of how those ISPs work and create something that

became BowieNet? What if we could use the leverage of David Bowie and create more of a fun, more media-centric, music-centric, art-centric community?" And that's really where we separated ourselves, because instead of trying to be really big – all things for all people – we went in the opposite direction. We wanted to create this really tight community of passionate music people.'[5]

The idea, in all its vast, apparently insane ambition, swiftly came together. Bowie would be attached not just to a passive website, but an internet service provider that would charge a monthly fee which would simultaneously undercut the market leader AOL and offer world-exclusive content, including occasional, strictly controlled access to the star himself through webchats and Q&A sessions. It would blur the boundaries between musician and fan, and be hugely lucrative for the former. You could even describe it as a forerunner of the vastly successful adult-oriented website OnlyFans, which lures in the libidinous with promises of interaction with your favourite 'entertainers', in exchange for subscription fees and extra payments for exclusive content. The ideal, then, would be for the punters to indulge themselves to such an extent that, sated by the flexible whores, they 'fall wanking to the floor', as Bowie wrote in his 1973 song 'Time'.

Goodale and Roy did not have this particular happy ending in mind.* Instead, when they met Bowie's personal manager Bill Zysblat, they emphasised how the project would be innovative and lucrative alike, while remaining true to Bowie's reputation as a quixotic, individually minded artist. If he became Mr Corporate, as he had verged on doing in the '80s, then it would be the death knell for his credibility, however much money was on offer. Zysblat was interested but cautious, noting that it would need an established technology partner to stand any chance of success, but promised to put the idea in front of Bowie. It helped, of course, that Goodale and the musician already had an existing relationship, so the four men later

---

* Although it should be noted that the gallery section of BowieNet did feature some candid pictures of Bowie in his underwear, which he captioned 'where's my trousers?'.

convened in New York in the autumn of 1996 and the meeting went well enough for Bowie to give his approval to the plan. Roy was duly given licence to contact potential partners and inform them that 'David Bowie is going to be the first private label music ISP in the history of the internet'.

If this were a film, then this grandiose announcement would now result in a montage of big tech companies desperately producing their chequebooks and attempting to outbid one another for the rights to be a partner in this grand endeavour. However, in late 1996, David Bowie had not had a significant hit record in the United States in a decade, and while the previous year's *Outside* was undeniably a *succès d'estime*, he was not the commercial titan that he had been, briefly, around the time of *Let's Dance*. AOL sadly shook their heads and declined; Prodigy Communications muttered something about having to take a rain check. The idea looked as if it might fizzle out before it achieved fruition.

It was rescued by Concentric Network Corporation, a California-based firm who had made their money from, and established their expertise working with, traditional blue-chip clients, such as investment banks and hospitals. Providing services to a rock 'n' rollin' bitch like Bowie may have seemed a stretch, but it was also an opportunity for them to diversify into new and lucrative territory. They would take on all the administrative necessities for the website – the dull but essential business side – and in turn allow Goodale and Roy to look for more exciting partners for the website design itself. Bowie was drawn to the company Nettwerk, which had specialised in providing extra content on so-called 'enhanced CDs' for artists. According to Roy, he had clear ideas for how his website should look. 'In the beginning, he wanted something dark. He also wanted a design that was unique, that you just didn't see anywhere else.'[6]

As the website design and build progressed, Bowie proved to be a committed, hands-on collaborator, treating the nascent BowieNet with as much care as if it were another album of his. He had grandiose, possibly impossible plans of turning his particular corner of the internet into a 'stately pleasure dome' for the turn of the millennium, allowing, perhaps empowering, his admirers to become part of the whole endeavour by post-ing their own pictures, music and even – this may have been a step too far, admittedly – short poems. It was not intended as an informational or promotional endeavour, although this would be an inevitable, perhaps welcome by-product of raising his profile. Still, as Roy said, 'the last thing he needed was another electronic billboard of who David Bowie was. He didn't want a marketing site to try to sell albums or concert tickets. He wanted this to be an interactive community of people who could go to the site to contribute and learn. . . and have fun!'[7]

The project percolated throughout 1997 and 1998, including an ambi-tious but technologically unsuccessful attempt to livestream an *Earthling* gig from Boston, until, with rumours growing in intensity thanks to a leak from EMI, Bowie's management company put out a press release on 17 July confirming the imminent launch of BowieNet on 1 September. Subscribers would be offered 'high-speed Internet service across North America and, by year end, throughout the world', plus features includ-ing 'a fully customizable home page, davidbowie.com e-mail address (your.name@davidbowie.com), news groups, chat rooms, online share-ware, multiplayer gaming, and much much more'. This would include 'previously unreleased audio tracks, videos and photos and numerous live performances and Q&A sessions from Bowie, as well as special guest collaborators and contributors'.

Bowie himself commented that the site would be 'for all music lovers', rather than just for his own committed fans, but promised that it would contain 'unique proprietary content'. He then went on to make a further promise that, these days, would seem unexceptional but was positively revolutionary for 1998. Bowie suggested that BowieNet would be 'a single place where the vast archives of music information could be accessed, views stated and ideas exchanged'. In other words, it would be a democracy, not a dictatorship, albeit one with a musician's name and face emblazoned all over it. 'Uncensored internet access' was promised, but it would be anchored within the Bowie world, as long as its users could draw upon a

56k modem connection to be able to access the videos and music clips that the site would boast. It was ahead of its time, and the technological reach of the day, and it showed its creator and guiding spirit as a pioneer once again. 'If I was 19 again,' Bowie declared, 'I'd bypass music and go right to the internet.'[8] He did not need to say that both could coexist alongside one another, peacefully, and that he was the pioneering facilitator of such a union.

In the run-up to the launch, Bowie began contributing brief, often gnomic entries to an online journal that he had begun. The first, dated 23 August 1998, stated: 'I should suppose that an interesting and nicely arbitrary way of starting these journals is to make a few notes on various stories and rumours that have been floating around on the Net, write a little on what day-to-day life seems to hold, and maybe go back a few years, try to catch a glimpse of all that.'

Yet he flitted about, rather than try and tantalise his readers with anything revelatory. There was a tease about music – 'Tried some new song ideas this morning. I'd been listening to the sweet sound of the Semar Pegulingan, regularly called the gamelan or Balinese orchestra. It never fails to transport me to another place and way of thinking' – and allusions to current work ('I did just do a track of the old Gershwin song "A Foggy Day in London Town"'). But mostly, Bowie, understandably, kvetched and worried about the imminent launch. Behind-the-scenes drama was alluded to ('Is the work on-line getting serious or what. Nettmedia is going crazy trying to up-load everything on time. There are still major plumbing problems in some areas but everything should look halfway decent when we go on Monday night') and some not wholly believable insights were teased into his daily life at home. 'This is supposed to be the day of rest but as soon as we get back from our walk Iman goes to make coffee and I tunnel my way into the computer room, checking on content for the ISP.'

Finally, it was ready and BowieNet could launch. As its creator prepared to step through the door once again, almost 30 years to the day since Major Tom had floated in a most peculiar way, he uploaded a message that mixed anticipation with anxiety. 'THIS IS IT THEN. I have to submit this journal right now or I'll miss the deadline for tonight.' He referred to his 'constant fidgeting and last-minute changes and additions and moans', and ended appropriately with '. . . and here we go'. History would be made one way or another. But did Bowie have what it took to pull off something daring and innovative, or would it end up another *Johnny Mnemonic*,* an expensive cyberflop that failed to understand its medium?

BowieNet, at first, achieved all its goals, and more besides. Whatever Bowie, ever the innovator, had understood was that his millions of admirers were not simply interested in having yet another website to visit on a daily, weekly or monthly basis. Until the release of *hours. . .* in October 1999, there was little concrete news to report, and the endless rumour and scuttlebutt that made up a generous proportion of the online conversation about him was ignored entirely. Instead, the monthly subscription fee had to be earned in esoteric and creative ways, and Bowie understood that the easiest – if most exposing – means of doing so was to allow greater interaction with him.

He was, naturally, torn between wishing to exploit the possibilities of his new toy and still wary about the risks of giving up any degree of privacy in exchange for money. He had been able to manage the interview process for a considerable time, perhaps the entirety of his career, but he now had to skip the intervening journalist and offer unfiltered access to his thoughts, ideas and creative process. Naturally, it would be conducted purely on his terms. Over a series of apparently informal but carefully policed 'webchats', he would anticipate the internet's later penchant for 'AMA' (Ask Me Anything) exercises in public candour. BowieNet

---

* The unsuccessful 1995 sci-fi action film, based on a William Gibson short story and starring Keanu Reeves as a hapless futuristic data courier.

subscribers were able to quiz Bowie and a range of his friends and collaborators – including, bizarrely, Boyzone's Ronan Keating in early 1999 – about anything that took their fancy and he answered carefully selected questions during these chats.

The results were both valuable and variable. Bowie, as ever, anticipated something that would become commonplace a few years later, until the rise of social media made the webchat a largely passé concept. Yet from the first occasion that he dipped an elegant toe into the murky waters of the internet on 30 September 1998, greeting his subscribers with 'How about now?' in response to the frantic question 'WHEN ARE WE STARTING?', he seemed torn between repeating the usual high-blown platitudes ('The great flowering of the individual as an artist started in the 18th Century . . . Unfortunatley [sic] the idea that art was cut off from most of society started there too') and apparent outrage at the idea that one admirer might ask for his artwork to be sold as more affordable limited-edition posters. There are nuggets of inconsequential gossip, allusions to famous friends and alternation between silliness and apparent sincerity. The fanbase had been tipped into hysteria by the presence of their idol and celebrated this by asking, apparently at random, about his interests in Nietzsche and whether he had ever visited Walmart.

Bowie the internet entrepreneur is in evidence – 'We set up a relationship with tripod* to give BowieNet members 11 megabytes of web space to build sites on any subject they desire in the BowieNet pod customized for our ISP' – and, when asked what he thought about the early days of his project, he was balanced rather than ecstatic. 'I think we've made a pretty reasonable start. The man hours involved are tremendous. I guess I should say the person hours involved are tremendous. If we can live up to our own expectations, within a few months it should be quite formidable. As not only an archive, but also as an interactive community base.

---

* Tripod was a '90s web-hosting company that allowed the technologically savvy to build their own websites.

No doubt you will let us know how we're doing and believe me we take your comments very seriously.'[9] This was Bowie the salesman, a figure last seen in public asking his fans to vote for their favourite songs to be played on the Sound + Vision tour a decade before. He was not simply a musician now; he was the CEO of a tech start-up, earnestly eliciting feedback and comment from subscribers. Then the conversation ended as abruptly as it began, with jokes about hair transplants and Viagra. Bowie's first foray into fan interaction concluded.

He would engage in a further 15 or so webchats between late 1998 and the release of *Heathen* in the early summer of 2002. Looked at in retrospect, there are numerous interesting details about contemporary artistic and musical enthusiasms, interspersed with occasional flashes of irritation at slow internet connections, banal or repetitive questions or anything that dared to impugn Bowie's essential brilliance. But even the most intrepid Bowie admirer – or biographer – would struggle to elicit any more than the odd nugget of information from the conversations, which ended up being as purposefully unrevealing as the interviews that he gave during this period.

Even when Coco Schwab was prevailed upon to appear on BowieNet in July 2001, her responses were similarly dry. Those who had questioned her Svengali-like role in Bowie's professional (and, some disgruntled collaborators would suggest, personal) life would be unenlightened to find out that 'my efforts to get the job done was [*sic*] sometimes seen at best as overzealous and at worst as God (and the tabloids) knows what . . . [but] David's friendship and understanding and the importance of what he tries to achieve helped me see fear and jealousy for what it is and not to take on other people's stuff'.[10] These were noble and selfless sentiments, but anyone who wished to find out anything more revealing about one of the closest and most enduring relationships in Bowie's life would be frustrated and disappointed by the blandness with which anything revealing was batted back. BowieNet was not an environment for candour.

What it was, however, was a place for experimentation and gamesplaying. When he wasn't conducting these inevitably stilted public conversations, Bowie was a more relaxed, informal presence in his website's chatroom, where it was believed he would occasionally appear under the username 'Sailor' – presumably a reference to the 'Red Sails' lyric 'Sailor can't dance like you' – and offer fleeting nuggets of interaction before he would swoop away again, leaving his admirers tantalised until his next appearance. He never owned up to being this character; debate still exists as to whether it was really him or just a merry prankster pretending to be him.

Still, even if this was artificial and performative, it was more than, say, Mick Jagger or Bruce Springsteen were doing in the final years of the '90s. And it was in this spirit that Bowie launched a competition that would blur the lines between his fans' fervent but limited adoration and full collaboration: via BowieNet, he would offer them the chance to co-write a song with him, which would then appear on his forthcoming album.

In October 1998, Bowie posted a demo of an unfinished track, 'What's Really Happening', and outlined the deal. Between November and December, he would run a competition for an ardent admirer to complete the lyrics to the song: three verses, four lines each, seven syllables a line. In return, they would record the song with him, receive a co-writing credit (and resulting royalties), a $15,000 recording contract from Bowie's publishing company Bug Music and numerous other treats such as gift cards, a BowieNet subscription and vouchers to buy CDs with. But by far the most exciting aspect of the competition was that a fan would be allowed to enter the Bowie universe, giving his admirers a sense of democracy and wish-fulfilment coming true. That the whole thing acted as a not-so-subtle plug for his new website – and the reams of publicity that the stunt secured meant that it paid off – did not pass unnoticed.

The competition received more than 80,000 entries, ranging from professional musicians who saw this as an opportunity to get Bowie's attention to timewasters and provocateurs who, anticipating the internet's later penchant for trolling and backchat, did everything from send in altered lyrics to 'The Laughing Gnome' to carefully worked-out parodies of his earlier work. As Bowie later remarked, many of these were 'so flip they're almost successful, because they were written with such a lack of responsibility attached. Often things work really well when you don't feel the pressure of having to make them good. To play at something is often more productive than earnestly striving.'[11] Still, there were also, in his recollection, 'a lot of potty ones'. The internet had given everyone a voice, and, unfortunately, sometimes this was more an unhinged howl than a considered conversation.

The 80,000 were whittled down to 25 and then, via a mixture of BowieNet member voting and Bowie's own imprimatur, the winner was decided upon. It was a 20-year-old Ohioan, Alex Grant, who was crowned on 20 January 1999. Bowie remarked of his '360-degree interactive adventure' that 'it was impertinent, it scanned well, and it was easy to sing'. It helped that the winning lyrics were about the displacing effects of the internet and the culture it was breeding. Grant himself suggested that 'when I first logged on three years ago, [the internet] was this beautiful magic thing, but after a certain amount of time, I was getting stuck inside of that. My whole life became the internet.'[12] If *hours. . .* was a curious mixture of the old and the new, both musically and thematically, then its first instalment, 'What's Really Happening', prefigured both. The song owes a debt to Bowie's late-'70s output, while Grant's lyrics, all glass clouds and plastic boxes, teeter between inspiration and pretension. Like 'Telling Lies', it was far from the strongest song on the album, but its innovative creation meant that it garnered far more attention than it would have done had it been recorded in more conventional circumstances.

This innovation continued into 24 May 1999, when Bowie, Grant, Reeves Gabrels, Mark Plati and other musicians assembled at Looking Glass Studios in New York to complete the song, with the earlier backing tracks having already been laid down. Grant and his friend Larry sang backing vocals, something that Bowie later described as 'the most gratifying part of the evening', and the entire experience was livestreamed on BowieNet, complete with commentary from those involved. The transcript of the

recording, complete with remarks of varying surrealism and usefulness from watching BowieNetters, saw Bowie praise Grant again – 'he writes a mean lyric' – and later call his one-time collaborator 'a born writer'.\*
Then the session finished, the song was recorded and the Bowie machine returned to business as usual.

Bowie may have praised the internet for replacing music as a mass communicative force – '[music] doesn't have that cachet any more . . . it's been replaced by the internet which has the same sound of revolution to it'[13] – and, until the end of the century, he remained a steadfast admirer of its potential and possibilities, continuing to participate in regular BowieNet chats and extolling its virtues in interviews. Shortly before his *Newsnight* conversation, Bowie declared that 'there's a breakthrough happening where there's an on-line community. Nobody's quite sure what this animal is and what characteristics it's going to have. It's being born, so there will be as many downsides as upsides, and the fact that we should be comfortable with this fragmented and chaotic universe is only just starting to come in. It's only dawned on us in the last 20–30 years that this universe is not black and white with clear-cut rules, ways of doing things, and established patterns and traditions. It's an existence we've never gauged before, and I really feel this creature will be our next quantum leap, this creature can almost surf through life in a way we didn't know was possible before.'[14]

The central difficulty with Bowie's belief – which, almost incidentally, was spectacularly vindicated over the next decades – was that the democratisation of both knowledge and experience that the internet brought meant that there was less attention paid to those who had, before instant worldwide connectivity, been revered as gurus and prophets. BowieNet offered previously never-seen and little-known live recordings of songs, but before long these could be recorded and distributed on the internet, just as, even in the pre-iPhone era, any gig-goer could record a concert and

---

\*   Like many others in the Bowie narrative, Alex Grant vanished after the recording. He would now be in his late forties and has resisted the temptation to come forward and tell his story. Perhaps there would be a book in it.

turn it into their own live CD to be sold for profit or given away for free, depending on how mercantile their instincts were.

Bowie, however, had grander plans for his online presence. He briefly resurrected his artistic entrepreneurial instincts in October 1999 by hosting a virtual version of the notorious 1997 show *Sensation: Young British Artists*, which would introduce the likes of Bowie's friends Tracey Emin and Damien Hirst to an American audience. It opened at the Brooklyn Museum that month; Bowie lending his fame and influence to promote the show so directly was a considerable coup for the organisers, as well as reflecting something of the energy and vitality of the artists onto Bowie and his website. And his entrepreneurial instincts would expand, albeit without noticeable or lasting success. As the *Financial Times* tactfully described it, these innovations were 'unrelated to what business strategists might call his core competencies'.[15]

If you had been an enthusiastic teenager, thrilling to the songs performed by the drug-addled but still vital and dangerous Bowie on the Diamond Dogs or Station to Station tours in the mid-'70s, it may have come as a surprise to find, a quarter of a century later, the same man had reinvented himself as your bank manager, deciding whether or not you would be allowed a mortgage or credit card. Yet this was briefly the case in early 2000, when Bowie, by now fully immersed in the world of virtual possibility, collaborated with the long-obsolete USABankShares.com to launch BowieBanc. His most ardent admirers would receive BowieNet access, along with such fripperies as a debit card emblazoned with Bowie's face. In exchange for lending his name, Bowie was paid a marketing fee.

This was greeted with a degree of understandable ridicule. A few years before, Bowie had been recording *Outside* with Brian Eno and playing Andy Warhol for Julian Schnabel. Now he was toying with the idea of being a banker. Although the musician himself had no day-to-day involvement with the mechanisms of the accounts, BowieBanc was still promoted around his name and fame. As one rival banker observed cattily, 'as an account holder, I would certainly hope that David Bowie wasn't responsible for my portfolio'.[16] Unsurprisingly, the endeavour did not prove to be a success and was quietly wound up after a few years. But the image that it suggested – of Bowie as rapacious, money-obsessed capitalist – was one that had already been percolating since the '80s, and this, along with the Bowie Bonds scheme – of which more to follow – appeared to confirm it. It was too minor and inconsequential a mistake to be seen as a genuine misstep, but the excitement of the unknown now curdled into the cynicism of opportunism.

The main website continued, but Bowie gradually lost interest in interacting with his fans so directly. It was briefly suggested in 1999 that BowieNet had a potential value of $300 million, but this soon dissipated as the novelty factor wore off and as Bowie no longer devoted himself to the project with the enthusiasm with which he began it. The final webchat that he undertook was in the summer of 2002, to promote the release of *Heathen*, and was hosted by MSN, rather than his own website.

The BowieNet chats themselves limped on, somewhat unbelievably, until October 2004, with a typically spirited and good-natured conversation with Gail Ann Dorsey, but the momentum had long since passed. The gradual demise of BowieNet as anything other than a straightforward promotional website was inevitable as Bowie withdrew his own input and moved on to other projects. Like everything else in his life and career, it had a sell-by date, which duly came in 2006. He even suggested this in an interview in July 2003 when it was suggested that the internet was not finished. 'It is as far as I'm concerned,' was his curt reply. 'Have you ever tried to buy anything lately online?'[17]

Even the potential for the democratisation of music – something that other acts ably capitalised on long after Bowie appeared to retire from the industry – was something that he came to dismiss. 'You're still as hidden on the internet. There must be a million bands on the internet now; and how many are you gonna stumble across?' The now-56-year-old Bowie inadvertently struck a grandfatherly note when he suggested that 'the more worrisome part is that there's so much that one can find out through the

Internet; but I don't think people take advantage of it in quite the right way'. Quite what 'the right way' was, or could be, remained unclear; Bowie inadvertently anticipated the wilder world of online disinformation by extolling the virtues of the website Truthout, suggesting that 'it's really a fabulous storehouse of information of what's written in the alternative press, or the rest of the world's press, that never really sees the light of day here. I know that not that many people go to it, and it seems a great shame.'[18]

Bowie, like anyone in the twenty-first century, continued to be an avid correspondent until the end of his life. Several people who I interviewed for this book spoke of how they would receive brief emails from him out of the blue, recommending a book, film or album. He was unusually good at remembering birthdays, when the celebrator could usually expect a brief but warm message. Yet he did not have any public online presence to speak of after he first vanished from public view in 2004; he ignored Twitter, Facebook, Instagram and the like when they all appeared, whereas once he would have been one of their most committed early adopters.

There was one strange exception to this, which still remains mysterious. At the end of 2013, someone purporting to be Bowie released a cryptic statement online that suggested that new music would be released next year, before wishing his admirers a happy Christmas. At the time, this was said to be the work of an imposter – of whom there were a vast number around – and it was swiftly forgotten. Yet at the same time, Bowie delivered a Christmas message in the style of Elvis to the Radio Clash show on BBC6 Music, in which he declared 'Hello everybody, this is David Bowie making a telephone call from the US of A. At this time of the year, I can't help but remember my British-ness and all the jolly British folk, so here's to you and have yourselves a Merry little Christmas and a Happy New Year. Thank you very much.'

A few months later, a similar message was read out at a charity event for the Terrence Higgins Trust, when Bowie declared: 'This city is even better than the one you were in last year, so remember to dance, dance, dance.

And then sit down for a minute, knit something, then get up and run all over the place. Do it. Love on ya. More music soon. David.' The promised music soon appeared, in the form of the Maria Schneider* version of 'Sue (Or in a Season of Crime)', and, of course, the album *Blackstar* was waiting in the wings. So whether the Bowie impersonator was simply suggesting something optimistically that proved to be accurate, or if it was Bowie himself, making a final, fleeting return to the world of online communication, it was an appropriate epilogue to this most febrile, and prophetic, of periods in Bowie's life and work.

---

\* The composer and orchestra leader, not the *Last Tango in Paris* actress.

# BOWIEBONDS, *HOURS*. . . AND GLASTONBURY

## 'The gods forgot they made me'

*'I am only the person the greatest number
of people believe that I am'*

Bowie at Glastonbury, 2000. A legendary performance.
Hayley Madden/Getty

When Bowie walked on stage at Worthy Farm in Somerset on 25 June 2000, received wisdom has it that the gig he performed over the following two hours was not just the highlight of that year's Glastonbury Festival, but one of the greatest performances – if not *the* greatest performance – in the history of the festival. In terms of Bowie's own career, it is commonly believed to be the single moment that he regained his crown as the reigning monarch of contemporary music, transforming him at a stroke from a figure whose best work was behind him to a peerless performer who inspired and impressed audiences, and artists, who were not even born when he began his career. It was a revitalising, extraordinary performance, which saw him embrace a past that he had spent the past decade trying to escape from, and established the basis on which he would conduct the remainder of his career.

This, at least, is the story that has now passed into public consciousness. Many of those who were involved in the Glastonbury gig, whether as performers or organisers, have described it as their finest hour. Mike Garson comments that 'people still talk about it as the best show ever',[1] while co-organiser Emily Eavis said, 'I often get asked what the best set I've seen here at Glastonbury is, and Bowie's 2000 performance is always one which I think of first.'[2] Bowie's PR Alan Edwards recalls that 'David knew when he came off stage it had been a seismic moment. Everything changed from that day on.'[3] Contemporary reaction to the show might best be gauged by Caitlin Moran's ecstatic review in *The Times*, when she wrote of 'the sheer love of how amazing every minute, every *second* can be, when you are in thrall to something supreme', concluding that 'You will never take David Bowie at Glastonbury, 2000, for granted again.'

Moran's final paragraph also notes: 'O, my God, you will miss him, when he's gone! You will miss him so much it will feel like half the lights go out, and never come back.'[4] A decade and a half later, the painful accuracy of this became inarguable. Yet every writer has an article somewhere that they are ashamed of having written and I am sure that Moran would now regret the earlier piece she wrote in January 1997, on the occasion of Bowie's fiftieth birthday.

It's a remarkably vicious takedown of him, describing him as 'a 50-year-old man with no new ideas, wonky eyes, manky hair, LA teeth and a tartan suit, who talks like an animatronic statue in Piccadilly's Rock Circus'. Moran complains that 'there are a million ways of illustrating how embarrassing Bowie is now; how he has become sunblind from staring into the brilliant white light of the cutting edge; why a man who has spent two decades being a millionaire can't even tell a good joke, let alone sing a good album; and why music journalists, on spotting the name "David Bowie" on a new album, listen to it with rose-tinted ears that they wouldn't lend to any other lost, desperate AOR scene-jumper'.

Although Moran allowed that his heyday was full of great records ('When playing the heroically ruined *Low*, one would finally see the point of Bowie, and indeed come to love him as one loves one's own internal organs'), she briskly dismisses the previous decade as 'ten years of appalling albums' and reserves especial scorn for *Earthling*, writing that 'his involvement with drum'n'bass is simply embarrassing, and brings to mind the dozens of third-rate bands in the late Eighties who noticed the "Madchester" scene was lucrative, and suddenly developed a "dance element" to their music. Bowie's adventures in drum'n'bass are quite clearly normal, sixth-rate Bowie songs with drum'n'bass loops tacked to them — and even *that* stunt isn't original: Everything but the Girl were doing it two years ago.' She concluded, despairingly, 'What is the *point* of David Bowie now?'

Three and a half years later, she could answer her own question with her usual eloquence; the point of David Bowie was to play Glastonbury and sweep up a quarter of a million spectators into his thrall. Yet in the intervening period, Moran had articulated something, bluntly, that many more conservative or adulatory Bowie fans were almost afraid to suggest. *Earthling* was not a good album, any more than *Black Tie White Noise* or *Tin Machine* were. She singled out *Outside* as weak – which seems unfair, but at the time it had not been best served by its tour – and given that *The Buddha of Suburbia* had barely been released, she could be forgiven for not having heard it. In other words, to suggest that Bowie in early 1997 was coasting on former glories was harsh but, in many regards, accurate.

The admiration that I, and millions of others – including, of course, Moran – feel for Bowie is inordinate without being unconditional. To take 1998 as an example, it was a transitionary year. The BowieNet project dominated, but Bowie would also make three films: *Everybody Loves Sunshine, Gunslinger's Revenge* and *Mr Rice's Secret*. None of them could be described as wholly successful. *Everybody Loves Sunshine* was a low-budget British gangster film, mainly filmed on the Isle of Man and featuring Bowie as an old-school criminal who attempts to intervene in a gangland dispute. His presence inevitably gives the film a certain degree of class, but his friendship with the film's star Goldie – who had shortly before released an inexplicably self-indulgent* album, *Saturnz Returns*, on which Bowie had guested – was the major reason for his involvement.

It did not trouble the box office, but then neither did *Gunslinger's Revenge* nor *Mr Rice's Secret*. The latter, at least, represents a change of pace for Bowie. His first children's film since *Labyrinth*, it saw him stepping in for Peter O'Toole as a man who lived to the age of 400, courtesy of a magical elixir: shades of *The Hunger*, but with less vampirism and lesbianism. It is pleasantly executed but without any particular interest, and had it not starred Bowie, it would probably have disappeared into Family Channel purgatory forever. However, because of the presence of its star, it received greater attention after Bowie's death, thanks to a line of dialogue that many took to be a statement of the actor rather than the character:

---

\* To listen to the opening track, 'Mother', which lasts for more than an hour and features Goldie attempting to make sense of his life over a mixture of drum'n'bass beats, a choir and a 30-piece string section, is to be bewildered at the realisation that albums like this were ever recorded and released in the late '90s. It can be blamed, like most of life's ills, on cocaine.

'It's what you do in life that's important, not how much time you have or what you wish you'd done.'

A similar sentiment was expressed in a short film narrated and scored by Bowie, Francis Whately's *In Stillness and in Silence* (*Sacred*), an appreciation of a piece of sculpture by the artist Richard Devereux. It is a haunting two minutes, in which, over various shots of the sculpture, 'Sacred', Bowie recites a prose poem of sorts as a soundtrack of 'Ian Fish, UK Heir' from *The Buddha of Suburbia* plays. As often with Bowie's artistic endeavours, pretension is not dodged entirely ('it washes over you, having a dialogue with something arcane that's maybe not mortal'), but the narration over the conclusion of the film, in which Bowie deals with mortality, is deeply affecting:

'And all at once, the outward appearance of meaning is transcended, and you find yourself struggling to comprehend a deep and formidable mystery: I'm dying. You're dying. Second by second, all is transient. Does it matter? Do I bother? Yes, I do. Life is fantastic. It never ends. It only changes. Flesh, to stone, to flesh, and round, and round.'

There was also another film in 1998, *Velvet Goldmine*, which was to be a less happy experience for Bowie. Written and directed by Todd Haynes, it was a fantasia on glam rock in general and the Ziggy Stardust era in particular, focusing mainly on the character Brian Slade, a bisexual gender-bending singer who fakes his own death at the height of his success, only to return at the film's conclusion as a bland, homogenised mainstream pop star. (Shades here of *The Buddha of Suburbia*.) The presentation of Slade, an avatar for early '70s Bowie, is not a wholly flattering one, but Haynes, then as now a leading figure in American alternative cinema, may still have been surprised at Bowie's contempt for the picture.

Although Haynes was allowed to use various songs from the period on the soundtrack, including the Bowie-produced 'Satellite of Love', Bowie flatly refused to give permission for any of his songs to feature, despite

Haynes asking for the rights to seven, including 'Moonage Daydream', 'All the Young Dudes' and, naturally, the title track. Although the film's producer Michael Stipe sent Bowie a lengthy letter asking him to reconsider his decision, Bowie claimed that he was planning his own Ziggy film and that he was not prepared to cooperate with rival projects until such a picture was made.

The finished film was a commercial failure and remains an intriguing curiosity, if unsuccessful. It looks superb on a limited budget (Sandy Powell's costumes were deservedly Oscar-nominated) and is drenched in allusions to Bowie's heroes, most notably Jean Genet and Oscar Wilde. There are characters based on everyone from Coco Schwab to Lou Reed and Iggy Pop, and Bowie's old mentor Lindsay Kemp has a cameo as, amusingly, a pantomime dame. And when it came to its soundtrack, necessity led to invention: the film led to the temporary formation of a supergroup, the Venus in Furs, which featured Thom Yorke on vocals and Jonny Greenwood and Bernard Butler on guitar, as well as none other than an original figure of the period, Andy Mackay from Roxy Music. This band covered various Roxy songs including '2HB' and 'Ladytron' with predictable class.

What stops *Velvet Goldmine* from being a classic is that its script is erratic, its lead (Jonathan Rhys-Meyers) weak and the general ethos of the film uncertain. It has nothing original to say about Bowie, glam rock or sexual liberation, which means that it's ultimately a superbly mounted *jeu d'esprit* rather than the renegade Bowie biopic that audiences may have wished for (and, indeed, still wish for at the time of writing). And it suffered from Bowie's refusal to endorse it or to give any kind of promotional support to it. Instead, he clearly loathed the screenplay and the finished picture, and was unafraid to bad-mouth the film in interviews.

A couple of months after he saw it, he told the *Big Issue* that 'when I saw the film, I thought the best thing about it was the gay scenes, the only successful part of the film frankly. The film didn't understand how innocent everyone was then about what they were getting into.'[5] A few years later, he was even less guarded. He ridiculed Rhys-Meyers's performance, saying

'I thought he was as charismatic as a glass of water. I thought "Surely I've got more zing than that",' and bemoaned it being made by Haynes, complaining 'that film came from a distinctly American perspective. And glam never happened in America. It was so intrinsically a British thing. You had to understand the idea of these bricklayers and blokes like that who suddenly put on make-up. It was just funny.'[6]

A few months later, Bowie was more measured, perhaps as the result of seeing Haynes's breakthrough picture, 2002's *Far from Heaven*. He called him 'a good filmmaker' and said 'I suspect he'll make great movies', but sighed that *Velvet Goldmine* was 'not the best thing he's ever made'. His objection – understandably – was that Haynes had taken it all too seriously, complete with high-blown allusions to *Citizen Kane*. 'I just found all the characters very colourless. Everybody kind of lacked personality, and the main thing was that if he was trying to catch an essence of glam in London in '72, '73, whatever, he really missed the humour. It was a very serious movie. It was hilarious in those days! A scream! It was really a riot, you know, it was a lot of fun. And this seemed like a cold world he'd painted, dry as a bone, yeah?'[7]

Even as Bowie railed against another imitator, he was in danger of vanishing from sight. In late 1997, he had had a showy cameo on a BBC all-star cover of his old friend Lou Reed's 'Perfect Day' – which he had produced on the *Transformer* album – and managed to make the line 'You made me forget myself' come alive anew, imbuing those five words with a world-weary gravitas that showed up much of the rest of the version for the effortful karaoke it was. Yet he hadn't released any new music since *Earthling*, spending most of 1997 touring the album instead, and the suspicion began to grow that after the creatively hectic – if artistically variable – few years that had produced four separate albums, Bowie was turning into a dilettante, amusing himself with acting, art and the internet, but failing to fulfil his true potential. And then the Rugrats came calling, and everything changed.

In his 2007 memoir *Bowie, Bolan and the Brooklyn Boy*, the producer Tony Visconti describes his falling-out with Bowie as having occurred because the musician hired Nile Rodgers, rather than him, to produce *Let's Dance*, and lacked the guts to tell him the 'devastating' news face to face. In Visconti's recollection, Bowie then reached out to make amends by asking the producer to remix the sound on his Serious Moonlight tour in 1984, which Visconti refused to do, leading to a 14-year fall-out between the two, of which he said, 'I'm not sure what the silence was really all about.' When Bowie finally got back in touch in 1998 to discuss future collaborations, Visconti recounted being moved to tears, saying 'I'm so happy to hear your voice after 14 years, David.'[8]

It makes for an affecting anecdote, but when I asked Visconti about it in 2023, his recollection was subtly different. He said instead that 'David and I never fell out. We gave each other permission to work with other people.'[9] This open creative marriage meant that Bowie worked with Rodgers, Eno and Gabrels, among others, in the intervening 14 years, but Visconti was his most enduring collaborator – and, in the fullness of time, would become little less than his 'representative on earth', giving candid interviews in Bowie's place. Yet this was still considerably in the future and, for the time being, there was a song to record for *The Rugrats Movie*.

Although albums such as *Ziggy Stardust* and *Hunky Dory* had been enhanced by lavish orchestral arrangements, Bowie had largely eschewed strings on his music over the previous decades. A gloopy cover of 'God Only Knows' on *Tonight* was an exception, but even such epic tracks as 'The Motel', 'Strangers When We Meet' and his cover of 'I Know It's Gonna Happen Someday' were devoid of violin-soaked ballast. There was a simple reason for this: Visconti and Mick Ronson had been Bowie's go-to string arrangers. The former was (supposedly) estranged and the latter was dead.

When it came to the song that he composed for the Rugrats, 'Safe in This Sky Life', Bowie had pulled out all the stops to deliver what the film's producer Kathryn Rachtman called 'a proper David Bowie song', which she ambitiously described as 'a little bit of "Space Oddity", '"Heroes"' and "Absolute Beginners" rolled into one'. Bowie and Gabrels composed a sweeping, knowingly self-referential song that was not only miles away from the *Earthling* sound of the previous year, but cried out for a producer and string arranger who could rise to the occasion.

Re-enter Visconti. The trio of musicians worked harmoniously on the song, only for it to be deleted from the film when the scene it was accompanying was cut. Rachtman complained to MTV that '[Bowie] delivered a song far beyond my wildest dreams, and now I can't even use it'. Bowie – who also recorded a cover of John Lennon's 'Mother' for a cancelled tribute album in the same sessions – shrugged and put the song in his capacious vault, muttering 'These things happen.' But the reconciliation with Visconti had been formative, and the subsequent results for his career would be vital.

❡

If *Earthling* is fondly remembered by those who worked on it, *hours*. . . inspires the opposite reaction. Gabrels says bluntly that 'if it didn't go wrong, it certainly went different to what I'd anticipated it would be',[10] and Plati calls it 'really not the same experience I'd had before'.[11] Garson, who did not play on the album but was recruited for the eventual tour, describes it as '*Hunky Dory* but not produced as well . . . It could have been a great album, and it isn't a great album.'[12]

A quarter-century after its release, *hours*. . . is regarded as being in the lower tier of Bowie records, far beneath *Heathen* and *Reality* and the last gasp of a directionless, aimless artist,* before his reunion proper with Visconti rescued him from his torpor. This is a commonplace critical standpoint and it is also somewhat unfair. Yet in order to understand the creative and economic process that led to its creation, it is necessary to skip back decades in time, and meet Tony Defries.

In *Velvet Goldmine*, Eddie Izzard plays a cigar-chomping caricature of an exploitative manager named Jerry Devine. In fact, the role isn't all that

---

* No 'his best since *Scary Monsters*' comparisons this time around, alas.

much of an exaggeration of Defries, who took over Bowie's management in 1970 and proceeded to turn the fey singer-songwriter into a global star, via his company MainMan. He saw Bowie's potential from an early stage, declaring that 'As far as RCA in America are concerned, the young man with red hair sitting at the end of this table is the biggest thing to come out of England since the Beatles. And if we get this right, there's every possibility we will be as big as the Beatles, if not bigger.'[13] He was to be proved correct, but Defries's savviness when it came to Bowie's potential was matched by his own rapaciousness in business. He negotiated a hitherto unheard-of deal, whereby not only would he and Bowie own the copyright to the master recordings, but Defries himself would take 50 per cent of Bowie's earnings on some of his most famous albums, including *Hunky Dory*, *Ziggy Stardust* and *Young Americans*, apparently for perpetuity, after all expenses – including Defries's exorbitant salary and tour costs – had been paid, solely by Bowie.

The relationship between the two soured by 1975, with Defries prudishly disapproving of Bowie's drug use and general licentiousness, and the musician resenting the Mephistophelean contract he had become embroiled in. (In 2003, Bowie commented that 'in the early days, all the greats like Mick Jagger and John Lennon were forever telling me the same thing: don't have anything to do with managers. They were always very adamant about that and, in hindsight, it was good advice. But it was usually just after I'd signed a contract with another one.'[14]) Yet the deal that Bowie struck to leave his contract was a punitive one. Defries continued to retain the royalty rights to albums that he had nothing to do with, up until and including *Scary Monsters*, and this would last forever. Little wonder that Bowie was continually rueful about the deal.

Between 1975 and 1996, Bowie was undeniably a wealthy man, but the occasional penny-counting that some of his collaborators noticed had its origins in the miserable knowledge that a vast amount of his earnings was being siphoned off by a man he despised. Some of his work during this period – not least Sound + Vision – could be seen as undertaken from financial necessity rather than artistic fulfilment, and it is not fanciful to suggest that Bowie's showy reluctance throughout the '90s to revisit his past work arose from the knowledge that Defries would be taking a substantial cut every time he performed one of his most famous songs. He needed a vast cash injection in order to buy out his keeper, and his method of acquiring it was breathtakingly bold and original. Once, he had been the man who sold the world. Now, he would be the man who sold himself.

This does not, however, mean that Bowie marketed himself as the real-life equivalent of Paul, the army officer-turned male prostitute he played so disastrously in *Just a Gigolo*. Instead, he collaborated with the banker David Pullman on an innovative scheme in which he would forgo all the royalties from all the albums that he had recorded prior to 1990 for a period of ten years. Instead, the royalties would be translated into bonds, which were sold for $1,000 apiece and would attract an interest rate of 7.9 per cent for the next decade, before self-liquidating upon expiry. In other words, there was a sell-by date to this scheme, meaning that an investor was betting that one of the world's most famous musicians would continue to be a going concern during the time of their investment. It was a safe bet, or so it appeared, and the upfront amount that Bowie earned from his participation in the deal was considerable, too: $55 million, according to reports.

It is not known how much of the revenue Bowie spent on paying off Defries and reacquiring the rights to his back catalogue – from which, of course, he would not be making any money directly until 2007 – but well-informed reports have indicated that Defries made as much as $27.5 million from the deal,* which he promptly used to buy a lavish estate in Virginia. The cynical might have observed that Virginia was historically popular

---

* Although it's commonly assumed that Bowie did the deal to pay off Defries, Edwards demurs, saying: 'I don't think the decision to do the Bowie Bonds was directly related to his feelings about the Tony Defries deal. Whilst he certainly wasn't a fan of Defries and in general didn't like "managers", I don't think he was in a position where he had to do this deal. It just seemed like an interesting concept. It was very important to him that he retained the ultimate ownership of the songs.'

with the slave owners of the United States. Yet Bowie was, at last, free from the financial tyranny that he had suffered over the past two decades. Unshackled, he took the opportunity to look back, no longer in anger, but with excitement and curiosity.

The origin for much of the music on the *hours. . .* album was an unconventional one. Rather than being inspired by Bowie's travels, or literature, or Eno-led improvisation, it came about from him and Gabrels being asked to compose original songs for a computer game, *Omikron: The Nomad Soul*. As Gabrels recalls, the idea of Bowie albums beginning their lives as something different was not unheard of. 'The second Tin Machine record started out as the soundtrack to a West End production of Steven Berkoff's *West*, and it could well have ended up like that, if Berkoff had been a bit less Berkoff. Then the songs were angled towards being part of a George Miller film, *The Crossing*,\* which was not the kind of George Miller film we should have been doing. We should have been doing *Mad Max*.'[15]

Therefore, it did not come as a huge surprise that, in early 1998, Gabrels received a call from Bowie. 'David asked me to come to this meeting with this video games company Eidos, about doing songs for a game for them. David, Iman and I were there, and as the conversation progressed, we ended up saying "Yeah, we could do that. We could do all the instrumental music." I have a tendency to say yes and then figure out how the fuck I'm going to do it. But I always felt safe about that with David, because it always helps to have David Bowie take the heat if it doesn't work. But then it was becoming this other thing and I started to wonder *What happens if it all goes wrong?*'[16]

The answer would be the eventual dissolution of their artistic partnership, but at the inception of the *Omikron* project, everything seemed possible. Instead, with Gabrels and Bowie already having travelled to

---

\* Presumably what became the Nick Nolte–Susan Sarandon medical drama *Lorenzo's Oil*. Miller kept something of the rock ethos in the picture; the musician and actor Kathleen Wilhoite has a leading role, and the score was composed by the Police drummer Stewart Copeland.

Bermuda to work on new music, there were the bones of a new album, and it seemed a simple case of using *Omikron* as a testing ground for the songs, all at Eidos's expense. At the time, the company was flush with cash thanks to the success of the *Tomb Raider* games, so offering Bowie and Gabrels artistic leeway was straightforward.* Yet Gabrels was chafing at being the sideman. 'I'd put one solo record out and I was working on the next one. What fed into my dissatisfaction with my situation was having done records of my own and worked with musicians of my choosing and made all the final decisions myself. I had gotten a taste of what it was like to be the artist as opposed to being one of the guys.'[17] Change had to come and the result would be significant creative tension.

Mark Plati describes the situation with an outsider's detachment. 'Reeves and David had written a bunch of songs together, more acoustic songs, and went to England to try to record them, but they weren't happy with them. Then the idea was to put the songs in *Omikron*, and then David decided that he could do the video game *and* an album.'[18] Gabrels felt existentially dissatisfied. 'I was willing to work with David on what became *hours*. . ., but it was not intended to be the soundtrack for a video game. It was meant to be a record, like our previous records. Then the direction moved away from what I wanted it to be, but it was David's record, not my record. I was writing songs with my friend David, which he's asked me to co-produce, and I should be happy with that. But what I feel went wrong with that album was that it got misunderstood as being the soundtrack for *Omikron* when, in fact, it was it was an album that got used as the soundtrack.'[19]

If this has shades of *The Buddha of Suburbia* situation, then at least *hours*. . . was a far higher-profile endeavour than *Omikron*, which was a financial flop. The most interesting feature of the game is the way in which Bowie, Gabrels and Iman appear as characters that can be interacted with, albeit to a limited extent. Still, it was hardly *Tomb Raider* and was swiftly

---

* The other musicians mooted for the project included Massive Attack and Björk.

forgotten, meaning that *hours*. . . should have been able to stand on its own merits as an album. Yet by the time that Plati had been recruited to work on the songs in Looking Glass Studios in New York, it was apparent that something had gone awry in the process. As he says, 'it was a kind of push-pull between David and Reeves about how electronic they should be; should it be *Earthling* part two?' The answer was 'definitely not'. Instead, it was a largely acoustic album that nodded towards *Hunky Dory*, with songs that attempted to marry the tremulous naivete of that record with something more world-weary and adult. Throw in reflections on anything from the internet to religion, and you have an album that, conceptually, was rich in the kind of intellectualism that Bowie had been straining for over the past decade.

*hours*. . . should have been a masterpiece. It *could* have been a masterpiece. Plati even suggests, half-jokingly, that 'there's another version of *hours*. . . that I don't think I've ever heard since it's just locked up away. But I have no idea what that sounds like. It was mixed, and then mixed again, because we were like "Oh, it's not working this way".' Although he describes the recording process as being fun and harmonious, with Bowie again being an open-minded and playful collaborator, Gabrels suggests that it was riddled with arguments over the recording budget (hence, presumably, the decision to record what should have been string parts with synths, which makes it sound oddly dated) and even the instrumentation.

At one point, Plati was playing fretless bass, which Bowie was unconvinced by but which Gabrels believed had a pleasingly funky aspect to it. What began as a civilised discussion, in front of none other than Nancy Berry, the Virgin vice-chairman, soon escalated into a screaming argument, with Bowie shouting, 'You're a white guy from the suburbs! You're not funky!' Gabrels replied, 'OK, I understand. Because when I want to know what funky is, I'll ask a 52-year-old white Englishman from Brixton', before walking away. As he says, it was the beginning of the end of their artistic partnership. 'It was at that point that I knew I was leaving. I always knew when the emperor was naked, but I never told anybody. I would raise an eyebrow at him and he'd know that his secret was always safe with me. But for the first time, I felt that he was pulling rank and conning me. And that was the point I decided to leave. I felt pretty burnt out.'[20]

What made Gabrels's decision to leave all the more poignant is that, lyrically, the album is largely about his and Bowie's relationship, told from the perspective of Bowie. As he says, 'David has said that the lyrics on *hours*. . . were biographical, but not autobiographical. He says "I'm writing from the point of view of someone close to me." So if that is true, and that's what other people have told me, then he was putting himself in my shoes. *hours*. . . is full of stuff like that, and that's a thing that has blown my mind, years later.'[21]

Listened to from this perspective, many of the songs, most notably the excellent 'Something in the Air' and 'Survive', are no longer about romantic relationships, but intense friendships that have reached the end of their viability. It is an album suffused with sadness and a sense of loss that most critics either ignored or put down to Bowie in his pre-millennial mode, musing on what the 2000s held for mankind, without considering that its lyrical origins were far simpler than they had imagined. The same would later be true of *Blackstar*.

Not that it's solely about Gabrels. The album's rockiest song, 'The Pretty Things Are Going to Hell', simultaneously alludes to Bowie's 'Oh! You Pretty Things' and the Stooges' 'Your Pretty Face Is Going to Hell'. Lyrically, it refers to one of Bowie's lifelong literary idols, Evelyn Waugh, and his novel *Vile Bodies*, which was the basis for 'Aladdin Sane' and would again be alluded to on 'How Does the Grass Grow?' on *The Next Day*. As Bowie said of Waugh's 'bright young things', 'I think their day is numbered. So I thought, *Well, let's close them off*. They wore it well but they did wear themselves out . . . There's not much room for that now. It's a very serious little world.'[22]

Fittingly, *hours*. . . is a serious album, made by a serious man. The cover alone, with its pietà-inspired artwork of a long-haired Bowie cradling his short-haired *Earthling* persona, was rich in allusion, albeit spoilt by some fussy, immediately dated typography and a sense of undue self-importance that may have put record purchasers off. It was perhaps just as well that one mooted cover, of Bowie burning on a crucifix, was not used (it can instead be seen on the inside artwork), as this would have probably excited yawns, rather than controversy – although he would return to this concept in the video of 'The Next Day'.

Yet blasphemy was not his intention so much as a reckoning with immortality. Garson calls 'Seven', a Bowie–Gabrels co-write, 'an amazing song . . . an absolute cast-iron masterpiece, but it needed better production, someone like Visconti or Ken Scott working on it'.[23] Lyrically and musically, it's in a different league to anything else on *hours. . .*, with one of Bowie's most dramatic lines ('The gods forgot they made me, so I forgot them too'), harking back to 'Word on a Wing', but with agnostic despair rather than religious desperation as its guiding principle. It's a highlight of a fascinating, frustrating album that, had it been recorded under different circumstances, would now be regarded as one of Bowie's most interesting achievements, rather than a flawed endeavour that did little for his commercial or critical standing.

*hours. . .* was Bowie's first album to be released under the auspices of BowieNet; predictably enough, he went all out in cross-promotion. Firstly, there had been the elaborate competition to write the lyrics of 'What's Really Happening', and now each song was teased out with 45-second snippets on his website, before the entire album was available for download on 21 September 1999, a fortnight before it was available in the shops: the first major record to be available in digital format. 'I am hopeful that this small step will lead to greater steps by myself and others,' said Bowie, 'ultimately giving consumers greater choices and easier access to the music they enjoy.' Even as record chains fulminated about the unfairness of this as a commercial strategy, it proved that Bowie could be a clear-sighted pioneer about the future of music's distribution, even if the album he was releasing this way could not match its marketing chutzpah with musical innovation.

When *hours. . .* was released, Bowie tried a variety of different approaches to his usual publicity juggernaut. There would be no elaborate tour, no blitzkrieg of interviews, but instead he would play a few promotional gigs in small venues, as well as a six-song set at the NetAid concert at Wembley Stadium on 9 October. It was here that he resurrected various songs that had not been heard live in a decade or longer, including 'Life on Mars', 'Rebel Rebel' and 'Drive-In Saturday', delighting an audience who remembered his defiant refusal to play his old songs again. That, like so many other edicts, had long since been binned, but there was no apology, no grand explanation for his change of heart. In one of the interviews that he did grant, to David Quantick in *Q*, Bowie typically made a joke out of it. 'Why didn't I stay with the *Young Americans* sound?! I could still be doing that. Ooh, I wouldn't half be unhappy.'

He also said of his songs: 'I think people have – quite rightly – gotten used to interpreting the lyrics in their own way. I am only the person the greatest number of people believe that I am. So little of it has anything to do with me, so I just have to do the best I can with what I've got – knowing that it has a complete second life by the time it leaves me.'[24] Yet if he was expecting millions of people to take interest in the lyrics of *hours. . .*, he would only have been disappointed. Despite generally bland reviews, commercially it performed reasonably well in the UK, reaching number five in the charts – his highest placing since *Black Tie White Noise* – but it was a complete flop in the US, reaching an unimpressive 47 in the *Billboard* chart: his weakest result since *Hunky Dory*, suggesting that Bowie's love affair with the US was in danger of becoming unrequited.

It did not help that one of the album's least inspiring songs, the soporific 'Thursday's Child', was unaccountably released as its lead single, rather than the more intense 'The Pretty Things Are Going to Hell'. Gabrels calls it 'a lousy choice', one that was made over Nancy Berry and American radio's better instincts. The guitarist was preparing to quit. After half-heartedly playing a couple of final gigs with him, on *VH1 Storytellers* and for the BBC's *Top of the Pops*, Gabrels rang Bowie and asked if the two could talk. They then met at the studio and, over the course of their conversation, the artistic bond dissolved.

Gabrels recalled: 'I said "It's been 13 years and I couldn't be more proud of what we did. Everything that we did means a lot to me and our relationship means everything to me. But I need to leave, because I don't have anything new after this much time." We weren't finding anything new together, and there wasn't even a shitty experience to bring us back. We were just in each other's pockets constantly. And he was talking about starting something, his own version of Warhol's Factory. I could just see myself becoming 'the guy', with David saying, of each song, "Oh, make me three of those, one keyboard-based, one guitar-based and one percussion-based', and then him putting his name on it, giving it that "vitamin D". It may have been my own paranoia at that point, but I just didn't want that.'[25]

Bowie was sanguine and, publicly at least, always made a point of acknowledging Gabrels's contributions to the music that they made together. It may, or may not, be coincidental – a legacy of his Defries scourging, perhaps – that from the Glastonbury performance onwards, Bowie played virtually none of the songs that he had co-written with Gabrels in concert, preferring to concentrate on earlier and later music. The likes of 'Seven', 'The Pretty Things Are Going to Hell' and most of the songs on *Earthling* and *Outside* received highly infrequent outings. As with many other Bowie collaborators, once you left the inner sanctum, you were a part of his history: seldom loathed, but now surplus to requirements.

In any case, Gabrels now says that he regrets the abrupt manner of his departure, even as he reflects that 'I'm the only guy who ever quit working with Bowie, rather than being fired'. He says, 'I wish I had handled it differently. Today, I have evolved emotionally enough that I would have would have been more demonstrative of how much I appreciated the previous fourteen years. And I think I might have understood that I was closer to him than I realised. I remember going to his house and there was a table where he had pictures of his close family and friends. And there he was with Iman, and Coco, and Duncan, and Duncan's nanny Marion [Skene]. There was a picture of Marion siting in a Charles Rennie Mackintosh chair and then, at the other end of the table, he had a photograph of me sitting in exactly the same chair in almost exactly the same position, taken probably five years apart. It was proof then that he regarded me as not just a colleague, but a friend, and I regret I can't thank him for that, and everything, now.'[26]

If 1999 had had its share of personal and professional disappointments for Bowie, 2000 proved to be an *annus mirabilis*. The new millennium began with the happy realisation that, after years of trying – involving, supposedly, gruelling IVF treatments – Iman was now pregnant with their daughter, Alexandria 'Lexi' Jones. The news was announced on 13 February and Bowie put out a statement saying: 'It's been a long and patient wait for our baby but both Iman and I wanted the circumstances to be absolutely right.' She would be born on 15 August, a happy occurrence that would lead to her father reassessing his life, as well as reflecting on his mortality; he had already marked the news of the pregnancy by quitting a lifelong smoking habit.*

Bowie might have been forgiven for taking 2000 off, and, initially, this may have been his plan. But there was the small matter of the Glastonbury Festival looming in front of him, an event that he did not want to perform at, and which the organiser did not want him at. How he came to perform the iconic gig of the second half of his career is a fascinating story that combines high art, low chicanery, opportunism, luck and plain old-fashioned brilliance. As Edwards describes it, 'I wouldn't quite describe it as "underhand machinations": more like "accidental brilliance". . .'[27]

---

* Before – and, alas, after – this, Bowie was a committed smoker. Hanif Kureishi recounted the story of how, in 1994, 'Paul McKenna, who was a pal, tried to hypnotise Bowie into quitting smoking, but he clearly didn't want to be hypnotised and didn't want to quit, but he pretended for Paul. After, I remember him standing on the steps of my house, begging me to get him some fags. "Can't we go together?" I suggested. "But I can't go anywhere," he said, gesturing at Shepherd's Bush.'

Although there was no formal tour for *hours. . .*, Bowie performed several intimate gigs towards the end of 1999 in capital cities including Copenhagen, Paris and London. He played at the now-demolished Astoria in the latter, a 2,000-person venue in the centre of the city, on 2 December, where one of the invited guests was Michael Eavis. Eavis had a degree of history with Bowie, who had played the festival back in 1971, when it was known as Glastonbury Fayre and was a far more chaotic, bohemian event than it later became. Bowie did not appear until 5am, after being scheduled to play the previous evening, and performed a short, rapturously received set that featured many of the songs from *Hunky Dory* including 'Changes', 'Quicksand' and 'Kooks', although neither his biggest hit to date, 'Space Oddity', nor 'Life on Mars' featured. He later said of his appearance that '[the crowd] awoke benignly enough and gave me much encouragement as I fumbled through about nine songs. I accompanied myself on poorly played guitar and an even worse outing on a Woolworth's electric organ.'[28]

Matters had changed somewhat in the intervening three decades, and so Eavis came to the Astoria with an attitude of interest and expectation. This was soon dispelled by the set that Bowie played. It may have started with a stripped-back version of 'Life on Mars', with Mike Garson on piano, but the setlist then combined songs from *hours. . .* with more obscure tracks from earlier in his career, including 'Cracked Actor' and 'Repetition'. This would have been manna for committed fans but did not necessarily suggest that Bowie was performing at the level of a Glastonbury headliner. As Edwards tactfully puts it, 'my understanding was that Michael Eavis did indeed leave the Astoria gig half way through'.* Bowie himself regarded the idea of headlining the festival as somewhat retrograde. 'David also wasn't in any great hurry to do a festival like Glastonbury,' explains Edwards, 'as he was enjoying playing the new material and knew that if he headlined the event,

---

* A rumour has persisted that Bowie reinterpreted his songs as drum'n'bass numbers, but my editor, who was present, assures me that this is false.

he'd need to perform quite a few greatest hits.'[29] It is hard to imagine hundreds of thousands of people going wild for 'Thursday's Child'.

Yet business was business, and so Edwards idly trailed a story to the *Sunday Times* that suggested that Glastonbury would be interested in having Bowie perform. This is what public relations professionals call 'a punt', and what those not in that hallowed industry would describe as 'a lie'. Edwards now recalls that 'we leaked something to the *Sunday Times* to try and get speculation about the performance going, hoping it would generate interest. We hadn't anticipated how big the paper would go with it and, secondly, the seismic reaction from the public.' The headline simply said 'Bowie to Headline Glasto'. As Edwards observed, 'the Glastonbury ticket office was inundated with ticket enquiries like never before in their history'.

The last time Bowie had played Glastonbury, there had been 2,000 festival-goers, most not unused to recreational drugs, and backstage catering was nothing more glamorous than Eavis's kitchen, where performers were fed milk and eggs. This was an altogether different proposition. Edwards wrote in his memoir that, 'after a few days, neither [my colleague] Julian Stockton or I had heard from David and we were worried that he was annoyed. Then we got a message from him: "You're very naughty boys. Don't ever do that again. Well done."'[30]

Arrangements were made for Bowie to headline the final night of the 2000 festival and he assembled a live band that would include many recent collaborators including Mark Plati, who served as bandleader and musical director,* Gail Ann Dorsey, Garson and Sterling Campbell, as well as a return by his long-standing sideman and lead guitarist Earl Slick, who had previously appeared on the *Station to Station* and *Young Americans* albums, as well as on the Serious Midnight tour in 1983. Slick was the antithesis of the professorial Gabrels; he was not up on stage to showboat, but to support.

---

* In Plati's recollection, Bowie sold him the job by saying 'It's like being a producer but you're on the bus. And you can't sack anybody.' It would be the first time that anyone combined the roles of producer and musician for him since Visconti in 1970.

As he put it in an interview, 'You've got to look at it, like, it's David Bowie's name on the marquee. No matter how much we were mates onstage . . . the bottom line is, he was the company and I was the employee.'[31] This humility would serve him well professionally.*

Now that Bowie was committed to perform at Glastonbury, the planning began early. Rehearsals commenced at the end of March in New York, and three preview shows were booked in at the Roseland Ballroom in the city for mid-June. Campbell recalls that the band dynamic was, by now, fully cohesive. 'We got the right cast. This group felt tighter, and everyone gelled together. At that time, we just felt really comfortable. We had a little *Guardians of the Galaxy* dynamic going on because everybody was a character. It was a great time, with great energy, and I think David really enjoyed making music.'[32]

Adding to the sense of anticipation and build-up, Bowie was asked to keep a diary of preparations for the gig by *Time Out*. When *Q* had asked for something similar during the recording of *Outside*, he had obfuscated and produced something near-incomprehensible from the perspective of the album's protagonist Nathan Adler. Now, half a decade later, he was more straightforward and alluded to his unease about playing the festival: 'I find my present situation more than a little confusing actually, as I really don't remember why I agreed to close this year's Glastonbury Festival in the first place. It couldn't be more inconvenient in a way, now knowing that our pregnancy is well and truly for real. It means losing a clutch of days away from home. Days that I get more and more precious over.' He then set out his mission statement for the gig, alluding to the apparent retirement of

---

*    Slick had spent much of the '90s working in that least rock 'n' roll profession: timeshare sales. Bowie alluded to these misspent years by writing that 'the mystery man to all of us was Earl Slick. He seemed to have been swallowed up by the hills and time for many years. I came across him again when I stumbled into his website a few months ago. He had indeed been going through an almost reclusive period in his life but, oh my, when he started playing at that first day's rehearsal, it was clear that he is still all fire.'

his previous hits. 'Facing only a one-off show this year, I can safely gird up my loins, stand my ground and with steel like resolve, change horses midstream. Big, well-known songs shall litter the field this year at Glastonbury. Well, with a couple of quirks of course.'[33]

He offered similar apparent candour in subsequent weeks, whether it was his refusal to play 'Space Oddity' ('I can't face doing that one again yet . . . It is still extremely hard for me to sing songs that I no longer enjoy because of my over-familiarity with them'[34]), the wardrobe that he would be wearing on the night or how long the setlist would be. Yet in music, as in life, things go awry. Plati had fractured both of his elbows five weeks before the show and knew that there were several other musicians who would have killed to be in his position. Bowie briskly asked him 'What's your prognosis?' and when Plati replied that he would be able to play Glastonbury if he went through intensive physical therapy, nodded and regarded the matter as settled. Plati – who says that he was making 'awful faces' throughout rehearsal 'because I was in so much pain' – could not contemplate missing the gig. 'Now, it seems a little bit funny that I was playing guitar with a broken arm. But you're not gonna miss Glastonbury. What's the alternative? It hurts too much *not* to play the biggest show ever.'

Another, potentially more serious issue was that Bowie had expected to play a three-hour, career-spanning set, but was peremptorily informed before the festival that this was impossible. 'What crap news!' he wrote in his diary. 'I had my production manager phone England yesterday to ascertain how late into the following morning we could play at Glastonbury, only to find that if I dare cross the curfew mark, the promoter will be fined twenty thousand pounds a MINUTE if, that is, we survive the probability of the plug being pulled at the bewitching hour. This means I have to drastically cut my set by something like 12 songs. What a hopeless task. We love everything!'[35] 'Always Crashing in the Same Car' vanished, and nothing from *hours*. . . or *Black Tie White Noise* would make the cut, although he did perform 'Little Wonder' and 'I'm Afraid of Americans' from *Earthling* and 'Hallo Spaceboy' from *Outside*.

It is unclear whether Bowie ever seriously considered pulling out as a result of this, but instead he decided to make the best of the situation. The band would reconvene in the studio later that year, as well as immortalising most of the songs they played at Glastonbury in the BBC Radio Theatre in London two days after the show. The *Toy* sessions would be a time of creative fulfilment and excitement for Bowie, as well as the most obvious revisitation of his past to date, but he was coy about what they would involve, writing only that 'I've pulled together a selection of songs from a somewhat unusual reservoir and booked time in a studio. I still get really elated by the spontaneous event and cannot wait to sit in a claustrophobic space with seven other energetic people and sing till my tits drop off.'[36]

As he prepared for Glastonbury, Bowie struck an excited note in his final *Time Out* diary, writing: 'I can't resist the idea of encouraging all those slightly dazed and glazed peeps to give their voices full throttle to a chorus or two of a song or three. Just one last time. Oops! I'll never say "never again", again. Possibly.'[37] There was one more near-disaster in store: Bowie, who prided himself on never cancelling concerts, was unable to perform the second planned Roseland Ballroom show on 17 June, thanks to a case of laryngitis. Thankfully, it proved to be a 24-hour affliction, and he was back on stage for an invited audience of BowieNetters on 19 June, who were privileged enough to see the concert for free.

When Bowie arrived at the festival on 25 June to play the Pyramid Stage, he was atypically jittery.* The audience was considerably younger than his usual fans, and the atmosphere on site was rowdy and undisciplined, not least because gatecrashers had swelled the permitted numbers

---

* Possibly as a result of these nerves, he refused to allow permission for the entire show to be broadcast on the BBC, as was customary for headline acts. The BBC and those around him – including Alan Edwards – wanted his triumphant return to be shown in its glory, but Bowie only agreed to the first three songs being broadcast: 'Wild is the Wind', 'China Girl' and 'Changes'. All fine songs, beautifully performed, but an experience rather like going to The Ritz for dinner and having to leave after the amuse-bouche. In the end, a few more songs, including 'Life on Mars' and '"Heroes"' were broadcast, but the full gig was only commercially released in November 2018.

of 100,000 to around 250,000. Bowie was playing after the once-popular Scottish indie band Travis and modish electronic duo Chemical Brothers had headlined the previous nights, and he would be performing at the same time as the more upbeat act Basement Jaxx, who were headlining the Other Stage. He donned a remarkable outfit of Alexander McQueen frock coat and Oxford bags – one wag observed that his flowing hair seemed to be swept to the side in the manner of the film star Veronica Lake – which was a conscious visual homage to his previous appearance. Not that the vast majority of the audience cared: they wanted to be entertained, not edified.

'It was magical,' recalls Garson, 'but it could easily have gone wrong. When he walked out into the audience and saw a quarter of a million people, he got nervous. And he turned to me and said "Go and warm up the audience". I walk out there and I'm thinking "They don't want to see *me*." And then here's the wild thing. I sit down at the keyboard; no sound comes out. So there's 100 engineers plugging things in. It turns out I had shut the volume off. So imagine if we went out with a band, and we sit down and there's no piano. It would have ruined the whole show because you don't start on the right foot. You get thrown off, and you get depressed for the next two hours. So it was a blessing. And then he said "Play 'Greensleeves' for them", and so I play "Greensleeves", you know?'[38]

It was a surreal start to a legendary gig, but the next two hours saw Bowie at his artistic peak. He was usually a contained, even reserved presence on stage, but at one point he forgot himself sufficiently to enthuse 'This is so cool for us, it really is cool. I fucking love it!'* It may have been a greatest hits set, but there were curveballs – the show began with, of all

---

* Interestingly, Kureishi suggested that Bowie was miserable on the night and then it was not until afterwards that he realised what a success it had been. 'His voice was failing, he had to do a gig the next day at the BBC, and he was really worried. I remember going out and standing at the side of the stage, and the sound was terrible and it was freezing. As soon as it was finished, he rushed offstage, grabbed Duncan and then got in the car and went straight to bed. He hated it . . . It was incredible to me that someone could be so nervous, and yet still have the balls to go out there and make it all work.'

things, his 1976 cover of 'Wild is the Wind', and many of the best-known songs, such as 'Let's Dance', were subtly rearranged, not to Bob Dylan levels of obscurity, but enough to keep the audience guessing as to what they were listening to before the inevitable, vast chorus exploded. Plati says 'it was one of those times where you don't really believe you're doing this. At one point I'm standing next to Slick and he'd been real mellow, real conservative, right? Because he's just getting back into the groove, and I don't think he wants to push it too much. And then we start 'Station to Station', he lights up a cigarette, and starts bringing it. I'm like, "Oh, man. Earl's back. He's here."'[39]

The intense rendition of 'Station to Station' was, indeed, one of the evening's many triumphs, but virtually every song was performed and sung about as well as they had ever been. A particular highlight came with Bowie's Queen collaboration 'Under Pressure', in which Dorsey took over the Freddie Mercury vocal part: an intimidating challenge, to put it mildly. As she says, 'Freddie Mercury is the greatest performer I've ever seen in my life. I saw all the early Queen concerts. They're my favourite band. So I'd go into this trance and I would look up at the lights and I would think, *Freddie, Freddie, Freddie . . .* I have to give everything no matter what. This is the moment when I have to remember whose shoes I'm stepping into, and how much Freddie meant to me. So to be connected with that legacy on top of Bowie – talk about a challenge! So obviously David had a lot of faith in me and I am more grateful to him for that than anything else, for how he made me feel.'[40]

Caitlin Moran's adulation of the concert was widely shared, although one anonymous insider close to Bowie remarks that many music critics, believing that the show would be a lethargic trudge through half-forgotten songs, either left before he performed or went to see Basement Jaxx instead, who suffered the ignominy of playing to a half-empty field. The career-defining set was therefore not as widely reviewed as might be expected, although the *NME* praised 'the breadth and intent of this fantastic perform-ance' and Eavis, always a generous man prone to think and say the best of his acts, explained that Bowie had 'promised me the show of a lifetime, and he delivered it'.[41] Nevertheless, word of mouth from the enthusiastic gig-goers spread, and the performance was, and is, rightly venerated as an artist at the peak of his considerable powers.

Oh, how we would miss him when he was gone.

# TOY, 9/11 AND *HEATHEN*

## 'Everything has changed'

*'It just wasn't a sunny day anymore'*

Bowie performing at his Meltdown festival on London's
South Bank in support of *Heathen*, June 2002.
Chris Lopez/Getty

In *The Consolation of Philosophy*, Boethius writes that 'Ill fortune is better for men than good. When fortune smiles, she is always false. But when she is inconstant and whimsical, she shows her true self.' This could be applied to the ever-fickle music industry, doubly. Since the formation of Tin Machine, Bowie had observed his public standing oscillate between approval and ridicule without any apparent reason. Mediocre albums were praised to the skies, masterpieces ignored or misunderstood, and the likes of Caitlin Moran could suggest in 1997 that he was a forgotten relic of a former era before heralding him three and a half years later as nothing less than the ultimate rock 'n' roll messiah, sent down to Worthy Farm to show mankind how it's done.

Bowie was, in any case, a veteran of the business of more than three decades' standing and able to observe the vagaries of fashion with appropriately wry detachment. Yet when he had finished his Glastonbury performance and was able to realise that it really had been a considerable triumph rather than the disaster that he had feared, he was keen to take advantage of the momentum that he had accrued in his career. Firstly, there was the BBC Radio Theatre's performance on 27 June 2000, where he was able to play many of the songs that his band had rehearsed but had been unable to perform because of time constraints, including 'Always Crashing in the Same Car' and 'Seven'. Then, a couple of weeks after Glastonbury, Bowie reassembled his band and headed to two New York studios, his usual haunts of Looking Glass and Sear Sound, in order to record a new album that would be, in his own description, 'not so much a *Pin Ups II* as an *Up Date I*'. He had casually announced it in a BowieNet chat on 23 December 1999 – 'another exciting immediate project, Mark Plati and I will remake (with the band) a whole bunch of those '60s chestnuts' – and now its hour was at hand.

One of Bowie's most ephemeral '70s records is his 1973 album *Pin Ups*, a hastily recorded collection of covers that is most fondly remembered for its inclusion of the Merseys' 'Sorrow', which takes the original, a slice of tuneful but ordinary Merseybeat pop, and turns it into an elegant, string-laced piece that could easily have found a home on *Hunky Dory*. Since then, Bowie had often recorded covers on his albums, reaching an apotheosis on *Black Tie White Noise* where three of its twelve songs had been written by someone else; this would later be equalled on *Heathen*. Yet his intention with his latest work, which Bowie entitled *Toy*, was simultaneously self-regarding and conceptually brilliant. Rather than produce another album of covers of others' work, Bowie would cover his own songs from the late '60s with his newly assembled band and then Visconti would be drafted in to provide string arrangements where appropriate.

The rationale was clear. After spending the '90s fighting the influence of his past, Bowie had not only made peace with it, but was embracing it afresh, albeit entirely on his own terms. Anyone could cover 'The Man Who Sold the World' or "Heroes" or any of his other most famous songs, but the likes of 'The London Boys' and 'I Dig Everything' – both of which had been performed at the BBC – had been neglected throughout Bowie's later career, doomed to near-obscurity by their release on his earliest records.

Plati suggests that the impetus for *Toy* may have come from, of all people, Def Leppard's lead singer Joe Elliott. He came backstage after the NetAid gig at Wembley in October 1999 and, in Plati's recollection, said, '"Wow, it was great. You should do a whole record of those early songs." I don't know if that had any influence, a ton of influence or if David was already thinking something like that, but anyway, around December 1999, he called me to say "I want to do this '60s album, where we take these tunes and play them with our current band, and just kind of whack it out. And I want you to produce it with me."'[1] With Gabrels departed, and Visconti's contributions limited to string arranging, Plati now stepped up into the role of Bowie's key lieutenant and recording began with a spirit of excitement and spontaneity dominating.

'We went right in and aimed to make something live in the studio, to take and run with that. We'd do two or three takes and we'd have it, so that would be it. I'd never done that before. Records weren't made like that in the '90s. Either you're recorded live at a show, or you're in a studio, doing things piecemeal. We all had a really good time with *Toy*. It was such a fun record to play and to work on.' He brought in musicians he knew well and thrived on the spirit of spontaneity that Bowie engendered. 'The band was really just Sterling on drums, me on bass and guitars, and Lisa Germano on violin. It was as if I was saying "Oh, try this person, and here's why." And it all worked out great.'[2]

Nonetheless, Gabrels's departure had left a vacancy for a guitarist, which would be mainly filled by Earl Slick. However, to bolster the album's sound, Plati contacted his friend Gerry Leonard, the Irishman who would go on to become one of Bowie's key collaborators. As Leonard recalls, 'Mark came to me one fateful night, and said, "Would you like to play on a David Bowie record?" And I was like, "Are you kidding me? Of course, I want to play." So I ended up back in my flat in Brooklyn at 1am with this David Bowie song, which was kind of spooky. I did my thing and brought it back in the next day. David loved it and kept my playing on the track. And so I said "Can I meet him?" I did and he was smiling, and very, very warm. He had this golden glow about him.'[3]

Leonard's impression of Bowie may well have been coloured by the news that, on 15 August 2000, Iman gave birth to Alexandria – or Lexi – an event that was inevitably reported in *Hello!* magazine with a September photoshoot of the happy couple at home with their new baby. The pair were interviewed and Bowie seemed every bit the ecstatic father. 'It is amazing how a new child can refocus one's direction seconds after its birth. Everything falls into a feeling of "rightness". I have huge waves of parental love and protection pouring from me.' Lexi was temporarily housed in Bowie's library which became a substitute nursery – 'If Alex gets at all restless during the night, she has access to a few hundred really excellent books' – and Bowie stuck to the party line about his personal happiness, saying of his marriage: 'We've always been very close, but if it's possible, we've been drawn even closer. There's a joy or a contentment that's almost palpable to both of us. Overnight, our lives have been enriched beyond belief.'[4]

Most of the interview is pleasant but determinedly unrevealing: Bowie might have been any other middle-aged father, wryly mixing delight at the new arrival with a realisation that he was not as young as he once was. Yet the most interesting comment came not from him, but from Iman. Asked what knowledge she would hope to impart to her daughter, she replied: 'I think I would tell her to look for the satisfaction quota in whatever she chooses to do. To not do things merely to please other people, but to satisfy her own inner needs.'[5] Had she been giving her husband the same advice, he would undoubtedly have taken it. *Toy* was nothing if not an exercise in self-fulfilment, albeit conceived and executed at a sufficiently high artistic level to remove any taint of mere self-indulgence.

Bowie took two months away from recording to spend time with Lexi, but his commitment to his new album was just as absolute as his love for his new baby. Mike Garson, who was present at the recording, was, along with Slick, one of the only people who had known Bowie throughout his career and observed the change with affection. 'You look at the guy when he's in his early twenties and you say, "What can we do now?" You hear his voice now? He's singing it lower and different. Then I ask "What can I bring to this party that is not karaoke?" I love that album and I love the studio we made it at.' Garson was also sufficiently trusted to be with Bowie when the studio bravado dissipated and the private man took over. 'I remember specifically, when we finished one of the days of recording, he asked me to walk him downstairs over to his car that was going to take him home because he didn't want to be alone without any of his bodyguards. And so you would see the fragility and the vulnerability of the guy.'[6]

The only potential drawback with *Toy* from an artistic perspective was that, as Garson pithily describes it, 'some of the other songs were a little stupid, but some of them were just great'.[7] While there was no question of revisiting 'The Laughing Gnome', Bowie sat his band down and replayed the primitive '60s demos as if they had been recorded the previous day, before setting about recording the songs afresh. How much one enjoys the 2000-era versions of numbers such as 'Silly Boy Blue' and 'You've Got a

Habit of Leaving' depends firstly on your appreciation for the band line-up that Bowie was using at the time; there is a distinct sound showcased here which anticipates *Heathen* and *Reality*, unsurprisingly given the consistency of the personnel across all three albums.* Secondly, it depends how much you liked the songs in the first place. Only the most committed Bowie admirer would seriously argue that most of the music on *Toy* is a fine example of neglected genius that desperately needed to be brought back in this fashion. Instead, it's a fascinating exercise in revisiting one's past that makes for an engaging listen – I'd rather spend a day with *Toy* than *Earthling* or *Black Tie White Noise* – without making a serious case for their enduring qualities.

There were, of course, exceptions. The most successful of the older songs was Bowie's 'Conversation Piece' from 1969, which was now revamped with a beautiful Visconti string arrangement based on Garson's piano part. The latter calls the song 'one of my favourite pieces he ever wrote',[8] while Dorsey, who played on the album, describes it as 'a beautiful, truly lovely song'.[9] Its lyric is ambiguous; it seems to channel Thomas Mann in its depiction of a lonely intellectual, either a writer or academic, who lives above a shop. His only acquaintance of any note is the Austrian grocer, who 'jokes about his broken English' and tries to befriend him, but the song's protagonist bemoans that 'For all my years of reading conversation / [I] stand without a word to say'. It ends, heartbreakingly, with his reflection that 'I can't see the water through the tears in my eyes'. Its original recording was accomplished for a twenty-two-year-old, but this remake is essential.

The other oddity is that, for whatever reason, Bowie decided to include some newly written songs on the album, which, in retrospect, were clearly intended as a bridge between *hours. . .* and *Heathen*. His only comment on them was that they were written in conscious pastiche of how they might have been composed in the '60s and they could take their chances along

---

*   'Hole in the Ground', for instance, clearly anticipates 'Never Get Old' on *Reality*.

with what he called 'some of the songs from the '60s [that] were never recorded, let alone released, so will be as new to you as any of the new ones that I've written'.[10] In the latter category was the excellent 'Shadow Man', which was demoed during the Ziggy sessions and never released, and should have had its moment in the sun on *Toy*, rather than its eventual relegation of being a B-side to 'Everyone Says "Hi"'. Over another peerless Visconti string arrangement, it soars and swoops as Bowie meditates on how our actions in the present will one day influence the future. And in the former category was 'Uncle Floyd'.

Although the Bowie vaults have been somewhat opened over the past decade, many of his most interesting and much-discussed songs have yet to receive any official release, and one of these is what would, presumably, have been the epic centrepiece to *Toy*. The likely reason for 'Uncle Floyd' never being officially released is that it was transformed into 'Slip Away' and received its due prominence on *Heathen*, but the original version is, for my money, richer and better structured, and should be regarded as one of Bowie's greatest songs.

It takes as its subject the American children's television series *The Uncle Floyd Show*, which ran from 1974 until 1999. Amid Floyd's various she-nanigans, he would interact with Oogie, a wooden ventriloquist's doll who would, naturally, be voiced by Floyd. As often with Bowie, this would find an unexpected allusion more than a decade later, but for the time being, 'Uncle Floyd' the song was a heartbreaking examination of loss and passing time, epitomised by the lines 'Some of us will always stay behind / Down in space, it's always 1982'.

According to Plati, it was a late addition to *Toy*. 'David felt that we needed a little more colour, and so he came up with this song about these two folks, and Uncle Floyd in particular, and it really, really hit me. We recorded it and then, for the ending, we pulled in people from the studio just saying "Come on in and sing us with us." You know, Coco and Sterling and everyone singing it. We had such a good time. I really like the line about 1982. That whole last verse has something really visual about that.

It was just a brilliant song. Every time between what David's singing and what Gerry and Lisa are playing, it just kills me every time still, which is a good sign that we got something right and it will endure forever.'[11]

The ending, on which Bowie plays the Stylophone – an electronic toy that he used on 'Space Oddity' and had not seen, let alone played, in three decades* – came about through a piece of unexpected serendipity. As Sterling Campbell says, 'I brought a composer friend into the studio to watch David record and the Stylophone was there. We were kind of bored and we turned it on and start playing it and David's like, "Give me that!" That led to the haunting bit at the end. So that's how David was and how he worked, almost with found sounds. He was always interested in improvising and having new ideas and new material and stuff like that. That was always part of his working method. He knew how to pull a rabbit out the hat and it was just uncanny. And he always had that ability.'[12]

As Bowie recorded *Toy*, EMI reissued Bowie's back catalogue in handsome new editions – I remember buying a consistent run of everything from *Space Oddity* to *Tonight*, only demurring at *Never Let Me Down* – and all seemed set for *Toy* to be a major release for the spring of 2001. Bowie revealed on a BowieNet chat on 31 October that 'recording is wrapped – we just started the mixing yesterday. I think we'll have the whole thing done by about the 10th. Then as usual, the dinosaur corporate company takes over, and before you know it, in 5 months time the fucker will be on the street. We're hoping for about March.' Revealing that 'I really, really like all 12 [songs]' on the album, he suggested that there would be a few supporting gigs in New York, if not a full tour, and then that he would segue into recording with Visconti producing, of which he said 'the beginning of next year's album will be critical for both of us, as I'm sure that we've both learnt a lot over the ensuing years. Maybe [we] have gotten into some

---

* He later commented that 'Rolf Harris has never forgiven me for becoming really, really famous with the Stylophone. Poor Stylophone thought they were on a winner with "Space Oddity" after I featured it on that and brought out a really expensive model which nobody bought – and it sunk the company! Poor old Stylophone . . .'

bad recording habits as well. What Tony and I always found to be one of our major strengths is the ability to free each other up from getting into a rut. So no doubt there will be some huge challenges, but also some pretty joyous occasions. In short, really looking forward to this.'

And then matters went awry.

Over the years, there have been many famously unreleased albums, from the Beach Boys' *Smile* to Springsteen and the E Street Band's electric version of *Nebraska*. Some records are ditched because the narcotic or alcoholic intake of various band members made them impossible to complete; others – as in the case of Pink Floyd's *Household Objects* from 1974, a bold but perverse attempt to record an entire LP using only the eponymous utentils – were doomed from the outset by dint of their inherent lack of either practicality or listenability. Yet *Toy* was a straightforward, highly accomplished album, made by one of the most famous musicians in the world, that ended up going unreleased during Bowie's lifetime. What, precisely, went wrong?

Nobody who worked on the album was clear about why, exactly, it was shelved. 'I didn't like it not being released,' says Plati, 'but I wasn't privy to too many of the details, and I didn't want to be. My understanding was that it was record company stuff.' March 2001 came and went without any concrete news of *Toy*'s release, with Bowie remarking in June that 'EMI/ Virgin seem to have a lot of scheduling conflicts this year, which has put an awful lot on the back burner. *Toy* is finished and ready to go, and I will make an announcement as soon as I get a very real date.' The dreaded words 'scheduling conflicts' were used again in July, and then, in October, the bombshell was dropped: *Toy* would not be released.

A tetchy Bowie, dropping his usual ironic reserve, announced that 'Virgin/EMI have had scheduling problems and are now going for an album of "new" material over the *Toy* album. Fine by me. I'm extremely happy with the new stuff. I love *Toy* as well and won't let that material fade away.' Then there was a dig at the record company. 'If you've been following the newspapers, you will have seen that EMI/Virgin are having problems themselves. This has not helped.' His conclusion, though, was philosophical. 'But all things pass.'

Visconti commented that Bowie was 'hurt terribly' by EMI refusing to release the album, but apart from that, its non-appearance seemed to relate to the scheduling issues Bowie referred to. After all, the songs dribbled out, for the most part, over the next couple of years. As Bowie said in 2003, '*Toy* has actually started now to become a reservoir of B-sides and bonus tracks, so it's much depleted. From the original 14 or so that I did, I think seven are now out there. I think there's still enough in the past to be able to pop some more back and top it up, so to speak, but you know what? New writing just takes precedence. It always does.'[13]

This was true, as far as it went, but it was Bowie's publicist Alan Edwards who knew of the rather more unpalatable reality. EMI/Virgin had simply rejected the album altogether in early 2001, and Ashley Newton, the company's head of A&R, had announced the decision by sending Edwards an email simply entitled 'Bad news'. The year 2000 had been an extraordinary one for Bowie, culminating with his being named the most influential rock musician of all time by the *NME*. Yet, tellingly, this was an award for which he had been nominated for by his peers, rather than the general public. He ended the particularly self-congratulatory, back-slapping interview by suggesting 'it means more to me than any number of hit albums, this', but the cynical could have answered that the reason for Bowie's current predicament was that there had not been any hit albums in recent memory. Even the Glastonbury performance failed to send his more recent records – the ones that needed to sell well in order for his label to have any interest in him – up into the higher reaches of the charts. He had become the biggest cult artist in history, which was artistically impressive but commercially risky.

In Edwards's recollection, Newton had enjoyed *Toy* but was concerned that there was no obvious hit single, meaning that there was no chance that the album would ever recoup the money that would be needed to promote and release it. Edwards approached other record labels, but found, to his dismay, that nobody else was particularly interested either. As he wrote in his memoirs, 'it was more the end of an era than the end of David', as other similarly big-name heritage artists like Paul McCartney and Mick Jagger had also seen their latest solo albums flop.* Still, in his recollection, 'David was understandably a bit shaken when he heard the news'.[14] After all, he *was* David Bowie, and he had been with the EMI group for nearly 20 years, bar his four-album flirtation with Arista; he had returned to the fold for *hours. . .* and now may have regretted his decision.

The time for sentiment passed. The new music industry was a hard-nosed place, run by people with limited appetite for nostalgia. Ironically, just as Bowie had taken genuine pleasure in rediscovering his past, his potential paymasters lost interest in it. Ever the consummate PR man, Edwards put out a press release at the end of 2001 suggesting that Bowie had jumped rather than being pushed and that he was going to set up his own boutique label, giving him the freedom to sign interesting acts and work from his own studio. There was the usual intense back and forth in the media, but Bowie had managed to sidestep the potential humiliation of being perceived as a washed-up has-been. Yet events three months before had overshadowed this kind of petty squabbling and would have a considerable existential effect on Bowie's career and work for the rest of his life.

Bowie described the events of 9/11 without any irony or detachment. 'When the Twin Towers were attacked, I personally wasn't recording. I was up north, in Woodstock, in the album mines. Iman was there with our

---

\*   Largely because they weren't very good. McCartney's *Driving Rain*, a paean to his second wife Heather Mills, peaked at 46 in the UK charts, while Jagger's *Goddess in the Doorway*, christened 'Dogshit in the Doorway' by his bandmate Keith Richards, managed two places higher, at 44.

baby so, of course, psychologically it was unbelievably traumatic because I wasn't on the bloody spot. And it was all done by phone, until the phones were cut off. Oh man, I can't tell you how terribly scary that was . . . it was really awful.' But he was able to reflect on the likely outcome. 'In a way I suppose it was inevitable, especially with what's been happening politically. It's very easy to look at situations like these in a binary fashion, and the September 11 attacks encouraged us to look a little closer.'[15]

David Bowie could never be described as a political musician, ham-fisted dabblings on *Black Tie White Noise* aside. He had caustically sung on 'All the Young Dudes' that 'We never got it off on that revolution stuff / What a drag, too many snags', and his studied detachment from contemporary affairs was, depending on your perspective, either frustrating or refreshing. After the furore that greeted his remarks in the '70s\* – 'I believe very strongly in fascism' and 'Adolf Hitler was one of the first rock stars . . . [he was] as good as Jagger at working an audience'[16] – Bowie never again sought to ally himself with any particular ideology or movement. Many assumed, without clear evidence, that if he was anything, he was a wealthy transatlantic liberal, the kind of man who would be at home with Blairism and Clintonian democratic government, if more sceptical about the right-wing Republican administration ushered in by George W. Bush at the turn of the millennium.

Yet Bowie seldom, if ever, said anything in public that added credence to these beliefs. For all his public knew, he had never changed his mind from his 1975 statement declaring that 'You've got to have an extreme right front come up and sweep everything off its feet and tidy everything up. Then you can get a new form of liberalism.' He had even offered himself as the right man for the job: 'As I see it, I am the only alternative for the premier in England. I believe Britain could benefit from a fascist

---

\* In an interview conducted for *Playboy* by Cameron Crowe, who would later shift careers into filmmaking, and in whose excellent *Almost Famous* a Bowie-alike would make a brief cameo.

leader. After all, fascism is really nationalism.' Then he was photographed making what could have been a Nazi salute while arriving at Victoria station to the confected outrage of journalists, before recanting, calling his drug-addled antics part of 'an extraordinarily fucked-up nature at that particular time'.

It therefore almost came as a surprise to see Bowie opening the Concert for New York City on 20 October 2001. He had, of course, performed at numerous charitable and benefit galas over the previous decades, including Live Aid, the Concert for Freddie Mercury and 1999's NetAid, but the explicit way in which he allied himself with this patriotic, all-American event – alongside a wide variety of other British rock stars, including Jagger, Elton John, Paul McCartney and the Who – was new territory for Bowie. He performed two songs, Simon & Garfunkel's 'America' and his own '"Heroes"', and the latter, especially, was executed with particular vigour by Bowie and a scratch band that included Plati, Dorsey and the 11-piece Orchestra for New York City. It was a time of enormous significance to Bowie; he informed BowieNet members on 12 September that 'Life here will continue', and praised his fellow New Yorkers, saying '[They] are a resilient and fast-thinking people. In this way, they really do resemble my own Londoners. They came together quickly in massive community support and silent determination.'[17]

Bowie was an unlikely unifying figure and, after the Concert for New York City, he pivoted away from comfort into quiet despair. Unlike, say, Bruce Springsteen – an absentee from the benefit gig, but whose album *The Rising* is rightly regarded as perhaps the definitive musical response to the events of 9/11 – Bowie did not attempt to make a grand artistic statement about the atrocity, but it would permeate his thinking and work from September 2001 until his abrupt departure from public performance in June 2004. *Outside* had suggested a doom-laden reckoning with the millennium was approaching; the album that became *Heathen* replied that, yes, the twenty-first century had arrived, in a mixture of fire and blood and profanity. That it would become the album to restore Bowie to public prominence and regard, after years of near-misses and flops and *succès d'estime*, was a fortunate by-product.

Those around Bowie noted the change, both in the world and in him. 'We were all affected by 9/11,' says Plati. 'That was a cloud and you couldn't really escape that. The whole feeling around us was different to previous times we'd been together. It just wasn't a sunny day anymore. It was really hard to deal with that and, as bad as it looked on TV, it was worse being there. Those fires burned for a couple of months and you couldn't comprehend what it was like, being there. Things felt really dark and there wasn't the same spark again. There was a lightness missing from everything, and everyone felt it a little differently. Undeniably, it coloured things for years.'[18]

Even before the events of September, 2001 had been a year coloured by both reconciliation and loss, personally and professionally. Bowie's mother Peggy had died in April; he attended the funeral, and was photographed looking appropriately sombre. Visconti was now brought fully back into the fold as producer, after his work on string arrangements on the *Toy* album confirmed that he could collaborate harmoniously with Bowie once again. As he says, 'when we started working on *Heathen*, he came to stay in my home for four days, just catching up, watching rented films and going to the same Japanese restaurant night after night.'[19] The band who had played on *Toy* and at Glastonbury with Bowie were not dispensed with entirely, but new, shiny guest musicians, some of them extremely famous, were brought in to supplement – and, in many cases, replace – them. This may have seemed callous and ungrateful (they would be reinstated for the Heathen tour in 2002 and for *Reality*), but it also reflected Bowie's desire to move in a different direction and to produce something of lasting significance and interest. As he said to *Time Out*, 'I was keen to work with musicians neither of us had worked with before . . . I said [to my band] "Listen guys, for artistic reasons we won't be working together on the next album, but we'll pick up when I've finished and go back out as a band."'[20] He was as good as his word.

Film also occupied him. Bowie had a brilliantly amusing and self-mocking cameo in Ben Stiller's *Zoolander*,* which was filmed in September 2000 and released on 28 September 2001, while his music was also prominently featured in Baz Luhrmann's berserk musical fantasia *Moulin Rouge!*, which had premiered to great acclaim at Cannes earlier that year. Not only were covers of 'Diamond Dogs' and '"Heroes"' used, but Bowie himself contributed a sinuous cover version of the Nat King Cole standard 'Nature Boy' in a new arrangement by Massive Attack, which he called 'slinky and mysterious'. The film was an enormous hit and Bowie's cachet suffered no damage in being so closely associated with it. It also led to a friendship with Luhrmann thereafter: the two men considered heading to Berlin to work on a project together, but, like so many other ideas, it came to nothing.

In any case, Bowie had turned his attention to weightier matters. In an interview with the *Observer*, he insisted that his priority was now his infant daughter Lexi, rather than artistic or musical matters. 'I don't want to start doing what I unfortunately did with my son, inasmuch as I spent an awful lot of time on tour when he was a young child. I really missed those years and I know he did too. Fortunately, we were together by the time he was six and I brought him up from that point on. It was a one-parent family. I don't want to repeat the same mistakes with Lexi.' Yet, like many new fathers – especially those who were middle-aged or older – he felt fearful about the future. 'I had rosy expectations for the 21st century, I really did. The whole idea was lifting my spirits quite a lot during 1998 and 1999. But it has become something other than what I expected it to be. And it's obviously a pretty typical parental concern to wonder what type of a world you have brought your child into.'

---

* From his first line, peeling off his shades – 'If nobody has any objections, I believe I might be of service' – Bowie has a riotously good time playing himself, as he judges a 'walk-off' between Stiller and Owen Wilson's preening male models. His reaction shots, especially, are so drolly amusing that one regrets that Bowie didn't do more (intentional) comedy during his career.

227

This echoes David Fincher's *Se7en*, with that film's grim, misanthropic paranoia about the potential folly of bringing a child into the grim, dystopian world. (Even Fincher would not have been so bold as to imagine fires burning for months after a terrorist attack, as Plati and Bowie saw in New York.) When *Heathen* began recording in January 2001, Lexi was only a few months old and the necessity of looking after her meant that Bowie was unable to repeat his wham-bam-thank-you-ma'am technique of recording albums at speed. Instead, he had a new set of tricks and ideas when it came to his latest work. He would write the songs by himself, rather than with a Gabrels or an Eno, and he would allow his fears for the world and his daughter to influence the crepuscular atmosphere of the album.

*Heathen*, like *Outside* – the latter-day Bowie record that it most closely resembles, both sonically and thematically – is saturated with doubt and dread. It came as little surprise that Bowie admitted on BowieNet, shortly before the album came out, that 'misery is my default position . . . my soul flies erratically on the wings of a feeble bipolarism'. The rejection of *Toy* during *Heathen*'s recording did not help Bowie's mood, but he was sufficiently mature not to throw his toy(s) out of the pram and instead to concentrate on the music at hand. His influences while writing were an eclectic mixture – from Strauss and Mahler to his chief fanboy Moby and the French electronica duo Air – and while Bowie began recording sessions at his usual haunt of Looking Glass Studios, he soon decamped to the grander settings of Allaire Studios, deep in the Catskill Mountains and about two hours' drive away from New York.

Just as *Outside* had been influenced by its Swiss setting and the work of Thomas Mann, so *Heathen*'s more expansive recording surroundings led to the album feeling grander and more epic in scope than its predecessors. Visconti's string arrangements, performed by the Scorchio Quartet, had grace and beauty, and made one wish that he could have worked on several other intervening Bowie albums, too. *Heathen* drew on iconography that spanned everything from art – the album's artwork, designed by Markus Klinko, is full of desecrated and defaced pictures that function as a sequel to *hours. . .*'s re-evaluation of the pièta – to philosophy, with images of works by Freud and Nietzsche. The latter's 1882 book *The Gay Science* was the volume in which the German philosopher famously declared that 'God is dead'; *Heathen* appears to take as its central tenet the idea that, with Bowie now forgotten and cast off by whatever deities have ever existed, they themselves have ceased to matter in the world. Instead, we are all alone in the twenty-first century and must learn to make the best of what we have as the godless universe collapses around us.

This, as ever with Bowie, veers close to pretension. Most record buyers anticipating *Heathen* were hoping not for an impenetrable exercise in navel-gazing paranoia. Instead, the much-heralded reunion with Visconti and the presence of superstar guests Pete Townshend and Dave Grohl led to under-standably high expectations that this would be Bowie's Big Rock album, a statement comeback that would return to the artsy-yet-accessible tunes of *Scary Monsters*, his last studio record with Visconti. The Glastonbury comeback had permeated into the mainstream and Bowie was on the cusp of reaching an entirely new audience.

He was also aware that he needed a commercial hit. Some might argue that the presence of Grohl, in particular, on the album was a deliberate sop to younger record buyers, who idolised Nirvana and Grohl's subsequent band Foo Fighters, but *Heathen* was no collection of catchy three-minute pop songs. Bowie may have joked, mordantly, that childrearing had meant that 'the next album might have lyrics like "the wheels on the bus go round and round"', but he now knew that, after *Toy* was considered uncommercial in the current climate, he had to distinguish himself from other once-imperial rock stars who had fallen foul of shifting tastes.

The album was recorded – at some expense and without a record deal – over the course of 2001, mainly at Allaire, and the final mixing and overdubs took place in the wake of 9/11. 'It was easy to record *Heathen*,' Bowie later declared. 'It was as if it was lying in wait to be made. The songs themselves and the arrangements were very easy to organise. Strangely enough, the hard part was knowing which songs not to include.' By the beginning of 2002, the album was finished, ready to be released on Bowie's own independent label ISO; it would be distributed by Columbia Records, who gushed that Bowie was 'one of the most distinctive, influential and exciting artists of our time'. The revival could continue apace.

At the start of 2002, Bowie turned 55. It is not an especially old age and many artists and musicians have produced their greatest work after reaching their mid-fifties. Yet in a long, discursive and (apparently) candid conversation with *Interview* magazine, Bowie revealed that he had Strauss's *Four Last Songs* in mind as a musical inspiration, calling them 'the most terribly romantic, sad, poignant pieces that I think have ever been written', and noting that the songs, which Strauss wrote shortly before his death at the age of 85, were a reckoning with mortality. 'Especially in one's mid-fifties,' suggested Bowie, 'you're very aware that that's the moment you have to leave the idea of being young. You've got to let it go.' He went on to say, of *Heathen*, that he had 'no embarrassment about expressing the thoughts and experiences of an old man. There's a British nursery rhyme I carry with me. The first line is "This is the way the young men ride – clip-clop, clip-clop, clip-clop, clip-clop" and it ends with "This is the way the old men ride – hobbledy, hobbledy, hobbledy, down into the ditch". I had it in my mind that I'm in the "This is the way the old men ride" part.'[21]

Bowie would undoubtedly have had T.S. Eliot's 'The Hollow Men' in mind, too, which makes a similar use of a nursery rhyme,* building to the grim conclusion that 'This is how the world ends / Not with a bang but with a whimper'. There was, however, rather more of the bang than the whimper about Bowie's de facto comeback album. From its opening track, 'Sunday', he once again channels Scott Walker both vocally and musically, and wearily harkens back to 'Word on a Wing' once again as he explores *Heathen*'s central themes in the paradox 'Nothing has changed, everything has changed'.

---

* In Eliot's case, 'Here we go round the prickly pear / At five o'clock in the morning'.

If we leave aside the three covers on the album – all fine, all superfluous – then the record has nine original songs, which represent a strange grab-bag. 'Sunday', '5.15 The Angels Have Gone'.* 'Heathen (The Rays)' and 'I Would Be Your Slave', all name-checked by Bowie as owing the most to his Strauss influence, are atmospherically menacing, the perfect musical encapsulation of the legacy of 9/11. While both Bowie and Visconti insisted that the songs were all written before the attack, they bear the heavy, plangent feel of a city under siege and engulfed by fire. 'Afraid', resurrected from the *Toy* sessions, is an incongruous but pleasant addition, while 'Slip Away' sounds magnificently mournful, with Visconti's production giving it considerable heft. 'Slow Burn' is the album's apparently obligatory rocker, with Townshend's flamboyant guitar playing giving it an electrifying lift that the otherwise mundane songwriting and lyrics would not merit. And then there's 'Everyone Says "Hi"'.

Whenever I listen to *Heathen*, I have to resist the temptation to skip to my two favourite songs, 'Slip Away' and this one. 'Slip Away' is, of course, a rich broth made from the bones of 'Uncle Floyd', but 'Everyone Says "Hi"' takes Bowie's newfound fixation on mortality and offers a darkly comic spin on it, in the form of a three-minute pop song, on which one of the guitar players is none other than Bowie's long-standing sideman Carlos Alomar.

On first listen, it appears to be a paean to his son Joe, Duncan Jones – and how much his father is missing his now grown-up boy. However, Bowie's deliciously twisted lyrics, returning to the macabre humour of 'Please Mr Gravedigger' and the like, are not referring to temporary absence, but permanent bereavement; like much of the rest of *Heathen*, it is a song about death. Over a riff played on electric cello and a sumptuous string arrangement, phrases that sound innocuous – 'said you sailed a big ship, said you sailed away'; 'hope the weather's good and it's not too hot'

---

* Bowie declared that this was his favourite track on the album. 'It's been a joy working with Tony Visconti again and I believe he brings so much to my songs, not just support. He's a great musician and strings arranger as well.'

– become imbued with subversive glee when you realise the intent. By the time that Bowie is alluding both to Cerberus, in the form of 'your big fat dog', and whatever deity still exists, 'the guy upstairs', it's hard not to take giddy delight in the jest.

'Everyone Says "Hi"' would be released as *Heathen*'s second single, reaching the top 20 in the UK. But the album that it was taken from would be a considerably greater hit. It again reached the top five in Britain but, more auspiciously, got to number 14 on the *Billboard* charts, suggesting that Bowie's affection for his adopted country had finally been reciprocated by the record-buying public there. It helped that the reviews were outstanding. Bowie may have wryly anticipated that the critical cliché was to compare every album of his favourably to *Scary Monsters*, but David Quantick's words in *Q* were particularly glowing. Over the course of a warm, perceptive piece that acknowledged the undersung genius of *Outside* and the overlooked *hours. . .*, Quantick concluded that 'David Bowie, always much more than just a Greatest Hits, still makes music that no-one else has heard before, and still does it well. And *Heathen*? A return to form. Definitely.'

This was a simple narrative, and an easy one to sell. With the pungent glow of Glastonbury showing no signs of dissipating, the return of Visconti to production duties and the *Toy* debacle never having become public knowledge, *Heathen* was the first Bowie album since *Black Tie White Noise* that came with the genuine sense of being An Event. Although it wasn't as accomplished as *Outside*, it was far more accessible. Bowie was able to control the publicity around the album's release to his advantage. He discussed the idea of a full-on media saturation campaign with Edwards before rejecting it. Correctly, he decided that his reputation would not be served well by popping up on regional television and local radio. He may not have had the mystique that he did in his heyday, but there was no need to turn into a ubiquitous *Stella Street* caricature of himself, Dave from Beckenham stopping by *Never Mind the Buzzcocks* for a few cheeky gags.

He was also tired. In an interview with the *Observer*, he put his fatigue down to being the 55-year-old father of an infant daughter, but he was also weary of the demands of the increasingly corporate music industry. Once, he had thrived on the idea of fame, taking care to maintain the Ziggy persona both on and off stage and thrilling to the attentions and embraces of fans of both sexes. Now, he was contemptuous of such matters. 'I don't have views on celebrity,' he sighed. 'I'm indifferent to it. I think it's absolute crap. I cannot understand anybody who wants to be on the front page of a newspaper all the bloody time if they don't have something to sell.'[22] He was, instead, 55 going on 56, and did not, by his own estimation, feel like an 18-year-old inside. *Heathen* was a middle-aged man's record, its fear of mortality and godlessness that of a middle-aged man who had trouble sleeping at night.

Not that Bowie would confide such fears and doubts to anyone, least of all a journalist. Instead, he told the *Observer*'s Tim Cooper that 'there are no yearning ambitions any more. There are things I'd like to do but none are crucial. I have a sense that I've become the person that I always should have been. It's been a kind of cyclical, almost elliptical, journey at times, but I feel like I've finally arrived at being instead of becoming, which is kind of how I feel about being young – there's always a sense that you're becoming something, that you're going be shocked by something new or discover something or be surprised by what life has in store. I'm still surprised at some things, but I do understand them, I know them. There's a sense that I know where I am now. I recognise life and most of its experiences, and I'm quite comfortable with the idea of the finality of it. But it doesn't stop me trying to continually resolve it, resolve my questions about it. And I probably will. I think I'll still be doing it – hopefully – like Strauss, at 84.'[23]

Bowie prepared to support *Heathen* with a limited tour,* as well as agreeing to assume the artistic directorship of London's Meltdown Festival

---

* This was not done with glee. In a BowieNet chat, he commented: 'Touring has become harder and harder for me. This new set of shows that I'm doing this year are actually not too many to cope with really. I'm doing about a dozen in Europe and a little more than a dozen in the States. Which means I'll be able to get home.'

for the year, in which the director invites many of their favourite acts to perform at the Royal Festival Hall. Bowie was pilloried in the press for many of his choices – Coldplay, Supergrass, Suede et al. were hardly the stuff of experimental boundary-pushing – but this ignored his more esoteric selections, including the British debut of the choral symphonic pop group the Polyphonic Spree (supporting the Divine Comedy, who were entirely overshadowed the night I saw them), Television and the Legendary Stardust Cowboy, whose 'I Took a Trip on a Gemini Shadow' was covered by Bowie on *Heathen*.

Yet the most exciting show, appropriately enough, was Bowie's closing gig in late June, in which he performed the entirety of *Heathen*, as well as all of *Low*, back-to-back. It was typically ambitious, a simultaneous attempt to resurrect a much-admired part of his back catalogue and to contrast it with his latest work, all performed by the band that he had assembled for the triumphant Glastonbury gig, and now joined by Gerry Leonard. 'It was a brilliant move,' says Leonard. 'People do it all the time now, but back then people hadn't had that idea of pairing those two records and making an iconic gig.' He was recruited into the live band by dint of Bowie turning to Plati and saying, quizzically, 'Well, can Gerry rock?'[24] He could indeed and would become a mainstay of Bowie's live band, as well as on record.

The Meltdown gig was not only Bowie's most-praised appearance since Glastonbury, but it was arguably his last truly great live performance. Plati recalls that preparing for the show was a particular challenge. 'To me, it was almost a bigger deal than Glastonbury. This was a far more finessed situation, where everybody's got to be on point and very tuned into what they were doing. I found that much more of a challenge, the sense of being a bit more under a microscope.' Still, once rehearsals began, both the intent and, crucially, the ability to perform two technically complex albums was there. 'Once we started doing it,' says Plati, 'it was relatively straightforward. We found the multitrack original tapes of *Low*, transferred them into the computer and then I divided things up among the players. Arranging some of the weirder ones like "Subterraneans" was a little tricky. But people did all kinds of stuff and everybody was into it. At one point, David and I were on the same keyboard, split in half.'[25]

Although *Heathen* would not be widely performed, Bowie managed to head to Manchester a couple of weeks later for another headline gig at the city's Move Festival, which I attended. My expectations were high; I had missed out on tickets for Meltdown, given they had sold out in a matter of minutes – most, of course, were reserved for industry types, 'friends of David' and other licensed hangers-on – and heading to the Old Trafford cricket ground seemed the only realistic way of seeing him on the tour.

It was a phenomenally wet, miserable evening, and the support acts – Suede and the Divine Comedy,* both Meltdown holdovers – seemed intimidated, both by the weather and the company they were keeping. Then as Bowie, impossibly elegant in a dark, Edwardian-style, three-piece suit, complete with watch chain and pocket fob, took to the stage, accompanied by a solo Mike Garson playing 'Life on Mars' before the full band came in halfway through, all the discomfort and damp dissipated immediately.

Bowie played about half of *Heathen*, along with various hits old and new, including 'Ashes to Ashes', 'Fame' and 'Changes'. Over the course of a propulsive couple of hours, during which he managed to keep his cool while all around him became almost embarrassingly over-excited at being in his presence, Bowie effortlessly demonstrated why, after a long, fallow period, he was once again being feted as the great artist of his generation. Several of the songs, including '"Heroes"' and 'Let's Dance', were performed in the same arrangements that he had tested at Glastonbury, in which the giddy euphoria of the chorus was held back until an almost indecently lengthy period into the song, while others, including the magnificent

---

* The Divine Comedy's singer-songwriter Neil Hannon – the *other* figure who idolised Scott Walker –quipped that, when Bowie went on stage in Manchester, 'he brought the sun out with him, which proves he's in league with the devil'. He also said, of his fleeting meeting with him backstage before the festival – along with Brett Anderson – 'Bowie was very nice, and satisfyingly short, as well.'

'Hallo Spaceboy' and a suitably epic 'I'm Afraid of America' took their accustomed place in the Bowie canon with élan.

The *Heathen* songs, meanwhile, sounded better live – fuller and richer and more immediate than on record. 'There were things he just didn't bring me in for,' says Garson, 'and the only time I got my sweet revenge is when we played them on the road, and they got better. And he smiled, you know? You miss a few opportunities in life. That's how it is. But least I didn't miss the opportunity by finishing after eight weeks and never seeing him again. The fact that I kept going, and he kept calling me back, was one of the most beautiful things that occurred.'[26] The affection, warmth and trust between the two men was obvious, down to Bowie making a special point of singling out Garson as one of the original Spiders from Mars, which was met with appropriate clamour from the crowd.

The new millennium had seen one of the most tumultuous periods in Bowie's career, in which his own ambivalence towards large-scale, protracted touring that focused mainly on his back catalogue had been tempered by the pleasure he took from the recognition and love that the songs received. His domestic life was happy and, if he was verging on an existential crisis concerning his place in an apparently godless universe, then at least the music that he wrote about it was both understood and appreciated. A new album was on the horizon and everything seemed, for the first time in an aeon, quite assured and calm. What could possibly go wrong now?

# *REALITY*, A REALITY TOUR AND RETIREMENT

## 'I'm never gonna get old'

*'I desperately want to live forever'*

The Reality tour. It was long and lucrative but it eventually
took its toll on Bowie's declining health.

Gerry Leonard

'I'm so pissed off because the last ten months of this tour have been so . . . fantastic. Can't wait to be fully recovered and get back to work again. I tell you what, though. I won't be writing a song about this one.'

So David Bowie – or someone acting on his behalf – wrote on his website on 12 July 2004. At the time, most of his fans were aware that he had a health issue that was serious enough to lead to the emergency curtailment of the Reality tour in late June that year, with the final 11 shows cancelled. Yet the initial prognosis was that Bowie had had a trapped nerve that required emergency surgery and that, after a suitable period of rest and recuperation, he would once again be fit, ready to get back into the studio and on the road.

The first would not happen for nearly a decade and the second would never occur again. Nor was his illness simply a trapped nerve, but a full-on heart attack that nearly killed him. Had it done so, Bowie would have joined an unfortunate club that includes the likes of Tommy Cooper, the Deviants' singer Mick Farren and, most regrettably, the drummer Devon Clifford, who performed with the band You Say Party! We Say Die! and saw the act live up to its name when he expired mid-performance in Vancouver. Fortunately, Bowie survived, but the near-death experience, following an existential crisis that seemed to have begun in the final years of the millennium and had only grown since 9/11, led to a full reassessment of his career and life. And the conclusion that he came to was stark: no more touring, no more press interviews and, for a protracted period, no more recording of any original material.

For any long-standing fan of Bowie, it was hugely disappointing, if understandable, news. Throughout his career, he had been a consistent presence in public life. Even such relatively fallow years as 1981 and 1982 had seen him star in the Brecht adaptation *Baal* for the BBC, for which he also recorded the soundtrack with Visconti in Berlin – their last full collaboration together until *Heathen* – and begin writing the songs for *Let's Dance*. Since he began his career in 1963, Bowie had never had a full year away from the spotlight. He had been working and writing consistently for the past 40 years, and had recorded 25 studio albums over that period which, taken together, represent the greatest body of work that any individual British musician produced in the twentieth and twenty-first centuries. (It's a shame that *Never Let Me Down* and *Tin Machine* spoil the party, but every glittering gathering has its outcasts.)

Bowie was due a break, and the unqualified critical and commercial triumph of *Heathen*, his most popular album since *Let's Dance*, gave him the right to withdraw from the stage for a while. Yet, buoyed up by success, he now began to embrace a recording and touring schedule that would have exhausted a man half his age. The Heathen tour of 2002 was supposed to be a short jaunt across Europe and the United States, but it expanded into a five-month affair that saw him play everywhere from Paris to Philadelphia, as well as give myriad interviews and live performances on TV shows all over the world. If you'd watched the BBC's *Parkinson* show in September 2002, or *Late Night with Conan O'Brien* the following month, to name but two, there Bowie was, grinning away and looking fit and well, with a new blond hairstyle that bore more than a slight resemblance to that of another famous British DB: David Beckham.

Bowie concluded his 2002 tour with a nostalgic return to the Hammersmith Apollo in London, where he had famously retired his Ziggy Stardust character on 3 July 1973. As with his Manchester appearance earlier that summer, he began the set with 'Life on Mars' and played an extended gig in which songs that had seldom, if ever, made it onto previous setlists, such as the Brecht–Weill 'Alabama Song' and 'The Bewlay Brothers', were now performed in all their glory for the fervently partisan audience. It seemed almost incredible that, a few years previously, Bowie had showily disowned his back catalogue, claiming that he would never play these songs ever again. Even 'Rebel Rebel', which he had made a point of saying he would not perform as it no longer had any meaning for him, returned to the setlist, although this was on his own terms: it was in a new arrangement that he would later record in the studio,* and would be performed virtually every night on the Reality tour.

After another typical piece of showmanship – he played consecutive gigs in all of New York's boroughs, from Manhattan's Beacon Theatre to Jimmy's Bronx Café – Bowie ended 2002 rejuvenated and revitalised, having returned to the forefront of contemporary music. This newfound relevance was confirmed when he was nominated for the Mercury Music Prize, alongside such hip acts as the Streets, Doves and Roots Manuva. After many years in which Bowie had seemed like yesterday's man, the immaculately tailored, impeccably debonair 55-year-old was, in the knowingly excitable parlance of the music magazine *Smash Hits*, 'back, back, BACK!'

Bowie had form in segueing straight from one record to another with the same personnel, whether it was moving from *Ziggy Stardust* to *Aladdin Sane* or *Low* to *"Heroes"* and, more recently, the swift shift from *Outside* to *Earthling*. Now, he proposed to do the same once again. As Mark Plati puts it, 'the end of the Heathen tour was a bummer because the band was really hot by then and firing on all cylinders. So, fast forward to 2003, and we're back in Looking Glass Studios again in January, working up songs from scratch.'[1]

It was to be Plati's last album with Bowie, and a less satisfying experience than the previous records had been because he came close to being merely a hired hand. One trade-off of the return of Visconti was that the musicians now took a back seat, and so Plati, who had enjoyed his role as co-producer and bandleader, now viewed his reduced status as a demotion, not least because Visconti played many of the bass parts that he would have expected to. 'There were parts written for me by Tony,' he now says, 'which I found to be odd, because usually I came in and listened to a song and interpreted what David wanted. But I ended up just doing what I wanted anyway, because I didn't think they were that special, too. So it's

---

* One strange anomaly in Bowie's career is that, when he recorded songs for films, they were either very good – 'Cat People' comes to mind – or utterly token; his 'Rebel Rebel' redux was used on the soundtrack of, of all things, *Charlie's Angels: Full Throttle*.

fair to say that was a less enjoyable collaboration than my other ones. In fact, I didn't really consider it a collaboration. It just felt more like "I'm just coming here to play".'[2]

Bowie himself was heavily involved in the instrumentation of the album, playing everything from guitar and keyboards to percussion and baritone sax on it. He decided to record at Looking Glass Studios, right in the centre of Manhattan, which suited the ethos of the album he was making. Allaire had been perfect for the more ethereal, philosophical ambience of *Heathen*, but, with a couple of exceptions, *Reality* would be about as philosophical as a boot to the face. It was intended to be a hard-rocking, intensely guitar-driven album, largely worked up by Bowie and Visconti themselves. Its strange, coiled air of intensity owed something, in part, to the band all struggling to give up cigarettes. As Dorsey says, 'we were all trying to quit smoking and we all stopped around the same time, 2002 to 2003-ish. It was very hard, because we all used to smoke our brains out.'[3] Bowie, typically, replaced nicotine with tea-tree sticks, jokingly claiming that they were every bit as addictive.

Lyrically, Bowie now chose to make the 9/11 preoccupations of *Heathen* explicit, with the album's first track, the dynamic 'New Killer Star', opening with imagery of 'the great white scar over Battery Park', before switching into a 'Let's Dance'-esque groove that reminds the listener that Visconti believed that he would be producing *Let's Dance* right up until a few days before recording started. Still, there was no grudge left between the two men, whose friendship proceeded with renewed vigour and would last until the end of Bowie's life.

In one interview, Visconti suggested that *Reality* would be a less consequential album than *Heathen*. 'I'd referred to that album as his "magnum opus". I told him "That was more like a symphony, and you can't write too many of those." . . . *Heathen* consisted of very broad strokes and a grand sonic landscape – there were layers and layers of everything – whereas for *Reality* he wanted to change to something that he and his live band could play on stage with great immediacy, without the need for synthesiser patches and backing tracks. He wanted to make this more of a band album.'[4]

The irony is that it was less a band album and more a David Bowie solo album that happened to feature contributions from a group of talented musicians with whom he had worked, sporadically, for at least the last decade; even longer, in Mike Garson's case. It also felt rushed. *Heathen*, even if it was less cohesive than Bowie might have wished it to be, had the air of a significant and carefully thought-out work, taking the ashes of *Toy* and daubing a cathedral door with them. *Reality*, meanwhile, begins with a fine opening salvo of four extremely strong tracks, before deteriorating into plod-rock of the most undistinguished kind. Even the most committed Bowie fan would struggle to make any case for the likes of 'Fall Dog Bombs the Moon', 'She'll Drive the Big Car' or 'Days', three of the least memorable songs he ever wrote.

Still, it was an improvement on *Earthling* or *hours. . .* and its best songs were fabulous. A kinetic cover of Jonathan Richman's 'Pablo Picasso' benefitted from Gerry Leonard being allowed to let loose with some wildly inventive Spanish guitar playing, while a stately, harpsichord-driven cover of George Harrison's 'Try Some, Buy Some' momentarily conjures the idea of what it would have been like had Bowie been produced by Phil Spector in the '70s: a fascinating, if possibly destructive, pairing. The soulful, fragile ballad 'The Loneliest Guy' is one of the two songs that showcases Garson's peerless ability on the piano, while the title track has a punch that made it a firm live favourite whenever it was played.

There were also two other songs that were more interesting, both in the circumstances of their creation and in what they said about (the now 56-year-old) Bowie himself. 'Never Get Old' became the subject of much discussion in interviews, with speculation that it contained autobiographical overtones. He claimed that it was intended to be funny. 'It just brought a grin to my face singing it. I grow old hourly, but it was a line too good not to sing. One of my generation was going to sing it at some point, so I thought I'd do it.'[5] He elaborated further. 'The image of a rocker in his fifties singing petulantly "I'll never get old" is ludicrous and funny. It's an irresistible line to sing at this age.'

In fact, it was a return to a near-constant preoccupation of Bowie's: fear, amounting to Larkin-esque dread, of creeping mortality, self-consciously made light of with a wink and a smirk. He was once asked in 1987 whether it was more important to try for eternal youth or to grow old gracefully. Perhaps with his iconic role in the recent *The Hunger* in mind, in which his once-immortal vampire suddenly ages hundreds of years in a matter of a few days, he replied that 'I think the most important thing is to actually try and grow old . . . meaningfully.'[6]

He laughed as he said this, but 15 years later, the concept of ageing was an increasingly important one to him for the most personal of reasons. As he said to one journalist, 'I desperately want to live forever. You know what, I want to still be around in another 40 or 50 years. I just want to be there for Alexandria. She's so exciting and so lovely, so I want to be around when she grows up. I think, "When am I gonna let go of her? When she's 20?" Nah, I wanna see her get married. "When she's 30?" Nah, I wanna see what she's like as a mother. I don't want to let her go. If I didn't have my little three-year-old running around, I wouldn't be writing songs quite this way. Seeing in her eyes all the hope and joy and optimism of the future, I have to reflect that in what I'm doing.'[7]

The other song on the album that had especial significance for him was 'Bring Me the Disco King', written as far back as 1992 and intended, at various points, for both *Black Tie White Noise* and *Earthling*. It is entirely unlike anything else on the album, anticipating *Blackstar* in its use of jazz motifs and menacing piano and percussion, and gives Garson one of his greatest showcases on a Bowie album. Unsurprisingly, he remains deeply proud of his work. 'The thing about David is that he didn't ever want me repeating myself. So he was always looking for another piano element of me. He was like a forensic scientist going into my brain. He flew me in from LA in the midst of their recording *Reality* because they didn't get the result he wanted on "Bring Me the Disco King" and "The Loneliest

Guy". I was only there two or three days. I played those songs and then I was out of there.'

The recording process for the former was a complicated but worthwhile one. 'I'm proud of it because he didn't want an "Aladdin Sane"-style solo or a very romantic "Lady Grinning Soul" solo. If you listen to the last two minutes, it's a chordal solo, which is very unusual. It almost comes from the Dave Brubeck universe, circa 1960. I was listening to a two-bar drum track phrase by Matt Chamberlain, which was taken off *Heathen*, and Tony and David took this little loop from that song, brought it over and said "Play to that". I ended up recording it on my own piano because the one in Looking Glass Studio was broken. I went home and spent three days with my engineer. And then David said he liked the sound we got with the piano synth. I was freaking out. I got on the phone with him and eventually he just said, "Mike, it's my album". It was very humbling, because he remembered the feeling of him sitting right next to me with that piano. And even though sonically my piano sounds better, because it was a 100-grand, nine-foot concert grand versus a $2,000 synth, it was the sound he wanted. David put the music ahead of everything and I didn't have that instinct. I learned that from him. And now I will go with whatever feels great. But we did have a little bit of a fight for it, with the "It's my fucking album, fuck you" routine.'[8]

When *Reality* was finished, it was scheduled for release in early September, a little more than a year since *Heathen* came out. Bowie decided to support the album with a spectacular global tour, by far the most ambitious and lengthy series of shows that he had undertaken since the Outside tour of the mid-'90s. The cynical might even have suggested, given its short recording schedule, that *Reality* was primarily intended as a pretext for a lucrative series of shows, although this was a misreading of Bowie, who performed as and when he wanted to, rather than in a Rolling Stones-esque commercially driven fashion in which the new album was nothing more than a souvenir.

Bowie was openly ambivalent about touring. 'It was not something

I looked forward to very much. I've always loved the putting together of everything. I love the idea of making albums and writing albums and conceptualising and all that side of the thing, you know? The actual "going out on the road" side of the thing – one, I never thought I was that good at it, and two, I just didn't enjoy the process too much. I don't know, maybe because I didn't feel competent as an artist.' Yet now, he changed his tune, saying 'I'm finally starting to really enjoy performing as well . . . over this last eight years or so, since I've started working the first time around with Reeves, we went through the '90s, now I just got really comfortable on stage. Now I'm just like a duck in water out there.' Still, when the interviewer asked him how long this could continue, Bowie's reply was guarded. 'Yeah, I know. I wonder. I wonder. I have a horrible idea that's my answer.'[9]

For the release of *Reality*, which would again be distributed by Columbia, Bowie had a typically trendsetting idea; why not perform a live gig from London, which would be beamed around the world to cinemas, followed by an on-screen Q&A? It was the next step on from BowieNet: mass communication conveyed with originality and style. But it did not go entirely according to plan. As Alexis Petridis described it in the *Guardian*, 'there is a Europe-wide Q&A for the fans, which simultaneously recalls the Eurovision Song Contest and a particularly chaotic phone-in on 1980s kids show *Saturday Superstore*. Technical hitches abound. The questions are staggering. Josephine in Berlin wants to know what happened to a dog Bowie owned in the 1970s. Unsurprisingly, Bowie replies that the dog died. He wears a regretful expression. Whether he is regretting the passing of the hound or his decision to take part in the Q&A is unclear. His answers reveal less than his skin-tight trousers do.'

Still, all was not lost. Petridis wrote that 'an encore featuring a breathtaking version of 1979's "Fantastic Voyage" restores equilibrium. Bowie exits looking pleased, with good reason. After all, most of his 1970s peers would be hard pushed to fill a sporty hatchback with fans eager to hear their new material, let alone 68 cinemas.'[10] The touring band consisted of the same musicians who had been playing with him for the past few years, although Plati had bowed out, citing other work commitments with Robbie Williams.* Leonard was promoted to bandleader, something that he describes as 'an astonishing experience . . . it took me days to come to terms with it, and then it was a case of putting together the band, the crew, the setlist, everything.'[11]

When *Reality* was released, the reviews were respectful and appreciative, if less enthusiastic than they had been for *Heathen* – although some got round the potential risk of excessive enthusiasm by deciding that that album had, in fact, been overpraised. It would be *Q* that bravely grasped the nettle of cliché to call it 'Bowie's best music since *Scary Monsters*', with its reviewer writing that 'the best of *Reality* sounds like a man coming to terms with what was lost in [his] mad years and the saving graces of love and stability'.[12] That this could have been said of virtually every Bowie album from *Black Tie White Noise* onwards – and was particularly true of *hours. . .* and *Heathen* – did not get in the way of the critical consensus. Subsequently, its reputation has declined, with Pat Levy's 2018 judgement that it is 'a decent record in the pantheon of Bowie, nothing more, nothing less'[13] seeming like a fair summation of an accomplished, occasionally magnificent but also business-as-usual record.

Sales in the UK were good. It reached number three in the charts, Bowie's highest placing since *Black Tie White Noise*, although it did not linger in the top ten for long. Its US fortunes were more mixed, as it underperformed relative to *Heathen*, hitting a disappointing 29 in the *Billboard* rankings. It would be the tour, entitled A Reality Tour, that would define the album, and when it was announced, it proved that Bowie was still a commercial behemoth. At more than 110 shows over four continents – including a return to New Zealand and Australia for the first time since 1987 – it was ambitious on a scale that few of his peers would dare attempt.

---

* Bowie professed himself mystified by Britain's biggest solo pop star. 'I'm bemused by the whole Robbie Williams aspect of British pop. It all looks like cruise ship entertainment to me.'

A giant tour needed huge amounts of publicity, so Bowie gamely gave interviews to virtually anyone who wanted to speak to him,* as well as appearing in a splendidly self-parodying advert for Vittel water, in which he was shown interacting with his various best-known stage personae, thanks to the impersonator David Brighton and computer trickery, while 'Never Get Old' plays. The highlight comes when he is barked at by a Diamond Dog incarnation of Bowie; cameos by everyone from the Pierrot clown from 'Ashes to Ashes' to a toast-munching Thin White Duke contributed to a welcome sense of fun and self-deprecation.

When Bowie was not being affronted by his previous selves, the *Ottawa XPress* and the *Colombian* were just two of the titles that received an audience with him during the tour and to whom he spoke in a more expansive, apparently candid fashion than he had done for years. It was almost as if he had already decided that these would be the final press interviews he ever gave, on the final tour he would ever perform, and he wished to set the record straight. So along with the usual bits of PR flummery – 'I like all of the stuff I've written since around 1991', he cheerfully said. 'I think the last ten or 12 years have been really good to me as a writer'[14] – he decided to touch on matters that he had previously steered clear of.

Sometimes, this included the vexed question of a knighthood, which he hinted he had turned down ('I would never have any intention of accepting anything like that. I seriously don't know what it's for. It's not what I spent my life working for. It's not my place to make a judgment on Jagger, it's his decision. But it's just not for me.'[15]). And at others, he seemed to anticipate, and thrive on, a life post-celebrity. Referring to a friendship he had struck up in New York with another father in a local park, he explained that 'he's there every single weekend and we really buddied up to each other.

---

* Which nearly included me. I was the arts editor of a student magazine at the time and got in touch with his publicists to see if Bowie would be interested in answering questions via email. I received a warily positive response and sent over a carefully worked-over, hopelessly naive list of queries – 'You virtually never write love songs. Why is this?' – and never heard anything again. Ah well.

But we've only talked about music twice in all that time. [Still] the first time we started talking, he said: "I would never have thought I'd find you in a park." And it kind of upset me: why wouldn't you believe that I would take my own daughter out? But I suppose that's the impression that one has of celebrity.'

Warming to his theme, Bowie explained that 'it's about how you want to live your life, isn't it? I certainly don't want to live it in the full glare and I want to be able to go where I want to go in an anonymous fashion. Which is where my baseball cap comes in. I've found that, if I hide the hair under a cap, I somehow become almost invisible. I blend in so much with the rest of humanity it makes me feel almost normal!'[16] Which is, of course, exactly what Ziggy Stardust, Thomas Jerome Newton or any of Bowie's many other personae would have said.

Yet if he was asked about the future, he showed no indication that he was contemplating retirement, or even slowing down. With Visconti a renewed fixture in both his professional and personal life, he was bullish about continuing their working relationship, even bemoaning that they were not allowed to be more prolific. 'In the old days, we used to do maybe a couple of albums a year. But, of course, the industry can't really support that. We kind of have to restrict it to one a year, which will be OK, I guess. There's a whole syndrome that I felt that I'd fallen into where you can only do something once every two years or so because the company has a sell-off period, then it has a factory line, like, it's such a hard deal. The whole industry thing is hard to come to terms with, so Tony and I are pretty much going to go our own way.'[17]

A Reality Tour began on 7 October, after various invitation-only preview shows in August and September. Given how recently Bowie had been playing dates in Europe and the United States, it seemed almost as if he was conducting his own version of Bob Dylan's Never-Ending Tour, but the show was rather grander than the Heathen tour's concerts the previous year. Although Bowie attempted to play down what he had come up with, in conjunction with designer Thérèse DePrez and visual director Laura

Frank – 'I'm not really very keen to put on much of a theatrical show, in terms of big sets and elephants and fireworks and things like that'[18] – the arena shows were suitably lavish and opulent, delighting the million or so people who saw them. While they were by no means as choreographed, as, say the Glass Spider or Sound + Vision tours, the use of LED screens and moveable platforms – vital components of any large-scale tour of this kind – made for a visual spectacle that complemented the music.

Bowie had been sincere in his frustration at the Glastonbury gig being curtailed. Although he remained lukewarm about the experience of touring, which would take him away from his now three-year-old daughter for an extended period of time, he visibly enjoyed performing the gigs when he was on stage. He would play for two and a half, even three hours, if curfews and enthusiasm would allow. 'He was on great form,' says Leonard. 'He'd be saying "Dylan has 80 songs [in his setlist] and that sets an example, so we've got to keep going here." We started learning songs on the road. We would work them up in soundcheck, and he gave me a song to work on and I would work on it with the band, until we had 64, which was great.'[19]

I saw Bowie et al. at Wembley Arena in November 2003, on the first of two London gigs he played: as it turned out, they would be the last full concerts he ever played in the city. It was, as ever, an impeccably mounted affair, with an audience full of comedians who idolised Bowie – Steve Coogan, Ricky Gervais, Paul Merton and many others – and a finely picked setlist that featured 25 songs and included everything from 'Bring Me the Disco King' to 'The Man Who Sold the World'. It wasn't heavy on hit singles, but a singalong version of 'All the Young Dudes' – in which Bowie pretended to be infuriated that the audience had joined in with the chorus – was a particular highlight. Also, in their own different ways, were striking performances of 'The Motel', 'Five Years' and an acoustic 'Loving the Alien', which stripped away that fantastic song's dated production in favour of something sparse, clean and very beautiful.

There might also have been a surprise addition, too. 'We'd actually worked up an arrangement of "The Laughing Gnome",' explains Leonard, 'and soundchecked it at the London show. We definitely had something going on with it and it was very tongue in cheek. I think there was some anniversary coming and David was thinking, "Would it be fun to do it?"' To the disappointment – or relief – of many, Bowie decided against this particular trip down memory lane. 'I think maybe he caught himself and decided "No, actually, no, in these days of the internet, I'm not going to put that out there, because it'll haunt me.'

The thought of what 'The Laughing Gnome' in a 2003 incarnation might have been is fascinating – Leonard teases that 'we did our little arrangement with the full band and had a grand plan for doing it, but ultimately he decided not to put it out there' – but there were plenty of other compensations and rarities unearthed along the way. Future gigs featured everything from 'Diamond Dogs' and 'The Supermen' to his first ever single, 'Liza Jane', which had been re-recorded as part of the *Toy* sessions but was still languishing in obscurity. A surprised audience in Holmdel, New Jersey were therefore blindsided to be treated to it in June 2004.

While Bowie was travelling between gigs, he was both accessible and reserved. As Garson says, 'he considered those of us in the band his friends, but he had to be so protective, because of the way the world works and the fans. I mean, we roomed. We had two buses on those tours. The band was in one bus and I was with him with his tour manager and assistant. And because he wanted that pedigree, and that ancestral connection, so to speak, he wanted me there. And so we would talk in the middle of the night and our bunks were six inches apart. Mind you, he would close the screen, sometimes, and then he'd be reading books for three days. So then you wouldn't see him at all.'[20]

It proved to be a thrilling time, but also a nostalgic one. 'Through the years,' reflects Garson today, 'I didn't realise the amount of love and respect that was coming to me because all I was concerned about was the next piece and playing the right notes for the guy. On stage, when everyone else heard him announcing me, I wasn't hearing it. It was like "What's next?" So now I see those videos of the gigs, it really warms my heart. David trusted me and respected me. I was a year and a half older than him and he would ask me for suggestions and I would help him put the setlist together, right while everybody else was kissing his ass and tell him how great he was.'[21]

Still, there was also a more macabre element to their friendship. Garson had long been trusted in ways that few others had been; 'I helped with some first aid which might have saved his life at a Madison Square Garden concert, and I remember "Rock 'n' Roll Suicide" at Radio City, and he had so much make-up on his face that he fainted.' He was rewarded for this intimacy with a particular confidence. 'One morning, when we were on the bus, he told me that several years before, maybe in the late '70s or the early '80s, he met a psychic who told him when he was going to die. And he said it to me, quite matter-of-fact. He didn't think it was quacky or weird, because probably half the psychics are full of shit and some are real. And obviously, this guy was for real. So when I got the call, the first thing I thought, *This is what he told me* because he said, "I'm going to die when I'm 69."'[22]

There were other, inadvertently prophetic moments on the tour, too. During what would be his final show in Scotland in late November 2003, Bowie channelled Ziggy Stardust, announcing that 'not only is this the last show of the tour, but it's the last show we'll ever do. . . until T in the Park next summer.' The 2004 edition of the festival, at which he was due to headline, was feverishly anticipated by the Scottish media and Bowie gave a number of interviews to promote his appearance. But it would never come to pass. And some admirers were concerned that he was losing his lustre; the near-ubiquity with which he was being seen on tour was turning him into an almost predictable figure, removing years of mystique and turning him into just another millionaire rock star.

One dismissive review in the *Daily Telegraph* said 'Mostly, though, I think the problem was Bowie himself. The man famous for acquiring personae the way the rest of us acquire fridges has finally stripped away all those accumulated layers, and here he stood before us in plain jeans and jerkin, simply as himself. And do you know what? He's not terribly interesting. He's affable enough, and quite funny. "The Man Who Sold the World" was introduced thus: "1846 – England was at war with France, and I released this." He can still sing like a dream, he's got the songs, he's got the band, he's got the set. But I fear that, as part of that process of stripping away his old selves, he has lost almost in its entirety the one quality on which his whole career has been founded: charisma.'[23]

It was customary for Bowie to be photographed with other leading musicians while on tour or at festivals, but according to one anonymous but well-placed member of his camp, there were several rock stars who weren't bothered about meeting him, clearly deciding that he was yesterday's news. It would be invidious to mention most of their (household) names, but one was Alex Turner, then enjoying the first fruits of success with Arctic Monkeys. When the two met, it was unsuccessful. Turner later told *NME* his version of events. 'We didn't know what to say to him, you know. We were just overwhelmed. It was like a fucking runaway train in those days.'[24] 'Later on, things would change, given the vast debt that the Arctic Monkeys' 2022 album *The Car* owes to Bowie. It proves, if nothing else, that his influence lived on in unexpected but pervasive ways.*

I saw Bowie again, for his final full show in Britain, at the Isle of Wight Festival on 13 June 2004. By now, his band were eight months into a long and demanding tour, and the summer festival gigs, where they would be performing to non-partisan crowds, beckoned before they could all take a deserved rest. Alan Edwards had got into trouble with Bowie for arranging

---

* The ever-loyal Edwards denies that Bowie was ever disrespected. 'That wasn't my recollection really, at all. I thought younger acts held David in complete reverence: Nine Inch Nails, Smashing Pumpkins, Goldie, Damon Albarn, Noel Gallagher, Brett Anderson. A long list of people who he hung out with and collaborated with . . . Of course, some of the very young pop artists might not have understood, but I think anyone with the slightest musical depth or understanding knew exactly who he was. Frankly, younger artists seemed to be in awe of David and rightly so.'

an unauthorised *Sun* photoshoot en route to the festival. As he describes it now, 'the photographer Dave Hogan came along to take some pictures for the newspaper. We were looking to push sales for other shows on the tour, I think. Either way, David just wasn't in the mood for photographs and let me know exactly what he thought of the idea'.[25] The mood before the show was not helped by England having lost a match against Portugal on penalties in the Euro 2004 football championships, courtesy of star player David Beckham missing his spot-kick.

Bowie referred to this during the gig in an unexpectedly macho way – 'I'll be the only DB in Britain who hasn't got his nuts in a vice tomorrow' – but the 20-song set was lighter on singalongs than the audience might have expected, contributing to a vaguely funereal atmosphere. Those Bowie connoisseurs present may have thrilled to back-to-back performances of 'Station to Station' – for me, the highlight of the entire set – and 'Quicksand', but those expecting the hits would have been disappointed. No 'Life on Mars', no 'Let's Dance', no 'Changes', let alone 'Space Oddity', which had long since been retired from the tour setlist. It was a fascinating evening, but also a curiously disengaged one, as if Bowie was tiring of live performance. Perhaps he was. In any case, he would only play another five full gigs.

Gerry Leonard dismisses the idea that Bowie seemed in any kind of compromised health. 'I did not get that impression at all. He had a fitness guy on the road with him and was singing great. We were playing these long shows and he seemed to have great stamina. So it was very much out of the blue when he had that chest pain.' The first inkling that things were going wrong came when, at the Norwegian Wood festival in Oslo on 18 June, an over-enthusiastic – or oddly malicious – fan threw a lollipop at Bowie three songs into the show, catching him in the eye.

The angry singer shouted 'Where are you, you fucking creep?' before saying 'Yeah, I suppose it's easier to get lost in the crowd, you bastard.' After a moment, he recovered himself and said, with his usual suavity, 'Do remember I've only got one [eye] anyway. Fortunately, that's the one that works. The other one has just become a little bit more decorative than it was before . . . lucky you hit the bad one.' Just before he jokily announced that they would play an 'extra-long concert' as a punishment, he issued a request: 'Please keep your affection to yourself.' He was as good as his promise, playing 27 songs, as he would two nights later in Finland.

The problems began on 23 June, when Bowie and his band played the Park Kolbenova festival in Prague. Dorsey, who was standing next to him, describes what happened vividly, and distressingly. 'It was horrible, really horrible. I will never forget that night. He was about to have a surgery on his left arm for a rotator cuff thing, an old ski injury from when he lived in Switzerland, and he was taking cortisone, because it was a little painful. So when he had an ache in his shoulder, he thought something had gone wrong there. But anyway, when we were playing the song "Reality", he wasn't singing, just standing there in front of me with his arms stretched out, holding the microphone out as if he was posturing. Then he turned and looked over his left shoulder at me and his face was translucent. I could almost see through him, he was so pale. And he was gasping for air and his eyes were wide. I could see the front row looking up at him and their faces were in shock, before David's bodyguard came on and took him off.'[26]

Something had gone unexpectedly, terribly wrong. The band played through a couple of mostly instrumental songs – 'A New Career in a New Town' and 'Be My Wife', with tour backing singer Catherine Russell on vocals – and then Bowie returned to the stage. Somehow, he made it through a few more songs, but he had to leave for another half an hour after they attempted 'Station to Station', and then, after 'Changes' had just begun, he had to leave the stage, saying 'I can't do this. I'm sorry, everybody. I'm really, really sorry. We'll come back. We'll make it up to you. But I am in pain. And I have to get off this. I have to stop.'

Bowie had suffered a heart attack in front of tens of thousands of people. It was a terrifying and very public experience, and anyone who knew how dedicated he was to performing would have been aware that he rarely cancelled shows. 'I've done shows with him where he's been sick,' says Dorsey, 'and there's a bucket on the side of the stage. He's walked over to it, thrown up and then gone back again.'[27] Yet he had gone into cardiac arrest and this would last until the next show two days later at the Hurricane Festival, just outside Hamburg.

Most other artists would simply have cancelled, but Bowie dragged himself back on stage, saying to Garson, 'I went to the president's doctor in Czechoslovakia and he told me it's a pinched nerve.' Garson was unconvinced. 'I'm thinking to myself, *It's no pinched nerve.* On stage, because I had this telepathic tactile connection to him, I could feel something was wrong, because my hands were tightening up. And I could almost see him putting his hands on his heart.'[28] Bowie had been pumped full of painkillers and opiates – as a former drug addict, this was very much not something that he was happy about – but he managed to retain an air of black humour, saying to Dorsey as they went on 'Well, this will be an interesting night.'

It was, in the grimmest of ways. Although Bowie somehow managed to get through a 21-song set, videos of the concert show him clearly looking ill and below par, changing from his usual elaborate stage costume into a nondescript hoodie. After he finished performing 'Ziggy Stardust', he started to walk down a metal set of steps by the side of the stage, but it was all too much for him. As Dorsey recalls, 'when he got to the very bottom of the stairs, he just threw up. He just lost it. And everybody freaked and they grabbed him and they put him in a car and they took him out of there with a police escort to the hospital. And that's when they said "You have been in cardiac arrest for 48 hours."'

Bowie had, admittedly, lived a more eventful life than most other 57-year-old men. His consumption of drugs and alcohol when younger had been heroic, even prodigious, and his smoking habits, only abandoned recently, had persisted for decades after the rest of his addictions had been conquered. Yet there was something deeply shocking about what happened to him in late June 2004. The rest of the tour was cancelled, the band dispersed and uncertainty reigned. The message that appeared on his website a couple of weeks later might have been intended to reassure, and it did. Most of Bowie's fans thought that he had simply had a serious but not life-threatening health scare and that, after a suitable period of rest, he would once again resume his recording and performing career.

They – we – were disappointed. He would never perform another full concert or give a press interview again, and it would be the best part of another decade before he would release another album, itself as delight-ful a surprise as his retirement had been an unpleasant shock. But Bowie was now about to enter a lengthy period in his career where he departed from public view, when the only activities that he undertook were things that he truly cared about. The resulting years would be both frustrating and fascinating.

# *THE PRESTIGE* AND THE WILDERNESS YEARS

## 'Making something disappear isn't enough'

*'So here I am, enjoying my retirement'*

Bowie in recovery. On the streets of Chinatown,
New York City, July 2004.

WireImage/Getty

'My, my, my, I hope I warrant that.' As David Bowie walked onto the stage at the Royal Albert Hall on 29 May 2006, to the undisguised joy of the audience, the applause was so long and so loud that the very ceiling seemed in danger of collapse. Bowie was arriving for the encore of a David Gilmour gig, as an unannounced special guest, and would perform 'Arnold Layne' and duet with Gilmour on 'Comfortably Numb', taking on the vocal parts that Roger Waters had sung on album. Bowie had never collaborated or performed with Gilmour before – although both had played at Live Aid, albeit separately – and the reason for the faintly unlikely appearance was that they shared a road manager, Nick Belshaw.

The event was seismic for several reasons: it was Bowie's first performance in Britain since his heart attack; it was the first time that he had played at the Albert Hall – almost unbelievably – since 1970; and, with his performance on the ever-popular 'Comfortably Numb', it was a superstar collaboration of a kind seldom seen outside mega-gigs. According to Gilmour, the guest appearance came along quite organically. 'We were thinking it would be interesting and amusing to get different people up to guest in places. We wanted to get someone to take Roger's part on "Comfortably Numb" since it's such a two-person sort of conversation. Our tour manager guy had been working a lot with David Bowie and said he had lunch with him. I said, "Ask him if he wants to come and do 'Comfortably Numb'." He said he'd love to and could he do another song as well. I said, "What would you like to do?" So he did "Arnold Layne" as well.'[1]

In truth, Bowie was a better fit for 'Arnold Layne' than he was for 'Comfortably Numb'. Pink Floyd keyboardist Rick Wright, who usually performed the Waters part live, commented that 'he turned it into a David Bowie song', which could be seen either as a compliment or an elegantly couched put-down. On 'Arnold Layne', Bowie was able to summon up the spirit of his '60s work, going full south London in a manner that simultaneously paid homage to Syd Barrett and reclaimed the song as one that he might have written himself. On the more epic finale, Bowie's singing was far more dramatic and histrionic than the flat, measured verses usually demanded, meaning that he was in danger of overshadowing Gilmour altogether. Still, he could be excused his moment of showboating. After all, 18 months before, it had looked as if he would never perform live, or do anything else, again.

What happened to David Bowie between his last full live performance at the Hurricane Festival in 2004 and the release of 'Where Are We Now?' almost a decade later remains one of the most mysterious aspects of his life and career. He gave no in-depth press interviews, performed live a total of five times – encompassing ten and a half songs in total – and, after 2007, apparently faded from view, bar a couple of fleeting cameo roles in low-profile films. With Bowie no longer the accessible figure he had been a few years before, BowieNet acknowledged the end of an era and ceased to function in 2006, a tacit admission that there would be no more webchats or exclusive access to its founder. Rumours began to circulate. I was solemnly told by people who claimed to know these things that Bowie had had multiple heart attacks, was suffering from terminal cancer or that he was battling early onset dementia.

Some of the stories of ill health were better sourced than others, but the more fanciful stories came about simply because Bowie chose not to comment or offer any credence to the gossip. His PR team, led by Edwards, was increasingly kept out of the loop too, with Edwards's dealings with his employer increasingly limited to brief, business-like emails and the exchange of birthday and Christmas gifts. Yet even before *The Next Day* sessions began in November 2010, in circumstances of the utmost secrecy, Bowie was hardly the Norma Desmond figure that he was painted as. He acted, made high-profile guest appearances with other musicians, was photographed at parties and film premieres, and generally appeared to enjoy the life of a wealthy retired man-about-town. The question remained – which would be answered definitively a few years later – whether retirement was enough for him.

After Bowie was operated on for a severely blocked artery and an angio-plasty performed, he returned to New York in July 2004, with the remaining dates of A Reality Tour cancelled. His recuperation went well enough for him to be photographed shopping in the city's Chinatown later that month and he spent the rest of the year catching up with theatre, films and con-certs. A relentless touring schedule over the previous couple of years had meant that he had only limited opportunities to see new bands, but now he offered his patronage and support to the likes of Franz Ferdinand and Arcade Fire, both of whom were performing music that owed a consider-able debt to his '70s and early '80s work.

Throughout his career, Bowie, like many other musicians of similar standing, had made guest appearances on his friends' and collaborators' albums. By far the best-known examples of this came in the '70s, when Bowie produced, co-wrote and sang backing vocals on many of Lou Reed and Iggy Pop's most famous songs, including 'Lust for Life', 'Perfect Day' and 'Satellite of Love'. He was usually happy to appear on his guitarists' solo works, too; Mick Ronson's *Slaughter on 10th Avenue*, Adrian Belew's *Young Lions* and Reeves Gabrels's *Ulysses* all feature significant vocal con-tributions by Bowie. This generosity towards his old friends remained a consistent aspect of his career. In 2003 alone, he popped up on Reed's Edgar Allan Poe concept album *The Raven*, singing 'Hop Frog', and guested on Earl Slick's *Zig Zag*.

Bowie was also a patron of lesser-known bands, especially if he was introduced to them by his trusted producers. He appeared on Rustic Overtones' 2001 album *Viva Nueva* after he was introduced to them by Visconti, and it was also because of his long-standing ally that he would return to the studio for the first time since the *Reality* sessions in April 2005 to appear as a guest singer on 'The Cynic' on the Visconti-produced album by Danish band Kashmir *No Balance Palace*, along with Lou Reed, who guested on 'Black Building'. As Visconti recalled, 'David arrived in the studio late in the morning one day, fresh as a daisy, and enthusiastic-ally sang the be-Dickens out of 'The Cynic' as if he had written it himself.

Not only did David sing to perfection, but he also treated us to selections from his iPod. It was a fabulous day! The Danes seem to be cool, even-tempered people, but there was an explosion in the control room as soon as David left . . . something akin to the Mardi Gras.'[2]

He had also taken a tentative step back into the studio earlier that year on what would be the last song until *The Next Day* to have a Bowie writing credit on it – '(She Can) Do That'. That summer, it was used in the forgotten Jamie Foxx flop blockbuster *Stealth* – another reminder that, when it came to his original music being used in films, Bowie had a surprisingly low hit rate. It was co-written with the then-modish electronic artist BT and produced at Looking Glass Studios by Visconti. Its now dated stuttering electronica bears no relation sonically to anything that Bowie was doing at the time, or after, and its lyrics, mainly consisting of repetition of the title, are inconsequential to the point of irrelevance. On its own terms, '(She Can) Do That' is entirely forgettable, the weakest song to have Bowie's name on it in years, but is remarkable as an indication that, less than a year after a near-fatal heart attack, Bowie was still creating music and that any idea of retirement seemed exaggerated.

Perhaps because of this fleeting return to recording, Bowie agreed to participate as a guest artist in the Fashion Rocks concert at Radio City Music Hall in New York on 8 September that year. He turned down the chance to take part in the higher-profile Live 8 in July, making his three-song appearance in New York something of a coup for the organisers. Firstly, he performed a version of 'Life on Mars', accompanied by Garson, before joining an awestruck Arcade Fire for performances of 'Five Years' and their 'Wake Up', almost casually demonstrating in the process how much the latter owed to his own work. The performance took place in the aftermath of Hurricane Katrina and, acknowledging the coup the organisers had managed by enticing Bowie back to live performance, it would be his trio of songs that would be released as a download, with the money raised donated to Katrina charities.

Although Bowie did not give a formal interview after the show, he was sufficiently relaxed and pleased with how the concert had gone to offer a few passing remarks to eager journalists. He took the party line, as might be expected. 'It's great to be back. I loved every minute of being on stage. I didn't want to come off – I could have stayed up there all night. I feel fantastic at the moment.' He was now open about having suffered a heart attack, explaining that 'I decided to take a year off and do nothing. I didn't do any work and just made sure I looked after myself. I go to the gym, I don't drink and I'm feeling really good today.'[3]

He made another public appearance the following week, again with Arcade Fire, singing 'Queen Bitch' and 'Wake Up' at their show in New York's Central Park. If anyone had been watching Bowie closely at this point, they would have suspected that he was on the verge of a comeback after an intentionally fallow year. This was not denied when he gave a brief interview to Dave Itzkoff to support the Fashion Rocks charity, in which he suggested that he was able to lead a fuller life because 'fortunately, I'm not working . . . so I'm resting. I get out a lot. I am a New Yorker, very much, and I get out in New York. It's just a place that I adore. And I love seeing new theatre, I love seeing new bands, art shows, everything. I get everywhere – very quietly and never above 14th Street. I'm very downtown.'[4]

At this juncture, Bowie seemed to be torn between the possibility of returning to the recording studio and the stage, or continuing his semi-retirement. Certainly, he valued his newly adopted anonymity away from the spotlight. He had mused to Ricky Gervais two years before, when asked whether he had abandoned the idea of being David Jones from Brixton, that 'I will always be fundamentally just a Jones. The moment I close the door behind me, slip off my crushed velvet skateboard shorts and throw myself into our heated Olympic-size, three-level swimming pool, I think to myself, *Self, is there a Jones next door that I should be keeping up with?* And do you know something? There always is. Though actually it's the Prestons in our case, but you know what I mean.'[5]

The jokes did not conceal the sense of bifurcation that he felt, and he was as clear with Itzkoff as he was with anyone about his identity when he said, 'The Bowie character, for me, is strictly to be used for the stage, so I can hide back away as David Jones. Right now, in the mountains, where I am at the moment, it's David Jones. With my family, I am David Jones, very much.' As 2005 came to an end, most might reasonably have expected that the Bowie persona would continue to return in various forms, that the appeal of live performance and recording would eventually be too much for him to resist. But then another far more unusual and interesting opportunity came along instead.

At the beginning of 2006, Christopher Nolan was not yet the all-conquering force in cinema that he has subsequently become, But the 35-year old director had already established himself as an unusual, even unique, filmmaker, someone whose pictures appealed to both large audiences and critics alike while adopting time-fracturing narratives that owed much to his heroes – *The Man Who Fell to Earth* director Nicolas Roeg and the novelist Jorge Luis Borges. He had made a total of four feature films, beginning with his low-budget debut *Following* in 1998, and had subsequently worked his way up the Hollywood ladder with each acclaimed picture, including 2000's *Memento*, 2002's *Insomnia* and 2005's superhero picture *Batman Begins*. It would be the latter's 2008 sequel, *The Dark Knight*, complete with the late Heath Ledger's indelible performance as the Joker, that truly turned Nolan into a household-name blockbuster director. But, until then, the last film that he directed on a more modest scale, on a budget of a relatively tight $40 million, was an adaptation of a 1995 Christopher Priest novel, *The Prestige*.

Nolan had shown interest in filming the book from late 2000, seeing enormous cinematic potential in its shifting timeframes, the protagonists doubling up as one another – both of its stars Christian Bale and Hugh Jackman play dual roles – and in its unreliable narration. It was an ambitious, arguably uncommercial endeavour, devoid of a sympathetic protagonist and concentrating instead on the rivalry between two magicians in Victorian London, each of whom has a dark secret that is only revealed in the film's final act. Yet Nolan's script, co-written with his brother

Jonathan, attracted a prestigious (pun fully intended) cast that included his regular collaborator Michael Caine, Scarlett Johansson, Rebecca Hall and Andy Serkis, all of whom excelled at bringing to life Priest and Nolan's characters. There remained one missing piece in the jigsaw, however: the casting of the sole real-life character depicted on screen, the Serbian electricity pioneer Nikola Tesla.

Nolan had always taken interest in offbeat and unusual casting in his pictures. He had cast Robin Williams, who tended to play comic or heart-warming roles, in the part of the villainous novelist Walter Finch in *Insomnia*, while the presence of Rutger Hauer as an untrustworthy business magnate in *Batman Begins* was an obvious nod to Nolan's adulation for *Blade Runner*.* Yet Tesla seemed an insuperable issue. 'When we were casting *The Prestige*,' Nolan explained, 'we had gotten very stuck on the character of Nikola Tesla. Tesla was this other-worldly, ahead-of-his-time figure, and at some point it occurred to me he was the original Man Who Fell to Earth.' Nolan – the self-confessed 'biggest Bowie fan in the world' who had used 'Something in the Air' over the end credits of *Memento* and would later choose 'Loving the Alien' as one of his picks on *Desert Island Discs* – recalled that 'he seemed to be the only actor capable of playing the part. He had that requisite iconic status, and he was a figure as mysterious as Tesla needed to be.'[6] Accordingly, Bowie was offered the role: the first part he had been put forward for in a studio picture since *The Last Temptation of Christ* and the first serious acting challenge he had had since *Basquiat*. And, unsurprisingly, he turned it down.

Bowie never discussed his motivations for first refusing, then accepting, the part of Tesla, but it is not hard to speculate why. The shoot was in California, and even though he would only be required for a few days, it represented a cross-continent trip, which would be a hassle. He would be required to portray a well-known historical figure, and attempt an accent

---

* This is even true of small parts in his pictures. Edward Hibbert, best known for playing the haughty restaurant critic Gil Chesterton in *Frasier*, appears in a minor, atypically serious role in *The Prestige* as the theatrical agent Ackerman.

to boot, something that he was always instinctively uncomfortable with. Lastly, it was a film that was likely to be seen by more people than anything he had done in decades. Bowie routinely turned down overtly commercial projects, not least *A View to a Kill*, and the idea of appearing in a picture by the man who had directed the most recent Batman film – thereby reintroducing himself to the public in the grandest, most flamboyant way imaginable – may well have been anathema to him.

After he rejected the part, the cerebral, restrained Nolan all but panicked. 'It was the only time I can ever remember trying again with an actor who passed on me. I petitioned to let me explain why he was the right actor for it. In total honesty, I told him if he didn't agree to do the part, I had no idea where I would go from there. I would say I begged him.'[7] The entreaty had the desired effect and Bowie joined the cast. It would be a tight, quick shoot; filming began in mid-January in Los Angeles and was scheduled to end in early April, with a premiere set for early October. Bowie would join the production in March, shooting his scenes solely with Jackman and Serkis.

Nolan called him 'terrific' to work with, praising his 'otherworldly quality and extraordinary charisma'[8] and later declaring that 'the experience of having him on set was wonderful. Daunting, at first . . . I've never seen a crew respond to any movie star that way, no matter how big. But he was very gracious and understood the effect he had on people . . . Normally when you meet stars, no matter how starry they are, when you see them as people, some of that mystique goes away. But not with David Bowie. I came away from the experience being able to say I was still his biggest fan, and a fan who had the very miraculous opportunity to work with him for a moment. I loved the fact that after having worked with him, I had just the same fascination with his talent and his charisma. I thought that was quite magical.'[9]

Serkis was struck by Bowie's self-deprecation and modesty. 'As an actor, he always felt like he was slightly an imposter, which was quite interesting that he was kind of like, was this really his thing? But he'll give it a damn good shot, you know? So he laughed at himself a lot.' Bowie told Serkis that 'I think my Nikola Tesla, who was from Belgrade, sounds a little bit like Inspector Clouseau!' Jackman, meanwhile, made the mistake of telling Bowie that he had resold a sold-out ticket for one of his Australian concerts at a profit when he was younger. A faux-outraged Bowie promptly christened Jackman 'the Scalper'; the nickname stuck for the rest of the shoot.

*The Prestige* is one of Nolan's most underrated films, a picture that eschews fancy special effects or large-scale action scenes in favour of a psychological thriller in which, without wishing to spoil it for anyone unfamiliar with its twists and turns, both lead characters end up getting exactly what they deserve, in unexpected ways. It is compulsively watchable and owes much of its power, as Nolan anticipated, to Bowie's brief but iconic appearance. As with his performance in *The Last Temptation of Christ*, he is only on screen for a few moments, but Nolan, like Scorsese, knows how to use him effectively.

From his introduction, striding through a force field of electrical flashes to greet Jackman's aristocratic magician, to his departure, fleeing Colorado before he is lynched, Bowie's Tesla is an extraordinary creation, given many of the script's best lines, which have a thrillingly self-reflective quality. Tesla muses that 'society only tolerates one change at the time. First time I tried to change the world, I was hailed as a visionary. Second time, I was asked politely to retire. So here I am, enjoying my retirement.' It is immediately clear why he was Nolan's only conceivable choice for the role.

There is another aspect to the film, too, which Bowie absorbed. The 'prestige' of the title refers to a piece of misdirection, which is explained thus by Michael Caine's character Cutter, a veteran stage engineer: 'Every great magic trick consists of three parts or acts. The first part is called "The Pledge". The magician shows you something ordinary: a deck of cards, a bird or a man. He shows you this object. Perhaps he asks you to inspect it to see if it is indeed real, unaltered, normal. But of course . . . it probably isn't. The second act is called "The Turn". The magician takes the ordinary something and makes it do something extraordinary. Now you're looking for the secret . . . but you won't find it, because of course you're not really looking. You don't really want to know. You want to be fooled. But you wouldn't clap yet. Because making something disappear isn't enough. You have to bring it back. That's why every magic trick has a third act, the hardest part, the part we call "The Prestige".'

If one of the most famous men in the world had continued his musical career in public view, that would simply be a pledge. Should he appear to retire from touring and recording, removing himself from this public view and devoting himself to other interests instead, this would be a turn; an unexpected twist. But if he had other ideas altogether, which even he would take years to formulate – the ultimate example of hiding in plain sight – then Bowie's own version of the prestige would come to spectacular, epoch-defining fruition. But not yet.

The film premiered in October 2006, without Bowie present. However, it had hardly been a quiet year for him. After completing his appearance in *The Prestige*, he headed to England for a period, where he had accepted a cameo role in his friend Ricky Gervais's sitcom *Extras*. The idea behind the show was that Gervais's hapless would-be actor Andy Millman was forever seeking to thrust himself into fame and fortune, and, when he achieved his aim at the conclusion of the first season, the second instalment was an illustration of the term 'be careful what you wish for'. Millman, now the writer and star of an old-fashioned sitcom, finds himself patronised and belittled by the more successful celebrities who he is now on shoulder-rubbing terms with.

Most of the A-list figures who participated in the show are the subjects of mockery; Kate Winslet is shown acting in a Holocaust drama in an attempt to win an Oscar,* while Patrick Stewart is guyed as a sex-obsessed

---

* As she would eventually do for the would-be artistic, actually tawdry 2009 picture *The Reader*, which would once have been released as an exploitation B-movie called *I Was A Teenage Nazi Sex Slave* and been all the better for it.

pervert who has written a script in which various women lose their clothes at his behest ('but I've seen everything . . . I've seen it all'). Bowie's performance, however, was presented without a hint of mockery towards him, with the laughs purely at the Gervais character's expense. Millman, frustrated by the lack of appreciation that his show has received, heads to a VIP area of an upmarket club, only to see Bowie nearby. After Millman confesses his doubts and insecurities, Bowie, seizing the opportunity, begins to compose an impromptu song, 'Little Fat Man', aka 'Pug Nosed Face', which mocks the 'little fat man who sold his soul . . . chubby little loser', which turns into a riotous, *Hunky Dory*-meets-*Diamond Dogs*-style singalong, as the assembled guests sing 'He's banal and facile / He's a fat waste of space / See his pug-nosed face . . .'

The show's producer Charlie Hanson has warm memories of filming the show and of Bowie's participation in it. 'Bowie was friends with Ricky and was a fan of the show, and everyone had seen the first series by then, so they knew what it was about. He was happy to take part, especially after Ricky showed him the lyrics he'd written for the song, but said he wouldn't be able to play the piano and act at the same time, so he asked me to find someone that could play the piano behind the scenes. I found a guy called Clifford Slapper, a pianist who's a massive Bowie fan, and showed him the lyrics. Then Clifford came up with the melody for the song, which, to be honest, Bowie didn't even hear until he arrived.'[10]

The sequence involving Bowie was filmed at Elberts Bar in Hertford over two days in early June 2006. Hanson recalls that, on the first day, 'he arrived at lunchtime and then we rehearsed in the afternoon. Clifford played what he'd done and Bowie altered it a bit and sang it in his way. Then the next day, he came back with his son Duncan, because he hadn't seen him much over the previous years and was trying to rebuild his relationship with him. Filming was great. Obviously, Bowie enjoyed himself and Ricky was howling with laughter all the time because it's very funny.' Between takes, Bowie sang 'Starman' to the appreciative crew. 'Everybody, to be honest, was starstruck,' says Hanson, 'more so than a lot of the actors that we worked with. He was very friendly and polite and chatty, wanted to talk about theatre and writers and plays, which wasn't what I was expecting. And he was lovely about Clifford, too, saying "Where did you find this guy? He's perfect!"'[11]

The episode was broadcast on 21 September to an appreciative UK audience of 3.84 million. Had *The Next Day* and *Blackstar* never been recorded, it is a strange idea that the last song that Bowie would ever have been associated with would be a skit in a sitcom: he may well have enjoyed the irony of beginning his public life with jingles for adverts and ending it with a self-parodying song, with the years of megastardom and fame in between.

Bowie soon undertook another couple of acting roles, albeit as less demanding voiceovers. He was the antagonist Maltazard in Luc Besson's 2006 *Arthur and the Invisibles*, in which he took his (virtual) place alongside Madonna and Snoop Dogg. Although the film, a convoluted and visually unappealing fantasy adventure, is of little interest to anyone other than Bowie completists and children, he offers a suitably ripe vocal performance, treading a line between menace and humour that will be familiar to anyone who remembers Bowie's friend Gary Oldman's appearance as the deranged villain Norman Stansfield in Besson's masterly *Léon*.* And he also jumped at the opportunity to go fully over the top in the role of Lord Royal Highness in 'Atlantis SquarePants', an extended episode of the cult animated show *SpongeBob SquarePants*. When he was offered the part, Bowie called it 'the Holy Grail of animation gigs'; 'nothing else need happen this year. Well, this week anyway.'[12]

Bowie's gift for comedy, for impersonations and wackiness, has been remarked upon by many of his collaborators who I interviewed. The predominantly American musicians with whom he worked in the second half of his career were surprised but pleased to be introduced by him to anything from *The Office* to the work of Peter Cook and Dudley Moore. Yet it

---

* Amusingly, when Bowie proved unable, or unwilling, to take on the role in the sequels, Besson cast Lou Reed instead.

was a disappointment that Bowie was never given the chance on screen to fully cut loose with the sillier, funnier side of his persona – bar, perhaps, his work in *Zoolander*. His best-known performances tend to be deeply serious, even sombre, in nature, or fantastical figures like Jareth, the Goblin King from *Labyrinth* or Agent Jeffries from *Twin Peaks*.

It was only in *SpongeBob SquarePants* that he was given the opportunity to demonstrate his love of silliness, as Lord Royal Highness essays a fruity upper-class accent and obviously relishes the knowingly absurd dialogue – 'Seize these hostile bubble poppers!' – written for his character. And, as often happened with Bowie, there was even a line that came to be much revered outside of the context of the show, when Lord Royal Highness tells SpongeBob that 'art is what happens when you learn to dream'. Few would argue with that.

The Gilmour guest appearance, acting for Nolan, a pug-nosed face: 2006 was as busy a year for Bowie, in a non-musical capacity, as might be expected, but he would not perform any of his own songs in public until 9 November, when he and Garson appeared at the Hammerstein Ballroom in New York to play at the Keep a Child Alive Black Ball charity gala. Bowie played three songs, an unexpected reprise of Glastonbury opener 'Wild is the Wind' and 'Fantastic Voyage', before he duetted with Alicia Keys on an energetic performance of 'Changes'. By all accounts, the evening was a success, but Bowie, feeling self-conscious about both his appearance and performance skills, would not allow the show to be filmed; the photographer Kevin Mazur observed 'it was a great show, but he looked a little heavy'.[13] One can only imagine the cocktail of drugs and statins that a post-heart attack Bowie was prescribed, but anyone seeing his appearance in *Extras* or *The Prestige* can note the difference between this older, statelier Bowie and the preternaturally youthful figure that he was still cutting on the tour two years before.

Bowie had reached a crossroads. He could either re-immerse himself in public life fully, think about recording another album or, at the very least, undertake a series of one-off gigs. Or he could step back from the spotlight altogether: no more guest appearances, fewer cameos on songs or films, no more responsibility. A Reality Tour had been hugely lucrative – it grossed $46 million, one of 2004's highest-earning tours – and the boost to his reputation that *Heathen* and *Reality* had engendered meant that the latest compilation of his work, *Best of Bowie*, had sold handsomely. Bowie did not need to tour again from a financial perspective. But was he short-changing those around him if he did not?

Bowie rang Garson after their Hammerstein performance together. In Garson's account, 'He said "Do you think we should tour?" And, as my wife says to this day, "Why don't you say yes?" I said, "David, only if you're hearing it and feel it". He wasn't, but he felt bad for us, because he wanted us to have the work. We were working musicians. But my integrity superseded my pocketbook.' Garson expresses no regrets about the advice he offered Bowie. 'If you push someone against their free will, there's no good ending.'[14]

There had been a brief flurry of excitement in May 2006 when a Bowie-curated extravaganza was announced, the High Line Festival in Manhattan. It was suggested that he would give a one-off performance at what was clearly intended as an updated, New York version of his 2002 Meltdown festival. Yet for whatever reason, he withdrew from performing at the event shortly after he turned 60 on 8 January 2007; an event marked by rather less fanfare than the exultant Madison Square Garden concert the previous decade. The only, vague reason given for Bowie not performing was 'ongoing work on a new project', which was almost certainly code for his deciding against what would have been a potentially exhausting and exposing endeavour. He had no new material to perform and even a single two-hour show would have required weeks of rehearsals, assembling the band once more and, of course, the potential for something going awry. It was a disappointing change of heart, but those around Bowie were used to such things.

While 2007 may not have been as busy as 2006, it was still clear that the erstwhile Lord Royal Highness was in no mood to retire. The High Line shows went ahead without Bowie's stand-alone concert, but he did appear to introduce Gervais's show at Madison Square Garden on 19 May, singing an apparently impromptu a cappella rendition of 'Pug Nosed Face', leading the comedian to sigh that he would probably be called 'the Fat White Duck' or 'Piggy Stardust'. A few weeks later, he laid the ghost of BowieNet to rest when he accepted a lifetime achievement award at the Webby Awards, making an amusingly meta speech. Claiming he had only been given five words to say thanks, he said, 'I only get five words? Shit. That was five. Four more there. That's three. Two', before disappearing, leaving the audience, as ever, hungry for more.

And Bowie was still happy to take on the odd guest appearance, too. He made a brief cameo in May in the finance drama *August* as Cyrus Oglivie, an icy asset-stripper who delights in pricking the illusions of Josh Hartnett's arrogant dotcom financier. Bowie described his undemanding appearance as 'a little like wandering down the road for a morning paper, dropping into a quiet building and making a quick cameo appearance in a movie and continuing on home to read. Nice.'[15] As a cane-wielding tycoon who conveys an appropriate sense of menace in his few lines of dialogue, Bowie did his job splendidly, outclassing the rest of the production: no wonder the director Austin Chick later commented 'I spent the day saying "Oh God, I'm directing David Bowie".'[16] The film was not a success.

A more interesting guest spot came later in the year, when Bowie reunited with the producer Dave Sitek. He had previously recorded a guest vocal for the song 'Province' by Sitek's band TV on the Radio in 2006, having been an admirer of theirs since their 2004 debut *Desperate Youth, Blood Thirsty Babes*. Sitek was a remarkably successful and prolific figure, who the *NME* named the most forward-thinking person in contemporary music in 2008, and he and Bowie danced around one another for a period, flirting without ever quite going the full distance. (It would be fascinating to imagine what *Reality* or *The Next Day* produced by Sitek would sound like.) The album on which Bowie now appeared was *Anywhere I Lay My*

*Head*, a collection of Tom Waits covers sung by the actress and occasional musician Scarlett Johansson, who had also appeared in *The Prestige* but had no scenes opposite Bowie, to her chagrin.

She eventually met her idol at a party and briefly discussed Sitek with him, before inviting him to participate in the recording sessions down in Louisiana. Bowie expressed non-committal interest but was unable to join her, so she assumed that their conversation was little more than pleasantries. It was to Johansson's delight that, while she was filming Woody Allen's *Vicky Cristina Barcelona* in Spain, Sitek rang her to tell her that, apparently on a whim, Bowie had recorded backing vocals for two songs on the album, something that she later called 'the best phone call I ever got'. A suitably overawed Johansson thanked Bowie in the liner notes for 'sifting your stardust over this album'.

In the penultimate guest appearance Bowie made on another artist's work, he played down his contribution as 'these "oohs" and "aahs" on a couple of tracks', and suggested that 'the record company wanted to spin my involvement a little more than it actually warrants'. This was excessively modest. Sitek asked him to sing on the songs 'Falling Down' and 'Fannin' Street', which Bowie made evocative and inimitable contributions to, beautifully complementing Johansson's Nico-esque lead vocals. He praised her as '[creating] a mood that could have been summoned by someone like Margery Latimer or Jeanette Winterson', and, of the many disappointments in Bowie's career, a minor one is that he and Johansson never collaborated again, either as musicians or actors.

*Anywhere I Lay My Head* was released in May 2008, to critical acclaim, shortly after Bowie filmed a brief cameo in the family-oriented musical comedy-drama *Bandslam*. Like his role in *August*, it was an undemanding part, what he called 'a ten-second scene of absolute silence', in which he played himself, sending an encouraging email to the protagonist, a would-be musician who idolises Bowie. It was the last appearance he made in a feature film – although, as we shall see, far from the final time that he appeared on screen – and although it's an inconsequential part, it's a pleasant surprise in the context of the film, the equivalent of seeing an old friend you haven't encountered for a while popping up unexpectedly.

Bowie did not entirely withdraw from public life after this, but nor was he a constant presence, either. He was a familiar face on the New York social scene, once again appearing at the Met Gala in 2008 – appropriately themed around superheroes, with the subtitle 'Fashion and Fantasy' – and various *Vanity Fair* parties. He showed up at the premiere screenings of his son Duncan Jones's debut film *Moon* in January and April 2009, and returned to the Keep a Child Alive Black Ball, this time in a non-performing capacity, with Iman in October that year. He judged the 2009 Tribeca Film Festival,* went to gigs and to the theatre, read voraciously and enjoyed his anonymity when he wasn't attending public events. But he showed no signs of wanting to record any further music, to tour, to act or to do any of the things that he was associated with. David Bowie, it appeared, had quietly left the building. David Jones was enjoying the opportunities associated with his alter ego's fame, but he was coasting on past glories and a peerless reputation.

For those who had been playing and recording with Bowie, it was another matter. He could be present one moment, albeit often at a distance, and then absent the next. This was frustrating. According to Sterling Campbell, 'we'd go and see Arcade Fire together and Interpol and Gnarls Barkley. We saw a lot of shows together. We hung out, you know, not constantly, but we hung out a lot.'[17] Leonard, a more recent addition to the Bowie camp, was less in contact – 'we emailed a bit, saw Gail [Ann Dorsey] play, but it was generally pretty quiet' – and describes the new situation as 'disappointing for everybody . . . What people don't seem to realise is that if you work with somebody like David Bowie, and then you stop, everybody assumes that you're busy, or they can't afford you anymore. Mentally,

---

\* The film that won, incidentally, was Tomas Alfredson's excellent vampire picture *Let the Right One In.*

you've now switched over to be part of this bigger operation, and you're back to finding your feet again. So it took a while to get back.'[18]

Dorsey saw matters differently. 'I heard he was well, and I was happy, because that's all I cared about. I didn't care if he made music again. The next time we spoke was when Alexander McQueen committed suicide [on 11 Feb 2010], because McQueen had done a lot of clothes for me and for David, like the Union Jack coat on the *Earthling* cover. We had a little commiseration over that, and then I asked him "What are you up to? I'm glad you're there." And he said, "I'm doing my charcoals. And I'm taking Lexi to school." I thought, he's enjoying his family, which is something I think he really missed that time on the road. I remember saying to him, before one gig, "Are Iman and Lexi coming?" and he said "I don't want to take them out of their routine. We're in our world and if you pull them out of their world, it's disruptive." He really missed his family, so I think he was really enjoying being at home in the last few years. They were very close, they were very much in love and I was happy that he was happy that he was doing that, because why would you want to be without your kid?'[19]

Bowie seemed to have made his mind up. After his own dysfunctional family background, an unsuccessful first marriage and an absence from much of Duncan's life, he was determined not to make the same mistakes. If he never recorded another song, his reputation and fame were assured. He would always be the man who wrote '"Heroes"' and 'Let's Dance', a global superstar who had transformed the music industry. There was no need, financial or otherwise, for him to write or perform ever again. A happy, fulfilled home life was the most important thing for the now 63-year-old Bowie: sentimental, perhaps, but also true.

Which is why it came as a surprise to several of his former musicians, who had long since assumed their services were no longer needed, to get a call from Visconti early in 2011. As the world wondered whether Bowie would ever make another record, or if he had retired for good, the producer said, tongue firmly in cheek, 'There's a young singer-songwriter in town, David Jones from Brixton, and he wants to cut an album. Can we help him?'

# THE NEXT DAY AND DAVID BOWIE IS

## 'Here I am, not quite dying'

*'The switch-hitting, bisexual, senior citizen from London has resurfaced'*

*David Bowie Is* breaking new ground at the Victoria and Albert Museum, London 2013.

Rune Hellestad/Getty

L ate in the evening of 7 January 2013, a strange rumour began to circulate on social media. A few high-profile music journalists and known Bowie fans, such as Caitlin Moran and Alexis Petridis, had been sent a terse email suggesting that they should wake up – or, for the more nocturnal, check in – at 5am the following morning and look at their emails, where news was promised. That the message was coming from Bowie's publicists at Outside suggested that it concerned the long-absent musician, but no further details were forthcoming. Where there is a lack of information, gossip immediately takes hold.

The first suggestion was that there was a Bowie box set or high-profile reissue announced to coincide with his 66th birthday. It was news, undoubtedly – anything connected with Bowie was of interest, especially since his withdrawal from the public eye nearly a decade ago now – but it wasn't *seismic* news. The next idea was a grimmer one. Stories about Bowie's ill health had been circulating through the industry for several years now, and Outside and his management had refused to dignify them with any further information, not even a rebuttal. But perhaps things had reached the stage where something had to be announced, if only to dispel the tittle-tattle. Two decades before, on 23 November 1991, Freddie Mercury had publicly announced that he was HIV positive, knowing that his death was imminent; he died the next day. If Bowie's condition was similarly serious, then he may have wished to issue a similar pre-emptive statement. Had this been the case, then it would have made for a uniquely morbid birthday present.

The third rumour was the least likely of all. A couple of the better-informed music critics surmised that Bowie was about to release a new single, his first recording for a decade. Yet this seemed wildly unlikely. Bowie was, after all, one of the most famous men in the world, someone who was scrutinised and had his movements (such as they were) logged and reported and carefully dissected by his admirers. How on earth would he have managed not only to record a single – let alone an album – without anyone noticing? It was an outlandish suggestion. Yes, he had been an innovator in the past, with the download-only release of 'Telling Lies' among other things, but the possibility that, in the era of smartphones and mass communication – one that he had foretold in his *Newsnight* interview in 1999 – someone as iconic as Bowie could simply have returned to an industry that virtually everyone assumed that he had long since left behind seemed both fanciful and impossible.

Many sensible figures, the self-appointed custodians of the Bowie legacy, were quick to dismiss the murmurings. The usual refrain – 'Let the Dame alone!' – was sounded. And although a few curious figures set their alarms for 5am the following morning, preparing to be disappointed – perhaps a new expanded Tin Machine box set would be announced, or a five-disc *Earthling* drum 'n' bass release would be visited upon us all – most decided that this was just another excitable story, put about by the terminally optimistic, who seemed incapable of accepting that Bowie's career was over.

A few hours later, things were rather different.

The circumstances under which *The Next Day* came into being remain mysterious. While it would have been immeasurably useful for any Bowie fan – or biographer – for him to have sat down with a trusted confidante and explained exactly why he decided to start writing and recording songs again, after a significant creative hiatus, such information was not forthcoming. Even those who worked on the album with him were not given any such insight. Instead, the facts are as follows.

In the autumn of 2010, Bowie had not been in a recording studio for three years and had apparently lost all interest in writing music. On the occasions that Visconti and his former collaborators saw him socially, he was far more interested in discussing the current music scene than he was in talking about any of his own projects. Everyone believed that he was retired. So it came as a huge surprise to Visconti, Leonard and Campbell when he contacted them in November that year to say, diffidently, 'Would you be interested in coming down to the studio and working on some demos with me?'

Campbell has a clear recollection of what happened. 'I was down at my studio and David called me one day. We had a chat about how everything was going and then he asked what my availability was, but to keep it hush hush. And so we started demoing. A couple of months after the call, we found a really rinky-dink basement studio and began rehearsing stuff that would become *The Next Day*.'[1] It was a thrilling experience, especially for Leonard, a relatively new addition to the Bowie machine, but one not without its risks. 'I'd resigned myself to it not happening, so it was amazing that he was going to come back and do music again. I think we all knew how important this was, when he said to us, "Look, can you keep a secret?" And we knew that if we kept it secret, David can come back and make this record, but if we didn't, he's just going to shove it. And you don't want to be the person who caused that. So it was very easy to make that decision.'[2]

The four worked together for a week at 6/8 Studios in Manhattan's East Village. The circumstances were challenging – Campbell mentions that 'I was playing on a really crappy drumkit, which kept moving around' – but it barely mattered. Leonard recalls that they rehearsed intensively but did not record anything until the final day, a process that he describes as 'kind of miraculous'. Bowie was his old self, or so he appeared, anyway. 'He seemed like the same person and excited to be back and doing it again. At first, he was a little nervous, bringing out the songs in front of us, but then he quickly became encouraged by the fact that we were excited, and we thought they were good ideas, and we brought them to life. He just kept pulling out the songs and "Where Are We Now?" came out. And all these songs for *The Next Day* were there in demos, which was amazing.'[3]

While previous albums had been largely improvised in the studio, it was now clear that Bowie had a different intent. Visconti suggested that this was music that he had been working on for some time. 'You could tell from the beginning that the songs were stunning even in primitive form. They were obviously things that had built up over the past ten years, sketches he had all along.'⁴ So much for the idle retirement years. Yet after the week's recording was finished, Bowie gathered up the demos that they had prepared, thanked the musicians and disappeared, saying 'I'm going to start writing now' as a sign-off.

Silence then followed for another six months and the musicians felt a sense of having marched up to the top of the hill before having no clear idea of where to head to next. In fact, one of the reasons for Bowie not contacting them again was an uncertainty about where the songs could be recorded. In the intervening decade between albums, Looking Glass Studios had closed down, and the first studio that he approached decided that having none other than David Bowie record there would be an excellent opportunity to drum up some publicity.* When Visconti was telephoned and asked 'Is it true that you're making a record at such and such a studio?', it was clear that they would have to move on swiftly. At last, Magic Shop Studios, a few minutes' walk from Bowie's home in Tribeca in New York, was settled upon and, on 2 May 2011, the recording sessions for Bowie's 26th album began.

One of the reasons for *The Next Day*'s coherence was that it was recorded using musicians who Bowie both rated and trusted. After a lengthy career in which he had moved from band to band with both alacrity and ruthlessness, he had now settled upon his rep company and they included the likes of Earl Slick, Zachary Alford – subbing in for Campbell, whose work commitments with the B-52s meant that he was unable to play on most of the record – and Gail Ann Dorsey. Her reaction to being brought into the fold again remains touching. 'He called me again and said, "I'm doing another album". I never thought I'd get that call again. Then he stressed "This is all very special, because this time, we can't tell anybody

---

* The name of the studio has not been publicly disclosed, but one of those involved in the abortive recording suggests that it was Oven Studios, Alicia Keys's personal recording studio – which would make sense, given the previous collaborations between her and Bowie.

that we're doing it. We have to keep everything completely secret. And if you're not in on it, then I can't count on you. So you're either in or you're out." And I said "I will do anything for you, David." I lied to people. I said I was making an album for some Swedish artist who had a bunch of money and who nobody had ever heard of.'[5]

Alford was similarly glad to be asked to return for his first Bowie album since *Earthling*. 'It was actually a really low point in my career. I'd just bought a house and I was struggling. So when that call came through, it was like "Right, I'm back." At first, I just thought it would just be like things carrying on as before. But when I was back with him, I realised that I felt different. I felt so lucky to be back. I had to cherish this opportunity, because it was a blessing. In a way, I probably wasn't as carefree or as nonchalant as I had been in the '90s with him, because I was trying harder to stay. It sounds almost hokey, but the gravity of the situation was apparent to me.'[6]

The May 2011 sessions were prolific, with a degree of seriousness and focus that all the participants relished. Bowie played the earlier demos to the band, as well as sketches that he'd recently written, and then the musicians would flesh them out into songs. There would only be a few takes; on occasion, tracks would be finished in a single recording session. Alford kept a diary of proceedings and it led to slight friction with Bowie.

'I wanted to remember everything. And David got upset with me, because I was writing all the time and he would be making fun of me writing. And I shrivelled and shrunk back, but replied "I want to remember this".'[7] Everyone who played with Bowie concurred that he was never an overbearing or bullying presence in the studio, but the light-heartedness of previous recording sessions was largely absent. Alford acknowledges that he may have suspected that this would be the last time he worked with Bowie and that this particular sense of fatalism fed into the atmosphere, even as everyone tried their best to pretend that it was business as usual.

When the sessions concluded, there was a break for Bowie to assess the songs recorded, but it would also provide a rare opportunity for Leonard to see the musician in another sphere, as well as co-writing songs with him. 'I was living in upstate New York and I knew that David was in the neighbouring town, Woodstock. So I rang and asked him if he fancied a coffee and he came over several times. He liked espresso, I liked espresso and I had a very good espresso machine. So we were chatting and then he said, "Do you want to have a crack at this song?" I had a very simple setup and we just worked, the way I would have worked with bands back in Dublin. And we wrote three songs together, two of which ended up on *The Next Day*. It's a testament to his feeling comfortable around me and that he trusted me. The best place to be with somebody like David is to feel like you're part of their lexicon and part of their vocabulary, that they can rely on you. So it is kind of incredible that it happened, and yet it felt wholly natural in its own way.'[8] The two Leonard co-writes – 'Boss of Me' and 'I'll Take You There' – were two of the last songs to appear on a Bowie album that he was not solely credited with. There would, perhaps unsurprisingly, be no cover versions on *The Next Day*.

As the recording sessions wore on in separate blocks – September 2011, November 2011, March–April 2012 and July 2012 – individual personnel came and went, with band members excusing themselves because of previous commitments. Eventually, nearly 20 musicians would be credited for their work on the album; hardly a record-breaking amount, but the necessity of working with session players meant that everyone who contributed to *The Next Day* would sign an unusually stringent NDA, meaning that they were sworn to a remarkable level of secrecy. As Visconti described it, 'the NDAs were necessary because we didn't know everyone that well. We got lucky with the studio . . . Normally there are interns at studios, but whenever we were there, they gave their interns time off. They didn't want them to witness it. When we were working there, they had a skeleton staff of two, which is not normal. We had to talk about [the secrecy] as a group, share our experience of the insanity, the frustration. And David would just sit there smiling. The fun we were having in the studio overshadowed all the neuroses. But there definitely were neuroses.'[9]

Along the way, there were strange near-misses. Robert Fripp, whose guitar playing had been such a central part of "'Heroes'" and 'Teenage Wildlife', wrote on his blog in October 2011 that he had had a dream that he had been asked to play on a new Bowie album, but declined. He was never approached to participate in *The Next Day*, so it was pure coincidence that he wrote 'it gradually appeared that David had some remarkable new ideas in process, not yet public. These he presented indirectly, to allow the penny to drop without prompting. Eno also got involved, and what a flowering of ideas!' Visconti may later have complained that this innocent reverie nearly led to the cover being blown, but loyalty to Bowie overcame a natural desire to boast about participating in the recording. As Slick, who came in to play guitar for a week in the final sessions, complained, 'it was rough. I was bursting to tell people that I'd been back in the studio with David, that he looks good, he's singing his ass off, that we got this great album. And I couldn't say a thing.'[10]

Once the album was completed in late October 2012, the question arose about what was going to be done with it. It would have been easy enough to start up the promotional machine again, to coordinate a global release with interviews, an expensive campaign and whatever live perform-ances Bowie could be persuaded to participate in, but this would have run the risk of making the album's arrival in the world seem almost mundane. Undoubtedly, the return of Bowie after a near-decade of silence would be an event, but there was a difference between excited pleasure and some-thing truly epochal, an initiative that would attract attention on a hitherto unparalleled scale. Lazarus had risen from the dead; now he had to show the world that he had returned.

Visconti described the promotional decision that was taken with con-siderable, indeed almost misleading, precision. '[Rob Stringer, Sony Music president] came to the studio. He was thrilled. He said "What about the PR campaign?" And David said, "There is no PR campaign. We're just going to drop it on 8 January. That's it." It's such a simple idea, but Bowie came up with it.'[11] In fact, what happened – according to Alan Edwards – was that Bowie, who his ever-loyal publicist described as looking 'quite frail', greeted him in New York by saying, 'I've recorded a new album and I want to release the first single from it.' When asked when this would take place, he said 'Tuesday. It's my birthday and I want to release a track as my birthday gift to the world.'[12]

Rush-releasing an album, and the sudden appearance of a new single, was not a wholly new idea in the music industry. Radiohead's much-admired 2007 album *In Rainbows* had been announced on 1 October and was released ten days later, with fans able to pay any amount they wanted for it, including nothing. It was an innovative, and commercially hugely successful, strategy, which bypassed the industry's usual gatekeepers and reinforced the sense that the Oxford band were some of the great innovators in the business. Bowie, a long-term admirer of Radiohead, watched from afar in New York and took notes. It helped, of course, that *In Rainbows* was excellent; the surprise at its sudden advent soon gave way to delight at the brilliance of its songwriting. Yet Bowie was similarly bullish about *The Next Day* and the song that he had earmarked as its first single, 'Where Are We Now?' He was right to be.

Edwards suggested that the album's release should not be regarded merely as a piece of music news, but as a major news story that would play well with the *Today* programme and thereby establish Bowie as not just a cultural heavyweight but an internationally important figure. It was a daring, even provocative strategy, but his client's long absence from the spotlight meant that there was – in his estimation, at least – a hunger to hear from Bowie once again, even if there was to be no direct comment from him. Edwards was not regarded as one of the industry's most successful PR men for no reason and he put together a list of important people who could break the news most effectively, led by the Sky News presenter Kay Burley. Such was Bowie's concern that matters be kept secret until first thing in the morning of 8 January 2013 that Edwards found himself in the unusual, and potentially compromising, position of having to tell Britain's leading news and music journalists alike that there was a major story on the verge of breaking, but that he was unable to give more details until just before it did.

The explosion of excitement and delight that greeted the announcement of Bowie's return was without parallel in my lifetime. I still vividly remember waking up early on 8 January to endless messages from friends, all wanting to discuss the happy news, and then reaching bleary-eyed for my phone to watch the Tony Oursler-directed video for 'Where Are We Now?' Like every other Bowie fan, I had heard that his retirement had been occasioned by severe ill health and I feared that any developments concerning him would be bad. Yet as the first Bowie music video to have been released in nearly a decade unfolded, and the song that accompanied it built in majesty and power, hopes I didn't even know I had were fulfilled. David Bowie was back, and *how*. It was little wonder that Edwards triumphantly wrote in his autobiography that 'this was one of the greatest PR campaigns of my career. In its simplicity and clarity, it distilled everything I've learned since 1975.'[*,13]

Visconti – who became Bowie's de facto spokesman during the publicity campaign, the responsibility for which didn't seem to irk him – suggested in early interviews that 'Where Are We Now?' was not representative of the rest of *The Next Day*, either musically or vocally. He called it 'very different' to the other songs. 'I think it's a very reflective track for David. He certainly is looking back on his Berlin period and it evokes this feeling . . . it's very melancholy, I think. It's the only track on the album that goes this much inward for him.'[14]

It was a bold, and unusual, choice for *The Next Day*'s lead single. Of

---

* Edwards suggests that Bowie himself had to vanish from the onslaught of publicity for a day or so, feeling overwhelmed by it, but when he returned, he was sufficiently pleased to quip to Tilda Swinton that 'I've finally got more press than Elvis'; the joke, of course, being that the two men shared a birthday.

his recent albums, only *hours. . .* had a ballad as its first offering and that was widely felt to have been a perverse mistake, with the more commercial 'The Pretty Things Are Going to Hell' the more obvious release. Had Bowie released 'The Next Day' or 'The Stars Are Out Tonight', it would have been far more closely in line with his decision to prioritise songs like 'Slow Burn' and 'New Killer Star' over 'Slip Away' or 'The Loneliest Guy'. Yet, understandable though that would have been, it would also have missed a unique opportunity.

For the first time in his musical career, the Bowie singing on 'Where Are We Now?' sounds old. After years in which he had appeared to defy the ageing process, thanks to a mixture of expensive dentistry, carefully managed fitness regimes and, naturally, impeccable tailoring, he now adopted the quavering voice of an older man, looking back over his life in Berlin. It was a song without vanity, as its narrator reminisces on his youth and calls himself 'a man lost in time'. In its explicit call-back to Bowie's swashbuckling, legendary years in Germany, it comes to resemble his very own version of Beckett's *Krapp's Last Tape*. The elegiac, mournful solemnity of 'Where Are We Now?' seems like a farewell to a city, and a life, that Bowie would never return to.

If this was all that the song was, it would be far easier to admire than to love; the initial tune is pleasant without being memorable and the chorus intentionally underwhelming. However, just over halfway through, the song changes in pitch, rhythm and intensity, as Alford's drumming turns into a martial beat, Leonard's guitar becomes moody and yearning, the piano strikes demonstrative chords and Bowie declares a repetitive, enormously affecting, paean of fidelity and love over the swelling music:

> As long as there's sun
> As long as there's rain
> As long as there's fire
> As long as there's me
> As long as there's you.

It is simple but breathtakingly effective: the most straightforwardly beauti-ful song that Bowie had written since 'Uncle Floyd' and even richer and more emotionally accessible than that, too. It would reach number six in the UK charts, Bowie's highest placing since 'Absolute Beginners' got to number two in 1986 and his first top-ten hit since 'Jump They Say' in 1993. Some of this can, of course, be put down to the overwhelming success of the hype behind it, but 'Where Are We Now?' is also a magnificent song, one of the very best that Bowie ever wrote, and universally acclaimed as such.* That there was at least one even better offering on *The Next Day* was a truly thrilling prospect.

The Tony Oursler-directed video that accompanied its release, meanwhile, was full of enigmatic hints and Easter eggs for the Bowie trainspotters: footage of Berlin here, images of juxtaposed diamonds and dogs there, as a disembodied Bowie sings, his face mapped onto a puppet. Visually, it also appeared to refer back to 'Slip Away'/'Uncle Floyd', with an ageing Bowie now becoming Floyd (and Oogie) himself. Yet it is not until almost the end of the clip that the musician himself appears properly, dressed in a *Song of Norway* T-shirt – a reference to his former girlfriend Hermione Farthingale, who appeared in the film of that name – and strik-ing suitably dramatic attitudes. For those of us who had believed, and feared, that Bowie was in severe ill health, seeing him in the video was a reassuring sign that he was, indeed, returned to us. The only questions concerned what would come next and whether *The Next Day* could live up to the considerable hype that its audacious opening salvo had engendered.

'Here I am, not quite dying.' As soon as the chorus to the album's title song kicks in, at precisely one minute and 12 seconds, it is obvious that Bowie is having fun: with the music, playing with preconceptions of his absence from the spotlight and toying with his listeners. That the first song is a deliberate sonic callback to 'It's No Game' on the *Scary Monsters*

---

* The only naysayer was Reeves Gabrels's wife, who said after first hearing the song 'Why did he just go and write "Thursday's Child" all over again?'

album suggests that this is Bowie (admirably aided by Visconti) at ease with his legacy, ready to take risks and experiment. It sounds like little that he produced over the previous three decades, but is instead filled with fresh, exciting and brilliantly constructed songs.

If *The Next Day* is examined in the context of Bowie's wider career, it feels wholly the album that he not only wanted but needed to make. (That the record company were only informed of its existence a matter of a few weeks before its release – thus rendering any idea of corporate interference wholly moot – proves that this was not recorded in order to satisfy bean counters.) Over its 14 songs, there are Brecht/Weill homages that nod to Bowie's casting in *Baal* ('Dirty Boys'), an Evelyn Waugh-alluding anti-war track ('I'd Rather Be High') and a brilliantly conceived character sketch of a high-school shooter ('Valentine's Day'). Bowie off the leash always produced his best and most interesting work – as with *The Buddha of Suburbia* and *Outside* – and by the time that the record concludes with another finely woven homage to Scott Walker and 'The Electrician' in the form of the haunting 'Heat', a comeback that had once seemed not only implausible but impossible had resulted in a masterpiece.

It is not a perfect album. The second single, 'The Stars (Are Out Tonight)' has a splendidly chilly, cinematic quality to its promotional video – as directed by his regular collaborator Floria Sigismondi – but the song itself is strictly Bowie-by-numbers, sounding like an offcut from *Reality*. Likewise, it's a lengthy record, at 53 minutes and 14 songs, and if 'Boss of Me' and 'Dancing Out in Space' had been removed, I doubt that anyone would have been particularly disappointed. The recording sessions were so fruitful, in fact, that several other songs were later released as an EP in November 2013 – *The Next Day Extra* – and it is hard not to feel that the likes of 'Atomica' and 'The Informer' would have been stronger inclusions than a couple of the less distinguished tracks. But this is nitpicking. If Bowie had returned with an album of the calibre of *Tin Machine*, it would still have been an event. That he had chosen to re-enter the fray with a record as intelligent, beautiful and sophisticated as *The Next Day* was a remarkable accomplishment. Had he released it instead of *hours. . .*, *Earthling* or *Reality*, it would have, rightly, been regarded as one of his finest records. That it was his grand return made it the more momentous.

Although Bowie chose not to give any interviews to promote the record, even if he had done so it's doubtful that he would have sat down with some diligent scribe and carefully explained the thought process behind each song. One of the few occasions that he had been forthcoming had come in 2008, when he put together – or, in today's parlance, 'curated' – a selection of his 12 favourite songs, *iSelect*, for an exclusive compilation for the *Mail on Sunday*. With the exception of 'Life on Mars', most of the songs on this album tended towards the obscure – 'Some Are', a bonus track on a *Low* reissue, was unknown except to the most committed of the musician's admirers – and so Bowie contributed an appropriately tongue-in-cheek essay, in which he wrote 'I've selected 12 of my songs that I don't seem to tire of. Few of them are well known, but many of them are still sung at my concerts. Usually by me.'[15]

There were nuggets for Bowie completists thrown in. For instance, we learn that 'Teenage Wildlife' remains one of his most beloved compositions ('I'm still enamoured of this song and would give you two "Modern Loves" for it any time') and that 'Time Will Crawl' was a reaction to Chernobyl. But if anyone seriously expected that Bowie would choose to explain his creative inspiration in any satisfactory manner, they would be disappointed.

He did, however, continue to enjoy toying with the expectations of those who hung on his every word, and so, in apparent acquiescence to a request from the novelist Rick Moody for some kind of explanation as to the creative processes behind *The Next Day*, he supplied 42 of them: 3 for each song. It was hard not to feel that he was doing so with tongue firmly in cheek: how else could one explain summarising 'The Next Day' as 'effigies', 'indulgences' and 'anarchist'?[16]

It was all the more interesting, then, that for *The Next Day*'s standout track, 'You Feel So Lonely You Can Die', Bowie chose the words 'traitor', 'urban' and 'comeuppance' to describe it, in addition to its lyrical allusion to his birthday-brother Elvis's 'Heartbreak Hotel'.* If the pulsatingly operatic, string-drenched vigour of the song – Bowie returning to the bedsit drama of 'Rock 'n' Roll Suicide', quite literally with a vengeance – was not enough, the force and passion with which he delivers his vocals suggests that he has it in for someone and that he is delivering his own, very English version of something commonplace in American music by 2013: the diss track. And the target of his opprobrium probably would have relished such an attack, too.

The relationship between Bowie and Morrissey, which initially seemed to be one of the more interesting in music† – the two bookish outsiders together, one a Londoner and one a Mancunian – soon fizzled out after Morrissey abruptly left the Outside tour, citing a mysterious illness and believing that he had not received sufficient attention from Bowie's fans. Thereafter, the two men severed contact, not least because Morrissey, who now christened his former idol 'David Showie', lost no opportunity to criticise him, saying in 1999 that 'Bowie is principally a business and I can't imagine he would have telephoned his own mother without considering the career implications'.[17]

Bowie was tight-lipped about Morrissey's departure, commenting in one MTV interview that 'I was disappointed that he hasn't shown for any of the other shows, because I really enjoyed working with him ... the audience seemed to like him, and the chemistry was really interesting.' However, a more accurate indication of his feelings could be discerned from another conversation with a local Scottish television station, in which he revealed that '45 minutes before the show, we were suddenly told that Morrissey wasn't going to be working that night, when in fact he went back to London. The promoter told the crowd and, to be honest, there was

---

*    Which features the lyric 'You'll be so lonely, you could die'.

†    Dylan Jones said of Bowie: 'I have only ever encountered two interviewees blessed with both an unusual level of self-regard and a very likeable ability to laugh at themselves; the other, oddly enough, being Morrissey.'

hardly a murmur. Four hundred and twenty-two disgruntled Morrissey fans asked for their money back, leaving many, many thousands to enjoy the show.' He concluded, 'I'm old-fashioned enough to believe that a standing ovation generally means the audience enjoyed the show.'

He took care to blame tabloid exaggerations, rather than Morrissey himself, but he had been disrespected – those 422 refunds had been carefully noted – and so when his former collaborator worked with Visconti on his (excellent) 2006 album *Ringleader of the Tormentors*, Bowie not only refused Visconti's suggestion that the two men should collaborate on a cover of the Righteous Brothers' 'You've Lost That Lovin' Feelin'', but would undoubtedly have listened to the centrepiece of *Ringleader of the Tormentors*, 'Life Is a Pigsty', with a certain degree of irritation. Morrissey had already aped Bowie in 'I Know It's Gonna Happen Someday' and the master had reclaimed the song for his own accordingly. Now, Morrissey's second overt pastiche of Bowie – complete with 'Space Oddity' drums and the 'Five Years'-esque pronouncement that 'Even now, in the final hour of my life, I'm falling in love again' – could not help but seem like a declaration of intent. Bowie listened, brooded and then responded.

What makes 'You Feel So Lonely You Can Die' so glorious is that the contrast between the soaring rapture of the music and the hilarious pettiness of the lyrics reveals that Bowie was not merely spending his time out of the spotlight as a loving husband, father and retired cultural icon, but meditating on those who had done him wrong. There were other figures in the music industry, of course, who had few kind words to say about Bowie. Elton John was no great admirer of his,* despite or because of 'Rocket Man' being a straightforward lyrical lift from 'Space Oddity', and the relationship between Gary Numan and Bowie was notoriously poor,

---

* Sir Elton commented in his excellent autobiography *Me* that 'I was never *great* friends with Bowie. I loved his music and we socialised a couple of times, visiting the Sombrero with Tony King and having dinner together in Covent Garden while he was rehearsing for the Ziggy Stardust tour. But there was always something distant and aloof about him, at least when I was around.'

albeit mainly from the former's perspective. But clearly there was something about the continued disrespect and embarrassment that Morrissey had caused him that rankled.

Therefore, the song's lyrical thrust might best be described as the anti-'Rock 'n' Roll Suicide'. On that track, Bowie-as-Ziggy presented himself as the saviour for the lonely and disaffected, repeating 'you're not alone'. Morrissey, who saw Bowie numerous times on the Ziggy tour, and beyond, took comfort from such a statement. Yet now, 40 years later, Bowie brutally cast off his one-time admirer, hoping that he would die very much by himself. There are specific, pointed references to Smiths lyrics ('I hear you moaning in your room / Oh see if I care, oh please, please make it soon'*) and Bowie confronts the idea of the miserabilist as poseur, sneering 'Death alone will love you'. For those around him who saw him as unceasingly amicable, professional and likeable – *nice* is a word used more than once in interviews – the song is a bracing reminder that Bowie was as human as everyone else.

As if to reclaim his own legacy, the song ends with Alford beating out the famous opening drumbeat from 'Five Years', an implicit riposte to Morrissey's 'I Know It's Gonna Happen Someday', which ended with a similar quotation from 'Rock 'n' Roll Suicide'. A score was settled, and in the most dramatic and enjoyable of fashions. If nothing else, Morrissey – who has never commented publicly on the song – should feel proud to have inspired something so remarkable.

Whether the warmth of the album's reception was because of its excellence, the skilfully managed PR campaign or because of a large number of disaffected former Smiths fans, *The Next Day* became Bowie's most

---

\* I see these as brief, brutal parodies of 'How Soon Is Now?' and 'Please, Please, Please Let Me Get What I Want', but to be honest, there are plenty more Smiths songs that fit the bill.

commercially successful album since *Let's Dance*. It reached chart positions that had seemed impossible even a few years before: it topped the UK charts, reached number two in the US *Billboard* rankings (beating *Let's Dance*, which only peaked at number three) and achieved success in markets where Bowie had barely ever toured or featured before. The likes of South Korea, Mexico and Hungary were all fresh converts to him. As the album reached the country's top five, he was, like Spinal Tap, big in Japan.

The music industry had changed immeasurably in the previous decade. In 2003, Bowie may have pioneered the idea of downloading music on the internet, but most consumers bought their albums as physical products, usually as CDs. Ten years later, the arrival of streaming music on platforms such as Spotify, to say nothing of YouTube, meant that the primacy of the record itself had been reduced, along with sales. I was living in Putney at the time, and was unable to find anywhere selling the record, as there was no specialised music shop there.*

It was worth owning a physical CD for Jonathan Barnbrook's witty cover art, which took the cover of *"Heroes"* and placed a white square over it. It was the opposite of the tiresome, instantly dated cartoonish art for *Reality*, being a knowing deconstruction of a famous image. 'With *The Next Day*,' Barnbrook said, 'he saw that there was something new here and reassured me when I was worried that the idea would be misunderstood . . . There was quite a lot of discussion behind the scenes with the record company about that cover, because it was taking quite a big chance. It's confusing, it doesn't make sense. But I do think, of all the covers we did, it is the most unusual . . . It's quite an original idea, taking your own album cover and defacing it.'[18]

Critics had exhausted their superlatives for *Heathen*, and describing *The Next Day* as his best album since his penultimate one did not come close to conveying the sense of event that the album clearly deserved. Andy Gill boldly, and accurately, captured the general zeitgeist in the *Independent* by

---

* Eventually, I bought a copy in Sainsbury's, of all unlikely places.

calling it 'the greatest comeback album in rock 'n' roll history'[19] while others strove to simultaneously convey their *bona fides* when it came to objective criticism and to allow their readership to sense their excitement. Alexis Petridis struck a more cautious, if still enthusiastic, note in the *Guardian* when he wrote of the adulation that 'people were welcoming back an exhilarating, distant memory of Bowie, rather than the reality'. Nonetheless, Petridis still went on to praise the album as 'thought-provoking, strange and filled with great songs', observing that 'Bowie has earned himself the exalted position where one takes for cultural richness the kind of thing you'd ordinarily dismiss as agonising pretension'.[20]

In the wake of the release of *Blackstar* nearly three years later, some critics back-pedalled on their initial adulation for *The Next Day*, suggesting that it was 'merely' a hugely accomplished collection of songs rather than the Schubert-in-winter masterpiece that his final album was. This is a perfectly fair and credible reaction. Yet little more than a decade later, and judged purely on its own terms, *The Next Day* holds up remarkably well. There are several Bowie albums from the period covered in this book – including some of my favourites – which I have to take a deep breath and mentally prepare myself to be able to appreciate ('enjoy' is too simplistic) them fully.* No such loin-girding is necessary for *The Next Day*, which combines its near-miraculous existence with a quality of old-fashioned songwriting that reminds the listener that, had Bowie been born a decade or so earlier, he would undoubtedly have been a Tin Pan Alley stalwart, knocking off three hits in the morning before a deservedly long lunchbreak.

According to those who recorded the album with him, there was never any serious discussion about touring it. Bowie would occasionally make fleeting remarks about 'Oh, this would sound great live', but although many of those who played with him offered enthusiastic comments in contemporary interviews about the possibility of at least a one-off gig,

---

* Yes, I'm talking about *Outside* in particular.

whether in London or New York, it was never publicly contemplated.\*
There was not even a compromise solution suggested, as with the Beatles'
farewell rooftop gig at their headquarters on Savile Row, of a filmed live
performance or similar. Instead, those who wanted to see more Bowie
had to be content with a series of videos that he released from the album,
including a Louis Vuitton promotional film for a harpsichord-based remix
of 'I'd Rather Be High' and an oddly half-hearted clip for 'Valentine's Day',
in which Bowie wielded a guitar as if it were a gun: something that might
have been provocative half a century before.

If he wished to stir up some good old-fashioned controversy to go
with the worship, then the video for 'The Next Day' more than fulfilled
its brief. Once again directed by Sigismundi, it featured Bowie performing
in a subterranean hell-hole bar, wittily called 'The Decameron', where the
clientele seem to be purely clergymen or prostitutes. With guest appearances from Bowie's friend Gary Oldman and the Oscar-winning French
actress Marion Cotillard, and suitably grim and disturbing quasi-religious
imagery that included everything from flagellation and stigmata to the
spectacle of severed eyeballs being presented on a plate (an allusion to
the early Christian martyr Saint Lucy), it was undeniably Bowie's most
shocking and provocative promotional film since 'The Heart's Filthy
Lesson' and seemed precision-engineered to upset the easily offended.

The outrage duly followed. The Catholic League had not taken kindly
to Bowie apparently posing as Christ for a 1997 Tower Records promotional
image ('If this is supposed to be cute, it fails') and now the League's president Bill Donohue stepped forward to criticise his latest video. Sighing that

---

\* The closest he probably came was to consider a one-off appearance at the London
Olympics opening ceremony in 2012. He was sufficiently interested in the idea to
allow the event's artistic director Danny Boyle to come to New York to pitch it to him,
and although Boyle had used his music dynamically in *Trainspotting*, he turned down
the chance to perform, saying 'I don't want to do anything in the past. I am working
on stuff for the future.' Boyle later confessed to being 'a nervous wreck' waiting to
meet him and that he found it far more demanding than meeting the Queen – who
did participate.

'the switch-hitting,* bisexual, senior citizen from London has resurfaced', Donohue offered up his own prayer – 'David Bowie is back, but hopefully not for long' – before describing the video as '[reflecting] the artist – it is a mess'. Dismissing Bowie's previous comments on religion, Donohue concluded that he was 'not sure what he believes in today (anyone who is "not quite an atheist" is not an atheist), but it's a sure bet he can't stop thinking about the Cadillac of all religions, namely Roman Catholicism. There is hope for him yet.'[†,21] On the other side of the Christianity scale, George Carey, the former Archbishop of Canterbury, sighed that the video was 'juvenile' and that 'I doubt that Bowie would have the courage to use Islamic imagery – I very much doubt it.'[22]

Entertaining though the rumpus was, it merited no more than a day or so's headlines, not least because, by then, something rather grander had begun. In late 2010, around the time that Bowie began to record the demos for *The Next Day*, he authorised an informal approach by one of his archivists to see if the Victoria and Albert Museum in London – the V&A – might be interested in staging an exhibition of items from his personal archive. The V&A, perhaps the world's most respected collection of arts and crafts, was then under the inspirational directorship of Martin Roth, who wished to expand the museum's repertoire into something more contemporary after the success of a Kylie Minogue show in 2007. The curators Victoria Broackes and Geoffrey Marsh visited Bowie's American archive in early 2011 to assess its viability for a potential show.

The exhibition, which would eventually be titled *David Bowie Is*, existed in a strange hinterland somewhere between being authorised and

---

\* A 'switch-hitter' is a baseball player who can bat with both hands.

† Other spokespeople for Christian groups also tried to ridicule Bowie. Jack Valero of the Catholic Voices group said 'I wouldn't give him the time of day, it is just desperate. He used to be famous, why does he need to do this?', while Andrea Williams of Christian Concern lamented that 'It is actually just a bit sad – what is he seeking to achieve?'

unauthorised. As Marsh later said, 'the agreement was that we could borrow anything from the archive and that Bowie would have no involvement at all and the only agreement was that all the text in the exhibition would be checked by his archivist for historical accuracy – the interpretation itself would be the museum's entirely'.[23] Broackes described Bowie as being 'top of a very short list of people the V&A would cover as a single artist' and that the opportunity to stage the exhibition was 'almost too good to be true', although she also described Bowie's refusal to have any direct input as 'of course disappointing, but we also felt it was a unique opportunity and we were honoured to have it'.[24] His only binding request, which was honoured, was that the exhibition would begin in London and finish in New York: it would eventually run, off and on, for more than five years, making it the grandest virtual tour imaginable.

The curators were helped by Bowie's magpie-like tendencies when it came to amassing objects. As his touring guitarist Eric Schermerhorn recalls, 'when we were on the bus, he collected everything; he took Hunt Sales's drumsticks, guitar picks, and everything for his personal collection of stuff. I remember once we were in Japan, going back into the dressing room and there's this little suit on our hanger, a Ziggy suit, that a fan had and gave back to him. It was as if it was designed for a 14-year-old boy. He was laughing and said "Well, how did I fit into this?" But he collected everything, drumsticks upwards.'[25]

'Everything' proved to be a horde of 75,000 objects, which Broackes and Marsh were given the run of and which would eventually be whittled down to a display of around 500 objects. Unsurprisingly, the V&A's exhibition focused on the best-known items from the collection, such as the blue suit that Bowie wore in the 'Life on Mars' video, his handwritten lyrics to 'Station to Station' and the Union Jack coat worn on the cover of the *Earthling* album. Even this selection felt comprehensive, at times overwhelmingly so, but there was space for irreverence, too; two of the exhibits included Bowie's cocaine spoon from the height of his drug period in the mid-'70s and a warm 1976 note from his 'birth twin' Elvis Presley – who

Bowie had hoped would sing 'Golden Years' – wishing him good luck with his forthcoming Station to Station tour.

David Bowie Is opened on 23 March 2013, a fortnight after The Next Day was released, and was a direct beneficiary of the admiration and publicity that that album had received. At the press preview shortly before opening, arts journalists battled for space with incognito celebrities, all of them desperate to experience what would be, in its own way, the final David Bowie gig; a situation helped by the state-of-the-art music mix, designed by Visconti, to be played on the supplied Sennheiser headphones. There may have been initial concerns before its launch that it was too parochial to be a true success – when it began, London was the only venue that was booked to host it – but when the ecstatic reviews and high-profile private view dominated the papers, yet again, the museum found itself inundated with requests for transfers. David Bowie Is would eventually be shown at 12 museums on five continents, and in countries from Australia and Canada to Japan and Brazil. Around two million tickets were eventually sold, 300,000 of them in London alone.

Bowie was not to be found at the private view and dinner on the opening night, but nor had he been expected to be present. Had he reappeared for his first public appearance in Britain since his cameo with David Gilmour seven years before, he would undoubtedly have been mobbed and the event would have come to resemble a particularly hysterical backstage riot rather than a seemly launch for a major exhibition. There was a great deal of discussion in the media about whether he would see the show before it finished on 11 August, but no announcement or press opportunity was imminent. If he and his family were to visit, it would be a purely private affair.

Eventually, whether out of curiosity or because it had been planned all along, Bowie, Iman, Lexi and Coco Schwab headed to London and visited early on the morning of Sunday 7 July. They were greeted and given a private tour by Broackes, who would later tell Nicholas Pegg that Bowie was 'sincerely moved by the experience', and that he spent around an hour and a half wandering around, looking at his life spread out before him.

By the time he and his family left, there was a queue of 200 people patiently waiting to be admitted when the exhibition opened at 9.30 that morning, none of them with the slightest idea that, a few moments before, the subject of the show had been walking round the gallery.

On the few occasions that Bowie did return to Britain late in life – carefully choreographed and planned occasions that he undertook with the support of his long-standing tour manager, so as to minimise the potential for recognition or hassle – he usually kept his plans and movements low-key. It was therefore a surprise that Iman, in an interview with the *Observer*, casually disclosed that the family had visited London that summer. 'No one knew we were there! We flew in on the jet to Luton and every day we went and did different things and the press never knew! It's absurd this idea that celebrities can't be anonymous. We even went on the London Eye. We queued separately, Lexi had a friend with her and they went with the bodyguard and then we all met on board.' Bowie even took his daughter to revisit a specific aspect of his past. 'He took her to Brixton. They went and took a photo outside the house he grew up in.'[26]

It is debatable as to when Bowie realised that the decline in his health was terminal. Received wisdom is that he was diagnosed with liver cancer in the summer of 2014, but that he did not realise that it was inoperable until November 2015. This has been questioned by some well-placed figures in the Bowie camp, who have suggested that he knew that his health was poor long before then, but are reluctant to speak about this on record for fear of betraying confidences placed in them by those who are still around today. Yet what seems clear is that Bowie's final visit to Britain had a valedictory quality to it, and one that he would come to remember a couple of years later, when he wrote 'Dollar Days', with its lines 'If I never see the English evergreens, I'm running to / It's nothing to me.' Lazarus had risen from the dead. But even the resurrected must meet their end eventually.

## 14

# *LAZARUS* AND *BLACKSTAR*

## 'Look up here, I'm in heaven'

*'Thank you for our good times. They will never rot'*

On 25 February 1631, the metaphysical poet-turned-Dean of St Paul's John Donne dragged himself into the pulpit one final time to preach his own funeral oration. Donne had been riddled with illness for much of the previous decade, whether it was typhus, fever or the many agues that Jacobean England was home to, and so it was something of a wonder that he survived until the age of 59. Yet his decision to settle accounts with his great sparring partner, Death, was simultaneously a piece of grim pragmatism and a last stab of theatricality.

Donne was neither the first nor the last figure to turn his imminent death into a literary or artistic statement, but the uncompromisingly public way in which he did so established a precedent that few dared to emulate. When the sermon was published, entitled 'Death's Duel', the bookseller who sold it added a note: 'It was preached not many days before his death, as if, having done this, there remained nothing for him to do but to die; and the matter is of death – the occasion and subject of all funeral sermons. It hath been observed of this reverend man, that his faculty in preaching continually increased, and that, as he exceeded others at first, so at last he exceeded himself.'

Just less than four centuries later, Bowie – a figure worthy of comparison with Donne in many regards, not least his approach to the inevitable – sent out his own version of 'Death's Duel' into the world. When *Blackstar* was released on his 69th birthday, 8 January 2016, the initial reaction was warm, if slightly confused. Even by Bowie's standards, critics appeared to suggest the lyrical content of this album was opaque, almost frustratingly so. What was the near-obsession with Lazarus and strange, philosophical themes of death, rebirth and change? Nobody had expected 'The Laughing Gnome' or 'Let's Dance', but this was esoterica for its own sake, surely. Bowie had returned, once again, which was welcome, but *Blackstar* was not the continuation of the comeback that anyone had expected.

And then, on the morning of 11 January, it became overwhelmingly clear that Bowie had played his final 'prestige' – and had preached his own version of 'Death's Duel' in the process.

It is easy, in retrospect, to regard the period between the release of *The Next Day* plus an additional EP in November 2013 and the coming of *Blackstar* in January 2016 as being one of Bowie's most intensely active, despite or because of the impact of his diagnosis in mid-2014 of liver cancer. He had recorded a brief vocal cameo for the title song of Arcade Fire's *Reflektor* in early 2013, and although he continued to keep a low profile in public, was not above pieces of post-modern japery.

When he was awarded Best British Male Artist at the Brit Awards on 19 February 2014, he did not appear at the event, but instead sent Kate Moss,* dressed in Bowie's original Ziggy Stardust costume, to read out a speech on his behalf as 'his representative on earth'. Showing that there is more joy in heaven over one sinner that repents, the once-agnostic Noel Gallagher presented the award, saying 'You maniacs didn't think David Bowie was actually here? David Bowie's too cool for that. He doesn't do this shit!'

After the usual whimsical platitudes ('I'm completely delighted to have a Brit for being the best male – but I am, aren't I, Kate? Yes. I think it's a great way to end the day'), Moss then delivered a piece of provocation, in which Bowie, apparently randomly, weighed in on the then-pressing question of Scottish independence, when he declared 'Scotland, stay with us'. Bowie's unexpected intervention caused the then-prime minister and noted Bowie fan David Cameron, who was campaigning fervently against independence, to 'let out a little cry of joy'.[1] The referendum result was 55–45 in favour of Scotland remaining part of the United Kingdom, although even the most devoted of Bowie's admirers would find it difficult to suggest that his contribution made any significant difference.

---

\* Unlikely though this connection sounds, there was an existing relationship between the two; Moss had interviewed Bowie for *Q* in late 2003.

In any case, he had other matters on his mind. For many years, Bowie had been exploring the possibility of a Ziggy Stardust musical. Although sometimes he made light of it ('I've forgotten the number of times I've been asked to revive Ziggy as a musical. Everybody sees money, they look at *Tommy*★ and a lightbulb goes off in their heads'[2]), he was sufficiently interested in doing so to approach his old *Buddha of Suburbia* collaborator Hanif Kureishi, telling him that Pete Townshend had 'what he called a gusher – you know, money just pouring through your reservoir forever'. The two collaborated for a while, but the potential for a fruitful and lucrative show was stymied by what Kureishi saw as Bowie's mercurial intentions, 'He didn't want it to be a sort of narrative . . . He wanted it to be really modern, really avant-garde. He didn't really quite know how to do that . . . I don't think Bowie really knew what he wanted or what he was doing at the time.'[3]

Bowie eventually abandoned the idea, complaining that 'it just didn't come together in the way that I thought it might . . . The more I wrote into it, the smaller and smaller it just seemed to be.' He also made a joke out of it, quipping to *Rolling Stone*: 'Can you imagine anything uglier than a nearly 60-year-old Ziggy Stardust?'[4] Yet he continued to be interested in working on a piece of musical drama – rather than simply a musical – and so, when he returned to London in the summer of 2013, he sought an audience with the theatrical impresario Robert Fox, with a view to exploring a new project: a show entitled *Lazarus* and based on *The Man Who Fell to Earth*, for which he would need a writer.

Fox suggested Enda Walsh, who had achieved considerable early success with his 1996 play *Disco Pigs* and had also done a credible job of turning the popular film *Once* into a Tony award-winning Broadway musical. Bowie was already familiar with Walsh's work and so when Fox introduced the two of them in New York, it was a seamless meeting. Bowie embraced

---

★ Pete Townshend's adaptation of the Who's rock opera was a conspicuous success when it opened on Broadway in 1993.

Walsh and said, 'You've been on my mind for three weeks', before discussing his work and recurrent themes with a fan's enthusiasm, which led the playwright to '[spend] that whole morning and now this first hour of our first meeting in a state of serene self-confidence'[5].

However, Bowie had not come simply to praise the writer, but to begin what Walsh would call 'a year and a half of really wonderful, open collaboration' by handing him four pages of notes – an extension of the character and themes both from the film of *The Man Who Fell to Earth* and from the Walter Tevis novel on which it was based. Bowie's character Thomas Newton had returned and would be accompanied by a (possibly imaginary) female character, The Girl; a mass murderer named Valentine; and another woman, Emma, who was named after Emma Lazarus, the American poet whose sonnet 'The New Colossus' – with its famous lines 'Give me your tired, your poor, / Your huddled masses yearning to breathe free' – is inscribed upon the Statue of Liberty. Bowie was vague on details, but suggested that the play had to revolve around the idea of escape, and that Newton, who had been stuck on Earth for years, would attempt to return home one final time, or die in the attempt.

At this stage, Bowie seemed ambivalent about whether it would be a so-called 'jukebox musical', consisting of existing numbers, or scored by a new collection of songs, before he eventually split the difference and decided that it would be largely new arrangements of some of his best-known tracks, along with some original music. He handed Walsh a selection of 69 lyrics and songs ('Some of these you'll know') and suggested that the playwright would be best placed to decide what did or didn't fit with the loose narrative that was being proposed. Eighteen would eventually make it into the show: four new songs, including, appropriately, 'Lazarus', four cuts from *The Next Day* and new arrangements of everything from 'It's No Game' to 'Life on Mars' and 'Changes'.

For the first couple of months, in the spring of 2014, Bowie and Walsh collaborated closely, both in person and over Skype and email. 'He would play Thomas and I would play everyone else,' says Walsh. 'David really felt that role and came up with some of the best lines. But there was no intention of David ever taking the part in the theatre.' Instead, Michael C. Hall, the actor best known for his role as the supposedly ethical serial killer in *Dexter*, would eventually be cast in the role of Newton and would do a magnificent job. When the two first met, Bowie tacitly acknowledged Hall's career-long preoccupation with death – from *Dexter*'s murderous antics to his breakthrough role in the funeral-themed *Six Feet Under*, and now *Lazarus* – by saying 'What is it with you?' If Bowie had any health concerns, he hid them well. 'At this point, David seemed completely fine and in great shape,' said Walsh. 'He was wonderful, inspiring company.'[6]

The script was completed by the summer of 2014 and credited to both Walsh and Bowie. In truth, if it had not had two such illustrious names attached to it, it may have struggled to generate the interest that it subsequently received. Bowie was scathing about back-catalogue musicals, which crowbar in character names and situations so that famous songs can be used,* but *Lazarus* almost went to the other extreme. It contained elements of everything from *Outside* and *Low* to *Ziggy Stardust*, but even the most committed Bowie scholar may have found aspects of the storyline incomprehensible. However, with its starry creator making the project viable, Bowie began approaching potential collaborators to make his dream a reality.

The ideal director was Ivo van Hove, a fiercely individual and cultish talent who was about to stage a new revival of Arthur Miller's *A View from the Bridge* in London. Van Hove, who had used 'The Motel' in a Dutch-language staging of *Angels in America*, was a committed admirer of Bowie's and responded positively to the way that the musician wanted someone who would bring visual pizzazz to the show – in his words, 'someone who would push the production to the extreme'.[7] Nonetheless, van

---

* This arguably reached its nadir in the Queen musical *We Will Rock You*, with its characters Galileo, Scaramouche and Killer Queen. Still, it made a lot of money.

Hove was concerned about the secrecy surrounding the show. 'That was the most scary moment for me in the whole process. They didn't give the script to me the day before. It was just there on the table and then they started to read [the first act] aloud.' Bowie was playing all the characters and it became obvious that this was a project that he was as deeply committed to as any of his albums. As van Hove said, 'Of course, I knew that they would ask afterward, "What do you think?" What if I hated it?'[8]

He did not, though, and signed up to the project straight away. Bowie suggested that he would like to begin work on the staging of *Lazarus* in early 2015, with a view to it premiering late that year. When van Hove demurred, saying that it would be a better fit for 2016, Bowie was adamant that time was pressing. 'I could really only [do the show] in 2016,' recalled van Hove, 'but he was in a hurry. I asked him why, and he said: "I'm fucking 68!" I cancelled another major international project for him.'[9]

After hiring Henry Hey, who had played keyboards on *The Next Day*, as musical director and giving him responsibility for the new arrangements that the songs would require, Bowie turned his attention away from *Lazarus* to recording new music. The four songs that he had written for the show were similar to the style that he had been working in on *The Next Day*, but he was also interested in a broader, more complex kind of composition. He contacted Zachary Alford in spring 2014 to ask him if he would return to the studio with him. The drummer was thrilled to help.

Still, something had changed. As Alford says, 'just prior to that recording session, Tony Visconti had his 70th birthday party, so we were all there, but David seemed a little cranky. He was fine, but there was a weight on his shoulders. Then we went back into the studio. We had a new guy on keyboards,* I'm not sure where from, and Tony was playing bass. It was a much smaller group, with no guitarist; David was playing the guitars. The vibe wasn't as loose. It felt a little bit more private.' And Bowie himself had altered, too. 'I did notice a slight difference. He looked older than he

---

* Presumably Henry Hey.

was assumed to be. He was getting close to the end, but I still had no clue that he was sick.'[10]

The demos that Alford recorded with Bowie and Visconti, the embryonic *Blackstar*, remain an intriguing 'what if' in the Bowie canon. 'I was still having difficulty divorcing myself from David's past, because my dream would be to be on *Station to Station*. So I was trying to recreate that, and he was really, really trying to go in a new direction. And hearing what *Blackstar* ended up being, it was way different from my approach.'[11] There was a reason why Bowie wished to switch styles and it came from his interest in the work of the jazz musician Maria Schneider, who performed Grammy Award-winning music with her eponymous orchestra. He had flirted with jazz before on previous records, from Lester Bowie's contributions to *Black Tie White Noise* to Mike Garson's playing on 'Bring Me the Disco King', but his albums had always remained within the sphere of rock. Now, however, he wanted to try something wholly new and unexpected, and to transform his interest in jazz into his own album.*

Bowie visited Schneider at her apartment in the summer of 2014 to discuss a potential collaboration. Details of what he was after were initially unclear – 'maybe vampires,' he quipped – but, as she said, 'David wanted dark and I went dark'. After she passed on the chance to record Bowie's demo 'Bluebird', which would later turn into 'Lazarus', the two began work on a piece that would become a seven-minute experimental jazz epic, 'Sue (Or in a Season of Crime)', with lyrics revolving around sexual jealousy and inspired by everything from John Ford's Jacobean tragedy *'Tis Pity She's a Whore* to the poetry of Robert Browning. It was considerably different to the more straightforward songwriting on *The Next Day*, sharing similarly elliptical lyrics but with a far more challenging musical arrangement and sensibility. This was no hummable 'Where Are We Now?', but something altogether darker and more uncompromising. More than ever

---

\*    Visconti commented: 'We always held the jazz gods on a pedestal above us.'

before, Bowie was recording for himself and nobody else. If others happened to appreciate what he was doing, it was merely a bonus.

Bowie recorded 'Sue' with Schneider's jazz orchestra and Visconti at Avatar Studios on 24 July 2014, the first new music that he had recorded in two years.* The guitarist Ben Monder, who played on the track, was intrigued to meet the star – and was not disappointed. 'My impression of him was immediately positive. Both he and Tony were at the first rehearsal and they were both very nice, really enthusiastic about the whole process, and took pains to put us all at ease. You know, I think one characteristic that struck me of him was he tried to dispel the whole "rock deity" thing. And he just exuded kindness, which I appreciated a lot. At the same time, he had a really wicked sense of humour and wasn't afraid to wield it.'[12]

The song, which would be backed up by ''Tis a Pity She Was a Whore' as its B-side – on the initial version of which Bowie played all the instruments and curtly described it as 'if vorticists wrote rock music, it might have sounded like this' – was intended to be the initial single from the latest Bowie best-of compilation, *Nothing Has Changed*, and was released on 17 November 2014. The album cover featured another Jonathan Barnbrook design, this time of the singer coolly examining himself in a mirror. It was typical of Barnbrook's, and Bowie's, attention to detail that the three formats it was released in – CD, LP and Deluxe CD – each featured a different image, mirroring the three eras that were being explored across the compilation. The feeling of what would usually seem like a cash-in record being freighted with greater import – a pause and a reckoning before the final account was prepared – was strengthened by 'Sue' being the first song on the album.

---

* The bassline apparently uses a great deal of Plastic Soul's 1997 song 'Brand New Heavy', meaning that, alongside Bowie and Schneider, the members of the act are co-credited with its composition, thereby making them some of Bowie's last ever collaborators.

The seven-and-a-half minute track was not greeted with the same warmth that *The Next Day* had been. Alexis Petridis quipped in the *Guardian* that 'it would be wrong to say that his collaboration with New York's Maria Schneider Orchestra hasn't got a tune, but you have to search for it', before suggesting 'it feels as much a statement as a song'.[13] A new release from Bowie was always an event, but it was the first release since 2013's comeback that was not greeted with universal praise, peaking at an unimpressive 81 in the British charts. Still, more unexpected and interesting developments lay close at hand, even as Bowie now found himself diagnosed with the liver cancer that would eventually kill him.

Those who spent a considerable amount of time around Bowie are notable for two things in particular: the affection in which they held – and hold – him, and their discretion about issues that he and his family would prefer not to be made public. Therefore, if you ask about Bowie's health in the period between 2004 and 2016, you are likely to be batted back with a non-reply, with the implication that it barely matters, after all. He survived a heart attack, recuperated, returned to the music industry, released two albums and then died.

This has not satisfied those who want to know about every aspect of the man's health. His biographer Wendy Leigh told the BBC that 'physically, he didn't just battle cancer. If that's not enough, he had six heart attacks in recent years'; she claimed that 'I got this from somebody very close to him'. The photographer Mick Rock, who worked on a 2002 account of Bowie's Ziggy career with him, *Moonage Daydream*, said: 'I knew about the strokes, and I knew there had been a complication and he had to go back in [to the hospital], but I didn't know he was as ill as he was.'[14] And one member of the Bowie circle, speaking under condition of anonymity, told me: 'There were problems going on for the last ten years before he died, and those problems were quite severe at times. On at least one occasion, he was lucky to survive and that was a few years before he died.'

Bowie undoubtedly knew that he was ill by the time that he came to record 'Sue', but rather than his condition leading him to retreat from the industry, as he had done in 2004, he was now galvanised into producing another record. After the session with Alford and Visconti, Bowie retreated into seclusion, only interrupted by the release of the *Nothing Has Changed* compilation. He then contacted several of the musicians who had played on 'Sue' including Monder, saxophonist Donny McCaslin and drummer Mark Guiliana, and asked them whether they would be interested in recording a new album with him in early 2015 (the first person he had asked was Schneider, but she was unavailable). McCaslin would bring his quartet of himself, Guiliana, bassist Tim Lefebvre and keyboardist Jason Lindner, and the album would be recorded at Bowie's new haunt, the Magic Shop studio in SoHo, once again under the stewardship of Visconti.

*Blackstar* is an extraordinary record, and a Visconti comment – 'If we'd used David's former musicians, they would be rock people playing jazz . . . Having jazz guys play rock music turns it upside down'[15] – is the perfect encapsulation of its success. Although Bowie had been loyal to many of the musicians who had played on his last tour with him, even down to bringing Alford back into the studio for the demos, he now wished to move on from the style and approach that he had adopted, in one form or another, for the past three albums and 15 years. It would be the first time since the Tin Machine project that he recruited a wholly fresh group of musicians for his new record, but he had the courtesy to contact those people he had been working with beforehand. 'He didn't ask me to play on *Blackstar*,' Garson recalls, 'and he apologised to me. He said there's not a lot of piano on the songs and it just didn't seem right. He was very nice about it.'[16]

Monder, who had been on a retreat when McCaslin called and asked if he wanted to play on the record ('I said "Yeah, I think I can clear my calendar"') describes the run-up to the recording sessions. 'There were no rehearsals. I just received a few demos that David and Tony had made with [Alford], and these were homemade demos without lyrics, just so I could get acquainted and have an idea of what I was going to do on these tunes. Not all of the demos even made it onto the record, but "Blackstar" itself was definitely one of the ones that did. It was good that I had a more or less clear idea of what I wanted to do entering the session, and those ideas turned out to work fairly well.'[17]

Unbeknown to the musicians, Bowie had started to undergo chemotherapy and broke the news to Visconti in early January by taking off his cap to reveal his newly bald head. 'There were days he couldn't come in,' said the producer, 'but when he got in front of the microphone, he sang his balls off. I'd never seen him happier.'[18] He told the musicians that he was unwell, but no further details were forthcoming; it was a private matter, for a deeply private man, and respected as such. And, as with *The Next Day*, stringent NDAs ensured that nothing would be leaked into the public domain.

The initial studio session was designed to record songs that would fit both the *Lazarus* stage production and a potential album, which included 'Lazarus' itself, the musical's songs 'No Plan' and 'When I Met You' and a full-band version of ''Tis a Pity She Was a Whore'. A working pattern developed; Bowie and the musicians would record in intensive blocks of four-to-six days, and then once these songs had been completed, Bowie would retreat once again to assess what they had before the next bout of recording began.

The time in the studio was undeniably intense and focused, but according to those who worked with Bowie, there was no clear sign of ill health. 'I was the only one in the room that had no idea that he was sick,' says Monder. 'He seemed healthy and I thought he looked great. I thought, *This guy was super-healthy for someone who had had a heart attack ten years prior.*' Bowie was relaxed and humorous, showing the band YouTube videos he found amusing and, at one point, delivering a deadpan and decidedly adult parody of his narration for *Peter and the Wolf*.

Yet when it came to work, he was the consummate professional. 'It was amazing to see how focused he was when he was singing,' said McCaslin. 'He was completely on point and he never seemed to really warm up.'[19] Monder echoes this, saying 'he was really open to everyone's input. He had a clear idea of what he wanted, and the material dictated a specific approach because it was idiosyncratic, but there was a lot of room within it for interpretation. Bowie himself was really enthusiastic and that was infectious. He was very excited to be making a record again and super-positive.'[20] And he enjoyed himself, albeit with black humour to the forefront. He sent McCaslin one email saying: 'I haven't had this much fun since my heart attack.'[21]

They would be joined in the studio by occasional guests, including LCD Soundsystem frontman James Murphy, who had remixed 'Love Is Lost' for *The Next Day Extra*. Bowie spoke matter-of-factly about his involvement playing percussion on the remake of 'Sue' and 'Girl Loves Me' by saying, 'We will have a new body in the studio as of Tuesday. He's a lovely bloke and he will get in the way and make lots of suggestions and we will have a ball.'[22] Murphy had an important but limited presence on the album and, in 2021, spoke candidly to Marc Maron about how he might have had greater input into the record. 'When I walk in, I see David sitting in his chair and the rest of the band are in the other room playing. I didn't know what I was supposed to do. I was struggling to find my way into this already-moving machine . . . I'm like: "Oh, excuse me while I insert myself . . . Oh hey guys, have you considered hearing what this fucking guy thinks? Maybe you've heard my songs?"'

Murphy knew that he had not been hired for his bonhomie but to be, in his words, 'the disturber of the process'. He was impressed by his collaborator; 'I didn't know [Bowie] at all, but he definitely seems to have a kind of confidence that they weren't handing out when I was born in 1970.' But he also felt that he could only contribute in very limited fashion. He eventually left the recording sessions, saying to Bowie: 'Look man, I think I need to take these things to my studio and work on these things myself – that's the instrument I play.' He concluded that 'it wasn't a good fit and it broke my heart. I had to leave: I kind of talked myself out of a job. I don't have that gene, man.'[23]

The entirety of the music was recorded by late March, at which point Bowie headed to the nearby Human Studios to lay down his vocal tracks and overdubs, all of which were completed by May, after which the album was mixed by Tom Elmhirst. When Monder left the sessions, he was unsure quite what he had played on. 'It was a really positive experience in every way. But I really had no idea what the final product was going to be like, because we recorded 12 songs and I didn't know what they were going to choose, what order it was going to be and how it was going to be edited. It was a giant jumble by the time I left, so I didn't have much of an impression of anything.'[24]

Compared to *The Next Day*, where the songs may have been musically and lyrically daring but were still very clearly self-contained pieces of rock music, *Blackstar* was pushing boundaries in a way that Bowie had not attempted to do since *Outside*. Over the course of the seven tracks that were included on the album – Bowie's briefest studio record since *Station to Station*, if we exclude his soundtrack to *Baal* – there was a remarkable degree of experimentation and innovation, always with the sense of his walking a tightrope above the figurative Niagara Falls. Succeed, and the result would be something remarkable. Fail, and it's down into the tempests, soon to be washed away, or washed up.

Under normal circumstances, Bowie would have been allowed a rest. His cancer had briefly gone into remission – 'don't celebrate too quickly', he warned Visconti – but it was now time to move on to the second major project of the year, in the form of *Lazarus*. He had spent the intervening months not only writing and recording the four new songs that would be included in the show's soundtrack, but supervising Henry Hey's arrangements of his existing music. There was a debate as to whether '"Heroes"' used at the end of the play, would be, in Hey's words, 'this giant triumphant rock anthem', or whether it would instead be made to sound in keeping with the more downbeat, reflective atmosphere. 'I sent David a demo,' Hey said, 'and that finally sealed it for him. It's very understated and melancholy. At no point does it ever arc up into this triumph.'[25]

While any show that had Bowie's imprimatur upon it could easily have been a sell-out Broadway triumph, the decision had long been made not to stage it at a large theatre, but instead at the 199-seater New York Theater Workshop, where Walsh's *Once* had received a try-out run before transferring to Broadway. Nonetheless, the show, which featured a live seven-piece band, complex video projections and the starry presence of Michael C. Hall in the lead, was not cheap to stage: its budget was more than $1 million, a modest amount for a big New York show but a fortune for something that stood no chance of recouping its investment through ticket sales alone.

Before rehearsals began, Bowie headed to Brooklyn to film the video for the title track of *Blackstar* with the director Johan Renck. Renck had contacted Bowie earlier that year, opportunistically, to ask him for music for his forthcoming television series *The Last Panthers*. To his surprise and delight, Bowie had sent him an early version of 'Blackstar' for him to use over the opening credits.

Afterwards, he contacted Renck and said 'Look, I've completed this song. Do you want to come over and have a listen to it?' After Renck listened to the extraordinary music, Bowie firstly asked him if he would be interested in making a video for it and then, shortly afterwards, confided that 'I have to tell you something. I have to tell you that I'm very ill and that I'm probably going to die.' To Renck's astonishment, he clarified this by saying, 'I feel I have to tell you this because I'm not sure I will be around to be in the video'. As Renck later said, 'he wanted death to be a third collaborator in this video. He wanted death to be there as a presence in terms of formulating all the ideas and lying as a middle instigator for all his thoughts.'[26]

The video for 'Blackstar' not only featured a dead astronaut – the final hurrah of Major Tom – but was rich in strange, disturbing imagery, not least a now grey-haired and drawn-looking Bowie portraying the final personae he would take on in his career: an Aleister Crowley-esque warped messiah, brandishing what looks like a sacred book embossed with, appropriately enough, a black star on it, and another figure, Button Eyes, who would reappear in the 'Lazarus' video and was described by Renck as 'introverted, a sort of tormented blind guy'.[27] The video was officially released on 19 November and was greeted with enthusiasm that was only mildly tempered with bewilderment. Ryan Dombal wrote in *Pitchfork* that the song was 'ten minutes of interstellar art-rock and ritualistic chanting and melodramatic balladry and even some playful funk. In scope and audacity, it's closer to the cocaine-fuelled fantasias of 1976's *Station to Station* than almost anything he's done since.'

Taken on its own, 'Blackstar' was, indeed, an extraordinary statement of intent. The longest song that Bowie had included on an album since *Station to Station*'s title track, it had a similarly multi-faceted quality, moving through various kinds of tempo and arrangement. One moment, it sounds like an ominous jazz funeral march, the next a beautifully fragile, even uplifting ballad about death and rebirth. The lyrics are intentionally opaque; McCaslin suggested that Bowie told him they were about the rise of ISIS, presumably because of the line 'On the day of execution / Only women knee and smile'. but this was firmly denied by Bowie's representatives, perhaps because it was too straightforward a reading of the song. The use of McCaslin's quartet, as well as Monder's guitar playing, lends it a fascinatingly unusual texture which raised expectations for the eponymous album that it came from. It may not have been 'Let's Dance', or even 'The Stars Are Out Tonight', but it was an elegantly complex suite of ideas that made it wholly clear that 'Sue' was the precursor to a new period in its ever-questing creator's work.

Between filming the video for 'Blackstar' in September and its release, Bowie was as involved as his health allowed in the rehearsals for *Lazarus*, which took place from 3 October until the show opened on 7 December. Because of the cast's limited availability, it would only be a short run.

Closing on 20 January 2016, it would only play for little more than six weeks. And shortly before workshopping the play could begin, Bowie's health meant that he would be unable to be with van Hove and the cast in person, necessitating the disclosure of his illness, which meant that rehearsals had an especially charged atmosphere to them. As the director explained, 'he was on Skype and he was clearly sick. Then he told us. I was blown away. I don't think I uttered two words because it was totally unexpected. But did it influence the work? No. Because I felt from the first time I met him that this project was for him very urgent and very important. Of course, it then became even more urgent to tell that story, to finish it, hopefully with him alive.'[28]

When he was well enough to attend rehearsals, Bowie was a vital, supportive and generous presence, enthusiastic and excited about the show and how it would be received. Comprehensive feedback was offered, and welcomed, but only ever sent after the day's work. A particular highlight came one day after a run-through when Hey anxiously asked the composer and co-writer 'Is everything OK? Would you like anything else?' 'Yes,' replied Bowie. 'I think I'd like to sing.'[29] For the final time in public, Bowie performed a song, launching into 'Lazarus' along with Hey and his band. It would be the only time that he ever sang any of the music from *The Next Day* or *Blackstar* outside the studio.

Yet the remission that had granted him a few extra months of vitality was soon, cruelly, to come to an end. In early November, he was told by his doctors that his cancer was terminal and that they were withdrawing all treatment, save for palliative care. Many might be forgiven for giving into despair, but Bowie remained a dedicated professional and filmed another video with Renck, this time for 'Lazarus'. It was shot in Brooklyn, at the same studio where 'Blackstar' had been filmed, and although the five-hour shoot was inevitably exhausting for its ailing star, he was utterly committed to perfecting what would be the final visual accompaniment he would leave to his music. It would eventually be released on 7 January 2016: the day before *Blackstar* and three days before Bowie died.

It is undeniably a disturbing watch. The Button Eyes character from the 'Blackstar' video returns, this time a prisoner or inmate in some kind of repressive hospital or institution. He is shown writhing in pain, goaded by mortality and another Bowie persona, as he tries desperately to offer the world a last testament, a final farewell of sorts. In the closing frames of the film, he is shown retreating into a coffin-like wardrobe, dressed in a diagonally striped suit – the last incarnation of the Thin White Duke*
– never to exit or return in this lifetime. The title of the song is therefore as ironic as '"Heroes"'; it is less the account of a resurrection and more a withdrawal from existence.

As Renck remarked, the final shots were improvised on the day 'Little did I know how extraordinarily powerful this was, to end the last video he ever did by him going into his own fucking coffin and closing the door and disappearing, for all eternity.' Yet even in extremis, Bowie retained his sense of humour. When the implications of this once-famously bisexual man eschewing life and love alike became clear, Bowie giggled and said, 'Yeah, look, David Bowie has come back into the closet! Fuck yeah, we've got to do that. Let's do that right away.' 'Even at the very end of things,' Renck observed, 'he would have a laugh and he would be audacious.'[30]

If 'Blackstar' was a complex, almost prog-like epic, 'Lazarus' remains a more conventional but nonetheless brilliant offering. It could be compared to 'The Next Day' in its lyrical sentiments, contrasting that song's defiance with something far wearier and more accepting of imminent death. Appropriately enough, the first lyrics, sung a minute into the song, are 'Look up here, I'm in heaven'. It has a measured grimness to it, but also, thanks to Bowie's astonishing vocals, a strange kind of uplift, particularly in the moment that the full band comes in behind him and he declares 'By the time I got to New York, I was living like a king.' Still,

---

* Even close to death, there was a final allusion to the past. The suit was pictured on the 1991 reissue of *Station to Station*.

the knowledge of Bowie's declining condition makes it impossibly moving. Never has a man sung 'I'll be free, ain't that just like me' to more heart-breaking effect.

After filming the video, Bowie's health moved into inexorable decline. He was far less of a presence at rehearsals, although no formal announcement needed to be made. As van Hove said, 'no one from the cast knew anything because he only came when he was feeling well. But I could see, when he looked at me, in his eyes there was really a troubled man, anxious about dying and also about leaving a family behind. You could see a heartbroken man in his eyes, if you knew it.'[31] Preview performances for *Lazarus* began on 18 November, nearly three weeks before opening night. The show was, naturally, sold out, and whatever the critical reaction was, it was undeniably one of the biggest events in New York theatre in that year, even the decade. But it was unclear whether a rapidly ailing Bowie would survive until the first night, let alone be able to attend.

In the end, a grey-haired, gaunt Bowie was able to attend the show's premiere on 7 December – the first time that he had publicly supported his own work in years and the last time that he would ever be seen in public. Getting to this stage had been hard. Robert Fox noted that 'the work was great and working with him was wonderful, but it wasn't great that he wasn't well. It was not good at all. Some days he just wasn't able to be around, but whenever he could be, it [his cancer] didn't interfere with his contribution. It was just horrible for him, rather than difficult for us.' He was photographed by hordes of fans and paparazzi, and managed to make it on stage at the curtain call, to tumultuous applause, but the strain exhausted him. He had to recover his strength backstage before van Hove helped him to his nearby car. 'I somehow knew it was the last time I would see him,' said the director.[32] He was, regrettably, correct.

It now seems incredible, but when the reviews of *Lazarus* came out the following day, the critics were oblivious to its creator's failing health, or the heavy hints of *memento mori* that hung over the play. It was reviewed on three separate levels: as the latest work by a hugely talented director, a superbly accomplished collection of new and rearranged songs, and, finally, as a narrative work. The broad consensus was that it worked very well on the first and second levels, and stuttered on the third; the *Hollywood Reporter*'s judgement – that 'the two intermission-less hours of *Lazarus* are predictably strange, often impenetrable and a tad pretentious, but always fascinating'[33] – was not uncommon.

It is almost impossible to assess *Lazarus* as a work of theatre on its own terms. Not only does it require at least some passing knowledge of the narrative of *The Man Who Fell to Earth* to be even remotely comprehensible, but the allusions to other parts of the Bowie canon – particularly *Outside* – are sufficiently pervasive, if at times vague, to mean that this is a show best appreciated by those with a postgraduate degree in Bowie studies. It has been revived several times, sometimes with Hey and van Hove involved and sometimes without them, and looks likely to be a staple of ambitious musical repertory theatre for years to come. What it isn't is a conventional (and lucrative) jukebox musical along the lines of *Mamma Mia!* or *We Will Rock You*. Bowie could easily have given permission for his songs to be used in something far less challenging that would probably still be running today, but he was never interested in doing the obvious. Far more intriguing challenges awaited him.

When Bowie left the New York Theater Workshop on 7 December, he had a little more than a month to live. He spent the final weeks that he was able to work undertaking as much activity as could manage; Visconti suggested that he was urgently demoing five new songs. 'I thought, and *he* thought, that he'd have a few months, at least. Obviously, if he's excited about doing his next album, he must've thought he had a few more months. So the end must've been very rapid. I'm not privy to it.'[34] *Blackstar* had originally been intended to be released on 30 October 2015, shortly before *Lazarus* opened, but it had been impossible to film his final video before November because of rehearsal commitments, to say nothing of his ill health, and so a delayed release date of 8 January 2016 – his 69th birthday – was decided upon instead.

Bowie had obsessively followed the critical and popular reaction to *The Next Day*, but would not be able to do the same for *Blackstar*. Nevertheless, he, and those around him, knew that he had produced something beautiful, strange and unique. In one of his final emails to his record company Sony, he modestly described it as 'not bad for an old rocker'.[35] As he realised, to his reluctance, that it would be his final album, he began to take stock in the last weeks that he had. Bidding farewell to his most trusted and beloved collaborators became his priority.

Alan Edwards visited him for the final time in late 2015. Summoned by Coco ('he'd like you to come and listen to the album'), he visited Bowie at Electric Lady Studios, where his client was watching *The Good, the Bad and the Ugly*, and observed that 'he looked tired and thin, but this was in no way unusual'. They listened to *Blackstar*, swapped stories and 'there was no business discussed'.[36] At the end, Bowie and his publicist embraced, and the musician departed.

Bowie wrote Eno a long, warm and irreverent email, alternating between in-jokes and proud summation of their peerless artistic achievements. He ended it by saying, 'Thank you for our good times, Brian. They will never rot', before signing off 'Dawn'. They had recently discussed the possibility of working on a follow-up to *Outside*. 'We both liked that album a lot,' noted Eno, 'and felt that it had fallen through the cracks. We talked about revisiting it, taking it somewhere new. I was looking forward to that.' But, as the producer later said, 'I realise now he was saying goodbye.'[37] Garson, his longest-standing lieutenant, received a similar note, saying 'Mike, we did an incredible body of work together', which led the musician to remark to his wife, presciently, 'I'm not going to hear from him again.'

He was proved correct, but subsequently learned that, on his deathbed, Bowie wanted to say more. 'I didn't find this out until about a year and a half after he passed, but he had sent a message through somebody when he was dying, basically saying, "Please, thank Mike for me." It was one of the most touching moments in my life.'[38] There were others who received similarly cryptic messages, but the idea was not to make a grand farewell statement of any kind. *Blackstar*, after all, would become his final artistic legacy. Bowie knew that the early response to the album had been favourable and could only hope that it would be at least as acclaimed as *The Next Day*, if not more so.

When *Blackstar*, with its enigmatic, almost empty Barnbrook-designed cover of a star, was released on 8 January, critical reaction to it was somewhere between giddy delight and pleasurable mystification. Alexis Petridis in the *Guardian* saluted it as 'rich, deep and strange',[39] while the *New York Times* described it as 'strange, daring [and] ultimately rewarding . . . at once emotive and cryptic, structured and spontaneous, and above all, wilful, refusing to cater to the expectations of radio stations and fans'.[40] It received unanimous praise, tempered only occasionally with the faint suspicion that Bowie was being obscure for obscurity's sake. But, as Visconti put it, 'I think he thought if he was going to die, this would be a great way to go. This would be a great statement to make.'[41]

Visconti also suggested, perhaps giddily, that 'I think *Blackstar* is his best album, his magnum opus . . . He just got better and better.'[42] Writing this nearly a decade after *Blackstar* was released, with the hype dissipated, it is possible to make a serious, although by no means unconditional, case for agreeing with Visconti's statement. The greatest albums that Bowie released in the period covered by this book – *The Buddha of Suburbia*, *Outside*, *The Next Day* and, up to a point, *Heathen* – are all supremely accomplished records, with brilliant songwriting that stands up alongside anything that Bowie recorded earlier in his career. Yet none of them are perfect. Each of them contain some duff tracks that could easily have been reworked or jettisoned altogether, and a couple of songs that are decent but no more than that. And the weakest records that Bowie put his name to (I would suggest *Earthling* and *Tin Machine*, but there are a couple of others that I haven't been rushing to listen to lately, either) were simply poor pieces of work that were recorded in a fit of misplaced zeal and can be regretted at leisure.

*Blackstar* is different. If it is considered alongside the excellent three original songs that Bowie recorded for *Lazarus* – 'No Plan', 'Killing a Little Time' and 'When I Met You' – then the ten songs that Bowie released in, to coin a phrase, the final hour of his life represent some of his most accomplished, interesting work. It seems particularly extraordinary that a man who could record something as pointless as 'Fall Dog Bombs the Moon' as a mature artist could return more than a decade later with this exquisite, disturbing collection of songs.

Describing it as a jazz album was a common critical lunge, but the genius of *Blackstar* is that it's a complex rock album performed by jazz musicians – and Bowie himself. The first singles were a fine curtain-raiser for what came subsequently, just as the 2014 versions of 'Sue' and ''Tis a Pity She Was a Whore' were refined and improved upon in the album versions. And then the three remaining songs are of the same level of attainment. 'Girl Loves Me' tips its bowler hat to *A Clockwork Orange* in its use of the made-up language of Nadsat, just as its arrangement sounds like watching Alex and his droogs take a menacing walk down a darkened alley. 'I Can't Give Everything Away', with the last vocal Bowie ever recorded, is a deceptively joyful piece of badinage with his admirers: he has spent most of his life in the public gaze, but there will always be the David Jones aspect of him that remains unreachable and unknowable, perhaps even to himself. And then there's what might be my favourite song on the album, 'Dollar Days'. More conventional than the rest of *Blackstar*, and recorded almost spontaneously in the studio, it comes on as a post-2013 meditation on Bowie's farewell to Britain and the knowledge of his impending mortality, expressed, heartbreakingly, in the repeated words 'I'm dying to'. Or, as it could easily be heard, 'too'.

*Blackstar* was released in a strange year for the music industry. Four major figures died in 2016 – the others were Leonard Cohen, George Michael and Prince – and when the record found its appropriate place in the 'album of the year' pantheon, it was jostling against Cohen's similarly mortality-fixated swansong, *You Want It Darker*, and Nick Cave's deeply affecting collection of songs, *Skeleton Tree. Blackstar* will always be remembered, fairly or otherwise, as its creator's 'death album', his very own version of Schubert's *Schwanengesang*. A decade later, it has yet to become ordinary or conventional. 'Blackstar' and 'Lazarus' are not being used to sell cars or home furnishings on TV advertisements, and it retains a strange, beguiling power that only *Station to Station* and *Low* equal.

If Bowie had been healthy enough to witness its release, he would undoubtedly have been both thrilled and amused by the reaction that it received. However, it was precisely because of his terminal illness that the album takes the form that it does. And so when Bowie died at his home in downtown New York on 10 January, two days after turning 69, he could at least have known that his corporeal body may have expired, but, as he anticipated on the title track of his final album:

> Something happened on the day he died
> Spirit rose a metre and stepped aside.

David Robert Jones – David Bowie – was no more. But the spirit that found its final flowering in his defiant, remarkable farewell to the world was about to receive the tear-stained acknowledgement and boundless love that it, and he, had always merited. Lazarus may have died, but only his wasted physical body was finished. His legacy would live on, as long as the artform that he had so excelled in lasted.

# EPILOGUE

## Hero: the afterlife of David Bowie

*'He was the best there is'*

I woke early on 11 January 2016 after an unsettled night. My wife Nancy was pregnant with our daughter and she was nearly a fortnight overdue, which meant that we had to go into hospital for labour to be induced. Yet I could tell from her expression that she had other news to tell me.

'David Bowie's dead.'

I can remember only a handful of occasions that I can say precisely where I was when I heard about the death of a celebrity who I had never met: Stanley Kubrick, Princess Diana, Michael Jackson, Heath Ledger. Yet finding out about Bowie's death, just a couple of days after I had started getting to grips with *Blackstar*, was an emotional blow quite unlike any of the others. Damp-eyed, I began writing a tribute to him on my website, while listening to 'Conversation Piece' over and over again. The line about being unable to see the water for the tears resonated in a way that it never had before.

I wrote quickly and emotionally, spewing thoughts and feelings out without pause or check. On any other day, I would then have retired to bed and done nothing else. But there was no time for self-indulgent griev- ing. We had to head to hospital; new life had to be born. I packed my bag and walked out of the house, feeling as if I had lost a friend, or a parent. I felt adrift.

This sense of universal shock and sorrow at the unanticipated death of Bowie was one that resonated with men and women across both sides of the Atlantic. When the news was announced, the world stopped its business to mourn. Not since the death of Princess Diana nearly two decades before had a public figure's demise led to such an emotional and unchecked outpouring. That night, vigils took place in London, New York and elsewhere, as strangers, united by love for Bowie and his music, gathered together to sing, exchange reminiscences and to celebrate and mourn the departure of a man who gave pleasure to millions for decades. As one sign said, 'the Starman has returned home'.

In Brixton that evening, hundreds of his fans gathered, seeking solidarity and comfort. I wished I had been there with them, rather than sitting anxiously in a Brighton hospital. Flowers were laid by a giant mural of him as Aladdin Sane, just around the corner from where he was born. The cinema was emblazoned with the sign 'David Bowie, Our Brixton Boy, RIP'. Some admirers had painted their faces with Ziggy lightning bolts; others played half-remembered snatches of Bowie songs on acoustic guitars. The area's pubs played nothing else on their sound systems and jukeboxes that evening. All ages, races, classes and backgrounds assembled, a melting pot of cultures and Londoners all united by a fierce love for their departed idol.

Yet amid the grief, there was also an appreciation for what he had left them. As one woman commented, 'people talk about him reinventing himself, but I don't think that's true. He invented and the decades struggled to catch him up. It's as simple as that.' Another suggested that *Blackstar* was the only appropriate way that he could have quit the stage. 'For him to have looked death in the eye and then create that – what an artistic way to go. He skidded into that grave, didn't he?'[1]

It was a similar story in Berlin and New York, the other two cities most closely associated with Bowie. Although he had not lived in Germany for years, and the country had its grim associations, being the site of his final full live performance before heart trouble forced him into semi-retirement, the indelible connection between artist and place was best expressed when – as hundreds gathered outside his former flat in Berlin's Schöneberg district and the Neues Ufer bar where he used to drink – the country's foreign ministry paid tribute to him. The institution wrote on social media: 'Good-bye,

David Bowie. You are now among #Heroes. Thank you for helping to bring down the #wall.' And Bowie's home at 285 Lafayette Street in New York became a place of pilgrimage and grief immediately, with dozens of floral tributes laid down outside the building. One affecting sign simply said 'Starman Forever'.

Bowie may have sung on 'Space Oddity', mockingly, that 'the papers want to know whose shirts you wear', but he would have been both gratified and, perhaps, a little embarrassed by the media response to his death. On Tuesday 12 January, virtually every English-language newspaper carried a full-page account of the news on its cover. In Britain, the *Guardian* and *The Times* both produced wrap-around editions, with suitably iconic portraits of Bowie and the dates he lived. The former used the 1978 Lord Snowdon picture of him looking youthful and beautiful, while *The Times* chose the 1983 Ralph Gatti image of Bowie promoting *Merry Christmas, Mr Lawrence* in Cannes. In both cases, he looked ineffably, impossibly stylish.

As soon as Bowie's death was announced, the famous rushed to pay tribute to their peer. Music aristocracy from Madonna and Kanye West to Paul McCartney and Pharrell Williams offered their condolences. Some were the usual anodyne placeholders – surely Jagger and Keith Richards could have come up with something more affecting and personal than 'as well as being a wonderful and kind man, he was an extraordinary artist and a true original' – but others bothered.

Peter Gabriel wrote: 'He meant so much to me and to so many. He was a one-off, a brilliant outlier, always exploring, challenging and inspiring anyone who wanted to push the boundaries of music, art, fashion and society. There are so few artists who can touch a generation as he did, we will miss him badly.' He concluded, 'Long live Lazarus.' Bowie's Freddie Mercury Tribute Concert duet partner Annie Lennox referenced the 'Blackstar' video; 'the bejewelled remains of Major Tom lie dormant in a dust-coated space suit . . . It leaves me breathless. You must see it to believe it . . . He knew. . . He could see through it all.' And his old friend and Berlin flatmate Iggy Pop, never naturally verbose, commented simply and affectingly that 'David's friendship was the light of my life. I never met such a brilliant person. He was the best there is.'

As is obligatory in these circumstances, politicians had to weigh in, too. The then- prime minister David Cameron, who had once claimed that *Hunky Dory* was his favourite album, talked of how 'today we are mourning the loss of an immense British talent . . . 'Genius is an over-used word but I think musically, creatively, artistically, David Bowie was a genius.' His predecessor Tony Blair, who had briefly enjoyed a wary friendship with Bowie in the '90s, declared that 'from the time I saw his Ziggy Stardust concert as a student, I thought he was a brilliant artist and an exciting and interesting human being. It was a great privilege when I got to meet him later in life.'

There would be no such encomium from US President Barack Obama, but his spokesman carefully commented, 'I am not sure whether President Barack Obama was a Bowie fan. But the broad outpouring of reaction to Bowie's death illustrates how his loss will be felt.' It was an accurate observation. And from the world of literature, J. K. Rowling, who had previously been public about her admiration and affection for Morrissey,* suggested simply 'I wish that he could have stayed on earth longer.'

Those closest to Bowie in the final years of his life were as affected by the unexpected news as complete strangers. Visconti wrote on his Facebook page that 'he always did what he wanted to do. And he wanted to do it his way and he wanted to do it the best way. His death was no different from his life – a work of art. He made *Blackstar* for us, his parting gift.' Alluding to the inevitability of Bowie's end, Visconti noted that 'I knew for a year this was the way it would be. I wasn't, however, prepared for it. He was an extraordinary man, full of love and life. He will always be with us. For now, it is appropriate to cry.'

---

* Who pointedly, and childishly, refused to include Bowie's name in a list of the celebrity deaths of the year at a Manchester gig he played in August, before performing his song 'All the Best Ones Are Dead'. This led, deservedly, to his being booed and called a 'cunt' by at least one offended member of the audience.

Gail Ann Dorsey, meanwhile, had sent him birthday wishes a couple of days before, and had heard from him a fortnight earlier. 'I'd had mail from him at Christmas time. I still have the message he sent, because it was a little bit out of character with him. He was sweet-natured, but he wasn't a mushy, kind of sentimental guy. That wasn't his thing. And then he sent me this kind of love message, and that was unusual for him.' Shortly afterwards, she understood why. 'I was staying in a hotel that night, and try-ing to get to sleep, but messages kept coming in. So I looked at my phone, and there was a message from Reeves, and it said "David Bowie's died". I turned on CNN and there was an image of Bowie, and I was in the shot. My heart just stopped. It was such a strange experience. From that moment on, my phone just lit up like a firecracker. We were all calling each other. The phone was just ringing off the hook. Other musicians, artists, every-body, we all freaked out.'[2]

The days after Bowie's death were a surreal experience for anyone who knew him and who were pestered by news agencies and broadcasters for quotes and information. Sterling Campbell recalls the maelstrom that he unwillingly found himself briefly caught up in. 'I didn't really know how to react to it. The internet's a weird place, especially when an event like this takes place, because everybody has something to say and something to do. And this was a huge event, and I was technically a part of it. People were reaching out to me who wouldn't normally do so and it was all so surreal. Everything went viral. For somebody who'd had nothing to do with it, it was like being in the midst of this kind of firestorm of information, and so I really did not process it. In my head, I was laughing with David, because this was just insanity.'[3]

By the time that Bowie died, Reeves Gabrels, like many former col-leagues, bandmates and friends, had lost contact with him. Now a member of the Cure – and therefore playing alongside another charismatic, eccentric British frontman in Robert Smith – he had no expectation of a reconciliation with his former collaborator. 'The last time I saw him was just prior to 9/11. We emailed occasionally, but I was in Nashville and he was in Manhattan, and I couldn't call the guy up and expect him to chat. But I listened to *Blackstar* the day it came out, and then the next night. I had a dream about David, in which we were arguing about which band was better, Blur or Pulp, which was the kind of conversation we always used to have before he died. He hadn't been on my mind in a long time, after all those years of being with him 24 hours a day, and so I went to bed, thinking "That's interesting . . . for me, *Blackstar* sounds like where we could have got to if we'd followed *Outside*." Then I woke up to a message from Duncan [Jones] at 2am, saying that his father had passed. The fact that I'd dreamt about him, and then suddenly he'd died, was really kind of freaky.'[4]

Bowie would not have been sentimental about the reaction to his demise. Appreciative, yes; gushing, no. His will was soon made public, and it was simple and unsurprising. Of his $100 million estate, Iman received half, his children a quarter apiece – with Lexi inheriting the family property near Woodstock too – and there were bequests of $2 million to Coco and $1 million to Duncan's former nanny Marion Skene. Bowie asked that his body be cremated privately immediately after he died and that no public funeral or memorial service be held. *Blackstar* would have to serve as his final testament, albeit one laden with mystery and enigma until the last. (As he himself sang, 'I can't give everything away.')

This has not stopped many from attempting to weigh in with their opinions about what Bowie would, and would not, have wished for. Gabrels deals with these types briskly. 'I can see what he would have found humorous and what he would have been irritated by. There have been a lot of people coming forward and saying "Oh, I knew David, this is what he would have said and done." And as someone who spent over ten years with him, I can say, "No, it really isn't."'[5]

In the days immediately after Bowie's death, many who had been close to him reflected on his final offering. Both William Boyd and Kevin Cann, who had little interest in the records Bowie had made over the previous decades, listened to *Blackstar* and considered it a masterpiece. 'I wasn't very interested in Bowie's later albums,' admits Boyd. 'I'd mainly been listening to classical and world music, and if I wanted rock, I'd go to South America or Africa. But I thought *Blackstar* was extraordinary. I listened to it many times and found it moving, eerie and spooky. I first heard it after he died, and that gave insight into how he was thinking, and the weight that it had, as well as his meditations on death.'[6] Cann, meanwhile, says 'I actually do like *Blackstar*, but from all of that work, there's always a gem or two. It's remarkable that there's that level of quality, where you can always find something that really stands out. I've got a huge amount of respect for everything that he's done.'[7]

Meanwhile, work – and life – had to continue. The *David Bowie Is* exhibition was being shown at the Groninger Museum in the Netherlands at the time of its subject's death. Although the exhibition was not usually open on Mondays, grieving fans were allowed special admission to it, along with the opportunity to sign a condolence book. Fifty people were already waiting outside when it opened and there was a constant flood of visitors throughout the day, all wishing to become part of something greater than themselves. Andreas Blühm, the museum's director, explained that 'we've been very involved with him over the last months, so it's as if a close friend has died, but a friend you haven't met in person. That's quite bizarre and everyone working at this museum is personally touched.'[8] Such was the demand that the exhibition was extended for a further four weeks before it headed on to its next berth in Bologna. It would run until 15 July 2018, concluding at the Brooklyn Museum.

*Lazarus*, meanwhile, carried on until 20 January, before transferring to London for an 11-week run between November and January 2017. By a strange stroke of chance – or irony – the cast recorded the show's soundtrack album on 11 January, shortly after learning of its creator's death. Michael C. Hall, who had lost his father when he was young and suffered from Hodgkin's lymphoma in his late thirties, described the emotions that he felt when he awoke to a blizzard of messages as 'a familiar internal fist clench'. He made it through the session through sheer force of will. Hall later described how 'some sort of old survival mechanism kicks in. I think it's about holding on, it's about mirroring what I see to not be victimised by trauma.'[9] His co-star Cristin Milioti explained that 'there was no better way to get through that day. We all held hands and curled up on the couch in the recording studio. I think all of us just cried, all day. It was so hard to sing those songs. And yet it was so intense and beautiful because it just felt like we were celebrating him.'[10]

It would have pleased Bowie that *Blackstar* became his most successful album of modern times. A mixture of its innate excellence and a desire by his admirers to commemorate him in some tangible fashion saw it hit the top of the *Billboard* 200 – his only album ever to do so – as well as virtually every other major chart throughout the world. In an age dominated by streaming, when an album by an established artist was increasingly not seen as a strongly commercial prospect, *Blackstar* sold nearly two million copies in its first year of release – a considerable achievement when its creator was neither available to publicise it, nor would have done so even if he had still lived.

Amid universal subsequent critical acclaim, the album won five Grammy Awards in February 2017, for Best Alternative Music Album, Best Rock Song and Best Rock Performance, among others. When Donny McCaslin collected the award for the latter, he announced that 'the course of my life as an artist and a person changed when I met David', praising Bowie as 'an artistic genius, a kind man and a funny-as-hell guy'. Few would disagree.

During the days after Bowie's death, I watched the international reaction and concentrated on more immediate matters. My wife's induction did not go as anticipated, and so, for a few grim days in January 2016, I felt an increasing sense of concern about her and our daughter. Eventually, she was born in the late afternoon of Friday, 15 January 2016, by C-section. The week's events had to be acknowledged somehow and so she would be called, appropriately enough, Rose Evelyn Bowie Larman. Rebl Rebl has, I am proud to say, lived up to her billing ever since.

The last professional photographs of Bowie that exist – the snatched images of him from the *Lazarus* premiere aside – were taken by his long-standing associate Jimmy King, who also took the pictures that adorn the cover of the *Nothing Has Changed* compilation from 2014. In these parting images, a suited and behatted Bowie is shown looking far more cheerful and carefree than in the other, more formal promotional shots taken after his semi-retirement in 2014. In the most famous picture, which is believed to have been taken in September 2015 or thereabouts, Bowie is grinning exuberantly at the camera, leaning forwards as if convulsed with laughter, but it's unclear who the joke is on. His millions of admirers? Himself? Someone or something else? Potentially all three? Bowie was never one for giving the game away easily.

He does not look like someone who knew that he was seriously ill and would die of his illness a matter of a few months after the pictures were taken. Yet, as I've discovered while researching and writing this book, expecting Bowie to behave in a conventional or, at times, even comprehensible fashion – to satisfy the whims of others – would be an exercise in impotent frustration. Whether you like or appreciate everything that he did over the period I have written about, nothing was done to satisfy anyone other than himself. His bloody-minded pursuit of this satisfaction remains impressive and admirable, if, at times, perverse. Like another sometime New York resident, he did it his way.

Writing this nearly a decade after his death, it is heartening to observe that Bowie's posthumous artistic reputation remains as exalted as it always merited. There have, of course, been many, *many* reissues and live concert releases, ensuring that the Bowie gravy train keeps on tootling away. The most ambitious of these projects was the wholescale re-recording of the *Never Let Me Down* album, fulfilling an (apparently) throwaway remark that he made when he chose a remix of 'Time Will Crawl' for the *iSelect* compilation in 2008. He wrote, 'Oh, to redo the rest of that album.' Two years after he died, producer Mario J. McNulty and an all-star cast of musicians – including Gabrels, continuing his work with Bowie one final time two decades after their professional partnership had ended – came together to re-record the music, swapping the original's synthesiser arrangements for Nico Muhly-arranged strings and allowing Laurie Anderson to step in on 'Shining Star' where once the actor Mickey Rourke had performed a rap.

It is impossible to say whether Bowie, whose passing comment was taken as giving consent to the project, would have approved of the re-recording or not, but it at least elevates his weakest album to listenability. 'Beat of Your Drum', in particular, is far more appealing than it once was, although the dismal lyrics and indifferent music can only be salvaged so far. It was briefly overpraised by some critics who were delighted to have a 'new' Bowie album to listen to, but they should have waited until early 2022, when *Toy* would finally be released, albeit with 'Uncle Floyd' still lurking in a vault somewhere. It is possible that, over the next few years, there will be some genuinely new songs released, including music recorded in the *Blackstar* and *The Next Day* sessions, but such a decision will be made by a very few people in the Bowie firmament. The rest of us will find out what's left in due course.

Professionally, Bowie's final statement was *Blackstar* and, as countless others have correctly observed, even if he could not have anticipated that his parting album and death would come as close together as they did, it has a thrillingly elegiac brilliance that few, if any, other artists have matched at any point in their career. He has entered a rare pantheon that few musicians are admitted to – of peerless genius. I'll let Garson, the man who knew him as well as any of his collaborators did, speak:

Like all of us, he had his character flaws and what have you. I never had to deal with any of that, but I was aware of it. But the essence of the guy was that as an artist, when you really look back – I started saying this back 20 years ago, and then I said it ten years ago, and I'm saying it again now – in a hundred years, you'll know the Beatles, you'll know Dylan, and you'll know Bowie. Those are the ones you keep coming back to. I've talked to so many actors and singers, and they were just in awe of who this guy was in his many talents. Even his acting ability was phenomenal. And ever since he passed, I keep saying that he's our Michelangelo/da Vinci. And, in 500 years, if the planet manages to exist then, people will still know who he is and tell stories about him. Alan Edwards would go even further. He had the audacity and balls and probably nerve and probably truth to say 'This guy's gonna be known in 5,000 years.'[11]

Other perspectives are available, from the slightly to the considerably less laudatory, and I have tried to bring as many of them into this book as I can. As a person, Bowie was as flawed as any of us. He was capricious, easily distracted and then just as easily bored, and could treat his collaborators in a high-handed fashion, expecting them to run when they were called and discarding them when they were no longer required. It is to his credit that, especially in the final decades of his life, this aspect of his personality became subsumed by a desire to forge meaningful working relationships with the hugely talented people he played with both on record and live. But many of those I have profiled or featured here – Erdal Kizilçay, Nıle Rodgers and, particularly, Reeves Gabrels, to name but three – could find his often-dictatorial behaviour frustrating and counterproductive.

I have not included some of the off-the-record comments that a couple of interviewees made about Bowie's reminiscences of his behaviour in the '70s and early '80s; firstly, because they do not come under this book's purview, and, secondly, because although he never openly confessed to anything illegal, the impression given was that of a man taking full advantage of the opportunities he was offered, for good and sometimes for ill. Should I ever have cause to write about this earlier period of his life, these comments would become rather more germane to the story I would be telling.

In any case, our perception of who the 'real' Bowie was may yet one day be superseded by a high-profile cinematic or televisual account, although Bowie himself has previously defied fictionalised portrayal. Since his death, there has been a low-budget biopic, *Stardust*, in which the usually excellent Johnny Flynn – himself both an estimable musician and a fine actor – was miscast in an account of Bowie's first visit to the United States in 1971. It was a box-office flop. Likewise, we have no way of knowing whether the conversation between Bowie and Danny Boyle in 2011 went particularly badly; not only did Bowie decline to perform at the Olympics in 2012, but he also refused permission for Boyle to use his music in a biopic about the relationship between Bowie and Iggy Pop that he wished to direct, based on a script by Frank Cottrell Boyce. It was a decision that Boyle later said left him 'in grief'.

Big-budget music pictures – such as *Rocket Man*, *Bohemian Rhapsody* and the Robbie Williams biopic *Better Man* – have all been critically or commercially successful in the years since Bowie died and it is possible that his estate may yet give their support to a conventional biopic. It is rumoured that a script, entitled *Starman*, exists; one day, it might be filmed. In any case, it will now be easier for filmmakers to use Bowie's music in a picture, if they are sufficiently well-funded. His entire publishing catalogue was sold to Warner Chappell in February 2022, for a reported $250 million. For a man who was more conscious of his financial limitations than many of his peers were until he was well into middle age, this would have been an amusing, and rewarding, turnaround. If only he had still been alive to see it.

At the time of writing, Bowie would have been nearly 80 years old. Once, this would be an unimaginably ancient age for a rock star, but now it seems almost unexceptional. His friends and peers like Paul McCartney, Mick Jagger, Bruce Springsteen and Bob Dylan are either approaching their ninth decade or are well into it, and it is tempting to wonder what Bowie would have done if he had survived his illness. Would he have continued to produce ground-breaking, brilliant music but refused to perform publicly?

Would *Blackstar* have been a final hurrah preceding a committed retirement? Or, like 2016's other casualty, Leonard Cohen, would Bowie have performed a last, extended valedictory tour, giving his fans a final chance to hear songs old and new once again?

We shall never know, although nobody I interviewed, save Garson, suggested that he had any interest in performing live after 2004. However, we should not regret the songs that Bowie never wrote or the films that he never acted in – or directed – but instead be humbly thankful for the bold and generous legacy that he bequeathed us. He inspired countless people not only to produce art and music that have made the world an infinitely greater and richer place, but did so with a calm, reserved brilliance that made him one of the most purely likeable figures ever to attain the level of fame that he reached. His influence, as both musician and man, was peerless. As long as we still enjoy listening to his records, reading his interviews, watching his performances or simply thrilling to the world that he did more than most to remake in his own image, David Bowie will live on. Lazarus, come forth; you're a fucking hero.

# BONUS TRACK

## The David Bowie Centre,
## September 2025

*'It is impossible to get him to relax'*

When *David Bowie Is* finally concluded its world tour in Brooklyn in 2018, the question as to where the Bowie archive would end up became pertinent. Should it be housed in some specially built warehouse in Manhattan, close to Bowie's final residence there, or might it merit its own wing of MoMA or Tate Modern? Questions over Bowie's identity were asked – not for the first time – and whether he should be regarded as an epoch-defining artist or a 'mere' musician. While it was never conceivable that the material would ever vanish into private hands, it was believed that whichever institution became the custodian of the archive would have to do something special with it, in order to honour an extraordinary legacy.

Appropriately enough, given the Bowie estate's pre-existing relationship with the V&A Museum in London, they won out. In 2023, it was announced that they had acquired the archive and that it would be displayed in a purpose-built space, the David Bowie Centre, held within the new V&A Storehouse East in Hackney, east London. Tristram Hunt, the V&A's Bowiephile director, called the acquisition '[a] new sourcebook for the Bowies of tomorrow'.[1] The knowledge that the archive, holding as many as 90,000 items owned by and relating to Bowie, would be a game-changer when it came to understanding its subject (not least for any biographer) meant that many, including me, tried their best to be allowed early access to some of the treasures held within. But the V&A, and the project's chief curator Dr Madeleine Haddon, stood firm. Until the centre opened, nobody, but nobody, was to be allowed to catch sight of anything save what had been previously exhibited in *David Bowie Is*.

At last, a launch date of 13 September 2025 was agreed upon, and the David Bowie Centre was finally opened to the public. When I visited, I found the experience both overwhelming and highly emotional. The centre lies on the second floor of the V&A East Storehouse, a vast collection of the museum's holdings that itself opened a few months before. It's a fitting repository for all things Bowie, looking like a gleamingly futuristic version of the warehouse where the Ark of the Covenant is entombed at the close of *Raiders of the Lost Ark*. Bowie's one-time detractor Jonathan Jones had praised the Storehouse upon its opening in a five-star review, saying: 'This is what the museum of the future looks like – an old idea that's now been turned inside out, upside down, disgorging its secrets, good and bad, in an avalanche of beautiful questions, created with curiosity, generous imagination and love.'[2]

Much the same could be said of the Bowie archive, designed by the London and Paris-based architects IDK. It is not a vast space – one main room, containing nine display cabinets – and only a carefully selected 200 objects are on show at any given time, meaning that less than 0.025 per cent of the total archive is on public view. (More items are available individually via the museum's 'Order an Object' service, allowing anyone to request up to five at a time.) Still, there are enough highlights to satisfy anyone, whether they are a casual Bowie fan, an obsessive admirer or, of course, a biographer desperately charging around to try to fill the gaps while on the tightest of production deadlines.

There are many fascinating details outside the chronological scope of this book that are still worth noting. An Apple Records letter of 15 July 1968 brusquely rejects the young Bowie as a potential artist for the label, saying 'we don't feel he is what we're looking for at the moment'.[3] Rather sweetly, it is placed next to a mid-'60s reference from Bowie's father Heywood, sent to W.A. Freshman, head of a Mayfair legal firm. Bowie Sr writes of his son that 'whenever he takes on an idea of any kind he never lets up and he puts everything he has got into it . . . it is impossible to get him to relax and once having made up his mind to do something nothing will stop him in his efforts to make a good job of it.'[4] Such a sentiment remained as true five decades later as it was when it was first written.

Yet what makes a visit to the David Bowie Centre so fascinating isn't so much the costumes on display (which included the Alexander McQueen frock coat as seen on the cover of *Earthling* and the original Freddie Burretti ice-blue suit from the video of 'Life on Mars') or the Bowie memorabilia, which includes a double-ended key from the Berlin flat that he and Iggy Pop lived in during the '70s. Instead, it's the tantalising details from his various projects that will be the most compelling for obsessive fans. We learn, for instance, that 'Lazarus' was originally known as 'The Hunger' – perhaps a nod to the 1983 Tony Scott horror film of the same name, in which Bowie played an eighteenth-century cellist-turned-vampire – and that he rewrote some of his dialogue for his character in *Everybody Loves Sunshine*. Still, changing the line 'I've had them cleaned' to 'Happy birthday, boys. No train set this year but I've brought shooters' – although a marginal improvement – does not suggest that Bowie's forte was script doctoring.

Thankfully, dodgy '90s gangster films aside, this is a celebration of Bowie's remarkable versatility and enduring prescience alike. A note written in the early '00s muses on the imminent rise of MP3 players and streaming services, even as he notes that 'I feel closer to Marshall McLuhan than Robbie Williams'.[5] A breakdown of the timeline for *Blackstar* publicity – given that Bowie wouldn't be giving any interviews or making any live appearances, for reasons that became sadly obvious two days after its release – shows how engaged and involved he was with the minutiae of marketing, even from afar, right up until the end.

His influence on a younger generation of artists is acknowledged both by an interactive exhibition, 'The Library of Connections', featuring objects with Bowie associations clear and spurious alike,* and by a 2013 letter from Lady Gaga. She gushingly writes: 'I cried in fact, listening to each song . . . I feel as though my entire career has been an artistic plea for you to notice me.' Although it led to a correspondence between the two, her wish that 'I would be so grateful and honoured to meet you'[6] was, alas, never fulfilled.

Of the nine display cabinets, there is a welcome tribute to Gail Ann Dorsey, recognition of Bowie's interest in jungle and drum and bass music (it comes as an amusing surprise to learn that, while he was engaged in putting his *New Afro/Pagan* show together in the mid-'90s, he was a regular visitor to the Metalheadz club night at the Blue Note jazz club in pre-gentrified Hoxton) and a selection of '70s artefacts. These were chosen by his former collaborator Nile Rodgers – all *Black Tie White Noise* animosity long since smoothed over – and the young British band the Last Dinner Party, whose music owes '70s- and '80s-era Bowie the most substantial debt that it might without obviously plagiarising his work. A huge video screen shows highlights from live performance and music videos alike, and, at the press preview, 'Let's Dance' could occasionally be heard coming into earshot, faintly, before disappearing all over again.

Still, the most compelling and surprising section was that marked 'unrealised projects'. This ranged from lyrical ideas that never went anywhere – a list that included such scattered and cryptic lines as 'you have no right to your next breath' and 'I shall wail my dirge before I die and never stop to calcify' – to larger-scale ambitions. In the early '80s, Bowie wished to adapt David Kidd's 1960 memoir *All the Emperor's Horses*, which deals with the end of imperial China, and to play Kidd himself, who was a first-hand witness to the events via his marriage to the daughter of the former chief justice. Although he was, apparently, serious about the idea (an excited letter from Kidd, whom Bowie had befriended, details precisely

---

\* Greta Gerwig's film *Barbie* is included, for instance, because she became obsessed with 'Moonage Daydream' when she was eighteen. She subsequently told *Desert Island Discs* that: 'This sounds wild, but I truly think if David Bowie hadn't existed, I wouldn't have made anything.'

the kind of velvet cape he would wear to the premiere), it went the way of so many other Bowie projects into obscurity.

Others proved more durable. Although a curious mid-'70s television screenplay, called *The Catastrophy* [*sic*] *Cabinet*,\* went nowhere, its idea of a haunted *Wunderkammer* (as cabinets of curiosities are traditionally known) would eventually inspire the visual concept of the video for 'Lazarus', with its conclusion of Bowie, in his 'button eyes' guise, backing into the closet for the final time. And while the musician's grandiose plans for the *Leon/ Outside* project never came to pass, images and details about a projected 1994 show, 'Leon in India: A Music Village Ritual' – which would have cost around $1 million and used actors, musicians and dancers in an attempt to bring the then-sprawling project to life against the backdrop of the Arabian Sea in Mumbai – demonstrate that he was entirely serious about doing something beautiful, and brave, and original. Whether the subsequent *Outside* tour can be thus described is another matter altogether.

When I visited, the archive – which included a heartening amount of fan-made memorabilia, all carefully collected and preserved by Bowie – was still being catalogued. When this book is first published, the cataloguing will be roughly at the midway stage; one archivist I spoke to suggested that they had earmarked the end of 2026 as its conclusion. After then, the full measure of how decisively the David Bowie Centre's holdings affect our understanding of the man and his work will be taken. I suspect that, for all the detail and revelatory information on offer, it will not make any material difference to our appreciation of Bowie as a musician and creative figure. After all, as Led Zeppelin once noted, the song remains the same. Yet even as we still mourn his loss, a decade and more after his death, the chance for a final, posthumous audience with Bowie is one the tens of thousands of visitors that the centre will surely receive will be unable to resist.

---

\*   The collection also confirms that Bowie's spelling was terrible.

And there is a final, wonderfully inimitable enigma, too. Shortly before the centre opened, information was given to the press about a musical that Bowie was working on at the time of his death, set amid the rogues, vagabonds and literati of the eighteenth century. It was to have been entitled *The Spectator*. His notes hint at a sweeping and provocative take on life in eighteenth-century London. The characters in *The Spectator* might have included everyone from the so-called 'Thief Taker General' Jonathan Wild, a master criminal who posed as a concerned and public-minded citizen, to his nemesis and rival Jack Sheppard, who Wild had executed in order to clear the path for his own nefarious activities.

Both men's names are visible on the assortment of cryptic records that Bowie kept, along with those of the artists Joshua Reynolds and William Hogarth. But what is even more fascinating is the way that Bowie had carefully judged the theatrical potential of the men and women written about in *The Spectator*, which took its name from the early eighteenth-century periodical founded by the wits and politicians Richard Steele and Joseph Addison.

Many of the characters were little known, but Bowie's gaze was wide-ranging. He seemed amused by everyone from a Mr Clinch of Barnet, who could imitate the sounds of horses, hounds and a bassoon 'all with his own natural voice, to the greatest perfection', to the potential for an interesting subplot about two sisters, one 'vain and severe' who lost her potential husband to her kindlier, less beautiful sibling. His lifelong interest in Stanley Kubrick's film of *A Clockwork Orange*, which influenced his stagecraft throughout the '70s, finds an echo in his fascination with the Mohocks, a criminal gang of youthful, well-born hooligans who were intended to attack whichever figure Bowie took from *The Spectator*'s pages to be his protagonist. And some of the notes are both amusing and telling; one simply reads 'Many sex scenes'.

It is, as with many of Bowie's unfulfilled projects, a tragedy that *The Spectator* never came to pass and we can only hope that a Bowie biographer-cum-cultural historian can resurrect his ideas and research in some form in the future. But until then, it – and all the other 89,999 projects and letters and costumes lurking somewhere in the depths of east London – sits waiting for someone to engage with it, all over again, in the hope that this particular rumour from Ground Control was one worth listening to, after all.

# DISCOGRAPHY

[with Tin Machine] *Tin Machine*, released 22 May 1989 (EMI)

[with Tin Machine] *Tin Machine II*, released 2 September 1991 (London Records/Victory)

[with Tin Machine] *Tin Machine Live: Oy Vey, Baby*, released 27 July 1992 (London Records/Victory)

*Black Tie White Noise*, released 5 April 1993 (Savage/Arista)

*The Buddha of Suburbia*, released 8 November 1993 (Arista/Virgin)

*Outside*, released 25 September 1995 (Arista/BMG/RCA/Virgin)

*Earthling*, released 3 February 1997 (Arista/BMG/RCA/Virgin)

*hours...*, released 21 September 1999 (Virgin)

*Heathen*, released 10 June 2002 (ISO/Columbia)

*Reality*, released 15 September 2003 (ISO/Columbia)

*The Next Day*, released 8 March 2013 (ISO/Columbia)

*The Next Day Extra EP* (released November 2013)

*Blackstar*, released 8 January 2016 (ISO/Columbia)

*Toy* (released 2021)

# FILMOGRAPHY

Pontius Pilate, *The Last Temptation of Christ*, 1988, dir. Martin Scorsese

Sir Roland Moorecock, *Dream On*, 1991 (TV)

Monte, *The Linguini Incident*, 1991, dir. Richard Shepard

Phillip Jeffries, *Twin Peaks: Fire Walk With Me*, 1992, dir. David Lynch

Himself, *Full Stretch*, 1993 (TV)

Andy Warhol, *Basquiat*, 1996, dir. Julian Schnabel

Jack Sikora, *Gunslinger's Revenge*, 1998, dir. Giovanni Veronesi

Bernie, *Everybody Loves Sunshine*, 1999, dir. Andrew Goth

Various roles, *The Hunger*, 1999–2000 (TV)

Mr Rice, *Mr Rice's Secret*, 2000, dir. Nicholas Kendall

Himself, *Zoolander*, 2001, dir. Ben Stiller

Himself, *The Rutles 2: Can't Buy Me Lunch*, 2003, dir. Eric Idle

Himself, *Extras*, 2006 (TV)

Nikola Tesla, *The Prestige*, 2006, dir. Christopher Nolan

Emperor Maltazard, *Arthur and the Invisibles*, 2006, dir. Luc Besson

Lord Royal Highness, *SpongeBob SquarePants*, 2007 (TV)

Cyrus Ogilvie, *August*, 2008, dir. Austin Chick

Himself, *Bandslam*, 2009, dir. Todd Graff

# BIBLIOGRAPHY

David Buckley, *Strange Fascination: David Bowie, the Definitive Story* (Virgin, 2000)

Alan Edwards, *I Was There: Dispatches from a Life in Rock and Roll* (Simon & Schuster, 2024)

Sean Egan (ed), *Bowie on Bowie: Interviews and Encounters* (Souvenir Press, 2015)

Brian Eno, *A Year with Swollen Appendices: Brian Eno's Diary* (Faber, 2020)

Tom Hagler, *Bowie at the BBC: A Life in Interviews* (Welbeck, 2023)

Peter Howson, *Peter Howson: Bosnia* (Imperial War Museum, 1994)

Dylan Jones, *David Bowie: A Life* (Preface, 2017)

Robert Dean Lurie, *We Can Be Heroes: The Radical Individualism of David Bowie* (CreateSpace, 2016)

Thomas Mann, *The Magic Mountain* (Martin Secker, 1927)

Morrissey, *Autobiography* (Penguin, 2013)

Chris O'Leary, *Ashes to Ashes: The Songs of David Bowie 1976–2016* (Repeater, 2019)

Nicholas Pegg, *The Complete David Bowie* (Titan, 2016)

Sylvia Plath, *Ariel* (Faber, 1965)

Christopher Sandford, *Bowie: Loving the Alien* (Little Brown, 1996)

David Sheppard, *On Some Faraway Beach: The Life and Times of Brian Eno* (Orion, 2008)

Paul Trynka, *Starman: David Bowie, the Definitive Biography* (Sphere, 2012)

Richie Unterberger, *Unknown Legends of Rock 'n' Roll: Psychedelic Unknowns, Mad Geniuses, Punk Pioneers, Lo-Fi Mavericks & More* (Miller Freeman, 1998)

Tony Visconti, *The Autobiography: Bowie, Bolan and the Brooklyn Boy* (HarperCollins, 2007)

# NOTES

**Prologue**

1. Eric Schermerhorn, author interview, 2 February 2024
2. Michael Watts, *Melody Maker*, 22 January 1972
3. Roy Hollingworth, *Melody Maker*, 12 May 1973
4. Bill Wyman, *Entertainment Weekly*, 6 September 1991
5. Jonathan Bernstein, *Spin*, September 1991
6. Jon Wilde, *Melody Maker*, 2 September 1991
7. Schermerhorn, author interview, op. cit.
8. Dylan Jones, *David Bowie: A Life*, 2017, p.368
9. David Bowie interview, *Rolling Stone*, 31 October 1991
10. Schermerhorn, author interview, op. cit.
11. Ibid.
12. David Bowie interview, *Rolling Stone*, 31 October 1991
13. Ibid.
14. Ibid.
15. Adrian Deevoy, *Q*, June 1989
16. Schermerhorn, author interview, op. cit.
17. David Bowie interview with Charles Shaar Murray, *Q*, October 1991
18. Ibid.
19. Schermerhorn interview, David Bowie News, 6 November 2022
20. Schermerhorn, author interview, op. cit.
21. Ibid.
22. Ibid.

**Chapter 1**

1. Mark Blake, 'Born Again', *Mojo*, October 2008
2. Alan Edwards, author interview, 17 July 2024
3. David Sinclair, *Rolling Stone*, 10 June 1993
4. David Bowie, Q&A, *Q*, July 2000
5. Sinclair, *Rolling Stone*, op. cit.
6. Mick Brown, *Daily Telegraph*, 14 December 1996
7. Reeves Gabrels, author interview, 20 March 2024
8. Sinclair, *Rolling Stone*, op. cit.
9. Tim Palmer, author interview, 8 March 2024
10. Gabrels, author interview, op. cit.
11. Ibid.
12. Chris O'Leary, *Ashes to Ashes: The Songs of David Bowie 1976–2016*, p.231

13. Kevin Armstrong, author interview, 17 June 2024
14. Palmer, author interview, op. cit.
15. Christopher Sandford, *Bowie: Loving the Alien*, p.273
16. Adrian Deevoy, *Q*, June 1989
17. Ibid.
18. Robin Eggar, *Tin Machine II* interview, from Sean Egan (ed.), *Bowie on Bowie: Interviews and Encounters*, p.194
19. Gabrels, author interview, op. cit.
20. Palmer, author interview, op. cit.
21. Nicholas Pegg, *The Complete David Bowie*, p.589
22. Ibid., p.590
23. David Buckley, *Strange Fascination: Bowie, the Definitive Story*, p.471
24. Gabrels, author interview, op. cit.
25. Palmer, author interview, op. cit.
26. Ibid.
27. Ibid.
28. Gabrels, author interview, op. cit.
29. Schermerhorn, author interview, op. cit.
30. Sandford, p.296
31. Edwards, author interview, op. cit.
32. Tom Hagler, *Bowie at the BBC: A Life in Interviews*, p.209
33. Edwards, author interview, op. cit.

## Chapter 2

1. Sandford, p.300
2. Alan Edwards, *I Was There: Dispatches from a Life in Rock and Roll*, p.159
3. Edwards, author interview, op. cit.
4. *Hello!*, 13 June 1992
5. Ibid.
6. Ibid.
7. Gabrels, author interview, 22 March 2024
8. Hagler, op. cit., p.216
9. Sandford, op. cit., p.297
10. Sinclair, *Rolling Stone*, op. cit.
11. Ibid.
12. Jones, op. cit., p.374
13. Mike Garson, author interview, 29 February 2024
14. Sterling Campbell, author interview, 28 February 2024
15. Pegg, op. cit., pp.121–2
16. Gabrels, author interview, op. cit.
17. David Sinclair, *Q*, May 1993
18. Dave Thompson, the *Rocket*, May 1993
19. Buckley, op. cit., pp.486–7
20. Ibid.

21. Gabrels, author interview, op. cit.
22. John Adams, the *Independent*, 16 June 1993
23. Steve Sutherland, *NME*, 20 and 27 March 1993
24. Sandford, op. cit., p.309
25. Paul Trynka, *Starman: David Bowie, the Definitive Biography*, p.357
26. Lee Campbell, *Irish Times*, 27 March 2024
27. Buckley, op. cit., p.491
28. Trynka, op. cit., pp.357–8

## Chapter 3

1. Hanif Kureishi, the *Guardian*, 12 August 2017
2. Jones, op. cit., p.19
3. Ibid.
4. Hanif Kureishi, *Interview*, May 1993
5. Pegg, op. cit., p.421
6. Jones, op. cit., p.379
7. Ibid., p.369
8. David Bowie/Ricky Gervais, the *Observer*, 21 September 2003
9. Garson, author interview, op. cit.
10. Ibid.
11. Bowie/Gervais, op. cit.
12. Ibid.
13. David Bowie, *The Buddha of Suburbia* liner notes, 15 September 1993
14. Christopher Buckley, *Architectural Digest*, September 1992
15. Sandford, op. cit., p.310
16. Ibid.
17. Mat Snow, *Mojo*, October 1994
18. Thomas Mann, *The Magic Mountain*, p.670
19. Campbell, author interview, op. cit.
20. Ibid.
21. Gabrels, author interview, op. cit.
22. Campbell, author interview, op. cit.
23. Garson, author interview, op. cit.
24. Ibid.
25. Trynka, op. cit., p.364
26. Gabrels, author interview, op. cit.
27. Garson, author interview, op. cit.

## Chapter 4

1. Bowie, *Vanity Fair*, November 2003
2. Stephen Kijak, author interview, 25 January 2024
3. Ibid.
4. Richard Cook, *NME*, March 1984
5. Richie Unterberger, *Unknown Legends of Rock and Roll*, p.116

6.   Brian Eno, Q&A, *Q*, July 2001
7.   Brian Eno, *A Year with Swollen Appendices: Brian Eno's Diary, 1995*, p.17
8.   Pegg, op. cit., p.427
9.   Steven P. Wheeler, *Music Connection*, September 1995
10.  David Bowie, *Q*, January 1995
11.  Eno, op. cit., p.18
12.  Ibid., p.19
13.  Ibid., p.22
14.  Armstrong, author interview, op. cit.
15.  Eno, op. cit., p.25
16.  Ibid., p.27
17.  Ibid., pp.28–9
18.  Garson, author interview, op. cit.
19.  Simon Witter interview, *Rock's Backpages*, 5 October 1995
20.  Eno, op. cit., p.91
21.  Ibid., p.100
22.  David Bowie, Prodigy webchat, 1995
23.  David Bowie interview, *Humo* magazine, 1995
24.  Steve Pafford, StevePafford.com, 25 March 2019
25.  Pegg, op. cit., p.429
26.  Eno, op. cit., p.136
27.  Ibid.
28.  Gabrels, author interview, op. cit.
29.  David Sheppard, *On Some Faraway Beach: The Life and Times of Brian Eno*, p.416
30.  Gabrels, author interview, op. cit.
31.  Sandford, op. cit., p.320
32.  Paul Gorman, *Music Week*, January 1997
33.  Gabrels, author interview, op. cit.
34.  Witter, op. cit.
35.  Wheeler, op. cit.
36.  Charles Shaar Murray, *Mojo*, October 1995
37.  Wheeler, op. cit.
38.  Gail Ann Dorsey, author interview, 4 April 2024
39.  Ibid.
40.  Edna Gundersen, *USA Today*, 14 September 1995
41.  Garson, author interview, op. cit.
42.  Gabrels, author interview, op. cit.
43.  Ibid.
44.  Morrissey, *Autobiography*, p.47
45.  Pegg, op. cit., p.599

**Chapter 5**

1.   *Melody Maker* interview, 26 February 1966
2.   *Newsweek*, 9 October 1972

3. Pegg, op. cit., p.661
4. Charles Shaar Murray, *NME*, 29 September 1984
5. Jones, op. cit., p.348
6. Ibid., p.349
7. Chris Roberts, *Ikon*, October 1995
8. Kathy McCabe, *Daily Telegraph*, 19 February 2004
9. Richard Shepard, author interview, 22 January 2024
10. Ibid.
11. Ibid.
12. Ibid.
13. Ibid.
14. Tricia Jones, *i-D*, May 1987
15. Virginia Campbell, *Movieline*, April 1992
16. Ibid.
17. Ibid.
18. Andrew Grevas, 25yearslatersite.com, 20 September 2018
19. Daniel Dylan Wray, *Pitchfork*, 19 September 2017
20. Gabriele Niola, *Screen Daily*, 6 November 2017
21. Pegg, op. cit., p.24
22. Ibid., p.25
23. Ibid.
24. Sandford, op. cit., p.115
25. Ingrid Sischy, *ArtForum*, July 1996
26. Witter, op. cit.
27. Ibid.
28. Chris Roberts, op. cit.
29. Sandford, op. cit., p.317
30. Dan Jewel, *People*, 26 August 1996
31. Linda Laban, *Mr Showbiz*, March 1997
32. Ibid.
33. Phil Hall, *Film Threat*, 24 July 2002
34. Derek Jarman, *Dancing Ledge*
35. Robert Phoenix, *Dirt*, 5 October 1999

## Chapter 6

1. Hagler, op. cit., p.254
2. Ibid., p.255
3. Lucy O'Brien, *Q*, March 1996
4. Mark Beaumont, *NME*, 17 February 2017
5. Ibid.
6. Pegg, op. cit., p.430
7. Mark Plati, author interview, 23 February 2024
8. Ibid.
9. Gabrels, author interview, op. cit.

10. Dorsey, author interview, op. cit.
11. Plati, author interview, op. cit.
12. Ibid.
13. Ibid.
14. Garson, author interview, op. cit.
15. Zachary Alford, author interview, 9 April 2024
16. Plati, author interview, op. cit.
17. Garson, author interview, op. cit.
18. Plati, author interview, op. cit.
19. Pegg, op. cit., p.433
20. Trynka, op. cit., p.412
21. Brown, op. cit.
22. Hagler, op. cit., pp.261–71

**Chapter 7**

1. Michael Kimmelman, *New York Times*, 14 June 1998
2. Kevin Rawlinson, the *Guardian*, 11 November 2016
3. Jonathan Jones, the *Guardian*, 11 October 2016
4. Jonathan Jones, the *Guardian*, 25 April 2013
5. Mariko Finch, *Sothebys*, 6 October 2016
6. Mat Snow, *Mojo*, October 1994
7. Ibid.
8. William Boyd, author interview, 9 May 2024
9. Ibid.
10. Ibid.
11. William Boyd diary, 23 February 1994
12. Boyd, author interview, op. cit.
13. David Cohen, *Daily Telegraph*, 1 October 1994
14. Boyd, author interview, op. cit.
15. David Bowie, *Modern Painters*, Autumn 1994
16. Boyd, author interview, op. cit.
17. Ibid.
18. Peter Howson, *Peter Howson: BOSNIA*
19. Jones, op. cit., p.386
20. Libby Brooks, the *Guardian*, 5 June 2023
21. George Mair, *Edinburgh Reporter*, 10 October 2023
22. David Bowie, *Daily Mail*, 28 June 2008
23. Pegg, op. cit., p.696
24. Kevin Cann, author interview, 25 January 2024
25. Sandford, op. cit., p.314
26. Pegg, op. cit., p.697
27. Cann, author interview, op. cit.
28. Ibid.
29. Ibid.

30. Edwards author interview, op. cit.
31. Ibid.
32. Sandford, op. cit., p.314
33. Dan Aquilante, *New York Post*, 12 September 2003
34. Boyd, author interview, op. cit.
35. Ibid.
36. Barbara A. MacAdam, *ArtNews*, May 1998
37. Boyd, author interview, op. cit.
38. Ibid.

## Chapter 8
1. Edwards, *I Was There*, p.202
2. Ibid.
3. David Bowie, Q&A, *Q*, July 2000
4. Witter, op. cit.
5. Richard MacManus, *CyberCultural*, 10 January 2023
6. Ibid.
7. Ibid.
8. Keith Stuart, the *Guardian*, 11 January 2016
9. David Bowie, BowieNet chat transcript, 30 September 1998
10. Coco Schwab, BowieNet chat transcript, 13 July 2001
11. Chris Roberts, *Uncut*, October 1999
12. Alex Grant interview (from Chris O'Leary, 'What's Really Happening', Pushing Ahead of the Dame)
13. Pegg, op. cit., pp.704–5
14. Steffan Chirazi, *SOMA*, October 1999
15. Buckley, op. cit., p.545
16. J. Alex Tarquinio, *Forbes*, 4 March 2000
17. Ken Scrudato, *SOMA*, July 2003
18. Ibid.

## Chapter 9
1. Garson, author interview, op. cit.
2. Emily Eavis, DavidBowie.com, 10 February 2018
3. Edwards, author interview, op. cit.
4. Caitlin Moran, *The Times*, 26 June 2000
5. Andrew Davies, *Big Issue*, January 1999
6. Mikel Jollett, *Filter*, July/August 2003
7. David Wildman, *Weekly Dig*, December 2003
8. Tony Visconti, *The Autobiography: Bowie, Bolan and the Brooklyn Boy*, p.347
9. Visconti, author interview, 21 July 2023
10. Gabrels, author interview, op. cit.
11. Plati, author interview, op. cit.
12. Garson, author interview, op. cit.

13. Trynka, op. cit., p.348
14. Steve Lowe, *Q*, March 2003
15. Gabrels interview, 26 March
16. Ibid.
17. Ibid.
18. Plati, author interview, op. cit.
19. Gabrels, author interview, op. cit.
20. Ibid.
21. Ibid.
22. Pegg, op. cit., p.215
23. Garson, author interview, op. cit.
24. David Quantick, *Q*, October 1999
25. Gabrels, author interview, op. cit.
26. Ibid.
27. Edwards, author interview, op. cit.
28. David Bowie, *Time Out*, 11 June 2000
29. Ibid.
30. Edwards, op. cit., p.207
31. Ian Winwood, *Daily Telegraph*, 2 June 2024
32. Campbell, author interview, op. cit.
33. David Bowie, *Time Out*, 15 May 2000
34. Ibid., 19 May 2000
35. Ibid., 9 June 2000
36. Ibid.
37. Ibid., 11 June 2000
38. Garson, author interview, op. cit.
39. Plati, author interview, op. cit.
40. Dorsey, author interview, op. cit.
41. Pegg, op. cit., p.608

## Chapter 10
1. Plati, author interview, op. cit.
2. Ibid.
3. Gerry Leonard, author interview, 29 January 2024
4. Marquesa de Valera, *Hello!*, 19 September 2000
5. Ibid.
6. Garson, author interview, op. cit.
7. Ibid.
8. Ibid.
9. Dorsey, author interview, op. cit.
10. Pegg, op. cit., p.439
11. Plati, author interview, op. cit.
12. Campbell, author interview, op. cit.
13. Pegg, op.cit., p.440

14. Edwards, op. cit., pp.206–8
15. Jones, op. cit., pp.420–21
16. Cameron Crowe, *Playboy*, September 1976
17. Bowie, writing on BowieNet on 12 September
18. Plati, author interview, op. cit.
19. Viscont, author interview, op. cit.
20. Pegg, op. cit., p.443
21. Ingrid Sischy, *Interview*, June 2002
22. Tim Cooper, the *Observer*, 9 June 2002
23. Ibid.
24. Leonard, author interview, op. cit.
25. Plati, author interview, op. cit.
26. Garson, author interview, op. cit.

## Chapter 11
1. Plati, author interview, op. cit.
2. Ibid.
3. Dorsey, author interview, op. cit.
4. Pegg, op. cit. p.454
5. Steve Morse, *Boston Globe*, 16 September 2003
6. Tricia Jones, op. cit.
7. Billy Sloan, *Scottish Sunday Mail*, 23 November 2003
8. Garson, author interview, op. cit.
9. David Wildman, *Weekly Dig*, December 2003
10. Alexis Petridis, the *Guardian*, 10 September 2003
11. Leonard, author interview, op. cit.
12. Garry Mulholland, *Q*, October 2003
13. Pat Levy, Consequence of Sound, 7 June 2018
14. Alan Sculley, the *Columbian*, 9 April 2004
15. Dominic Mohan, the *Sun*, 12 September 2003
16. Tim Cooper, *Evening Standard*, 20 November 2003
17. Wildman, op. cit.
18. Pegg, op. cit., p.620
19. Leonard, author interview, op. cit.
20. Garson, author interview, op. cit.
21. Ibid.
22. Ibid.
23. David Cheal, *Daily Telegraph*, 19 November 2003
24. Luke Morgan Britton, *NME*, 10 April 2016
25. Edwards, author interview, op. cit.
26. Dorsey, author interview, op. cit.
27. Ibid.
28. Garson, author interview, op. cit.

## Chapter 12

1. Brian Hiatt, *Rolling Stone*, 24 September 2007
2. Tony Visconti, DavidBowie.com, 1 October 2005
3. Pegg, op. cit., p.627
4. Dave Itzkoff, Fashion Rocks, October 2005
5. Ricky Gervais/David Bowie, the *Observer*, 21 September 2003
6. Christopher Nolan, *Entertainment Weekly*, 19 January 2016
7. Ibid.
8. Pegg, op. cit., p.680
9. Nolan, op. cit.
10. Charlie Hanson, author interview, 23 January 2024
11. Ibid.
12. Pegg, op. cit., p.682
13. Jones, op. cit. p.437
14. Garson, author interview, op. cit.
15. Pegg, op. cit., p.682
16. Ibid.
17. Campbell, author interview, op. cit.
18. Leonard, author interview, op. cit.
19. Dorsey, author interview, op. cit.

## Chapter 13

1. Campbell, author interview, op. cit.
2. Leonard, author interview, op. cit.
3. Ibid.
4. Alexis Petridis, the *Guardian*, 12 January 2013
5. Dorsey, author interview, op. cit.
6. Alford, author interview, op. cit.
7. Ibid.
8. Leonard, author interview, op. cit.
9. Petridis, op. cit.
10. Pegg, op. cit., p.464
11. Petridis, op. cit.
12. Edwards, op. cit., p.294
13. Ibid., p.298
14. Matilda Battersby, the *Independent*, 9 January 2013
15. Bowie, *Mail on Sunday*, 29 June 2008
16. Rick Moody, *The Rumpus*, 25 April 2013
17. Michael Bracewell, *The Times*, 6 November 1999
18. Jones, op. cit., p.447
19. Andy Gill, the *Independent*, 25 February 2013
20. Petridis, the *Guardian*, 25 February 2013
21. Bill Donohue, Catholic League statement, 8 May 2013
22. John Bingham, *Daily Telegraph*, 8 May 2013

23. Artspace Editors, *Phaidon*, 27 February 2018
24. Pegg, op. cit., pp.701–2
25. Schermerhorn, author interview, op. cit.
26. Carole Cadwalladr, the *Observer*, 29 June 2014

## Chapter 14

1. Ben Riley-Smith, *Daily Telegraph*, 24 February 2014
2. Jones, op. cit., p.432
3. Ibid., p.379
4. David Peisner, *Rolling Stone*, 15 July 2003
5. Enda Walsh, *Lazarus* programme
6. Vincent Dowd, *BBC Culture*, 5 November
7. Pegg, op. cit., p.685
8. Bruce Handy, *Hollywood Reporter*, 20 December 2016
9. Rachael Revesz, the *Independent*, 11 January 2016
10. Alford, author interview, op. cit.
11. Ibid.
12. Ben Monder, author interview, 28 January 2024
13. Alexis Petridis, the *Guardian*, 12 October 2014
14. Jones, op. cit., p.465
15. Danny Eccleston, *Mojo*, August 2016
16. Garson, author interview, op. cit.
17. Monder, author interview, op. cit.
18. Jim Farber, the *Guardian*, 28 October 2023
19. Paul Sexton, UDiscovermusic, 11 January 2019
20. Monder, author interview, op. cit.
21. Handy, op. cit.
22. Pegg, op. cit., p.473
23. James Murphy, *WTF with Marc Marcon* podcast, 12 July 2021
24. Monder, author interview, op. cit.
25. Sarah Larson, *New Yorker*, 3 January 2016
26. Jones, op. cit., pp.477–8
27. Justin Joffe, *Vice*, 19 November 2015
28. Handy, op. cit.
29. Ibid.
30. Jones, op. cit., p.480
31. Handy, op. cit.
32. Joanna Walters and Edward Helmore, the *Guardian*, 16 January 2016
33. David Rooney, *Hollywood Reporter*, 7 December 2015
34. Brian Hiatt, *Rolling Stone*, 14 January 2016
35. Jones, op. cit., p.485
36. Edwards, op. cit., pp.1–2
37. Brian Eno statement, 11 January 2016
38. Garson, author interview, op. cit.

39. Alexis Petridis, the *Guardian*, 7 January 2016
40. Jon Pareles, *New York Times*, 6 January 2016
41. Hiatt, op. cit.
42. Jones, op. cit., p.467

## Epilogue
1. Various, the *Guardian*, 11 January 2016
2. Dorsey, author interview, op. cit.
3. Campbell, author interview, op. cit.
4. Gabrels, author interview, op. cit.
5. Ibid.
6. Boyd, author interview, op. cit.
7. Cann, author interview, op. cit.
8. Nina Siegal, *New York Times*, 11 January 2016
9. Hermione Hoby, the *Guardian*, 17 January 2016
10. Handy, op. cit.
11. Garson, author interview, op. cit.

## Bonus Track
1. Ben Beaumont-Thomas, the *Guardian*, 4 July 2025
2. Jonathan Jones, the *Guardian*, 28 May 2025
3. Peter Asher to Kenneth Pitt, 15 July 1968, David Bowie archive/V&A
4. Heywood Jones to W.A. Freshman, undated, *c.* 1966, Bowie archive
5. Bowie note, undated, *c.* early 2000s, Bowie archive
6. Lady Gaga to Bowie, undated, *c.* 2013, Bowie archive

# ACKNOWLEDGEMENTS

Writing a biography of someone who has lived, and died, within living memory comes with its advantages, but also its pitfalls, too. It is not enough simply to skulk off towards the cuttings library and produce an artful cut-and-paste job. Instead, it was clear from the outset that *Lazarus* needed to have the first-hand input of as many of Bowie's close collaborators from this period as it was possible to feature. I am therefore eternally grateful that virtually everyone I approached was generous with their time, input and memories of working with and knowing Bowie. I hope that their graciousness and patience has been justified by the finished book.

Bowie was, first and foremost, a musician, and those who worked with him in that capacity have been the most valuable contributors to *Lazarus*. My deep thanks must go to Zackary Alford, Kevin Armstrong, Sterling Campbell, Gail Ann Dorsey, Gerry Leonard, Ben Monder, Tim Palmer, Mark Plati and Eric Schermerhorn. Their thoughtful and at times uproarious contributions to the book were deeply welcome.

Particular gratitude must go to Bowie's longest-serving collaborator Mike Garson, whose lengthy and fascinating conversation with me enabled me to place many of Bowie's actions in a wider, career-spanning context, and to the great Reeves Gabrels, who has long been underappreciated in his vital contributions to Bowie's music throughout the '90s. We spent many enjoyable and fascinating hours in conversation together and I hope that his candid input gives much of the book an authority and rigour that it would not otherwise have possessed. While Tony Visconti graciously declined to be interviewed for *Lazarus* due to his own commitments to a forthcoming memoir, I was able to draw on a previous conversation that I conducted with him and to use some of his insights from that to offer a fascinating account of this most important of artist–producer relationships.

# ACKNOWLEDGEMENTS

Bowie was a Renaissance man and one of my key intentions with *Lazarus* was to examine his other achievements during this period, especially in the fields of art and film. To this end, I am eternally grateful for the contributions offered by Bowie's co-conspirator William Boyd, his artistic collaborator Kevin Cann, *Extras* producer Charlie Hanson and the filmmakers Stephen Kijak and Richard Shepard. My thanks also to Bowie's peerless publicist Alan Edwards, who offered some invaluable up-close details of life working for (and with) Bowie, and the filmmaker Francis Whatley. Finally, I spoke to several people whose off-the-record contributions, particularly in the early stages of my research, were invaluable to my understanding of what Bowie was really like. I thank you for your generosity.

While Bowie never gave formal approval to a biography, some works published in his lifetime won greater appreciation from him than others. I am accordingly grateful to several writers who have spent considerable periods thinking about Bowie and for their input into the book. My thanks to Christopher Sandford, Chris O'Leary, Robert Dean Lurie, David Buckley, Dylan Jones, Paul Trynka and Nicholas Pegg, all of whom contributed to *Lazarus* either directly or through their published works. All their writing about this most glorious of subjects comes unreservedly recommended.

This book would not exist without my editor and publisher Pete Selby, whose initial enthusiasm for an apparently off-kilter delve into the life and work of an artist whom we both revere has continued throughout the editing process. I hope I speak for Pete when I say that examining our idol in this degree of detail has done nothing to dampen our veneration for him and it has been a true pleasure to begin what I know will be a long and happy collaboration with him. My thanks also to James Lilford, my other excellent editor on this project. Once again, Alan Samson was this book's first recipient in manuscript and his wise counsel has been greatly appreciated.

My agent Ed Wilson was a source of good cheer during this book's creation and it was a reciprocal pleasure on my part to introduce him to a greater variety of Bowie's work than he was previously familiar with. If I

366

were to list all the friends and colleagues who have been kind enough to offer me their thoughts on Bowie's music and personae over the years, this would turn into a long recitative, but you know who you are. I look forward to your mockery when I next launch into an ill-advised public display of contortions when 'Let's Dance' comes on the figurative jukebox.

Finally, my greatest thanks must go to the two true heroes in my life. My wife Nancy knows that Bowie has, at times, been almost the third figure in our marriage, so greatly has my (strange) fascination with him endured. She has tolerated her husband's deep love of another with the good humour and tireless patience that have been hallmarks of our marriage for more than a decade now. And it seems appropriate that this book will be published just a few days before my beloved daughter Rose – Rose Evelyn Bowie Larman – turns ten. I am proud, once again, to dedicate *Lazarus* to her. Admittedly, I may not be much cop at punching other people's dads, but I hope that I have offered you, and will always offer you, all the love that I have to give.

The team at New Modern would like to thank the following individuals:

**Nige Tassell** for copy-editing

**Seán Costello** for proofreading

**Marie Doherty** for typesetting

**Stuart Tolley** for cover design

**Amanda Russell** for image research

**Lizzie Dorney-Kingdom** for publicity

**Marie Lecouturier, Charlotte Rose, Andreina Brezzo
and the team at Simon & Schuster UK** for sales and distribution